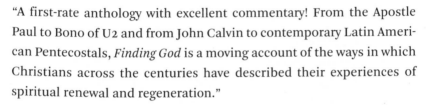
"A first-rate anthology with excellent commentary! From the Apostle Paul to Bono of U2 and from John Calvin to contemporary Latin American Pentecostals, *Finding God* is a moving account of the ways in which Christians across the centuries have described their experiences of spiritual renewal and regeneration."

> — JAMES H. MOORHEAD
> author of *Princeton Seminary in
> American Religion and Culture*

"*Finding God* contains powerful narratives that will be of value not only to people of faith but also to social scientists like me whose research interests come again and again to questions about conversion, why it happens, and what it means. Mulder's own story, courageously included here as a

Finding God

A TREASURY OF
CONVERSION STORIES

Edited by

John M. Mulder

with

Hugh T. Kerr

WILLIAM B. EERDMANS PUBLISHING COMPANY
GRAND RAPIDS, MICHIGAN / CAMBRIDGE, U.K.

Published 2012 by
Wm. B. Eerdmans Publishing Co.
2140 Oak Industrial Drive N.E., Grand Rapids, Michigan 49505 /
P.O. Box 163, Cambridge CB3 9PU U.K.

Printed in the United States of America

17 16 15 14 13 12   7 6 5 4 3 2

Library of Congress Cataloging-in-Publication Data

Finding God: a treasury of conversion stories /
edited by John M. Mulder with Hugh T. Kerr.
p.   cm.
Rev. ed. of: Conversions.
Includes bibliographical references and index.
ISBN 978-0-8028-6575-5 (pbk.: alk. paper)
1. Christian converts. 2. Conversion — Christianity.
I. Mulder, John M., 1946-   II. Kerr, Hugh T. (Hugh Thomson), 1909-1992.
III. Conversions.

BV4930.C63   2012

248.2′40922 — dc23

2012022980

www.eerdmans.com

In memory of
Hugh T. Kerr (1909–1992)
and for
Fred J. Hood, F. Morgan Roberts, and Joyce C. Tucker

Contents

Contents

Contents

Acknowledgments

This book is a revision and expansion of *Conversions: The Christian Experience*, subsequently reprinted under the title *Famous Conversions*, edited by Hugh T. Kerr and me. Since its publication by Wm. B. Eerdmans nearly thirty years ago, Hugh T. Kerr has died, but because of his tremendous contribution to the first version, this volume retains his name as co-editor.

Finding God: A Treasury of Conversion Stories seeks to accomplish what we could not do before. In the first edition, we sought diligently for the spiritual experiences of women and individuals outside the Western world, but we were only modestly successful. Because of the increased availability of such material, I have attempted to address that imbalance. In addition, this book contains the accounts of several contemporary Christians whose stories were either unavailable or eliminated the first time because of space. All criteria for selection are inevitably subject to criticism and debate, but I hope this selection is richer and will make for especially rewarding reading.

Several institutions have assisted in valuable ways in the preparation of this book, both in its first incarnation and now in a more expansive form. These include the libraries of Hope College, Louisville Presbyterian Theological Seminary, Princeton Theological Seminary, Second Presbyterian Church of Louisville, Southern Baptist Theological Seminary, Western Theological Seminary, and Yale Divinity School.

I also want to record my gratitude for the counsel and advice of several individuals: Allan Anderson, Jonathan Bonk, Joel Carpenter, Henri Gooren, Martin Han, Donald Luidens, Mark Noll, Dana Robert, Dae Young Ryu, Scott Sunquist, Arch Taylor, Grant Wacker, and Deokju Yi.

Unfortunately, I could not use all of the many individuals they recommended for inclusion. The leadership at Eerdmans has been extremely helpful in bringing this book to fruition, especially Jon Pott and David Bratt. Linda Bieze and Jenny Hoffman have been patient, understanding, and helpful in dealing with the tangled business of permissions to reprint material and listening to my complaints.

One individual stands out as deserving special appreciation for the assistance he has provided in preparing *Finding God:* Professor James D. Smith III of Bethel Theological Seminary (San Diego) and the University of San Diego. Jim and I shared lengthy emails and conversations about this book, and his experience in using the first edition in his classes and his knowledge of church history have immeasurably improved this book.

Finding God is dedicated to the memory of Hugh T. Kerr, who was my mentor at Princeton Theological Seminary, where he taught theology for many years. He was the editor of *Theology Today* for decades, taking it from its infancy to its place as the most widely circulated quarterly journal of theology in the world. "With" hardly describes Kerr's contribution to this volume, but in a deeper sense it gives me comfort to know that we are still working "with" one another. He always treated me as his colleague in our work together for more than a decade. He and his wife, Dorothy, became a second set of parents to my wife Mary and me, and our children knew them as "Grandma and Grandpa Kerr." We still miss them and the joy they brought to our lives.

Finding God is also dedicated in honor of Fred J. Hood, F. Morgan Roberts, and Joyce C. Tucker. They walked with me on a tortuous path of new life and ministry, and only they know how difficult that path was. To them I owe gratitude that is both indescribable and inexpressible.

My wife Mary, who has walked with me on many paths and who believed in me when I had lost hope, is the rock in my life. As a professor of English composition, she targeted many infelicities of expression and typos, and her critical perspective immeasurably improved the final product.

Both in its preparation and its publication, I hope that in some small way this survey of those who have found God will be a means of recovering what the Apostles' Creed means by the "communion of the saints." In manifold ways, in different tongues, and in various cultures, they testify to both the restlessness of the human spirit and its home in God's presence and kindness.

JOHN M. MULDER

Introduction

The English word "conversion" suggests the act of "turning around," moving from one place to another. The turning process can be physical, spiritual, emotional, theological, or moral. It is this physical-spiritual combination that lies behind the original Hebrew and Greek vocabulary in the Old and New Testaments.

The word "conversion" does not often appear in the Bible, but certain synonyms such as "repentance," "regeneration," and "being born again" occur almost everywhere and with great frequency throughout the Scriptures. The notion of "turning" can be variously stated, as for example "to turn," "to return," "to turn to," "to turn away from," "to turn toward," or "to turn around." To be converted is like making a "U-turn." It is "starting at square one again" or "going back to the drawing board."

Conversion, however it may be described, involves a complete change from one lifestyle to another. It may require abandoning an aimless and unsatisfying perspective in exchange for a new and promising incentive to live a more meaningful life. Sometimes the fact and experience of conversion are related to the search for intellectual truth or the longing for moral purity and goodness. At other times, and these make up the more graphic accounts of dramatic conversions, deep emotional earthquakes erupt out of the past, shatter the present, and make way for a new tomorrow.

I

In the Hebrew Scriptures, conversion is often associated with the divine challenge to the people of Israel to return from their false worship to the true faith of the Holy One, "the God of Abraham, Isaac, and Jacob." Especially in the prophetic literature, the perverse Israelites were confronted by the eloquence of Isaiah, Jeremiah, Ezekiel, and others, who urged them to forsake their idolatry and immorality and to turn toward the merciful God who created them, provided for them, and led them out of bondage into the new life of the promised land.

> Let the wicked forsake their way,
>   and the unrighteous their thoughts;
> let them return to the LORD, that he may have mercy on them,
>   and to our God, for he will abundantly pardon.
>
> (Isa. 55:7; see also
> Ezek. 18:30, 32; Hos. 14:2)

Elsewhere in the Old Testament, and particularly in the so-called penitential psalms, the longing for conversion grows out of a deep sense of sin, suffering, and frustration. Here we cannot be sure whether the psalmist speaks as an individual or for the people as a whole. But a profound sense of oppression and alienation, whether personal or corporate, pervades these lyrical expressions of religious faith. The stab of conscience, the shame of inward uncleanness, the remorse for sin, and the sensation of being lost and alone — all these agonies of soul are coupled with prayers for mercy, forgiveness, and a new chance to begin all over again.

> Create in me a clean heart, O God,
>   and put a new and right spirit within me.
> Do not cast me away from your presence,
>   and do not take your holy spirit from me.
> Restore to me the joy of your salvation,
>   and sustain in me a willing spirit.
>
> (Ps. 51:10-12; see also
> Pss. 6, 32, 38, 102, 130, 143)

There are also accounts of individual conversion experiences in the Old Testament, and indeed most of the pivotal figures — such as Abra-

xiv

ham, Jacob, Moses, Samuel, and the prophets — were summoned by an insistent God in such a way that they could only describe their call as an abrupt right-about-face. The dramatic episode of the prophet Isaiah is typical:

> I saw the Lord sitting on a throne, high and lofty; and the hem of his robe filled the temple . . . and the house filled with smoke. And I said: "Woe is me! I am lost, for I am a man of unclean lips . . . yet my eyes have seen the King, the LORD of hosts!" (Isa. 6:1-5)

The basic elements in this incident tend to be repeated in almost every Old Testament conversion experience. There is the flashing vision of truth, the conviction of sin and unworthiness, the joy of forgiveness and absolution, and the ready acceptance of a new life of mission and service.

II

In the New Testament, "conversion" and all its cognate terms, such as "repentance" and "new life," are directly related to the person and message of the Christ figure. Jesus began his public ministry by announcing that "the kingdom of God has come near; repent, and believe in the good news" (Mark 1:15). And his final words to his disciples commissioned them to convert the world: "Go therefore and make disciples of all nations" (Matt. 28:19).

The conversion experience summons up almost endless figures of speech in the New Testament writings. It can be a transfer out of darkness into light (1 Pet. 2:9), a spiritual rebirth or being born again (John 3:3), a restoration from impurity (Titus 2:14), a translation from death to life (John 5:24), a turning away from Satan to God (Acts 26:18), a totally new creation (2 Cor. 5:17), a getting rid of an old and acquiring a new humanity (Col. 3:9), a dying to self and rising again in Christ (Rom. 6:2-8).

The classic case of Christian conversion is, of course, that of the apostle Paul (Acts 9:1-19; 22:1-21; 26:1-23). The experience was dramatic, decisive, and determinative. Paul was never the same again, and in many ways the apostolic incident parallels Isaiah's prophetic vision. But the New Testament does not suggest a single stereotype for an authentic conversion experience. Nicodemus, for example, who provokes the dialogue with Jesus about what it means to be born again (John 3), is himself an ambiguous illustration of conversion. We don't really know whether Jesus persuaded Nicodemus or not. All we know is that later on he turned up at the time of Jesus' burial and entombment and gave some assistance (John 19:38).

The New Testament balances the sudden conversion of Paul with the more gentle and subtle changes wrought in people like Zacchaeus (Luke 19:1-10), Matthew (Matt. 9:9; see also Mark 2:13; Luke 5:27), Lydia (Acts 16:14), and Timothy (Acts 16), to say nothing of all those nameless souls who are lumped together as converts, saints, and martyrs in the book of Acts, the Pauline epistles, and the letter to the Hebrews.

If a new kind of life is what conversion implies in the New Testament, the consequence of the Christian conversion experience is a new sense of mission. The disciple as follower becomes the apostle, one sent out to proclaim the good news of the gospel. In the early apostolic church, conversion is seldom described as an experience to glory in, as if it were sufficient in itself as sheer emotional ecstasy. Conversion in the authentic Christian sense implies a commission to tell others and to follow in the footsteps of a Master whose commitment took him to the cross. That is one reason why Christians in the New Testament are such busy people. They are out to convert everyone and to turn the world upside down. So we read about Paul and Barnabas, in a typical description of their many travels: "as they passed through both Phoenicia and Samaria, they reported the conversion of the Gentiles, and they gave great joy to all the believers" (Acts 15:3; see also 17:6).

III

While a conversion experience may be for the convert the most real and significant event in his or her life, it is almost always difficult to interpret or explain to others. The reason is simply that conversion involves complex questions of theology, psychology, and sociology.

Theologically, it is not easy to say how the experience of conversion begins. Do human misery and the longing for a better life prompt the conversion quest? Or does God's grace within the human soul initiate the process? No doubt the human and the divine interact, but the paradox remains.

Psychologically, conversion can be readily related to, say, the crisis of adolescent identity or to the sense of moral and personal failure and the therapeutic need for acceptance. But while psychology can illuminate the dark places of the human spirit, it cannot explain the convert's assurance of being born again or that God has turned life upside down and inside out.

Sociologically, conversion can be put in the context of culture and history. Paul's conversion is not the same as Augustine's, and Pascal's testimony is not that of C. S. Lewis. Not only do times and seasons color the conversion experience, but certain historical and cultural factors seem to be especially propitious for mass revivals, group conversions on a large scale, and evangelistic preaching that calls for public decisions.

The Middle Ages illustrates very clearly how historical and sociological factors relate to conversion experiences. From the time of Augustine to the eve of the Protestant Reformation, personal conversion reports appear only infrequently. There are at least two cultural reasons for this medieval silence.

First, from the time of Constantine through the European expansion of Christendom and into the period of the Crusades, vast geographical areas and countless individuals became Christian. But it is an extremely delicate exercise to distinguish between authentic conversions and political conquests by might and sword.

Yet there is a second reason for the medieval gap. Monks in monasteries, aristocrats, and royal patrons might have possessed hand-copied manuscripts and might also have dictated to scribes and secretaries. But we must remember that Gutenberg's Bible was not printed until 1456. If one purpose for recording a personal conversion experience would be to persuade and convince others, many in the Middle Ages who might have given evidence of their faith were mostly restricted to oral rather than literary communication.

In any case, to recognize that there are not only theological but also psychological, historical, and sociological factors involved in conversion underscores the mystery of the relation between human questing and divine initiative. Those who have recorded their innermost thoughts and feelings about conversion also often confess to being puzzled by what happened, how, and why.

IV

This mysterious quality invariably accompanies the various ways the church has understood conversion throughout history and the different kinds of experiences that Christians themselves have described. To speak of "types" of conversion may do an injustice to the converted person, for each individual experience may well contain unique features. Even so, several common themes seem to emerge in the variety of Christian conversion accounts. Three may be noted here.

First, conversion is sometimes a dramatic and clearly identifiable experience, such as Paul's confrontation with Christ on the Damascus road. But it can also be a long and extended process, sometimes with no clear beginning and no clear end. In his classic discussion, *The Varieties of Religious Experience* (1902), William James described this as the difference between the "once-born" and "twice-born" individual. The "once-born" person is one of those fortunate people whose lives are not marked by radical breaks or deep crises; rather, they seem to go "from strength to strength," with confidence in God's sustaining love and trust in God's forgiveness and guidance. In the words of Horace Bushnell, an apologist for "Christian nurture," they seem to be people who never remember a time when they were not Christians.

The "twice-born" are those whose lives can be described as a series of signposts — of new directions taken, of ends and new beginnings, and specifically of a definite and certain experience of conversion at a particular moment. Many of the conversion accounts in this book are examples of this second type, in part because the stories of the life-long conversions of the "once-born" cannot be easily summarized or described. We may be tempted to accord spiritual superiority to the "twice-born," but throughout its history the church has always welcomed both kinds of Christians into fellowship — rejoicing in the joy of the new convert while, at the same time, sustaining the life of those who grow in grace day by day.

Second, the Christian church has also wrestled to understand the nature of the conversion experience and its importance within the church itself. Some Christians have argued that God's grace is so great and mysterious, and human sin so pervasive, that one cannot talk about a definite moment for becoming a Christian; such a claim, they insist, would be arrogant and would limit God. Others insist that God's love is so powerful that it breaks through at specific times in human life to bring certainty of forgiveness. Some even maintain that an individual can become perfect through a re-creation of the Holy Spirit. Each of these arguments emerges from different understandings of the church itself.

Is the church a body of "visible saints," as the New England Puritans assumed — people who have had a definite conversion and can narrate it publicly to others? Or is the church a combination of the "twice-born" *and* the "once-born" — both confessing Jesus Christ as Savior, but experiencing God's grace in different ways? These questions, and several other more complicated versions of them, have marked the history of Christianity and demonstrate the complexity of the nature of conversion itself.

It is also true, as several of the following accounts make clear, that conversions sometimes cross church and denominational lines. For all kinds of reasons, a particular creed or communion may be abandoned in favor of another. When vigorous and perhaps underhanded attempts are made to woo converts from one church to another, we castigate the process as unjustifiable "proselytizing." No doubt, examples of forced conversions can be found in Christian history at home and abroad. But, happily, there is little proselytizing among the churches today. Usually, when a person moves from one denomination to another, it is for personal, rather than pressured, reasons.

This also reminds us that "conversion" is an inclusive term and that Christian experiences come in many forms and varieties. As several of the personal accounts that follow clearly indicate, conversion is not necessarily limited to a radical shift from unbelief or doubt to Christian faith. Those who move, for example, from one branch of Christianity to another were obviously already Christian even if the new commitment also represents the renewing, as well as the widening and deepening, of Christian experience.

In addition, this book includes accounts from a few whose conversion experience seems more in the nature of vocational decision rather than emotional experience. And, although we do not raise the issue here, history sometimes shows us converted Christians who later lost the initial radiance of their experience.

Third, as the following accounts demonstrate, there is a remarkable, even exhilarating, variety in the way people describe their conversions. For some, it is obviously a highly emotional experience, shattering the very depths of their beings and reaching into the inner recesses of the human psyche. For other people, it seems to have been a much more intellectual matter — a recognition of the truth of Christianity and its doctrines without a deep emotional crisis. Sometimes the experience is primarily moral, leading the individual from a life that is seen as sinful or wrong into a pattern of behavior and a vision of existence that emphasize obedience, discipline, social justice. But at other times the experience seems to be aesthetic rather than moral — a glimpse of the beauty of holiness and a new way of perceiving the world and one's place in it. Some emphasize the power of God and their surrender to God's amazing grace, while others stress the decision they made to accept the forgiveness that was offered to them in Jesus Christ.

Given this variety, how can conversions be judged and evaluated? Many would insist that such judgment must be left to God. Even after Jesus told Nicodemus that he must be born again, he cautioned that "the wind blows where it chooses, and you hear the sound of it, but you do not know where it comes from or where it goes. So it is with everyone who is born of the Spirit" (John 3:8). Conversion is a mystery of God, and the varieties of conversion experiences testify to that divine initiative, seeking out those who are lost, finding them, and bringing them home.

And yet, on the basis of the Bible and the history of the Christian church, it is clear that faith must not be understood as merely an experience — even a conversion experience. Jesus admonished his followers, "Not everyone who says to me, 'Lord, Lord,' will enter the kingdom of heaven, but only the one who does the will of my Father in heaven" (Matt. 7:21).

Christianity is a way of life in which our thoughts and deeds and experiences are infused and transformed by the mystery of the love of God, a way of life witnessing to the love and forgiveness revealed in Christ Jesus. "You will know them by their fruits" (Matt. 7:16).

V

The conversion accounts included in this volume have been selected as *representative* of the wide variety of recorded experiences. Rather than attempting to "type" each one, we have simply listed the entries in more or less chronological sequence. Each is introduced briefly to set the author and the account in context, and in many instances the texts have been shortened and digested in the interests of uniformity.

The literary style and format of the original texts have been retained, including quaint and obsolete expressions as well as the masculinist language that many contemporary readers may find offensive and unacceptable. Many today, including the editors, wish to be more inclusive in our language, especially language about God, creation, and human nature. But that is a literary responsibility for today and tomorrow rather than an impossible assignment to rewrite the historical annals and classic texts of the past.

Extensive and diverse as the selections may appear, they still fall short of a full-scale roll call. But that, of course, is impossible. As the writer of the epistle to the Hebrews noted, "time would fail" to tell of all Christ's faithful witnesses (Heb. 11:32). If true in New Testament times, how much more so today!

Even so, some names that obviously belong here had to be ignored, either because there is no written personal record available or because the account is so short and ambiguous as to lack significant detail. For example, Francis of Assisi, according to his contemporaries and his later biographers, definitely did have a conversion experience. It was probably associated with one of three events: a heavenly voice that told him to restore and rebuild churches, a head-on confrontation with extreme poverty in Rome, or his identification with a leper begging alms. Biographers of Francis have written at great length about the legends of the saint, but the Little Friar wrote nothing about his experience, and it seems only proper to respect his reticence.

Thomas Aquinas, the foremost medieval theologian and the "doctor" of modern Catholicism, stopped writing his massive *Summa Theologiae* when he was in sight of the end. Apparently he experienced a mystical vision of some kind, for when a colleague asked why he didn't continue, Thomas replied: "I cannot go on. . . . All that I have written seems to me like so much straw compared to what I have seen and what has been revealed to me." But beyond that we simply don't know what happened.

Dwight L. Moody, who spent most of his revivalistic and preaching career calling for conversions and urging sinners to repent, himself left no extended account of his own experience. His application for church membership in Boston was deferred because of the vagueness of his beliefs. But shortly thereafter something must have happened, even though all he could write about was his joy to be alive. "I thought the old sun shone a good deal brighter than it ever had before — I thought that it was just smiling upon me; and as I walked out upon Boston Common and heard the birds singing in the trees, I thought they were all singing a song to me. . . . It seemed to me that I was in love with all creation."

At the center of the Christian missionary movement in its more expansive years stood the tall, elegant, and eloquent John R. Mott. An American emissary at home everywhere in the world, Mott's evangelism was inspired with his own enthusiasm and irrepressible optimism. At age thirteen, he wrote later, a Quaker evangelist "led my father, two of my sisters, and me to Christ." As a Cornell University student, he came to the point where he was able "with Thomas to say to Christ with intellectual honesty, 'My Lord and my God.'" In his own Methodist tradition, it was a sort of "second blessing." But he never wrote about it in any detail.

It would be intriguing to include, just to mention two more possibilities, Søren Kierkegaard and T. S. Eliot. Different in so many ways, both deeply influenced later generations, one as the father of existentialism, and the other by way of new modes and moods of poetry. The melancholy Dane sought all his life to define what it means to be a Christian, and Eliot in his mature years, quietly and without show, joined the Church of England, a symbol of his Christian commitment.

There is only one ambiguous note in Kierkegaard's *Journals,* entered with the exact moment — *"May 19* [1838]. *Half-past ten in the morning.* There is an indescribable joy. . . ." But we don't know whether it was joy at the prospect of returning to his father's house for a reconciliation, or whether the reference is more subtle, his spiritual joy at returning to his heavenly Father's true home.

Raised as a Unitarian in America and hating dramatic public conversions, T. S. Eliot arranged for a private baptism. Shortly thereafter he made his first confession and said that "the recognition of the reality of Sin is a New Life." Like Kierkegaard, Eliot's own person must be discovered behind his writing, and the best account of his conversion is between the lines of his poem *Ash Wednesday,* with the penitent turning and turning on the winding stairway. The image suggests the classic turning away from sin toward God.

Such tantalizing but terse accounts only make us wish for more. Alas, some who might have taught us by revealing their inmost experiences have chosen rather to remain silent about themselves.

Happily, there are so many others, as these representative selections indicate. And whether famous or not, the important thing for any Christian is not only to record what it means to be converted but to have one's own name "written in the Lamb's book of life" (Rev. 21:27).

Jesus answered [Nicodemus], "Very truly, I tell you, no one can see the kingdom of God without being born from above."

JOHN 3:3

"The wind blows where it chooses, and you hear the sound of it, but you do not know where it comes from or where it goes. So it is with everyone who is born of the Spirit."

JOHN 3:8

The Apostle Paul

The dramatic experience of Paul on the road to Damascus still constitutes for many the prototype and model of Christian conversion. It is true, of course, that not all authentic conversions follow the Pauline pattern. Yet there remains something normative in this early apostolic account.

Scholars and psychologists seem fascinated by Paul's conversion, and they try to interpret what it meant and why it happened as it did. Obviously, Paul regarded his experience as of monumental and life-changing importance. There are three more or less parallel accounts of the episode in the book of Acts, and Paul made passing references to the event on other occasions (e.g., Gal. 1:15-16; 1 Cor. 9:1; 15:8; 2 Cor. 4:6).

Before his conversion, Paul was known as a relentless persecutor of the new disciples of Jesus. On many occasions in his letters, Paul enumerates his credentials as a good Jew, a Pharisee in fact (see Rom. 11:1; 2 Cor. 11:22; Phil. 3:5). Paul wants to emphasize this side of his preconversion life simply because, in sharp contrast, his postconversion mission is to be an apostle of Jesus Christ whom he had persecuted. The radical difference of *before* and *after* links Paul's experience with so many later converts, even though their experiences may not have been as sudden or dramatic.

It is possible when interpreting Paul's conversion, or any other for that matter, to so dwell on the details or the discrepancies as to miss the main point. The essential ingredient in the three accounts in Acts, linking all three to a common confrontation, is the question-and-answer exchange: "Why do you persecute me?" . . . "Who are you?" . . . "I am Jesus." Perhaps, then, with this in mind, we can say that the Pauline experience is after all the common experience of all converts.

3

Act 9:3-19

Now as [Saul] was going along and approaching Damascus, suddenly a light from heaven flashed around him. He fell to the ground and heard a voice saying to him, "Saul, Saul, why do you persecute me?" He asked, "Who are you, Lord?" The reply came, "I am Jesus, whom you are persecuting. But get up and enter the city, and you will be told what you are to do." The men who were traveling with him stood speechless because they heard the voice but saw no one. Saul got up from the ground, and though his eyes were open, he could see nothing; so they led him by the hand and brought him into Damascus. For three days he was without sight, and neither ate nor drank.

Now there was a disciple in Damascus named Ananias. The Lord said to him in a vision, "Ananias." He answered, "Here I am, Lord." The Lord said to him, "Get up and go to the street called Straight, and at the house of Judas look for a man of Tarsus named Saul. At this moment he is praying, and he has seen in a vision a man named Ananias come in and lay his hands on him so that he might regain his sight." But Ananias answered, "Lord, I have heard from many about this man, how much evil he has done to your saints in Jerusalem; and here he has authority from the chief priests to bind all who invoke your name." But the Lord said to him, "Go, for he is an instrument whom I have chosen to bring my name before Gentiles and kings and before the people of Israel; I myself will show him how much he must suffer for the sake of my name." So Ananias went and entered the house. He laid his hands on Saul and said, "Brother Saul, the Lord Jesus, who appeared to you on your way here, has sent me so that you may regain your sight and be filled with the Holy Spirit." And immediately something like scales fell from his eyes, and his sight was restored. Then he got up and was baptized, and after taking some food, he regained his strength.

Acts 22:6-16

"While I was on my way and approaching Damascus, about noon a great light from heaven suddenly shone about me. I fell to the ground and heard a voice saying to me, 'Saul, Saul, why are you persecuting me?' I answered, 'Who are you, Lord?' Then he said to me, 'I am Jesus of Nazareth whom you are persecuting.' Now those who were with me saw the light but did not hear the voice of the one who was speaking to me. I asked, 'What am I to do, Lord?' The Lord said to me, 'Get up and go to Damascus; there you will be told everything that has been assigned to you to do.' Since I could not see because of the brightness of that light, those who were with me took my hand and led me to Damascus.

"A certain Ananias, who was a devout man according to the law and well spoken of by all the Jews living there, came to me; and standing beside me, he said, 'Brother Saul, regain your sight!' In that very hour I regained my sight and saw him. Then he said, "The God of our ancestors has chosen you to know his will, to see the Righteous One and to hear his own voice; for you will be his witness to all the world of what you have seen and heard. And now why do you delay? Get up, be baptized, and have your sins washed away, calling on his name.'"

Acts 26:12-18

"With this [persecution] in mind, I was traveling to Damascus with the authority and commission of the chief priests, when at midday along the road, your Excellency, I saw a light from heaven, brighter than the sun, shining around me and my companions. When we had all fallen to the ground, I heard a voice saying to me in the Hebrew language, 'Saul, Saul, why are you persecuting me? It hurts you to kick against the goads.' I asked, 'Who are you, Lord?' The Lord answered, 'I am Jesus whom you are persecuting. But get up and stand on your feet; for I have appeared to you for this purpose, to appoint you to serve and testify to the things in which you have seen me and to those in which I will appear to you. I will rescue you from your people and from the Gentiles — to whom I am sending you to open their eyes so that they may turn from darkness to light and from the power of Satan to God, so that they may receive forgiveness of sins and a place among those who are sanctified by faith in me.'"

Constantine

(ca. 280–337)

In the history of Christianity, few conversions rival Constantine's for its impact on the church and all of Western culture. Converted in his youth, he united the Roman empire under his rule and gave protection to the beleaguered band of early Christians. Constantine declared Christianity to be the official religion of the empire, thus beginning the Christianization of Europe and the shift of Christian power away from its origins in the Middle East to Europe and subsequently elsewhere throughout the world.

This union of church and state became the dominant pattern in Western church history — at least until the eighteenth century — and today it is often described as Constantinian Christianity. In short, Constantine's conversion marked a revolutionary turning point for Christianity.

The enduring effects of this conversion are fairly obvious; the conversion itself is difficult to describe. We have no account by Constantine himself, but Eusebius (260?–340?), known as the "first" church historian, recorded an early version in his *Ecclesiastical History*. Another description appears in *The Life of Constantine the Great,* which is supposed to have been written later by Eusebius. The second account emphasizes the powerful vision revealed to Constantine, and this dimension of the story was probably picked up from a very brief narrative of Constantine's conversion by Lactantius, a Christian tutor in Constantine's family. Reprinted here are the two versions by Eusebius.

Despite the differences, it is clear that Constantine was converted in A.D. 312 and that his victory over Maxentius at the Milvian Bridge ended a Roman civil war and assured Constantine's control over the Roman empire. But the variations in the texts raise difficult problems. Was there a vision? Was Constantine's conversion a genuine religious experience or a matter of astute political policy? What influenced him to accept Christianity? Did he become a full Christian at once or did he accept Christianity as only one of many forms of worship of an all-powerful deity?

An account from Constantine himself would probably not answer these questions, for they are tied to the mystery of the conversion experience itself. It may have been good politics to give the empire a common religion, but there was no compelling reason why it had to be Christianity. Yet Constantine became a Christian; with that the history of the world changed, and the church today still lives with the results of Constantine's decision for Christ.

~

When Constantine, whom we have already mentioned as an emperor, born of an emperor, a pious son of a most pious and prudent father; and Licinius, second to him, — two God-beloved emperors, honored alike for their intelligence and their piety, — being stirred up against the two most impious tyrants by God, the absolute Ruler and Saviour of all, engaged in formal war against them, with God as their ally, Maxentius was defeated at Rome by Constantine in a remarkable manner, and the tyrant of the East did not long survive him, but met a most shameful death at the hand of Licinius, who had not yet become insane. Constantine, who was the superior both in dignity and imperial rank, first took compassion upon those who were oppressed at Rome, and having invoked in prayer the God of heaven, and his Word, and Jesus Christ himself, the Saviour of all, as his aid, advanced with his whole army, proposing to restore to the Romans their ancestral liberty. But Maxentius, putting confidence rather in the arts of sorcery than in the devotion of his subjects, did not dare to go forth beyond the gates of the city, but fortified every place and district and town which was enslaved by him, in the neighborhood of Rome and in all Italy, with an immense multitude of troops and with innumerable bands of soldiers. But the emperor, relying upon the assistance of God, attacked the first, second, and third army of the tyrant, and conquered them all; and having advanced through the greater part of Italy, was already very near Rome. Then, that he might not be compelled to wage war with the Romans for

---

Excerpted from Eusebius, *The Ecclesiastical History*, IX.9.1-12, and *The Life of Constantine the Great*, I.xxvi-xxxix, in *Nicene and Post-Nicene Fathers of the Christian Church*, 2nd series, ed. Philip Schaff and Henry Wace (New York, 1890; Grand Rapids: Eerdmans, 1952), 1:363-64, 489-93.

the sake of the tyrant, God himself drew the latter, as if bound in chains, some distance without the gates, and confirmed those threats against the impious which had been anciently inscribed in sacred books, — disbelieved, indeed, by most as a myth, but believed by the faithful, — confirmed them, in a word, by the deed itself to all, both believers and unbelievers, that saw the wonder with their eyes. Thus, as in the time of Moses himself and of the ancient God-beloved race of Hebrews, "he cast Pharaoh's chariots and host into the sea, and overwhelmed his chosen charioteers in the Red Sea, and covered them with the flood," in the same way Maxentius also with his soldiers and body-guards "went down into the depths like a stone," when he fled before the power of God which was with Constantine, and passed through the river which lay in his way, over which he formed a bridge with his boats, and thus prepared the means of his own destruction. In regard to him one might say, "he digged a pit and opened it and fell into the hole which he had made; his labor shall turn upon his own head, and his unrighteousness shall fall upon his own crown." Thus, then, the bridge over the river being broken, the passageway settled down, and immediately the boats with the men disappeared in the depths, and that most impious one himself first of all, then the shield-bearers who were with him, as the divine oracles foretold, "sank like lead in the mighty waters"; so that those who obtained the victory from God, if not in words, at least in deeds, like Moses, the great servant of God, and those who were with him, fittingly sang as they had sung against the impious tyrant of old, saying, "Let us sing unto the Lord, for he hath gloriously glorified himself; horse and rider hath he thrown into the sea; a helper and a protector hath he become for my salvation"; and "Who is like unto thee, O Lord; among the gods, who is like unto thee? glorious in holiness, marvelous in glory, doing wonders." These and the like praises Constantine, by his very deeds, sang to God, the universal Ruler, and Author of his victory, as he entered Rome in triumph. Immediately all the members of the senate and the other most celebrated men, with the whole Roman people, together with children and women, received him as their deliverer, their saviour, and their benefactor, with shining eyes and with their whole souls, with shouts of gladness and unbounded joy. But he, as one possessed of inborn piety toward God, did not exult in the shouts, nor was he elated by the praises; but perceiving that his aid was from God, he immediately commanded that a trophy of the Saviour's passion be put in the hand of his own statue. And when he had placed it, with the saving sign of the cross in its right hand, in the most public place in Rome, he commanded that the following inscription should be engraved upon it in the Roman tongue: "By this salutary sign, the true proof of bravery, I have saved and freed your city from the yoke of the tyrant; and moreover, having set at liberty both the senate and the people of Rome, I have restored them to their ancient distinction and splendor." And after this both Constantine himself and with him the Emperor Licinius, who had not yet been seized by that madness into which he later fell, praising God as the author of all their blessings, with one will and mind drew up a full and most complete decree in behalf of the Christians, and sent an account of the wonderful things done for them by God, and of the victory over the tyrant, together with a copy of the decree itself, to Maximinus, who still ruled over the nations of the East and pretended friendship toward them. But he, like a tyrant, was greatly pained by what he learned; but not wishing to seem to yield to others, nor, on the other hand, to suppress that which was commanded, for fear of those who enjoined it, as if on his own authority, he addressed, under compulsion, to the governors under him this first communication in behalf of the Christians, falsely inventing things against himself which had never been done by him.

*   *   *

Thus then the God of all, the Supreme Governor of the whole universe, by his own will appointed Constantine, the descendant of so renowned a parent, to be prince and sovereign: so that, while others have been raised to this distinction by the election of their fellow-men, he is the only one to whose elevation no mortal may boast of having contributed.

While . . . he regarded the entire world as one immense body, and perceived that the head of it all, the royal city of the Roman empire, was bowed down by the weight of a tyrannous oppression; at first he had left the task of liberation to those who governed the other divisions of the empire, as being his superiors in point of age. But when none of these proved able to afford relief, and those who had attempted it had experienced a disastrous termination of their enterprise, he said that life was without enjoyment to him as long as he saw the imperial city thus afflicted, and prepared himself for the overthrowal of the tyranny.

Being convinced, however, that he needed some more powerful

aid than his military forces could afford him, on account of the wicked and magical enchantments which were so diligently practiced by the tyrant, he sought Divine assistance, deeming the possession of arms and a numerous soldiery of secondary importance, but believing the co-operating power of Deity invincible and not to be shaken. He considered, therefore, on what God he might rely for protection and assistance. While engaged in this enquiry, the thought occurred to him, that, of the many emperors who had preceded him, those who had rested their hopes in a multitude of gods, and served them with sacrifices and offerings, had in the first place been deceived by flattering predictions, and oracles which promised them all prosperity, and at last had met with an unhappy end, while not one of their gods had stood by to warn them of the impending wrath of heaven; while one alone who had pursued an entirely opposite course, who had condemned their error, and honored the one Supreme God during his whole life, had found him to be the Saviour and Protector of his empire, and the Giver of every good thing. Reflecting on this, and well weighing the fact that they who had trusted in many gods had also fallen by manifold forms of death, without leaving behind them either family or offspring, stock, name, or memorial among men: while the God of his father had given to him, on the other hand, manifestations of his power and very many tokens: and considering farther that those who had already taken arms against the tyrant, and had marched to the battle-field under the protection of a multitude of gods, had met with a dishonorable end (for one of them had shamefully retreated from the contest without a blow, and the other, being slain in the midst of his own troops, became, as it were, the mere sport of death); reviewing, I say, all these considerations, he judged it to be folly indeed to join in the idle worship of those who were no gods, and, after such convincing evidence, to err from the truth; and therefore felt it incumbent on him to honor his father's God alone.

Accordingly he called on him with earnest prayer and supplications that he would reveal to him who he was, and stretch forth his right hand to help him in his present difficulties. And while he was thus praying with fervent entreaty, a most marvelous sign appeared to him from heaven, the account of which it might have been hard to believe had it been related by any other person. But since the victorious emperor himself long afterwards declared it to the writer of this history, when he was honored with his acquaintance and society, and confirmed his statement by an oath, who could hesitate to accredit the relation, especially since the testimony of after-time has established its truth? He said that about noon, when the day was already beginning to decline, he saw with his own eyes the trophy of a cross of light in the heavens, above the sun, and bearing the inscription, CONQUER BY THIS [*In Hoc Signo*]. At this sight he himself was struck with amazement, and his whole army also, which followed him on this expedition, and witnessed the miracle.

He said, moreover, that he doubted within himself what the import of this apparition could be. And while he continued to ponder and reason on its meaning, night suddenly came on; then in his sleep the Christ of God appeared to him with the same sign which he had seen in the heavens, and commanded him to make a likeness of that sign which he had seen in the heavens, and to use it as a safeguard in all engagements with his enemies.

At dawn of day he arose, and communicated the marvel to his friends: and then, calling together the workers in gold and precious stones, he sat in the midst of them, and described to them the figure of the sign he had seen, bidding them represent it in gold and precious stones. And this representation I myself have had an opportunity of seeing.

Now it was made in the following manner. A long spear, overlaid with gold, formed the figure of the cross by means of a transverse bar laid over it. On the top of the whole was fixed a wreath of gold and precious stones; and within this, the symbol of the Saviour's name, two letters indicating the name of Christ by means of its initial characters, the letter P being intersected by X in its centre: and these letters the emperor was in the habit of wearing on his helmet at a later period. From the cross-bar of the spear was suspended a cloth, a royal piece, covered with a profuse embroidery of most brilliant precious stones; and which, being also richly interlaced with gold, presented an indescribable degree of beauty to the beholder. This banner was of a square form, and the upright staff, whose lower section was of great length, bore a golden half-length portrait of the pious emperor and his children on its upper part, beneath the trophy of the cross, and immediately above the embroidered banner.

The emperor constantly made use of this sign of salvation as a safeguard against every adverse and hostile power, and commanded that others similar to it should be carried at the head of all his armies.

These things were done shortly afterwards. But at the time above specified, being struck with amazement at the extraordinary vision, and resolving to worship no other God save Him who had appeared to him, he sent for those who were acquainted with the mysteries of His doctrines, and enquired who that God was, and what was intended by the sign of the vision he had seen.

They affirmed that He was God, the only begotten Son of the one and only God: that the sign which had appeared was the symbol of immortality, and the trophy of that victory over death which He had gained in time past when sojourning on earth. They taught him also the causes of His advent, and explained to him the true account of His incarnation. Thus he was instructed in these matters, and was impressed with wonder at the divine manifestation which had been presented to his sight. Comparing, therefore, the heavenly vision with the interpretation given, he found his judgment confirmed; and, in the persuasion that the knowledge of these things had been imparted to him by Divine teaching, he determined thenceforth to devote himself to the reading of the Inspired writings.

Moreover, he made the priests of God his counselors, and deemed it incumbent on him to honor the God who had appeared to him with all devotion. And after this, being fortified by well-grounded hopes in Him, he hastened to quench the threatening fire of tyranny. . . .

And already he was approaching very near Rome itself, when, to save him from the necessity of fighting with all the Romans for the tyrant's sake, God himself drew the tyrant, as it were by secret cords, a long way outside the gates. And now those miracles recorded in Holy Writ, which God of old wrought against the ungodly (discredited by most as fables, yet believed by the faithful), did he in every deed confirm to all alike, believers and unbelievers, who were eye-witnesses of the wonders. For as once in the days of Moses and the Hebrew nation, who were worshipers of God, "Pharaoh's chariots and his host hath he cast into the sea, and his chosen chariot-captains are drowned in the Red Sea," — so at this time Maxentius, and the soldiers and guards with him, "went down into the depths like stone," when, in his flight before the divinely-aided forces of Constantine, he essayed to cross the river which lay in his way, over which, making a strong bridge of boats, he had framed an engine of destruction, really against himself, but in the hope of ensnaring thereby him who was beloved by God. For his God stood by the one to protect him, while the other, godless, proved to be the miserable contriver of these secret devices to his own ruin. So that one might well say, "He hath made a pit, and digged it, and is fallen into the ditch which he made. His mischief shall return upon his own head, and his violence shall come down upon his own pate." Thus, in the present instance, under divine direction, the machine erected on the bridge, with the ambuscade concealed therein, giving way unexpectedly before the appointed time, the bridge began to sink, and the boats with the men in them went bodily to the bottom. And first the wretch himself, then his armed attendants and guards, even as the sacred oracles had before described, "sank as lead in the mighty waters." So that they who thus obtained victory from God might well, if not in the same words, yet in fact in the same spirit as the people of his great servant Moses, sing and speak as they did concerning the impious tyrant of old: "Let us sing unto the Lord, for he hath been glorified exceedingly: the horse and his rider hath he thrown into the sea. He is become my helper and my shield unto salvation." And again, "Who is like unto thee, O Lord, among the gods? who is like thee, glorious in holiness, marvelous in praises, doing wonders?"

Having then at this time sung these and such-like praises to God, the Ruler of all and the Author of victory, after the example of his great servant Moses, Constantine entered the imperial city in triumph. And here the whole body of the senate, and others of rank and distinction in the city, freed as it were from the restraint of a prison, along with the whole Roman populace, their countenances expressive of the gladness of their hearts, received him with acclamations and abounding joy; men, women, and children, with countless multitudes of servants, greeting him as deliverer, preserver, and benefactor, with incessant shouts. But he, being possessed of inward piety toward God, was neither rendered arrogant by these plaudits, nor uplifted by the praises he heard; but, being sensible that he had received help from God, he immediately rendered a thanksgiving to him as the Author of his victory.

Augustine

(354-430)

Like the apostle Paul, with whom he had so much in common, Augustine's career as churchman and theologian began with a sudden, dramatic conversion.
With both men, the experience became determinative for all their subsequent
life and thought, and, in later years, each frequently reminisced about his conversion experience, indicating its enduring and normative influence.

Born in 354 in Tagaste, North Africa, Augustine was the last and the greatest of the so-called early church "Fathers." He also had one foot in the early
Middle Ages, so that both patristic and medieval theology were combined in
his own system. But "system" is hardly the right word for Augustine's theology. He was, especially in his youthful years, an eclectic sampler of various
schools of philosophy, religion, and morality. Even after his conversion and
during his prolific writing career, Augustine moved from topic to topic in an
endless succession of seemingly unrelated works. His two most important
theological foci were sin and grace, and the conflict that these two set up in
his own experience, as in his conversion, provided a trademark for nearly everything he did or wrote.

It is tempting to interpret Augustine psychologically at this point, for just
as his theology seems to combine opposing ideas, so does his personality.
His father, Patricius, was not a religious man and seemed mostly untroubled
by moral questions; but Augustine's mother, Monnica, was a Christian of rare
devotion. Perhaps Augustine was himself the mixture of the sensual father
and the Christian mother.

After some years of studying in various centers, and a long-standing relationship with a nameless mistress, by whom a son, Adeodatus, was born,
Monnica and a few friends persuaded Augustine to go to Milan to study with
the great Ambrose. It was while in Milan, in the year 386 and in the company

of a friend, Alypius, that Augustine experienced his moving conversion. He had been agonizing, as had Paul, about the power of sin and the failure of his will. "I do not do the good I want, but the evil I do not want is what I do. . . . Wretched man that I am!" (Rom. 7:19, 24).

Augustine's own description of the event needs no further commentary. It was included in one of the world's great devotional classics, the *Confessions*. Although written more than forty years later, we can be reasonably certain, because of its intensity, that Augustine remembered the experience vividly, even to the details.

~

There was a little garden belonging to our lodging, of which we had the use — as of the whole house — for the master, our landlord, did not live there. The tempest in my breast hurried me out into this garden, where no one might interrupt the fiery struggle in which I was engaged with myself, until it came to the outcome that thou knewest though I did not. But I was mad for health, and dying for life; knowing what evil thing I was, but not knowing what good thing I was so shortly to become.

I fled into the garden, with Alypius following step by step; for I had no secret in which he did not share, and how could he leave me in such distress? We sat down, as far from the house as possible. I was greatly disturbed in spirit, angry at myself with a turbulent indignation because I had not entered thy will and covenant, O my God, while all my bones cried out to me to enter, extolling it to the skies. The way therein is not by ships or chariots or feet — indeed it was not as far as I had come from the house to the place where we were seated. For to go along that road and indeed to reach the goal is nothing else but the will to go. But it must be a strong and single will, not staggering and swaying about this way and that — a changeable, twisting, fluctuating will, wrestling with itself while one part falls as another rises. . . .

Now when deep reflection had drawn up out of the secret depths of my soul all my misery and had heaped it up before the sight of my heart, there arose a mighty storm, accompanied by a mighty rain of tears. That

From *Augustine: Confessions and Enchiridion,* trans. and ed. Albert C. Outler, vol. 7 of the Library of Christian Classics (London: SCM Press; Philadelphia: Westminster Press, 1955). Extracts from Library of Christian Classics are copyright © SCM Press and are reproduced by permission.

I might give way full to my tears and lamentations, I stole away from Alypius, for it seemed to me that solitude was more appropriate for the business of weeping. I went far enough away that I could feel that even his presence was no restraint upon me. This was the way I felt at the time, and he realized it. I suppose I had said something before I started up and he noticed that the sound of my voice was choked with weeping. And so he stayed alone, where we had been sitting together, greatly astonished. I flung myself down under a fig tree — how I know not — and gave free course to my tears. The streams of my eyes gushed out an acceptable sacrifice to thee. And, not indeed in these words, but to this effect, I cried to thee: "And thou, O Lord, how long? How long, O Lord? Wilt thou be angry forever? Oh, remember not against us our former iniquities."[1] For I felt that I was still enthralled by them. I sent up these sorrowful cries: "How long, how long? Tomorrow and tomorrow? Why not now? Why not this very hour make an end to my uncleanness?"

I was saying these things and weeping in the most bitter contrition of my heart, when suddenly I heard the voice of a boy or a girl — I know not which — coming from the neighboring house, chanting over and over again, "Pick it up, read it; pick it up, read it."[2] Immediately I ceased weeping and began most earnestly to think whether it was usual for children in some kind of game to sing such a song, but I could not remember ever having heard the like. So, damming the torrent of my tears, I got to my feet, for I could not but think that this was a divine command to open the Bible and read the first passage I should light upon. For I had heard[3] how Anthony, accidentally coming into church while the gospel was being read, received the admonition as if what was read had been addressed to him: "Go and sell what you have and give it to the poor, and you shall have treasure in heaven; and come and follow me."[4] By such an oracle he was forthwith converted to thee.

So I quickly returned to the bench where Alypius was sitting, for there I had put down the apostle's book when I had left there. I snatched it up, opened it, and in silence read the paragraph on which my eyes first fell: "Not in rioting and drunkenness, not in chambering and wantonness, not in strife and envying, but put on the Lord Jesus

1. Cf. Ps. 6:3; 79:8.
2. This is the famous *Tolle, lege; tolle, lege.*
3. Doubtless from Ponticianus, in their earlier conversation.
4. Matt. 19:21.

Christ, and make no provision for the flesh to fulfill the lusts thereof."[5] I wanted to read no further, nor did I need to. For instantly, as the sentence ended, there was infused in my heart something like the light of full certainty and all the gloom of doubt vanished away.

Closing the book, then, and putting my finger or something else for a mark I began — now with a tranquil countenance — to tell it all to Alypius. And he in turn disclosed to me what had been going on in himself, of which I knew nothing. He asked to see what I had read. I showed him, and he looked on even further than I had read. I had not known what followed. But indeed it was this, "Him that is weak in the faith, receive."[6] This he applied to himself, and told me so. By these words of warning he was strengthened, and by exercising his good resolution and purpose — all very much in keeping with his character, in which, in these respects, he was always far different from and better than I — he joined me in full commitment without any restless hesitation.

Then we went in to my mother, and told her what happened, to her great joy. We explained to her how it had occurred — and she leaped for joy triumphant; and she blessed thee, who art "able to do exceedingly abundantly above all that we ask or think."[7] For she saw that thou hadst granted her far more than she had ever asked for in all her pitiful and doleful lamentations. For thou didst so convert me to thee that I sought neither a wife nor any other of this world's hopes, but set my feet on that rule of faith which so many years before thou hadst showed her in her dream about me. And so thou didst turn her grief into gladness more plentiful than she had ventured to desire, and dearer and purer than the desire she used to cherish of having grandchildren of my flesh.

5. Rom. 13:13.
6. Rom. 14:1.
7. Eph. 3:20.

Martin Luther

(1483–1546)

Martin Luther was unquestionably one of the most important figures in the history of Christianity and the history of Europe. He never intended to start a new church but to reform the Roman Catholic Church in which he was raised, baptized, and ordained. But by his life and writings, he launched both the ideas and the movements that would divide Western Christianity into Protestant and Catholic camps and mold what became modern Western culture.

Luther was a coal miner's son. His father yearned for and achieved financial success, and he hoped his son Martin would find similar prosperity. When Martin finished his liberal arts studies at the University of Erfurt, the elder Luther pressured him into studying law. Less than six weeks later, Martin Luther abandoned law to enter the Augustinian monastery at Erfurt. The abrupt decision was due to the first of three monumental crises in Luther's life. On a trip through a forest amid a violent thunderstorm, Luther cried out in terror, "Help me, St. Anne, I will become a monk."

As in virtually all things, Luther took to monasticism with a visceral commitment and emotional zeal. Throughout his early spiritual struggles, the central question was certainty: How could he be sure that he had been saved by God? He tried to abide by every discipline known to the monastery. Indeed, he later said, "I was a good monk, and I kept the rule of my order so strictly that I may say that if ever a monk got to heaven by his monkery it was I."

But as soon as he had satisfied the rigors of the rule of monastic life, he was afflicted by doubt again: Have I done enough? Is more required?

His second crisis came before he celebrated his first Mass. Plagued again by his doubts about his righteousness before God, he was barely able to perform the service and handle the holy elements with what he perceived were his unholy hands.

Interestingly for Luther, the third crisis was a quiet affair, known as his "tower experience." Luther was primarily a student and scholar of the Bible, earning a doctorate in biblical studies. His preoccupation was the study of the Scriptures, which he increasingly saw as the foremost authority for Christian life and faith. His spiritual imagination was captured most by the anguish of the apostle Paul, who, like Luther, wrestled with the question of how unrighteous individuals could find refuge in a righteous God.

The account that follows, written the year before he died, is Luther's "tower experience," a breakthrough in his study where he discovered again Paul's conviction that people are not saved by their works or deeds. Rather, they are saved by the love of God in Jesus Christ that sets them right with God. This insight — justification by grace through faith — would serve as one of the rallying cries of the entire Protestant Reformation and has shaped Protestantism ever since.

Luther's influence extended well beyond theology and church affairs. As a writer of hymns and lover of music, he nurtured the artistic impulse in Western culture. As a translator of the Bible into German, he set the standards of the modern German language and stimulated literacy and education. In politics, his legacy is ambiguous, for he not only blessed the stirrings of liberty but also condemned the uprising of peasants and contributed to the anti-Semitism of his age and subsequent European history.

But as a religious genius, he unquestionably grasped the reality of the question posed to Paul by his jailer: "What must I do to be saved?" (Acts 16:30). In answering that question, Martin Luther captured the biblical truth that we cannot save ourselves; only God can save us. In answer to the more modern question, "How can I be sure?" Luther declared in his most famous hymn,

> A mighty fortress is our God,
> A bulwark never failing.

~

Meanwhile, I had already during that year returned to interpret the Psalter anew. I had confidence in the fact that I was more skilful, after I

From *Luther's Works*, volume 34: *Career of the Reformer* IV by Martin Luther, edited by Lewis W. Spitz; Helmut Lehmann, general editor, pp. 336-38. Copyright © 1960 Fortress Press, 2011 Evangelical Lutheran Church in America admin Augsburg Fortress. Use by permission.

had lectured in the university on St. Paul's epistles to the Romans, to the Galatians, and the one to the Hebrews. I had indeed been captivated with an extraordinary ardor for understanding Paul in the Epistle to the Romans. But up till then it was not the cold blood about the heart, but a single word in Chapter 1 [v. 17], "In it the righteousness of God is revealed," that had stood in my way. For I hated that word "righteousness of God," which, according to the use and custom of all the teachers, I had been taught to understand philosophically regarding the formal or active righteousness, as they called it, with which God is righteous and punishes the unrighteous sinner.

Though I lived as a monk without reproach, I felt that I was a sinner before God with an extremely disturbed conscience. I could not believe that he was placated by my satisfaction. I did not love, yes, I hated the righteous God who punishes sinners, and secretly, if not blasphemously, certainly murmuring greatly, I was angry with God, and said, "As if, indeed, it is not enough, that miserable sinners, eternally lost through original sin, are crushed by every kind of calamity by the law of the decalogue, without having God add pain to pain by the gospel and also by the gospel threatening us with his righteousness and wrath!" Thus I raged with a fierce and troubled conscience. Nevertheless, I beat importunately upon Paul at that place, most ardently desiring to know what St. Paul wanted.

At last, by the mercy of God, meditating day and night, I gave heed to the context of the words, namely, "In it the righteousness of God is revealed, as it is written, 'He who through faith is righteous shall live.'" There I began to understand that the righteousness of God is that by which the righteous lives by a gift of God, namely by faith. And this is the meaning: the righteousness of God is revealed by the gospel, namely, the passive righteousness with which merciful God justifies us by faith, as it is written, "He who through faith is righteous shall live." Here I felt that I was altogether born again and had entered paradise itself through open gates. There a totally other face of the entire Scripture showed itself to me. Thereupon I ran through the Scriptures from memory. I also found in other terms an analogy, as, the work of God, that is, what God does in us, the power of God, with which he makes us strong, the wisdom of God, with which he makes us wise, the strength of God, the salvation of God, the glory of God.

And I extolled my sweetest word with a love as great as the hatred with which I had before hated the word "righteousness of God." Thus that place in Paul was for me truly the gate to paradise. Later I read Augustine's *The Spirit and the Letter,* where contrary to hope I found that he, too, interpreted God's righteousness in a similar way, as the righteousness with which God clothes us when he justifies us. Although this was heretofore said imperfectly and he did not explain all things concerning imputation clearly, it nevertheless was pleasing that God's righteousness with which we are justified was taught. Armed more fully with these thoughts, I began a second time to interpret the Psalter. And the work would have grown into a large commentary, if I had not again been compelled to leave the work begun, because Emperor Charles V in the following year convened the diet at Worms.

I relate these things, good reader, so that, if you are a reader of my puny works, you may keep in mind, that, as I said above, I was all alone and one of those who, as Augustine says of himself, have become proficient by writing and teaching. I was not one of those who from nothing suddenly become the topmost, though they are nothing, neither have labored, nor been tempted, nor become experienced, but have with one look at the Scriptures exhausted their entire spirit.

Bartolomé de Las Casas

(1484–1566)

It is a sad, tragic, and horrific fact that the settlement of North and South America — indeed, the colonization of the world by Western European nations — is also the story of slavery. It is also sad that in most cases, the Christian church helped justify and undergird the practice of slave-trading and slave-holding.

But there were exceptions, and one was Bartolomé de Las Casas, who was born just as Christopher Columbus was planning his explorations of what was later called the "New World." In 1493, as a young boy, Las Casas saw the return of Christopher Columbus to Seville after his first voyage. Las Casas's father Pedro and several uncles left with Columbus the same year and returned in 1498. His father's present to Bartolomé when he returned was the gift of a young native Taíno youth, Juanico, with whom Las Casas forged a friendship. Although Juanico was returned to the West Indies by royal decree two years later, this was Las Casas's first exposure to slavery.

Las Casas's father decided to return to the West Indies permanently, and after briefly studying for the priesthood, Las Casas accompanied him. After five years, Las Casas returned to Spain, and in Rome in 1507 he was ordained as a priest. He pursued additional theological studies, and then he returned to Hispaniola (now the Dominican Republic and Haiti). There Las Casas performed the duties of a priest but also presided over his own land-holdings and slaves. He also encountered a group of Dominican friars, whose opposition to slavery was clear and uncompromising. He asked for absolution for his own enslavement of the natives and was denied. Yet he made peace with himself because he was a humane and gentle slaveholder.

Las Casas departed Hispaniola in 1512, leaving behind his clerical duties, his land, and his slaves to become a chaplain to the Spanish forces in Cuba.

There he witnessed some of the atrocities of the Spanish military, and he became increasingly concerned about the brutality and injustice of enslaving the natives. It was in this context that Pentecost 1514 arrived. The conflict between God's design and human slavery became clear to Las Casas. And he had to preach about it.

That was the turning point — the moral conversion — of Las Casas. He gave up his slaves. He became the preeminent advocate against slavery of the native peoples of the West Indies and South America and was instrumental in the formulation of the New Laws (1542) that abolished the basic economic structure of slavery in Latin America. He eventually joined a Dominican monastery and turned to writing a history of Columbus's voyages and the history of the West Indies, from which the following account of his moral crisis is taken. (Las Casas wrote in both the first person and the third person, but readers should understand that he is describing himself throughout this passage.)

Las Casas became the moral compass of Spanish colonization. His writings and the New Laws he helped formulate represent the beginning of modern international law and presage the later United Nations Declaration of Human Rights. Though he failed to squash slavery's most violent and devastating consequences, he was a voice for equity and compassion in the midst of greed and acquisition.

He listened to God and tested himself against a biblical text: "The Lord is pleased only by those who keep to the way of truth and justice."

~

1. Seeing Conditions in Cuba

. . . We told how Diego Velásquez, in charge of Cuba for the admiral, marked out five places for settlement where all the Spaniards on the island were to live in groups. There was one already populated, Baracoa. The Indians who lived near each settlement were divided up and given to the Spaniards. Each Spaniard had an itch for gold and a narrow conscience. They had no thought that those natives were made of flesh and

---

Excerpted from *Bartolomé de las Casas: The Only Way*, Helen Rand Parish, ed., Francis Patrick Sullivan, S.J., trans. (New York: Paulist Press, 1992), 186-91. Reprinted with permission from the publisher via Copyright Clearance Center.

blood. They put them to work in mines and at other projects the Indians could accomplish as slave labor, put them to work so promptly, so pitilessly that in a few days' time many native deaths showed the brutality of Spanish treatment. The loss of people on Cuba was quicker, fiercer, during the early period than it was elsewhere. The explanation: the Spaniards roamed the island *pacifying* it. They took many Indians from the villages as servants for themselves. The Spaniards reaped but did not sow. As to the villagers, some fled; some, nervous and fearful, cared only to escape being killed as many another was killed. The fields were picked clean of food and abandoned.

Since greed fed the Spaniards, as I said, they cared nothing for sowing and reaping food; they cared only for reaping gold they had not sown, however they could, eating whatever scraps of food they could scrounge up. And they set men and women to work without food enough to live on, never mind work on, in the mines. It is a true story, one I told elsewhere, that a Spaniard recounted in my presence and in that of several others, as if he were telling a fine way of doing things. He had his allotted Indians raise so many thousand mound-rows. (That is how they grow [the root] cassava bread is made from.) He sent them every third day, or two on, two off, to the fields to eat whatever growth they found. With what they then had in their bellies he made them work another two or three days in the mines. He gave them not another bite to eat. Farm work means digging the whole day, a far harder job than tilling our vineyards and food gardens home in Spain. It means raising into mounds the earth they dig, three to four feet square, three to four hands high. And not with spades or hoes that are provided, but with pole-length, fire-hardened sticks.

Hunger, having nothing to eat, being put to hard labor, caused death among these peoples more quickly, more violently, than in any other place. The Spaniards took healthy men and women to do mine and other work. They left behind in the villages only the sick and the old, left no one to help them, care for them. So the sick and old died from anguish and age as well as from mortal hunger. I sometimes heard, back then when I traveled the island, as I would enter a village, voices calling from inside the huts. When I went in to find out what they wanted, they answered, *"Food!" "Food!"* There was not a man or a woman able to stand on two legs that they did not drag off to the mines. As for the new mothers with their small boy and girl children, their breasts dried: they had so little to eat, so much work, they had no milk left, the babies died. That was the cause of the deaths of seven thousand baby boys and girls in the space of three months. The event was described in a report to the Catholic king by a creditable person who had investigated it. Another event also occurred back then. An official of the king got three hundred Indians as his allotment. He was in such a hurry putting them to work in the mines and at the rest of his jobs that at the end of three months only a tenth of those Indians remained alive.

The crushing of Indians took this route and grew in ferocity each day. As greed grew and grew, so did the number of Indian dead. [While this was going on] Padre Bartolomé de las Casas (mentioned briefly above) was very busy looking after his own holdings. As the others did, he sent his allotted Indians to the mines to dig gold, to the fields to plant crops, profiting from his Indians as much as he could, though he was always careful to maintain them well in every way possible, and treat them kindly, and alleviate their hardships. But he took no more care than the others to recall that these were pagan peoples and that he had an obligation to teach them Christian doctrine and gather them into the bosom of the Church.

2. Hearing the Call in Cuba

Diego Velásquez and the group of Spaniards with him left the port of Xagua to go and found a settlement of Spaniards in the province, where they established the town called Sancti Espiritus. Apart from Bartolomé de las Casas, there was not a single cleric or friar on the whole island, except for one in the town of Baracoa. The feast of Pentecost was coming up. So he agreed to leave his home on the Arimao River (accent on the penult) a league from Xagua where his holdings were and go say mass and preach for them on that feast. Las Casas looked over the previous sermons he had preached to them on that feast and his other sermons for that season. He began to meditate on some passages of Sacred Scripture. If my memory serves me, the first and most important was from Ecclesiasticus 34:18 ff.:

> Unclean is the offering sacrificed by an oppressor. [Such] mockeries of the unjust are not pleasing [to God]. The Lord is pleased only by those who keep to the way of truth and justice. The Most High does not accept the gifts of unjust people, He does not look

well upon their offerings. Their sins will not be expiated by repeat-sacrifices. *The one whose sacrifice comes from the goods of the poor is like one who kills his neighbor. The one who sheds blood and the one who defrauds the laborer are kin and kind.*

He began to reflect on the misery, the forced labor the Indians had to undergo. He was helped in this by what he had heard and experienced on the island of Hispaniola, by what the Dominicans preached continually — no one could, in good conscience, hold the Indians in encomienda, and those friars would not confess and absolve any who so held them — a preaching Las Casas had refused to accept. One time he wanted to confess to a religious of St. Dominic who happened to be in the vicinity. Las Casas held Indians on that island of Hispaniola, as indifferent and blind about it as he was on the island of Cuba. The religious refused him confession. Las Casas asked him why. He gave the reason. Las Casas objected with frivolous arguments and empty explanations, seemingly sound, provoking the religious to respond, "Padre, I think the truth has many enemies and the lie has many friends." Then Las Casas offered him the respect due his dignity and reputation because the religious was a revered and learned man, much more so than the padre, but he took no heed of the confessor's counsel to let his Indians go. Yet it helped him greatly to recall his quarrel later, and also the confession he made to the religious, so as to think more about the road of ignorance and danger he was on, holding Indians as others did, confessing without scruple those who held or wanted to hold Indians, though he did not do so for long. But he had heard many confessions on that island of Hispaniola, from people who were in the same mortal sin.

He spent some days thinking about the situation, each day getting surer and surer from what he read concerning what was legal and what was actual, measuring the one by the other, until he came to the same truth by himself. Everything in these Indies that was done to the Indians was tyrannical and unjust. Everything he read to firm up his judgment he found favorable, and he used to say strongly that from the very moment he began to dispel the darkness of that ignorance, he never read a book in Latin or Spanish — a countless number over the span of forty-two years — where he didn't find some argument or authority to prove or support the justice of those Indian peoples, and to condemn the injustices done to them, the evils, the injuries.

3. Responding in Cuba

He then made a decision to preach his conclusion. But since his holding Indians meant holding a contradiction of his own preaching, he determined to give them up so as to be free to condemn allotments, the whole system of forced labor, as unjust and tyrannical, and to hand his Indians back to Governor Diego Velásquez. They were better off under the padre's control, to be sure. He had treated them with greater respect, would be even more respectful in the future. He knew that giving them up meant they would be handed over to someone who would brutalize them, work them to death, as someone did ultimately. Granted, he would give them a treatment as good as a father would give his children. Yet, since he would preach that no one could in good conscience hold Indians, he could never escape people mocking back at him, "You hold Indians nonetheless. Why not release them? You say holding them is tyranny!" So he decided to give them up completely.

To get a better understanding of all that happened, it would be right here to recall the close friendship the padre had with a certain Pedro de la Rentería, a prudent, deeply Christian man. We spoke of him earlier somewhat [saying that he was the only encomendero I remember who cared for the Indian soul]. They were not just friends, but partners also in the estate. They received together their allotments of natives. They had decided together that Pedro de la Rentería should go to the island of Jamaica where Pedro had a brother. The purpose: to bring back pigs to fatten and corn to plant, plus other things not found in Cuba since it was cleaned out, a fact already established. For the voyage they chartered a government ship for two thousand castellanos. So, since Pedro de la Rentería was away, and since the padre had decided to give up his Indians and go preach what he felt obliged to preach and thus enlighten those who were deep in the darkness of ignorance, he went on a day to Governor Diego Velásquez. He told him what he thought about his own situation, the situation of the governor, and of the rest of the Spaniards. He stated that no one in that situation could be saved, and he stated that he intended to preach this to escape the danger, and to do what his priesthood required. Thus he was determined to give back his Indians to the governor, to keep charge of them no longer. Therefore the governor should consider them available and should dispose of them as he wished. But the padre asked the favor that the business be kept secret, that the governor give the Indians to no one else until Rentería returned

27

from the island of Jamaica where he was at the moment. The reason: the estate and the Indians they held in common might suffer harm if, before Rentería returned, the person to whom the governor gave the Indians might move in on them and the estate prematurely.

The governor was shocked at hearing such an unusual story. For one thing, that a cleric who was free to own things in the world should be of the opinion of the Dominican friars — they had first dared to think it and dared to make it known. For another, that the cleric had such a righteous scorn for temporal possessions that, having such a great aptitude for getting rich quickly, he should give it up. Especially since he had a growing reputation for being industrious: people saw him most zealous about his property and his mines, saw other acquisitive qualities in him. But the governor was mainly stunned, and answered him more out of consideration for what touched the padre in the temporal realm than for the danger in which the governor himself lived as top man in the tyranny perpetrated against the Indians on that island.

> Padre, think of what you are doing. No need for scruples! It is God who wants to see you rich and prosperous. For that reason I do not allow the surrender you make of your Indians. I give you fifteen days to think it over so you can come to a better decision. After a fortnight you can come back and tell me what you will do.

The padre replied,

> My Lord, I am most grateful that you want me to prosper, most grateful for all the other kindnesses your grace has done for me. But act, my Lord, as though the fortnight were over. Please God, if I ever repent of the decision I broached to you, if I ever want to hold Indians again — and if you, for the love you have of me, should ever want to leave them with me or give them to me anew — if you accept my plea to have them, even if I wept blood, may God be the one to punish you severely, may God never forgive this sin. I ask your grace one favor, that this whole business be kept secret and that you do not allot the natives to anyone until Rentería returns, so his estate suffers no harm.

The governor promised. He kept his promise. From then on he had a far greater respect for the padre. And concerning his governance, he did many good things that touched on native matters and his own personal conduct, all due to the effect of the padre (as if he had seen him do miracles). The rest of the Spaniards on the island began to change their view of the padre from before, once they knew he had given up his natives. Such an action was considered then and always the consummate proof that could demonstrate sanctity. Such was and is the blindness of those who came out to the New World.

The padre made the secret public the following way. He was preaching on the feast day of the Assumption of Our Lady in that place where he was — [the town of Sancti Espiritus] mentioned earlier. He was explaining the contemplative and the active life, the theme of the gospel reading for the day, talking about the spiritual and corporal works of mercy. He had to make clear to his hearers their obligation to perform these works toward the native peoples they made use of so cruelly, he had to blame the merciless, negligent, mindless way they lived off those natives. For which it struck him as the right moment to reveal the secret agreement he had set up with the governor. And he said, "My Lord, I give you freedom to reveal to everyone whatever you wish concerning what we agreed on in secret — I take that freedom myself in order to reveal it to those here present." This said, he began to expose to them their own blindness, the injustices, the tyrannies, the cruelties they committed against such innocent, such gentle people. They could not save their souls, neither those who held Indians by allotment, nor the one who handed them out. They were bound by the obligation to make restitution. He himself, once he knew the danger of damnation in which he lived, had given up his Indians, had given up many other things connected with holding Indians. The congregation was stupefied, even fearful of what he said to them. Some felt compunction, others thought it a bad dream, hearing bizarre statements such as: No one could hold Indians in servitude without sinning. As if to say they could not make use of beasts of the field! Unbelievable.

Ignatius Loyola

(1491?–1556)

St. Ignatius Loyola was a contemporary of both Martin Luther and John Calvin, and like them he sought to reform the church. But unlike them, Loyola was completely devoted to the Roman Catholic Church, and his impact and the influence of the order he founded, the Jesuits, have decisively shaped the history of both Catholicism and Protestantism.

Born into a family of Spanish nobility, Loyola decided to become a soldier, and the discipline of military life affected him deeply. In 1521 he was seriously injured in the siege of Pamplona by the French, and he retreated to the castle of Loyola to recover. There he began reading devotional literature on the life of Christ and the saints, and he was converted. When his health permitted, he made a pilgrimage to Montserrat, where he conducted an all-night vigil before the altar of the Virgin Mary and hung up his sword. He then spent a year at Manresa near Montserrat, where he had several mystical experiences of Jesus Christ. These formed the basis of what later became the *Spiritual Exercises,* Loyola's most famous work and the manual for the Jesuit order. It is widely used even today, especially for spiritual retreats.

After a pilgrimage from Manresa to Rome, Loyola began his studies, first in Spain and then in Paris. In 1534 he laid the foundation for the Society of Jesus, or Jesuits, with six companions, including Francis Xavier. In 1540 the pope commissioned the new order; the Jesuits were placed under the direct control of the pope himself, and the priests took a special vow of papal loyalty.

The Jesuits were not founded to combat Protestantism, but they did become the vanguard of the papacy in the Counter-Reformation. Effective in reducing abuses within the Roman Church, they were also successful in winning back whole areas of Europe in allegiance to Rome. Throughout their history the Jesuits have been noted for their extensive missionary work, especially in some of the most difficult areas of the world, as well as for their contributions to scholarship and education. Since Vatican II, they have been significantly involved in improving ecumenical relations between Protestants and Catholics.

The following account of Loyola's confession was dictated by him, and characteristically he referred to himself in the third person, suggesting his modesty and self-denial. His piety was demanding and disciplined, and as a soldier of God he continually required "more" of himself and of others. His motto: "For the greater glory of God."

~

Up to his twenty-sixth year he was a man given over to the vanities of the world, and took a special delight in the exercise of arms, with a great and vain desire of winning glory. He was in a fortress which the French were attacking, and although the others were of the opinion that they should surrender on terms of having their lives spared, as they clearly saw there was no possibility of a defense, he gave so many reasons to the governor that he persuaded him to carry on the defense against the judgment of the officers, who found some strength in his spirit and courage. On the day on which they expected the attack to take place, he made his confession to one of his companions in arms. After the assault had been going on for some time, a cannon ball struck him in the leg, crushing its bones, and because it passed between his legs it also seriously wounded the other.

With his fall, the others in the fortress surrendered to the French, who took possession, and treated the wounded man with great kindliness and courtesy. After twelve or fifteen days in Pamplona they bore him in a litter to his own country. Here he found himself in a very serious condition. The doctors and surgeons whom he had called from all parts were of the opinion that the leg should be operated on again and the bones reset, either because they had been poorly set in the first place, or because the jogging of the journey had displaced them so that they would not heal. Again he went through this butchery, in which as

Excerpts from *St. Ignatius' Own Story, as Told to Luis González de Cámara,* translated by William J. Young, S.J. (Loyola Press, 1998). Reprinted with permission of Loyola Press. To order copies call 1-800-621-1008 or go to www.loyolapress.com.

in all the others that he had suffered he uttered no word, nor gave any sign of pain other than clenching his fists.

His condition grew worse. Besides being unable to eat he showed other symptoms which are usually a sign of approaching death. The feast of St. John drew near, and as the doctors had very little hope of his recovery, they advised him to make his confession. He received the last sacraments on the eve of the feast of Sts. Peter and Paul, and the doctors told him that if he showed no improvement by midnight, he could consider himself as good as dead. The patient had some devotion to St. Peter, and so our Lord wished that his improvement should begin that very midnight. So rapid was his recovery that within a few days he was thought to be out of danger of death.

When the bones knit, one below the knee remained astride another, which caused a shortening of the leg. The bones so raised caused a protuberance that was not pleasant to the sight. The sick man was not able to put up with this, because he had made up his mind to seek his fortune in the world. He thought the protuberance was going to be unsightly and asked the surgeons whether it could not be cut away. They told him that it could be cut away, but that the pain would be greater than all he had already suffered, because it was now healed and it would take some time to cut it off. He determined, nevertheless, to undergo this martyrdom to gratify his own inclinations. His elder brother was quite alarmed and declared that he would not have the courage to undergo such pain. But the wounded man put up with it with his usual patience.

After the superfluous flesh and the bone were cut away, means were employed for preventing the one leg from remaining shorter than the other. Many ointments were applied and devices employed for keeping the leg continually stretched which caused him many days of martyrdom. But it was our Lord Who restored his health. In everything else he was quite well, but he was not able to stand upon that leg, and so had to remain in bed. He had been much given to reading worldly books of fiction and knight errantry, and feeling well enough to read he asked for some of these books to help while away the time. In that house, however, they could find none of those he was accustomed to read, and so they gave him a Life of Christ and a book of the Lives of the Saints in Spanish.

By the frequent reading of these books he conceived some affection for what he found there narrated. Pausing in his reading, he gave himself up to thinking over what he had read. At other times he dwelt on the things of the world which formerly had occupied his thoughts. Of the many vain things that presented themselves to him, one took such possession of his heart that without realizing it he could spend two, three, or even four hours on end thinking of it, fancying what he would have to do in the service of a certain lady, of the means he would take to reach the country where she was living, of the verses, the promises he would make her, the deeds of gallantry he would do in her service. He was so enamored with all this that he did not see how impossible it would all be, because the lady was of no ordinary rank; neither countess, nor duchess, but of a nobility much higher than any of these.

Nevertheless, our Lord came to his assistance, for He saw to it that these thoughts were succeeded by others which sprang from the things he was reading. In reading the Life of our Lord and the Lives of the Saints, he paused to think and reason with himself. "Suppose that I should do what St. Francis did, what St. Dominic did?" He thus let his thoughts run over many things that seemed good to him, always putting before himself things that were difficult and important which seemed to him easy to accomplish when he proposed them. But all his thought was to tell himself, "St. Dominic did this; therefore, I must do it. St. Francis did this; therefore, I must do it." These thoughts also lasted a good while. And then other things taking their place, the worldly thoughts above mentioned came upon him and remained a long time with him. This succession of diverse thoughts was of long duration, and they were either of worldly achievements which he desired to accomplish, or those of God which took hold of his imagination to such an extent, that worn out with the struggle, he turned them all aside and gave his attention to other things.

There was, however, this difference. When he was thinking of the things of the world he was filled with delight, but when afterwards he dismissed them from weariness, he was dry and dissatisfied. And when he thought of going barefoot to Jerusalem and of eating nothing but herbs and performing the other rigors he saw that the saints had performed, he was consoled, not only when he entertained these thoughts, but even after dismissing them he remained cheerful and satisfied. But he paid no attention to this, nor did he stop to weigh the difference until one day his eyes were opened a little and he began to wonder at the difference and to reflect on it, learning from experience that one kind of thoughts left him sad and the other cheerful. Thus, step by step, he came to recognize the difference between the two spirits that moved him, the one being from the evil spirit, the other from God.

He acquired no little light from this reading and began to think more seriously of his past life and the great need he had of doing penance for it. It was during this reading that these desires of imitating the saints came to him, but with no further thought of circumstances than of promising to do with God's grace what they had done. What he desired most of all to do, as soon as he was restored to health, was to go to Jerusalem, as above stated, undertaking all the disciplines and abstinences which a generous soul on fire with the love of God is wont to desire.

The thoughts of the past were soon forgotten in the presence of these holy desires, which were confirmed by the following vision. One night, as he lay awake, he saw clearly the likeness of our Lady with the holy Child Jesus, at the sight of which he received most abundant consolation for a considerable interval of time. He felt so great a disgust with his past life, especially with its offenses of the flesh, that he thought all such images which had formerly occupied his mind were wiped out. And from that hour until August of 1553, when this is being written, he never again consented to the least suggestion of the flesh. This effect would seem to indicate that the vision was from God, although he never ventured to affirm it positively, or claim that it was anything more than he had said it was. But his brother and other members of the family easily recognized the change that had taken place in the interior of his soul from what they saw in his outward manner.

Without a care in the world he went on with his reading and his good resolutions. All the time he spent with the members of the household he devoted to the things of God, and in this way brought profit to their souls. He took great delight in the books he was reading, and the thought came to him to select some short but important passages from the Life of Christ and the Lives of the Saints. And so he began to write very carefully in a book, as he had already begun to move a little about the house. The words of Christ he wrote in red ink and those of our Lady in blue, on polished and lined paper in a good hand, for he was an excellent penman. Part of his time he spent in writing, part in prayer. It was his greatest consolation to gaze upon the heavens and the stars, which he often did, and for long stretches at a time, because when doing so he felt within himself a powerful urge to be serving our Lord. He gave much time to thinking about his resolve, desiring to be entirely well so that he could begin his journey.

John Calvin

(1509–1564)

It may not seem in character for John Calvin to talk at much length about himself, especially about his own religious experience. Solemn and rigid in many ways, neither Calvin nor many of his followers, as for example the Dutch and the Scots, indulged in subjective religious introspection.

But we catch a glimpse of another side to the stern Genevan reformer when he tells us in the preface to his *Commentary on the Psalms* (1557) that he once had "a sudden conversion." It is a brief, tantalizing reference, and scholars are puzzled not only about the date but about what it involved. Calvin himself provides few clues, insisting, perhaps too modestly, "I am by nature timid, mild, and cowardly."

Was Calvin's "sudden conversion" mostly an intellectual shift from the humanism of his youth to the study of the Scriptures in his maturity? Was it his "mind" (Latin *animus*) that changed, or, as in the French edition, his "heart" (French *coeur*)? Perhaps we must say it was both. In any case, Calvin's conversion marked a turning point in his reforming career. Except for faint hints elsewhere, as in his *Reply to Cardinal Sadolet* (1539), he never again referred to his conversion experience. His writings, notably his biblical commentaries and his definitive systematic theology, *The Institutes of the Christian Religion* (1559), attest to the validity and depth of his theological position, and with that legacy we must be content.

We can detect three significant features in Calvin's brief account of his conversion. (1) Since he was thinking of the book of Psalms, he likened himself to David with all his sin and weakness together with his agonizing struggle to hold on to the God who inspired his muse. (2) The conversion experience, for Calvin, is attributed to God's direct intervention and is not described in Christian terms. There is no question about the centrality of Christ in Calvin's theology, but he avoided the pious "accepting Jesus" language of so many contemporary accounts. (3) The description of his conversion as the result of God's providential grace fits exactly into Calvin's theological emphasis on election as the divine initiative in the process of redemption.

If it was uncharacteristic for Calvin to be emotional about his conversion, the depth of his inner personal gratitude at the undeserved mercy of God found poignant expression in his so-called crest or seal. Picturing a heart upon an open, outstretched hand, the motto reads, "My heart I give Thee, Lord, eagerly and earnestly."

My father intended me as a young boy for theology. But when he saw that the science of law made those who cultivate it wealthy, he was led to change his mind by the hope of material gain for me. So it happened that I was called back from the study of philosophy to learn law. I followed my father's wish and attempted to do faithful work in this field; but God, by the secret leading of his providence, turned my course another way.

First, when I was too firmly addicted to the papal superstitions to be drawn easily out of such a deep mire, by a sudden conversion He brought my mind (already more rigid than suited my age) to submission [to him]. I was so inspired by a taste of true religion and I burned with such a desire to carry my study further, that although I did not drop other subjects, I had no zeal for them. In less than a year, all who were looking for a purer doctrine began to come to learn from me, although I was a novice and a beginner.

Then I, who was by nature a man of the country and a lover of shade and leisure, wished to find for myself a quiet hiding place — a wish which has never yet been granted me; for every retreat I found became a public lecture room. When the one thing I craved was obscurity and leisure, God fastened upon me so many cords of various kinds that he

The text for Calvin's conversion is taken from the preface to the *Commentary on the Psalms*. From *Calvin: Commentaries*, ed. Joseph Haroutunian and Louise Pettibone Smith, vol. 23 in The Library of Christian Classics (London: SCM Press; Philadelphia: Westminster Press, 1958). Used by permission of Westminster John Knox Press. www.wjkbooks.com. Extracts from the Library of Christian Classics are copyright © SCM Press and are reproduced by permission.

never allowed me to remain quiet, and in spite of my reluctance dragged me into the limelight.

I left my own country and departed for Germany to enjoy there, unknown, in some corner, the quiet long denied me. But lo, while I was hidden unknown at Basel, a great fire of hatred [for France] had been kindled in Germany by the exile of many godly men from France. To quench this fire, wicked and lying rumors were spread, cruelly calling the exiles Anabaptists and seditious men, men who threatened to upset, not only religion, but the whole political order with their perverse madness. I saw that this was a trick of those in [the French] court, not only to cover up with false slanders the shedding of the innocent blood of holy martyrs, but also to enable the persecutors to continue with the pitiless slaughter. Therefore I felt that I must make a strong statement against such charges; for I could not be silent without treachery. This was why I published the *Institutes* — to defend against unjust slander my brothers whose death was precious in the Lord's sight. A second reason was my desire to rouse the sympathy and concern of people outside, since the same punishment threatened many other poor people. And this volume was not a thick and laborious work like the present edition; it appeared as a brief *Enchiridion*. I had no other purpose than to bear witness to the faith of those whom I saw criminally libeled by wicked and false courtiers.

I desired no fame for myself from it; I planned to depart shortly, and no one knew that I was the writer [of the book]. For I had kept my authorship secret and intended to continue to do so. But Wilhiam Farel[1] forced me to stay in Geneva not so much by advice or urging as by command, which had the power of God's hand laid violently upon me from heaven. Since the wars had closed the direct road to Strasbourg, I had meant to pass through Geneva quickly and had determined not to be delayed there more than one night.

A short time before, by the work of the same good man [Farel], and of Peter Viret,[2] the papacy had been banished from the city; but things

1. Guillaume Farel (1489-1565) was, like Calvin, a Frenchman. He was one of the circle of Reformers who gathered around Bishop Briconnet at Meaux near Paris. When, after much struggle in which Farel was active, the Reformed faith was established in Geneva in 1535, he was the leader of the church and induced Calvin to work with him. He was ousted with Calvin in 1538, and returned with him in 1541; but he left in 1542, and in 1544 settled in Neuchâtel. He remained Calvin's close friend, and died a year after Calvin in 1565 in Metz.
2. Pierre Viret (1511-1571), Swiss-born Reformer, helped Farel in Geneva and

were still unsettled and the place was divided into evil and harmful factions. One man, who has since shamefully gone back to the papists, took immediate action to make me known. Then Farel, who was working with incredible zeal to promote the gospel, bent all his efforts to keep me in the city. And when he realized that I was determined to study in privacy in some obscure place, and saw that he gained nothing by entreaty, he descended to cursing, and said that God would surely curse my peace if I held back from giving help at a time of such great need. Terrified by his words, and conscious of my own timidity and cowardice, I gave up my journey and attempted to apply whatever gift I had in defense of my faith.

Scarcely four months had passed before we were attacked on the one side by the Anabaptists and on the other by a certain rascally apostate who, relying upon the secret aid of certain important people, was able to give us much trouble. Meanwhile, internal dissensions, coming one upon another, caused us dreadful torments.

I confess that I am by nature timid, mild, and cowardly, and yet I was forced from the very beginning to meet these violent storms. Although I did not yield to them, yet since I was not very brave, I was more pleased than was fitting when I was banished and forcibly expelled from the city.

Then loosed from my vocation and free [to follow my own desire], I decided to live quietly as a private individual. But that most distinguished minister of Christ, Martin Bucer,[3] dragged me back again to a new post with the same curse which Farel had used against me. Terrified by the example of Jonah which he had set before me, I continued the work of teaching. And although I always consistently avoided public

---

stayed in the city when Farel and Calvin were expelled (1538-1541). Thereafter he worked in Lausanne, his birthplace, and also lectured on the New Testament in Bern, until he was ousted in 1559 and returned to Geneva. After a checkered career in France and much controversy with French Catholics, he died at Orthez (south of Bordeaux) in 1571. He was an extensive and respected writer as well as an effective preacher. Unfortunately he has not been studied fully or properly.

3. Martin Bucer (1491-1551) was the Protestant Reformer in Strasbourg, where Calvin stayed for three years (1538-1541) when he was forced out of Geneva. A man zealous for Christian unity, he had considerable influence upon Calvin, especially during this early period in the latter's activity. He commented extensively upon the Bible, and did his best-known work on the Gospels. His commentary on Romans was published in Strasbourg in 1536, shortly before Calvin began to work on his own. See Henri Strohl, *Bucer: humaniste chrétien*.

notice, somehow I was dragged to the imperial assemblies.[4] There, whether I wished it or not, I had to speak before large audiences.

Afterwards the Lord had pity on the City of Geneva and quieted the deadly conflicts there. After he had by his wondrous power frustrated both the criminal conspiracies and the bloody attempts at force, I was compelled, against my own will, to take again my former position. The safety of that church was far too important in my mind for me to refuse to meet even death for its sake. But my timidity kept suggesting to me excuses of every color for refusing to put my shoulder again under so heavy a burden. However, the demand of duty and faith at length conquered, and I went back to the flock from which I had been driven away. With how much grief, with how many tears, and in how great anxiety I went, God is my best witness. Many faithful men also understood my reluctance and would have wished to see me released from this pain if they had not been constrained by the same fear which influenced me.

It would make too long a story to tell of the conflicts of all sorts in which I was active and of the trials by which I was tested. I will merely repeat briefly what I said before, so as not to offend fastidious readers with unnecessary words. Since [in the Psalms] David showed me the way with his own footsteps, I felt myself greatly comforted. The holy king was hurt more seriously by the envy and dishonesty of treacherous men at home than he was by the Philistines and other enemies who harassed him from the outside. I also have been attacked on all sides and have had scarcely a moment's relief from both external and internal conflicts. Satan has undertaken all too often in many ways to corrupt the fabric of this church. The result has been that I, who am a peaceable and timid man, was compelled to break the force of the deadly attacks by interposing my own body as a shield. . . .

But this also was David's experience. He deserved well of his people, yet he was hated by many, as he laments in Ps. 69:4: *They hate me without a cause. . . . I returned what I did not rob.* When I was assailed by the undeserved hatred of those whose duty it was to help me, I received no small comfort from knowing of the glorious example [set by David].

Now these experiences were a very great help to my understanding of the Psalms, since, as I read, I was going through well-known terri-

4. At Worms in 1540 and at Regensburg in 1541, where the Catholics and the Protestants entered into futile discussions on reunion.

tory. And I hope my readers will realize that when I discuss David's thoughts more intimately than those of others, I am speaking not as a remote spectator but as one who knows all about these things from his own experience.

Teresa of Ávila

(1515–1582)

Teresa of Ávila, or St. Teresa of Jesus, was a Spanish mystic and reformer who combined a life of intense piety with significant practical accomplishments. She was one of ten children in a family of Spanish nobility and was considered the "most beloved of them all." Her mother died when she was thirteen, and approximately three years later Teresa entered an Augustinian convent where she lived for a year and a half. In 1536 she joined the Carmelite convent in Ávila but soon fell desperately ill. At one point she went into a coma and was presumed dead; although she recovered, she suffered paralysis in her legs for three years.

During her first two decades as a Carmelite nun, Teresa experienced not only poor health but also profound religious struggles, describing this period as "nearly twenty years on that stormy sea." Never abandoning the practice of prayer, she began to realize that she was "sometimes being addressed by interior voices," and she saw "certain visions" and experienced revelations. The account of her conversion comes after her twenty-year struggle, and it indicates the new peace she received.

With this sense of assurance, Teresa launched a reform of the Carmelite order, and with St. John of the Cross, another famous Spanish mystic, she assisted in establishing reformed Carmelite monasteries for monks as well. She corresponded widely, and her letters reveal a woman of great administrative skill, shrewd judgment, and a good sense of humor. Her highly disciplined practice of what she called "mental prayer" continued and ultimately led in 1572 to a "spiritual marriage" in which she said her soul remained absorbed in God.

Her greatest devotional writing is *The Interior Castle,* but she is also noted for *The Way of Perfection* (a manual for her nuns) and her autobiographical writings, *Life* and *Book of Foundations*. She was canonized in 1662, and in 1870 she was one of the first two women to be named a Doctor of the Church. Her consuming passion to see Christ symbolizes how, in her own life, she united the spiritual and the physical, contemplation and achievement.

~

By this time my soul was growing weary, and, though it desired to rest, the miserable habits which now enslaved it would not allow it to do so. It happened that, entering the oratory one day, I saw an image which had been procured for a certain festival that was observed in the house and had been taken there to be kept for that purpose. It represented Christ sorely wounded; and so conducive was it to devotion that when I looked at it I was deeply moved to see Him thus, so well did it picture what He suffered for us. So great was my distress when I thought how ill I had repaid Him for those wounds that I felt as if my heart were breaking, and I threw myself down beside Him, shedding floods of tears and begging Him to give me strength once for all so that I might not offend Him.

I had a great devotion to the glorious Magdalen and often thought of her conversion, especially when I communicated, for, knowing that the Lord was certainly within me then, I would place myself at His feet, thinking that my tears would not be rejected. I did not know what I was saying; but in allowing me to shed those tears He was very gracious to me, since I so soon forgot my grief; and I used to commend myself to that glorious Saint so that she might obtain pardon for me.

But on this last occasion when I saw that image of which I am speaking, I think I must have made greater progress, because I had quite lost trust in myself and was placing all my confidence in God. I believe I told Him then that I would not rise from that spot until He had granted me what I was beseeching of Him. And I feel sure that this did me good, for from that time onward I began to improve. My method of prayer was this. As I could not reason with my mind, I would try to make pictures of Christ inwardly; and I used to think I felt better when I dwelt on those parts of His life when He was most often alone. It seemed to

---

Excerpted from *The Life of the Holy Mother Teresa of Jesus*, in *The Complete Works of Saint Teresa of Jesus*, trans. and ed. E. Allison Peers (London and New York, 1944), 1:54-57. Reprinted by permission of Sheed and Ward.

me that His being alone and afflicted, like a person in need, made it possible for me to approach Him. I had many simple thoughts of this kind. I was particularly attached to the prayer in the Garden, where I would go to keep Him company. I would think of the sweat and of the affliction He endured there. I wished I could have wiped that grievous sweat from His face, but I remember that I never dared to resolve to do so, for the gravity of my sins stood in the way. I used to remain with Him there for as long as my thoughts permitted it: I had many thoughts which tormented me.

For many years, on most nights before I fell asleep, when I would commend myself to God so as to sleep well, I used to think for a little of that scene — the prayer in the Garden — and this even before I was a nun, for I was told that many indulgences could be gained by so doing; and I feel sure that my soul gained a great deal in this way, because I began to practise prayer without knowing what it was, and the very habitualness of the custom prevented me from abandoning it, just as I never omitted making the sign of the Cross before going to sleep.

To return now to what I was saying about the torture caused me by my thoughts: this method of praying in which the mind makes no reflections means that the soul must either gain a great deal or lose itself — I mean by its attention going astray. If it advances, it goes a long way, because it is moved by love. But those who arrive thus far will do so only at great cost to themselves, save when the Lord is pleased to call them very speedily to the Prayer of Quiet, as He has called a few people whom I know. It is a good thing for those who follow this method to have a book at hand, so that they may quickly recollect themselves. It used also to help me to look at a field, or water, or flowers. These reminded me of the Creator — I mean, they awakened me, helped me to recollect myself and thus served me as a book; they reminded me, too, of my ingratitude and sins. But when it came to heavenly things, or to any sublime subject, my mind was so stupid that I could never imagine them at all, until the Lord showed them to me in another way.

I had so little ability for picturing things in my mind that if I did not actually see a thing I could not use my imagination, as other people do, who can make pictures to themselves and so become recollected. Of Christ as Man I could only think: however much I read about His beauty and however often I looked at pictures of Him, I could never form any picture of Him myself. I was like a person who is blind, or in the dark: he may be talking to someone, and know that he is with him, because he is quite sure he is there — I mean, he understands and believes he is there — but he cannot see him. Thus it was with me when I thought of Our Lord. It was for this reason that I was so fond of pictures. Unhappy are those who through their own fault lose this blessing! It really looks as if they do not love the Lord, for if they loved Him they would delight in looking at pictures of Him, just as they take pleasure in seeing pictures of anyone else whom they love.

It was at this time that I was given the *Confessions of Saint Augustine,* and I think the Lord must have ordained this, for I did not ask for the book nor had I ever seen it. I have a great affection for Saint Augustine, because the convent in which I had lived before becoming a nun belonged to his Order, and also because he had been a sinner. I used to find a great deal of comfort in reading about the lives of saints who had been sinners before the Lord brought them back to Himself. As He had forgiven them I thought that He might do the same for me. There was only one thing that troubled me, and this I have already mentioned: namely that, after the Lord had once called them, they did not fall again, whereas I had fallen so often that I was distressed by it. But when I thought of His love for me, I would take heart once more, for I never doubted His mercy, though I often doubted myself.

Oh, God help me! How amazed I am when I think how hard my heart was despite all the help I had received from Him! It really frightens me to remember how little I could do by myself and how I was so tied and bound that I could not resolve to give myself wholly to God. When I started to read the *Confessions,* I seemed to see myself in them and I began to commend myself often to that glorious Saint. When I got as far as his conversion and read how he heard that voice in the garden, it seemed exactly as if the Lord were speaking in that way to me, or so my heart felt. I remained for a long time dissolved in tears, in great distress and affliction. Dear God, what a soul suffers and what torments it endures when it loses its freedom to be its own master! I am astonished now that I was able to live in such a state of torment. God be praised, Who gave me life to forsake such utter death!

I believe my soul gained great strength from the Divine Majesty: He must have heard my cries and had compassion on all my tears. I began to long to spend more time with Him, and to drive away occasions of sin, for, once they had gone, I would feel a new love for His Majesty. I knew that, so far as I could tell, I loved Him, but I did not know, as I should have done, what true love of God really means. I think I had not yet quite prepared myself to want to serve Him when His Majesty began to grant me favours again. It really seems that the Lord found a way to make me desire to receive what others strive to acquire with great labour — that is to say, during these latter years, He gave me consolations and favours. I never presumed to beg Him to give me either these things or tenderness in devotion: I only asked for grace not to offend Him and for the pardon of my grievous sins. Knowing how grievous they were, I never dared consciously to desire favours or consolations. His compassion, I think, worked in me abundantly, and in truth He showed me great mercy in allowing me to be with Him and bringing me into His presence, which I knew I should not have entered had He not so disposed it.

Richard Baxter

(1615–1691)

Doubt and certainty are often seen as the two extremes of the Christian life, but in Richard Baxter one can glimpse a person who knew God through faith but confessed something less than absolute certainty. He lived among people who fought for what they believed, and their beliefs were always definite and sure. To them he preached peace and toleration of different points of view, but he was scorned by partisans on all sides. "These are my fixed resolutions and desires," he wrote in 1658, "even to be Catholick in my Estimation and respect to all, Loving all Christians of what sort soever, that may be truly called Christians . . . and . . . with this Catholick Charity to have the Conversation of such as the world hath long called Puritanes; and in this state I desire to die."

Baxter's Puritanism emphasized the need for a personal experience of God's forgiveness, rather than mere assent to the doctrines of the Christian faith, and Puritans constantly contrasted this "saving faith" with what they called "historical faith." And yet, as Baxter's account of his own conversion indicates, perfect proof of one's salvation was not always the result of conversion, and conversion itself could be a series of experiences, each of which brought a deeper understanding of God's love.

In 1638, Baxter was ordained in the Church of England, although he was a Nonconformist minister, working within the Church of England but refusing to abide by some of its disciplines and patterns of worship. During the English Civil War he sided with the Parliamentary cause, but then he became a vehement critic of Oliver Cromwell. When the monarchy was restored in 1660, he became a royal chaplain but also worked to keep Nonconformists in the church. For this he was jailed in 1685 for eighteen months. During his pastorate in Kidderminster, he organized an association of all the ministers in the town, and he is often called the first leader of the ecumenical movement in England. He was an eloquent and powerful preacher, and he is renowned for *The Saints Everlasting Rest* (1650), a moving devotional book, and *The Reformed Pastor* (1656), a manual in pastoral theology.

~

My father had only the competent estate of a freeholder, free from the temptations of poverty and riches; but having been addicted to gaming in his youth, and his father before him, it was so entangled by debts that it occasioned some excess of worldly cares before it was freed.

We lived in a country that had but little preaching at all. In the village where I was born there [were] four readers successively in six years' time, ignorant men, and two of them immoral in their lives, who were all my schoolmasters. In the village where my father lived there was a reader of about eighty years of age that never preached, and had two churches about twenty miles distant. His eyesight failing him, he said Common Prayer without book; but for the reading of the psalms and chapters he got a common thresher and day-labourer one year, and a tailor another year (for the clerk could not read well); and at last he had a kinsman of his own (the excellentest stage-player in all the country, and a good gamester and good fellow) that got Orders and supplied one of his places. After him another younger kinsman, that could write and read, got Orders. And at the same time another neighbour's son that had been a while at school turned minister, one who would needs go further than the rest, and ventured to preach (and after got a living in Staffordshire), and when he had been a preacher about twelve or sixteen years he was fain to give over, it being discovered that his Orders were forged by the first ingenious stage-player. After him another neighbour's son took Orders, when he had been a while an attorney's clerk, and a common drunkard, and tippled himself into so great poverty that he had no other way to live. It was feared that he and more of them came by their Orders the same way with the fore-mentioned person. These were the schoolmasters of my youth (except two of them) who read Common Prayer on Sundays and Holy-Days, and taught

Excerpted from *The Autobiography of Richard Baxter,* abridged by J. M. Lloyd Thomas and ed. N. H. Keeble (New York: E. P. Dutton; London: J. M. Dent & Sons, 1931/1973), 3-11.

school and tippled on the week-days, and whipped the boys, when they were drunk, so that we changed them very oft. Within a few miles about us were near a dozen more ministers that were near eighty years old apiece, and never preached; poor ignorant readers, and most of them of scandalous lives. Only three or four constant competent preachers lived near us, and those (though conformable all save one) were the common marks of the people's obloquy and reproach, and any that had but gone to hear them, when he had no preaching at home, was made the derision of the vulgar rabble under the odious name of a Puritan.

But though we had no better teachers it pleased God to instruct and change my father, by the bare reading of the Scriptures in private, without either preaching or godly company, or any other books but the Bible. And God made him the instrument of my first convictions, and approbation of a holy life, as well as of my restraint from the grosser sort of lives. When I was very young his serious speeches of God and the life to come possessed me with a fear of sinning. When I was but near ten years of age, being at school at High Ercall, we had leave to play on the day of the king's coronation; and at two of the clock in the afternoon on that day there happened an earthquake, which put all the people into a fear, and somewhat possessed them with awful thoughts of the dreadful God. (I make no commentary on the time, nor do I know certainly whether it were in other countries.)

At first my father set me to read the historical part of the Scripture, which suiting with my nature greatly delighted me; and though all that time I neither understood nor relished much the doctrinal part and mystery of redemption, yet it did me good by acquainting me with the matters of fact, drawing me on to love the Bible and to search by degrees into the rest.

But though my conscience would trouble me when I sinned, yet divers sins I was addicted to, and oft committed against my conscience; which for the warning of others I will confess here to my shame.

1. I was much addicted, when I feared correction, to lie, that I might scape.
2. I was much addicted to the excessive gluttonous eating of apples and pears; which I think laid the foundation of that imbecility and flatulency of my stomach which caused the bodily calamities of my life.
3. To this end, and to concur with naughty boys that gloried in evil, I

have oft gone into other men's orchards and stolen their fruit, when I had enough at home.

4. I was somewhat excessively addicted to play, and that with covetousness, for money.
5. I was extremely bewitched with a love of romances, fables and old tales, which corrupted my affections and lost my time.
6. I was guilty of much idle foolish chat, and imitation of boys in scurrilous foolish words and actions (though I durst not swear).
7. I was too proud of my masters' commendations for learning, who all of them fed my pride, making me seven or eight years the highest in the school, and boasting of me to others, which, though it furthered my learning, yet helped not my humility.
8. I was too bold and unreverent towards my parents.

These were my sins, which, in my childhood, conscience troubled me [with] for a great while before they were overcome.

In the village where I lived the reader read the Common Prayer briefly, and the rest of the day even till dark night almost, except eating-time, was spent in dancing under a maypole and a great tree not far from my father's door, where all the town did meet together. And though one of my father's own tenants was the piper, he could not restrain him nor break the sport. So that we could not read the Scripture in our family without the great disturbance of the tabor and pipe and noise in the street. Many times my mind was inclined to be among them, and sometimes I broke loose from conscience and joined with them; and the more I did it the more I was inclined to it. But when I heard them call my father Puritan it did much to cure me and alienate me from them; for I considered that my father's exercise of reading the Scripture was better than theirs, and would surely be better thought on by all men at the last; and I considered what it was for that he and others were thus derided. . . .

About that time it pleased God of his wonderful mercy to open my eyes with a clearer insight into the concerns and case of my own soul, and to touch my heart with a livelier feeling of things spiritual than ever I had found before. And it was by the means and in the order following: stirring up my conscience more against me, by robbing an orchard or two with rude boys, than it was before; and, bringing me under some more conviction for my sin, a poor day-labourer in the town (he that I before mentioned, that was wont to read in the church for the old parson) had an old torn book which he lent my father, which was called *Bunny's Resolution* (being written by Parsons the Jesuit, and corrected by Edm. Bunny). . . . And in the reading of this book (when I was about fifteen years of age) it pleased God to awaken my soul. . . .

Yet whether sincere conversion began now, or before, or after, I was never able to this day to know; for I had before had some love to the things and people which were good, and a restraint from other sins except those forementioned; and so much from those, that I seldom committed most of them, and when I did, it was with great reluctancy. . . .

And about that time it pleased God that a poor pedlar came to the door that had ballads and some good books; and my father bought of him Dr. Sibb's *Bruised Reed.* This also I read, and found it suited to my state and seasonably sent me. . . .

When I was ready for the university my master drew me into another way which kept me thence, where were my vehement desires. He had a friend at Ludlow, Chaplain to the Council there, called Mr. Richard Wickstead; whose place having allowance from the king (who maintaineth the house) for one to attend him, he told my master that he was purposed to have a scholar fit for the university; and having but one, would be better to him than any tutor in the university could be. Whereupon my master persuaded me to accept the offer, and told me it would be better than the university to me. . . . He never read to me, nor used any savoury discourse of godliness; only he loved me, and allowed me books and time enough: so that as I had no considerable helps from him in my studies, so had I no considerable hindrance.

And though the house was great (there being four judges, the King's Attorney, the Secretary, the Clerk of the Fines, with all their servants, and all the Lord President's servants and many more), and though the town was full of temptations, through the multitude of persons (counsellors, attorneys, officers and clerks), and much given to tippling and excess, it pleased God not only to keep me from them, but also to give me one intimate companion, who was the greatest help to my seriousness in religion that ever I had before, and was a daily watchman over my soul. We walked together, we read together, we prayed together. . . . He was the first that ever I heard pray *ex tempore* (out of the pulpit), and that taught me so to pray. And his charity and liberality were equal to his zeal, so that God made him a great means of my good, who had more knowledge than he, but a colder heart.

Yet before we had been two years acquainted he fell once and a second time by the power of temptation into a degree of drunkenness, which so terrified him upon the review (especially after the second time) that he was near to despair, and went to good ministers with sad confessions. And when I had left the house and his company, he fell into it again and again so oft that at last his conscience could have no relief or ease but in changing his judgment and disowning the teachers and doctrines which had restrained him. . . . And the last I heard of him was that he was grown a fuddler and railer at strict men; but whether God recovered him, or what became of him, I cannot tell.

From Ludlow Castle, after a year and a half, I returned to my father's house, and by that time my old schoolmaster, Mr. John Owen, was sick of a consumption (which was his death); and the Lord Newport desired me to teach that school till he either recovered or died (resolving to take his brother after him if he died); which I did, about a quarter of a year or more.

After that old Mr. Francis Garbett (the faithful, learned minister at Wroxeter) for about a month read logic to me, and provoked me to a closer course of study, which yet was greatly interrupted by my bodily weakness and the troubled condition of my soul. For being in expectation of death by a violent cough, with spitting of blood, etc., of two years' continuance, supposed to be a deep degree of a consumption, I was yet more awakened to be serious and solicitous about my soul's everlasting state; and I came so short of that sense and seriousness which a matter of such infinite weight required, that I was in many years' doubt of my sincerity, and thought I had no spiritual life at all. . . .

Thus was I long kept with the calls of approaching death at one ear and the questionings of a doubtful conscience at the other; and since then I have found that this method of God's was very wise, and no other was so like to have tended to my good. . . .

It set me upon that method of my studies which since then I have found the benefit of, though at the time I was not satisfied with myself. It caused me first to seek God's Kingdom and his righteousness, and most to mind the one thing needful; and to determine first of my ultimate end; by which I was engaged to choose out and prosecute all other studies but as meant to that end. Therefore divinity was not only carried on with the rest of my studies with an equal hand, but always had the first and chiefest place. . . . And by that means all that I read did stick the better in my memory, and also less of my time was lost by lazy intermissions (but my bodily infirmities always caused me to lose or spend much of it in motion and corporal exercises, which was sometimes by walking, and sometimes at the plough and such country labours).

But one loss I had by this method which hath proved irreparable: that I missed that part of learning which stood at the greatest distance (in my thoughts) from my ultimate end (though no doubt but remotely it may be a valuable means), and I could never since find time to get it. Besides the Latin tongue and but a mediocrity in Greek (with an inconsiderable trial at the Hebrew long after), I had no great skill in languages. . . . And for the mathematics, I was an utter stranger to them, and never could find in my heart to divert any studies that way. But in order to the knowledge of divinity my inclination was most to logic and metaphysics, with that part of physics which treateth of the soul, contenting myself at first with a slighter study of the rest. And these had my labour and delight, which occasioned me (perhaps too soon) to plunge myself very early into the study of controversies, and to read all the Schoolmen I could get; for next to practical divinity, no books so suited with my disposition as Aquinas, Scotus, Durandus, Ockam and their disciples; because I thought they narrowly searched after truth and brought things out of the darkness of confusion; for I could never from my first studies endure confusion. . . . I never thought I understood any thing till I could anatomise it and see the parts distinctly, and the conjunction of the parts as they make up the whole. Distinction and method seemed to me of that necessity, that without them I could not be said to know; and the disputes which forsook them or abused them seem but as incoherent dreams.

And as for those doubts of my own salvation, which exercised me many years, the chiefest causes of them were these:

1. Because I could not distinctly trace the workings of the Spirit upon my heart in that method which Mr. Bolton, Mr. Hooker, Mr. Rogers and other divines describe; nor knew the time of my conversion, being wrought on by the forementioned degrees. But since then I understood that the soul is in too dark and passionate a plight at first to be able to keep an exact account of the order of its own operations. . . .

2. My second doubt was as aforesaid, because of the hardness of my heart or want of such lively apprehensions of things spiritual which I had about things corporal. And though I still groan under this as my sin and want, yet I now perceive that a soul in flesh doth work so much after the manner of the flesh that it much desireth sensible apprehensions; but things spiritual and distant are not so apt to work upon them, and

to stir the passions, as things present and sensible are; . . . and that this is the ordinary state of a believer.

3. My next doubt was lest education and fear had done all that ever was done upon my soul, and regeneration and love were yet to seek; because I had found convictions from my childhood, and found more fear than love in all my duties and restraints.

But I afterwards perceived that education is God's ordinary way for the conveyance of his grace, and ought no more to be set in opposition to the Spirit than the preaching of the Word; and that it was the great mercy of God to begin with me so soon. . . . And I understood that though fear without love be not a state of saving grace, . . . the soul of a believer groweth up by degrees from the more troublesome (but safe) operations of fear to the more high and excellent operations of complacential love. . . . And I found that my hearty love of the Word of God, and of the servants of God, and my desires to be more holy, and especially the hatred of my heart for loving God no more, and my love to love him and be pleasing to him was not without some love to himself, though it worked more sensibly on his nearer image. . . .

But I understood at last that God breaketh not all men's hearts alike. . . .

And it much increased my peace when God's providence called me to the comforting of many others that had the same complaints. While I answered their doubts I answered my own; and the charity which I was constrained to exercise for them redounded to myself and insensibly abated my fears and procured me an increase of quietness of mind.

And yet, after all, I was glad of probabilities instead of full undoubted certainties; and to this very day, though I have no such degree of doubtfulness as is any great trouble to my soul or procureth any great disquieting fears, yet cannot I say that I have such a certainty of my own sincerity in grace as excludeth all doubts and fears of the contrary.

Blaise Pascal

(1623–1662)

The most appropriate word for describing Pascal, according to his many biographers and interpreters, is "genius." Pascal belongs to that rare circle of creative souls who cram several lifetimes into a few fleeting years. Mathematician, physicist, philosopher, theologian, and litterateur, he achieved fame in all these areas within a period of about twenty years.

A person of rigorous, scientific precision, he was also a man of deep, abiding faith. Sometimes he deliberately related the two, sharpening his geometrical mind as an instrument in the service of religious persuasion. The best-known example of this apologetic method is his so-called "wager." If God, as Pascal argued, does not exist, the skeptic loses nothing by not believing; but if God does exist, then the skeptic gains eternal life by believing. So why not make a bet!

A devout Catholic, Pascal associated himself with the controversial Jansenist movement at Port-Royal. A sort of French Catholic Puritanism, Jansenism stressed simplicity and humility of life, protesting against the moral casuistry and doctrinal remoteness of the Jesuits. Theologically, Jansenism invoked the name of Augustine and his concern to relate religious knowledge, divine grace, and human piety or spirituality. The certainties of faith, Pascal maintained, cannot be proved by reason, partly because "the heart has its reasons, which reason does not know" (*Pensées,* IV, 277).

If it may be said that Pascal's first "conversion" turned him toward Jansenism, signifying a renunciation of worldly pleasures, his second "conversion" was surrounded with a much more dramatic and enduring religious experience. He documented the exact moment when a vision (some critics say hallucination) invaded his inner being and forced itself upon him like an ecstatic revelation. Pascal wrote it all down and sewed it into the lining of his jacket, where it was found by a servant after his death nearly ten years later. Known as the *Memorial,* the full text is given here with English translations of the Latin and with biblical references supplied. "Fire" is, of course, a familiar symbol in the Bible, implying the presence of God. Whether we remember Moses and the burning bush, Isaiah's coal of fire from the altar, or the tongues of flame at Pentecost, the imagery of mysterious divine presence is inescapable — "for our God is a consuming fire" (Heb. 12:29).

In poor health most of his life, Pascal suffered through his final years in constant physical anguish. We may speculate as to whether it was meningitis, cancer of the spine, or a malignant stomach ulcer; no matter, though, for he knew he was a dying man and so he prepared a prayer, asking God to use his illness for some good purpose. The prayer, a portion of which is reprinted here, provides a fitting epilogue to his unforgettable conversion experience.

As T. S. Eliot notes in his introduction to the Everyman's Library edition of Pascal's *Pensées:* "Because of his unique combination and balance of qualities, I know of no religious writer more pertinent to our time."

The Memorial

In the year of Grace, 1654,
On Monday, 23rd of November, Feast of St. Clement,
　　Pope and Martyr, and others in the Martyrology,
　　Vigil of Saint Chrysogonus, Martyr, and others,
　　From about half past ten in the evening until about
　　half past twelve,

FIRE

God of Abraham, God of Isaac, God of Jacob, not of the
　　philosophers and scholars (Ex. 3:6; Matt. 22:32).
Certitude. Certitude. Feeling. Joy. Peace.
God of Jesus Christ

The two texts for the *Memorial* and the *Prayer* are taken from *Great Shorter Works of Pascal,* trans. Emile Cailliet and John C. Blankenagel (Philadelphia: Westminster Press, 1948), 117, 220, 228.

Deum meum et Deum vestrum ("My God and your God," John
    20:17).
Forgetfulness of the world and of everything except God.
    He is to be found only by the ways taught in the Gospel.
    Greatness of the human soul.
    "Righteous Father, the world hath not known Thee,
        but I have known Thee" (John 17:25).
    Joy, joy, joy, tears of joy.
    I have separated myself from Him
Derelinquerunt me fontem aquae vivae ("They have forsaken me,
        the fountain of living waters," Jer. 2:13).
    "My God, wilt Thou leave me?" (Matt. 27:46).
    Let me not be separated from Him eternally.
    "This is the eternal life, that they might know Thee,
        the only true God, and the one whom Thou has sent,
        Jesus Christ" (John 17:3).
    Jesus Christ.
    Jesus Christ.
    I have separated myself from Him: I have fled from Him,
        denied Him, crucified Him.
    Let me never be separated from Him.
    We keep hold of Him only by the ways taught in the Gospel.
    Renunciation, total and sweet.
    Total submission to Jesus Christ and to my director.[1]
    Eternally in joy for a day's training on earth.
    Non obliviscar sermones tuos ("I will not forget Thy words,"
        Psalm 118:16).
Amen.

Prayer Asking God to Use Illness to a Good End

Lord, whose spirit is so good and so gentle in all things, and who art so
compassionate that not only all prosperity but even all afflictions that
come to Thine elect are the results of Thy compassion: grant me grace
that I may not do as the pagans do in the condition to which Thy justice
has reduced me; grant that as a true Christian I may recognize Thee as

---

1. Monsieur Singlin of Port-Royal.

my Father and as my God, in whatever estate I find myself, since the change in my condition brings no change in Thine own. For Thou art the same, though I be subject to change, and Thou art God no less when Thou dost afflict and when Thou dost punish, than when Thou dost console and when Thou dost manifest indulgence.

Thou hadst given me health that I might serve Thee, and I have profaned it; now Thou dost send me illness to correct my ways: do not permit me to use it to anger Thee by my impatience. I have misused my health, and Thou hast justly punished me for it; do not suffer me to misuse Thy punishment. And since the corruption of my nature is such that it renders Thy favors pernicious, grant, O my God, that Thine omnipotent grace may render Thy chastisements salutary to me. If my heart was filled with love for the world while it had some vigor, annihilate this vigor for my salvation, and render me incapable of enjoying the world not only through the weakness of my body, but rather through the ardor of a love which will render me capable of delight in Thee by rendering me capable of delight only in Thee.

O God, before whom I must give an exact accounting of my life unto the end of my life and unto the end of the world! O God, who dost permit the world and all things of the world to be, only that they may train Thine elect and punish sinners. O God, who dost leave hardened sinners in the delightful and criminal ways of the world and in the pleasures of the world. O God, who dost make our bodies to die, and who in the hour of death dost detach our soul from all that it loved in the world. O God, who dost wrest me in the final moment of my life from all things to which I had attached myself, and to which I had given my heart. O God, Thou who on the day of judgment must consume the earth and all creatures contained therein, to show to all men that Thou alone dost live, and hence that Thou alone art worthy of love, since nothing can endure without Thee. O God, Thou who must destroy all these vain idols and all these deadly objects of our passions, I praise Thee, my God, and I shall bless Thee all the days of my life, that Thou hast deigned to predispose this dread day in my favor, by destroying for my sake all things in the feebleness to which Thou hast reduced me. I praise Thee, my God, and I shall bless Thee all the days of my life because it has pleased Thee to lessen me so that I no longer have the capacity for enjoying the sweetness of health and the pleasures of the world. And I bless Thee for having somehow annihilated to my advantage the deceptive idols which Thou wilt indeed annihilate to confound the wicked on the day of

Thy wrath. Give me, Lord, the strength to judge myself in the wake of destruction that Thou hast made with regard to me, so that Thou mayest not judge me Thyself after the complete destruction which Thou wilt make of my life and of the world. For, Lord, just as at the moment of my death I shall find myself separated from the world, devoid of all things, alone in Thy presence to answer to Thy righteousness for all the impulses of my heart, so, Lord, grant that I may consider myself in this illness as in a kind of death, separated from the world, devoid of all the objects to which I am enslaved, alone in Thy presence to implore Thy mercy for the conversion of my heart; and thus may I find unbounded consolation in Thy sending me now a kind of death to exercise Thy mercy before Thou dost in fact send me death to exercise Thy judgment. Grant then, O my God, that as Thou hast anticipated my death, so may I anticipate Thine appalling sentence, and may I examine myself before Thy judgment in order to find mercy in Thy presence.

Grant then, Lord, that I may conform to Thy will, just as I am, that, being sick as I am, I may glorify Thee in my sufferings. Without them I cannot attain to glory; without them, my Saviour, even Thou wouldst not have risen to glory. By the marks of Thy sufferings Thou wert recognized by Thy disciples, and likewise by their sufferings Thou dost recognize those who are Thy disciples. Therefore recognize me as Thy disciple by the ills that I endure, in my body and in my spirit, for the offenses which I have committed. And since nothing is pleasing to God unless it be offered by Thee, unite my will with Thine and my sufferings with those that Thou hast suffered; grant that mine may become Thine. Unite me with Thee; fill me with Thee and Thy Holy Spirit. Enter into my heart and into my soul, there to bear my sufferings and to continue in me that part of the suffering of Thy passion which yet remains to be endured, which Thou art yet completing in Thy members until the perfect consummation of Thy Body, so that it shall no longer be I who live and who suffer but that it shall be Thou who dost live and suffer in me, O my Saviour. And thus, having some small part in Thy suffering, I shall be filled wholly by Thee with the glory which it has brought to Thee, the glory in which Thou dost dwell with the Father and the Holy Spirit, forever and ever. Amen.

George Fox

(1624–1691)

George Fox was the founder of the Quakers, also known as the Society of Friends. Emerging out of the tremendous religious turmoil in England during the seventeenth century, Quakerism had its roots in English Puritanism. But Fox and his followers went beyond strict Puritanism, for they were radicals in the sense that they tried to return to what they perceived as the basic root principles of New Testament Christianity.

William Penn, one of Fox's most famous followers, called it *Primitive Christianity Revived,* and he accurately described Fox himself as "an original, being no man's copy." From Fox the Quakers emphasized the priesthood of all believers and abolished all offices of an ordained clergy. Fox proclaimed a continuing revelation by God, a revelation that centered in the Inner Light of Christ in each individual, and was not restricted simply to the Scriptures. As Fox wrote about his conversion, "Though I read the Scriptures that spoke of Christ and of God, yet I knew him not [except] by revelation, as he who hath the key did open, and as the Father of life drew me to his Son by his spirit."

Fox's doctrine of the Inner Light and his ministry to the outcasts of English society ("that which the people do trample upon") contributed to the tradition of pacifism among the Quakers and their concern for all conditions of humanity. Persecuted and even imprisoned, Fox greeted adversity and hatred with peace and charity toward others, and by the force of his personality and his witness he won others to his side.

His conversion in 1647 came after a long period of "seeking Truth," as he described it. He was born into a family of deep piety, and for a brief time was apprenticed to a shoemaker. But in 1643, feeling that he was called to reject all his ties to his family and friends, he began to travel about England in search of religious security. Fox despaired not only of his sin but also of the sloth and ignorance of the priests and ministers whom he encountered. At last, Christ spoke to him directly. He began an itinerant preaching ministry, but it was not until 1652 that he attracted a significant number of converts. In 1669 he married Margaret Fell, the widow of a nobleman, and through a few such influential converts the Society of Friends developed a firm foothold in the religious landscape of England.

Fox had no intention of creating another church, but he did demonstrate a knack for organization, combining both the skills of leadership and the ability to keep the Society of Friends democratic in structure. He traveled extensively and tirelessly, making missionary journeys to Ireland, the West Indies and North America, and Holland. Although Fox dictated his famous *Journal,* his genius and spirit emerge clearly in its pages, and it has been widely read by Quakers and many others for centuries. Even those who cannot accept his theology can admire the simplicity and peaceful witness that he made. In William Penn's view, he stood alone: "Many sons have done virtuously in this day, but dear George thou excellest them all."

Now during all this time I was never joined in profession of religion with any, but gave up myself to the Lord, having forsaken all evil company, and taken leave of father and mother and all other relations, and travelled up and down as a stranger in the earth, which way the Lord inclined my heart, taking a chamber to myself in the town where I came, and tarrying sometimes a month, sometimes more, sometimes less in a place. For I durst not stay long in any place, being afraid both of professor [one who professes religion] and profane, lest, being a tender young man, I should be hurt by conversing much with either. For which reason I kept myself much as a stranger, seeking heavenly wisdom and getting knowledge from the Lord, and was brought off from outward things to rely wholly on the Lord alone. And though my exercises and troubles were very great, yet were they not so continual but that I had some intermissions, and was sometimes brought into such an heavenly joy that I thought I had been in Abraham's bosom. As I cannot declare the misery I was in, it was so great and heavy upon me, so neither can I set forth the

Excerpted from *The Journal of George Fox,* rev. ed., ed. John L. Nickalls (Cambridge: Cambridge University Press, 1952), 10-12, 14-15, 18-21. Copyright © Cambridge University Press. Reprinted with the permission of Cambridge University Press.

mercies of God unto me in all my misery. Oh, the everlasting love of God to my soul when I was in great distress! When my troubles and torments were great, then was his love exceeding great. Thou, Lord, makest a fruitful field a barren wilderness, and a barren wilderness a fruitful field; thou bringest down and settest up; thou killest and makest alive; all honour and glory be to thee, O Lord of glory! The knowledge of thee in the spirit is life, but that knowledge which is fleshly works death. And while there is this knowledge in the flesh, deceit and self-will conform to anything, and will say, "Yes, yes," to that it doth not know. The knowledge which the world hath of what the prophets and apostles spake is a fleshly knowledge; and the apostates from the life in which the prophets and apostles were, have gotten their words, the Holy Scriptures, in a form, but not in their life nor spirit that gave them forth. And so all lie in confusion and are making provision for the flesh, to fulfil the lusts thereof, but not to fulfil the law and command of Christ in his power and spirit; for that, they say, they cannot do, but to fulfil the lusts of the flesh, that they can do with delight.

Now after I had received that opening from the Lord that to be bred at Oxford or Cambridge was not sufficient to fit a man to be a minister of Christ, I regarded the priests less, and looked more after the dissenting people. And among them I saw there was some tenderness, and many of them came afterwards to be convinced, for they had some openings. But as I had forsaken all the priests, so I left the separate preachers also, and those called the most experienced people; for I saw there was none among them all that could speak to my condition. And when all my hopes in them and in all men were gone, so that I had nothing outwardly to help me, nor could tell what to do, then, Oh then, I heard a voice which said, "There is one, even Christ Jesus, that can speak to thy condition," and when I heard it my heart did leap for joy. Then the Lord did let me see why there was none upon the earth that could speak to my condition, namely, that I might give him all the glory; for all are concluded under sin, and shut up in unbelief as I had been, that Jesus Christ might have the pre-eminence, who enlightens, and gives grace, and faith, and power. Thus, when God doth work who shall let [prevent] it? And this I knew experimentally [by experience].

My desires after the Lord grew stronger, and zeal in the pure knowledge of God and of Christ alone, without the help of any man, book, or writing. For though I read the Scriptures that spoke of Christ and of God, yet I knew him not but by revelation, as he who hath the key did open, and as the Father of life drew me to his Son by his spirit. And then the Lord did gently lead me along, and did let me see his love, which was endless and eternal, and surpasseth all the knowledge that men have in the natural state, or can get by history or books; and that love let me see myself as I was without him. And I was afraid of all company, for I saw them perfectly where they were, through the love of God which let me see myself. I had not fellowship with any people, priests, or professors, nor any sort of separated people, but with Christ, who hath the key, and opened the door of light and life unto me. And I was afraid of all carnal talk and talkers, for I could see nothing but corruptions, and the life lay under the burden of corruptions. And when I myself was in the deep, under all shut up, I could not believe that I should ever overcome; my troubles, my sorrows, and my temptations were so great, that I thought many times I should have despaired, I was so tempted. But when Christ opened to me how he was tempted by the same Devil, and had overcome him and bruised his head, and that through him and his power, light, grace and spirit, I should overcome also, I had confidence in him. So he it was that opened to me when I was shut up and had not hope nor faith. Christ it was who had enlightened me, that gave me his light to believe in, and gave me hope, which is himself, revealed himself in me, and gave me his spirit and gave me his grace, which I found sufficient in the deeps and in weakness. Thus, in the deepest miseries, and in greatest sorrows and temptations, that many times beset me, the Lord in his mercy did keep me. . . .

And one day when I had been walking solitarily abroad and was come home, I was taken up in the love of God, so that I could not but admire the greatness of his love. And while I was in that condition it was opened unto me by the eternal Light and power, and I therein saw clearly that all was done and to be done in and by Christ, and how he conquers and destroys this tempter, the Devil and all his works, and is atop of him, and that all these troubles were good for me, and temptations for the trial of my faith which Christ had given me. And the Lord opened me that I saw through all these troubles and temptations. My living faith was raised, that I saw all was done by Christ, the life, and my belief was in him. And when at any time my condition was veiled, my secret belief was stayed firm, and hope underneath held me, as an anchor in the bottom of the sea, and anchored my immortal soul to its Bishop, causing it to swim above the sea, the world where all the raging waves, foul weather, tempests, and temptations are. But oh, then did I see my troubles, trials, and temptations more than ever I had done! As the Light appeared, all appeared that is out of the Light, darkness, death, temptations, the unrighteous, the ungodly; all was manifest and seen in the Light.

Then after this there did a pure fire appear in me; then I saw how he sat as a refiner's fire and as the fuller's soap; and then the spiritual discerning came into me, by which I did discern my own thoughts, groans and sighs, and what it was that did veil me, and what it was that did open me. And that which could not abide in the patience nor endure the fire, in the Light I found to be the groans of the flesh (that could not give up to the will of God), which had veiled me, and that could not be patient in all trials, troubles and anguishes and perplexities, and could not give up self to die by the Cross, the power of God, that the living and quickened might follow him; and that that which would cloud and veil from the presence of Christ, that which the sword of the Spirit cuts down and which must die, might not be kept alive. And I discerned the groans of the spirit, which did open me, and made intercession to God, in which spirit is the true waiting upon God for the redemption of the body and of the whole creation. And by this true spirit, in which the true sighing is, I saw over the false sighings and groanings. And by this invisible spirit I discerned all the false hearing and the false seeing, and the false smelling which was atop, above the Spirit, quenching and grieving it; and that all they that were there were in confusion and deceit, where the false asking and praying is, in deceit, and atop in that nature and tongue that takes God's holy name in vain, and wallows in the Egyptian sea, and asketh but hath not. For they hate his light and resist the Holy Ghost, and turn the grace into wantonness, and rebel against the Spirit, and are erred from the faith they should ask in, and from the spirit they should pray by. He that knoweth these things in the true spirit, can witness them. The divine light of Christ manifesteth all things; and the spiritual fire trieth all things, and severeth all things. Several things did I then see as the Lord opened them to me, for he showed me that which can live in his holy refining fire, and that can live to God under his law. And he made me sensible how the law and the prophets were until John and how the least in the everlasting kingdom of God is greater than John. . . .

And I heard of a woman in Lancashire that had fasted two and twenty days, and I travelled to see her; but when I came to her I saw that she was under a temptation. And when I had spoken to her what I had from the Lord, I left her, her father being one high in profession. And passing on, I went among the professors at Dukinfield and Manchester, where I stayed a while and declared Truth among them. And there were some convinced, who received the Lord's teaching, by which they were confirmed and stood in the Truth. But the professors were in a rage, all pleading for sin and imperfection, and could not endure to hear talk of perfection, and of an holy and sinless life. But the Lord's power was over all; though they were chained under darkness and sin, which they pleaded for, and quenched the tender thing in them.

About this time there was a great meeting of the Baptists, at Broughton, in Leicestershire, with some that had separated from them; and people of other notions went thither, and I went also. Not many of the Baptists came, but abundance of other people were there. And the Lord opened my mouth, and his everlasting Truth was declared amongst them, and the power of the Lord was over them all. For in that day the Lord's power began to spring, and I had great openings in the Scriptures. And several were convinced in those parts, and were turned from darkness to light, and from the power of Satan unto God, and his power they did receive and by it many were raised up to praise God. And when I reasoned with professors and other people, some were convinced and did stand.

Yet I was under great temptations sometimes, and my inward sufferings were heavy; but I could find none to open my condition to but the Lord alone, unto whom I cried night and day. And I went back into Nottinghamshire, and there the Lord shewed me that the natures of those things which were hurtful without were within, in the hearts and minds of wicked men. The natures of dogs, swine, vipers, of Sodom and Egypt, Pharaoh, Cain, Ishmael, Esau, etc. The natures of these I saw within, though people had been looking without. And I cried to the Lord, saying, "Why should I be thus, seeing I was never addicted to commit those evils?" And the Lord answered that it was needful I should have a sense of all conditions, how else should I speak to all conditions; and in this I saw the infinite love of God. I saw also that there was an ocean of darkness and death, but an infinite ocean of light and love, which flowed over the ocean of darkness. And in that also I saw the infinite love of God; and I had great openings.

And as I was walking by the steeplehouse side, in the town of Mansfield, the Lord said unto me, "That which people do trample upon must be thy food." And as the Lord spoke he opened it to me how that people and professors did trample upon the life, even the life of Christ was trampled upon; and they fed upon words, and fed one another with words, but trampled upon the life, and trampled underfoot the blood of the Son of God, which blood was my life, and they lived in their airy notions, talking of him. It seemed strange to me at the first that I should feed on that which the high professors trampled upon, but the Lord opened it clearly to me by his eternal spirit and power.

In Mansfield there came a priest who was looked upon to be above others, and all that professed themselves above the priests went to hear him and cried him up. I was against their going, and spoke to them against their going, and asked them if they had not a teacher within them: the anointing to teach them, and why would they go out to man. And then when they were gone to hear him, I was in sore travail, and it came upon me that I was moved to go to the steeplehouse to tell the people and the priest, and to bid them to cease from man whose breath was in their nostrils, and to tell them where their teacher was, within them, the spirit and the light of Jesus, and how God that made the world doth not dwell in temples made with hands. And many other things concerning the Truth I spake to them. And they were pretty moderate to hear the Truth, whereby, after, many were wrought upon. Then came people from far and near to see me; and I was fearful of being drawn out by them, yet I was made to speak and open things to them.

There was one Brown, who had great prophecies and sights upon his death-bed of me. And he spoke openly of what I should be made instrumental by the Lord to bring forth. And of others he spake that they should come to nothing, which was fulfilled on some, that then were something in show. And when this man was buried, a great work of the Lord fell upon me, to the admiration of many, who thought I had been dead, and many came to see me, for about fourteen days' time. For I was very much altered in countenance and person as if my body had been new moulded or changed. And while I was in that condition, I had a sense and discerning given me by the Lord, through which I saw plainly that when many people talked of God and of Christ, etc., the Serpent spoke in them; but this was hard to be borne. Yet the work of the Lord went on in some, and my sorrows and troubles began to wear off and tears of joy dropped from me, so that I could have wept night and day with tears of joy to the Lord, in humility and brokenness of heart. And I saw into that which was without end, and things which cannot be uttered, and of the greatness and infiniteness of the love of God, which cannot be expressed by words. For I had been brought through the very ocean of darkness and death, and through the power and over the power of Satan, by the eternal glorious power of Christ. Even through that darkness was I brought, which covered-over all the world, and which chained down all, and shut up all in the death. And the same eternal power of God, which brought me through these things, was that which afterwards shook the nations, priests, professors, and people. Then could I say I had been in spiritual Babylon, Sodom, Egypt, and the grave; but by the eternal power of God I was come out of it, and was brought over it and the power of it, into the power of Christ. And I saw the harvest white, and the Seed of God lying thick in the ground, as ever did wheat that was sown outwardly, and none to gather it; and for this I mourned with tears.

And a report went abroad of me that I was a young man that had a discerning spirit; whereupon many came to me from far and near, professors, priests, and people. And the Lord's power brake forth; and I had great openings, and prophecies, and spake unto them of the things of God, and they heard with attention and silence, and went away, and spread the fame thereof. Then came the tempter, and set upon me again, charging me that I had sinned against the Holy Ghost, but I could not tell in what. And then Paul's condition came before me, how, after he had been taken up into the third heaven and seen things not lawful to be uttered, a messenger of Satan was sent to buffet him again. Thus, by the power of Christ, I got over that temptation also.

John Bunyan

(1628–1688)

John Bunyan was born into a world of violence, war, and bitter disputes about Christian doctrine. During his lifetime, the continent of Europe was engulfed in the Thirty Years' War, pitting Protestant against Catholic in what amounted to a civil war within Christianity. England saw its own civil war in the 1640s — Puritans fighting Anglicans, defenders of Parliament battling the forces of the king.

This atmosphere of war and combat is reflected in Bunyan's conversion and his vision of life. For him the world is an arena of good and evil; an individual is constantly tempted to sin; the Christian life is spiritual warfare against Satan. Because of the power of sin, a person's conversion is rarely certain or final. Conversion thus becomes a process rather than a single event.

Bunyan's understanding of God's redemption first appeared in his spiritual autobiography, *Grace Abounding to the Chief of Sinners* (1666), written while he was in prison for refusing to stop preaching without a license. A classic of the church's devotional literature, *Grace Abounding* is a powerful and dramatic tale of Bunyan's many temptations and his experiences of grace and forgiveness.

Bunyan turned this story into an allegory in *The Pilgrim's Progress* (1678), an eloquent and beautiful description of a Christian's journey through dangers and pitfalls to safety with God. *The Pilgrim's Progress* is a landmark in English literature. With the exception of the Bible, it was the most widely read book in the English language until the twentieth century.

Bunyan says that as a youth he had "few equals . . . both for cursing, swearing, lying, and blaspheming the holy name of God." He was an impoverished tinker or general repairman who married an equally poor woman whose only dowry consisted of two devotional books: *The Practice of Piety* and *The Plain Man's Pathway to Heaven*. When he read these volumes, Bunyan began to examine his life, and one Sunday, while playing tipcat, he had a sudden and deep awareness of his sin and God's anger. He searched the Scriptures thoroughly, and despite occasional feelings of forgiveness, he continued to agonize over his salvation.

The selection reprinted here describes some of the heights and depths that Bunyan experienced and his final awareness of God's love. This conception of the Christian life as a journey or pilgrimage continues to be one of the most powerful and enduring ways in which Christians understand their own faith and experience, and it has been dramatically influenced by Bunyan's writings.

Bunyan's other works include *The Life and Death of Mr. Badman* (1680), *The Holy War* (1682), and seventy-four rhymes in *A Book for Boys and Girls* (1686). After being released from prison in 1672, he preached as a Baptist minister, and he died in 1688 of pneumonia after making a pastoral call.

Before many weeks were gone, I began to despond again, fearing, lest, notwithstanding all that I had enjoyed, that I might be deceived and destroyed at the last; for this consideration came strong into my mind, "That whatever comfort and peace I thought I might have from the word of the promise of life, yet unless there could be found in my refreshment, a concurrence and agreement in the Scriptures, let me think what I will thereof, and hold it never so fast, I should find no such thing at the end; for the Scriptures cannot be broken."

Now began my heart again to ache, and fear I might meet with a disappointment at last. Wherefore I began with all seriousness to examine my former comfort, and to consider whether one that had sinned as I had done, might with confidence trust upon the faithfulness of God, laid down in these words, by which I had been comforted, and on which I had leaned myself. But now were brought to my mind, "For it is impossible for those who were once enlightened, and have tasted the heavenly gift, and were made partakers of the Holy Ghost, and have tasted the good word of God, and the powers of the world to come, if they shall fall away, to renew them again unto repentance. For if we sin wilfully, and after we

---

Excerpted from *Grace Abounding to the Chief of Sinners*, in *The Complete Works of John Bunyan* (Philadelphia, 1874), 54-56, 59.

have received the knowledge of the truth, there remains no more sacrifice for sin, but certain fearful looking-for of judgment, and fiery indignation, which shall devour the adversaries; even as Esau, who for one morsel of meat, sold his birthright. For ye know how that afterwards, when he would have inherited the blessing, he was rejected; for he found no place of repentance, though he sought it carefully with tears."

Now was the word of the Gospel forced from my soul; so that no promise or encouragement was to be found in the Bible for me; and now would that saying work upon my spirit to afflict me, "Rejoice not, O Israel, for joy as other people." For I saw, indeed, there was cause of rejoicing for those that held to Jesus; but for me, I had cut myself off by my transgressions, and left myself neither foot-hold nor hand-hold, among all the stays and props in the precious word of life.

And truly, I did now feel myself to sink into a gulf, as an house whose foundation is destroyed: I did liken myself in this condition, unto the case of a child that was fallen into a mill-pit, who though it could make some shift to scrabble and sprawl in the water, yet because it could find neither hold for hand nor foot, therefore at last it must die in that condition. So soon as this fresh assault had fastened on my soul, that Scripture came into my heart, "This for many days." And indeed I found it was so; for I could not be delivered, nor brought to peace again, until well nigh two years and an half were completely finished. Wherefore these words, though in themselves they tended to no discouragement, yet to me, who feared this condition would be eternal, they were at sometimes as an help and refreshment to me.

For, thought I, many days are not for ever, many days will have an end; therefore seeing I was to be afflicted not a few, but many days, yet I was glad it was but for many days. Thus, I say, I could recall myself sometimes and give myself an help, for as soon as even the word came into my mind, at first I knew my trouble would be long, yet this would be but sometimes; for I could not always think on this, nor ever be helped by it, though I did.

Now while the Scriptures lay before me, and laid sin anew at my door, that saying in Luke xviii. 1, with others, did encourage me to prayer; then the tempter again laid at me very sore, suggesting, "That neither the mercy of God, nor yet the blood of Christ, did at all concern me, nor could they help me for my sin; therefore it was but in vain to pray." Yet, thought I, "I will pray." "But, said the tempter, your sin is unpardonable." "Well, said I, I will pray." "It is to no boot, said he." "Yet, said I, I will pray." So I went to prayer with God; and while I was at prayer, I uttered words to this effect: "Lord, Satan tells me, that neither thy mercy, nor Christ's blood is sufficient to save my soul; Lord, shall I honour thee most, by believing thou wilt, and canst? or him, by believing that thou neither wilt, nor canst? Lord, I would fain honour thee, by believing that thou wilt, and canst."

And as I was thus before the Lord, that Scripture fastened on my heart, "O man, great is thy faith": even as if one had clapped me on the back, as I was on my knees before God: yet I was not able to believe this, that this was a prayer of faith, till almost six months after; for I could not think that I had faith, or that there should be a word for me to act faith on; therefore I should still be, as sticking in the jaws of desperation, and went mourning up and down in a sad condition.

There was nothing now that I longed for more than to be put out of doubt, as to this thing in question, and as I was vehemently desiring to know, if there was indeed hope for me, these words came rolling into my mind, "Will the Lord cast off for ever? and will he be favourable no more? Is his mercy clean gone for ever? Doth his promise fail for evermore? Hath God forgotten to be gracious? Hath he in anger shut up his tender mercies?" And all the while they run in my mind, methought I had still this as the answer: "'Tis a question whether he hath or no; it may be he hath not." Yea, the interrogatory seemed to me to carry in it a sure affirmation that indeed he had not, nor would so cast off, but would be favourable; that his promise doth not fail, and that he hath not forgotten to be gracious, nor would in anger shut up his tender mercy. Something also there was upon my heart at the same time, which I now cannot call to mind, which with this text did sweeten my heart, and make me conclude, that this mercy might not be quite gone, not gone for ever.

At another time I remembered, I was again much under this question "Whether the blood of Christ was sufficient to save my soul?" in which doubt I continued from morning, till about seven or eight at night; and at last, when I was, as it were, quite worn out with fear, lest it should not lay hold on me, these words did sound suddenly within my heart, "He is able." But methought this word *able,* was spoke so loud to me, it showed a great word, it seemed to be writ in great letters, and gave such a jostle to my fear and doubt, (I mean for the time it tarried with me, which was about a day,) as I never had from that, all my life, either before or after. (Heb. vii. 25.)

70

But one morning as I was again at prayer and trembling under the fear of this, that no word of God could help me, that piece of a sentence darted in upon me, "My grace is sufficient." At this methought I felt some stay, as if there might be hopes; but oh! how good a thing it is for God to send his word! for about a fortnight before, I was looking on this very place, and then I thought it could not come near my soul with comfort, therefore I threw down my book in a pet; then I thought it was not large enough for me; no, not large enough, but now it was as if it had arms of grace so wide, that it could not only enclose me, but many more beside.

By these words I was sustained, yet not without exceeding conflicts, for the space of seven or eight weeks; for my peace would be in it, and out, sometimes twenty times a day, comfort now, and trouble presently; peace now, and before I could go a furlong, as full of fear and guilt as ever heart could hold; and this was not only now and then, but my whole seven weeks' experience. For this about the sufficiency of grace, and that of Esau's parting with his birthright, would be like a pair of scales within my mind, sometimes one end would be uppermost and sometimes again the other; according to which would be my peace or troubles.

Therefore I did still pray to God, that he would come in with his Scripture more fully on my heart; to wit, that he would help me to apply the whole sentence, for as yet I could not; what he gave, that I gathered; but further I could not go, for as yet it only helped me to hope there might be mercy for me, "My grace is sufficient": and though it came no farther, it answered my former question; to wit, that there was hope; yet because "for thee" was left out, I was not contented, but prayed to God for that also. Wherefore, one day, when I was in a meeting of God's people, full of sadness and terror, for my fears again were strong upon me, and as I was now thinking my soul was never the better, but my case most sad and fearful, these words did with great power suddenly break in upon me, "My power is sufficient for thee, My grace is sufficient for thee, My grace is sufficient for thee," three times together: and oh! methought that every word was a mighty word unto me; as "my," and "grace," and "sufficient," and "for thee"; they were then, and sometimes are still, far bigger than others be.

At which time my understanding was so enlightened, that I was as though I had seen the Lord Jesus look down from heaven, through the tiles upon me, and direct these words unto me. This sent me mourning home; it broke my heart, and filled me full of joy, and laid me low as the dust; only it stayed not long with me, I mean in this glory and refreshing comfort; yet it continued with me for several weeks, and did encourage me to hope; but as soon as that powerful operation of it was taken from my heart, that other, about Esau, returned upon me as before; so my soul did hang as in a pair of scales again, sometimes up, and sometimes down; now in peace, and anon again in terror.

Thus I went on for many weeks, sometimes comforted, and sometimes tormented; and especially at some times my torment would be very sore. . . .

But one day, as I was passing into the field, and that too with some dashes on my conscience, fearing lest yet all was not right, suddenly this sentence fell upon my soul, "Thy righteousness is in heaven"; and methought withal, I saw with the eyes of my soul, Jesus Christ at God's right hand; there, I say, as my righteousness; so that wherever I was, or whatever I was doing, God could not say to me, "He wants my righteousness," for that was just before him. I also saw moreover, that it was not my good frame of heart that made my righteousness better, nor yet my bad frame that made my righteousness worse; for my righteousness was Jesus Christ himself, "the same yesterday, to-day and for ever."

Now did my chains fall off my legs indeed; I was loosed from my afflictions and irons; my temptations also fled away; so that from that time those dreadful Scriptures of God left off to trouble me: now went I also home rejoicing, for the grace and love of God; so when I came home, I looked to see if I could find that sentence, "Thy righteousness is in heaven," but could not find such a saying; wherefore my heart began to sink again, only that was brought to my remembrance, "He is made unto us of God, wisdom, righteousness, sanctification, and redemption." By this word I saw the other sentence true.

For by this Scripture I saw that the man Christ Jesus, as he is distinct from us, as touching his bodily presence, so he is our righteousness and sanctification before God. Here therefore I lived, for some time, very sweetly at peace with God through Christ. Oh! methought, Christ! Christ! there was nothing but Christ that was before my eyes: I was now only for looking upon this and the other benefits of Christ apart, as of his blood, burial or his resurrection, but considering him as a whole Christ! as he in whom all these, and all other virtues, relations, offices, and operations met together, and that he sat on the right hand of God in heaven.

'Twas glorious to me to see his exaltation, and the worth and prevalency of all his benefits, and that because now I could look from myself to him, and would reckon, that all those graces of God that now were green on me, were yet but like those cracked groats and four-pence-half-pennies that rich men carry in their purses, when their gold is in their trunks at home: Oh! I saw my gold was in my trunk at home! In Christ my Lord and Saviour. Now Christ was all; all my righteousness, all my sanctification, and all my redemption.

Further, the Lord did also lead me into the mystery of the union with the Son of God, that I was joined to him, and that I was flesh of his flesh, and bone of his bone, and now was that a sweet word unto me, in Ephes. v. 30. By this also was my faith in him, as my righteousness, the more confirmed in me; for if he and I were one, then his righteousness was mine, his merits mine, his victory also mine. Now I could see myself in heaven and earth at once, in heaven by my Christ, by my head, by my righteousness and life, though on earth by body or person.

Now I saw Christ Jesus was looked upon of God; and should also be looked upon by us, as that common or public person, in whom the whole body of his elect are always to be considered and reckoned; that we fulfilled the law by him, died by him, rose from the dead by him, got the victory over sin, death, and hell, by him; when he died, we died; and so of his resurrection. "Thy dead men shall live together, with my dead body shall they arise," saith he. And again, "After two days he will revive us, and the third day we shall live in his sight." Which is now fulfilled by the sitting down of the Son of man on the right hand of the Majesty in the heavens, according to that of the Ephesians, "He hath raised us up together, and made us sit together in heavenly places in Christ Jesus."

Ah! these blessed considerations and Scriptures, with many others of like nature, were in those days made to spangle in mine eye, so that I have cause to say, "Praise ye the Lord God in his sanctuary; praise him in the firmament of his power: praise him for his mighty acts; praise him according to his excellent greatness."

John Wesley

(1703–1791)

John Wesley's conversion on May 24, 1738, has been widely recognized as an epoch-making date. It marks the beginning of Methodism, a denomination that has exerted a profound influence in Britain, the United States, and throughout the world. Signaling the rise of evangelicalism in Christianity, Wesley's conversion is a model of the datable, instantaneous, certain experience of grace that has become so characteristic of some forms of the evangelical movement.

Although Wesley emphasized the sinfulness of his life prior to this date, he was born into what would be called a Christian home. His father, Samuel, was a scholarly but somewhat prickly rector in the Church of England. His mother, Susanna, was an extraordinary woman of beauty, learning, efficiency, and piety. She gave birth to nineteen children, only nine of whom lived to adulthood. Among them were John and his brother Charles, the author of innumerable hymns, and together they transformed the history of Christianity. Their mother left a permanent imprint on their lives, perhaps greater in the case of John, who had difficulty relating to women throughout his life. She educated all the children not simply in the three R's but also in Latin, Greek, history, literature, and of course religion. She set aside one evening a week for each of her children to converse about the child's educational and spiritual development. When John left for Oxford University, he continued the rigorous pattern that his mother had taught him at home. He joined a group of students who trained themselves in Christian spirituality; and because of their disciplined life, the members of this "Holy Club" were derisively called "Methodists."

As a child, John Wesley nearly died in a fire that devastated the parsonage; and when he was saved by two men of the town, his mother praised God and exclaimed, "Is this not a brand plucked out of the burning?" The phrase stayed with Wesley throughout his life. He left Oxford for a disastrous missionary tour in Georgia, suffered through a disappointing love affair, and, in frail health, returned to England on a ship buffeted by terrible gales. The images of these experiences — fire, storms, illness — characterize much of his preaching and piety, as well as the ethos of this kind of evangelicalism.

It was in Georgia that Wesley first encountered the Moravians, who impressed him because of the serenity and certainty of their faith. When he arrived back in London, he met the Moravian Peter Böhler, to whom he confessed that despite his knowledge of Christianity, he still felt he lacked saving faith and wondered if he should stop preaching. "By no means," Böhler said. "But what shall I preach?" Wesley asked, and Böhler replied, "Preach faith till you have it; and then, because you have it, you will preach faith." Shortly after that, Wesley visited the house on Aldersgate where a group of Moravians were meeting, and as someone read from Luther's preface to his commentary on Romans, Wesley's heart was "strangely warmed."

The influence of Luther on Wesley is appropriate, for Wesley's conversion was a renewed sense that assurance of salvation came by grace through faith, not by works. But, as Wesley's own account reveals, he was afflicted by doubt immediately after the experience and resolved, "Well may fears be within me; but I must go on, and tread them under my feet." He almost literally did just that, beginning an itinerant ministry that lasted for fifty years — into his eighties — traveling 250,000 miles, and preaching 40,000 to 50,000 sermons. Early on, he wrote to his brother Samuel, "Leisure and I have taken leave of each other," and they never met again. He considered all the world his parish, and to a considerable degree, later Methodists and evangelicals have fulfilled his charge.

～

What occurred on *Wednesday* the 24th, I think best to relate at large, after premissing what may make it the better understood. Let him that cannot receive it ask of the Father of lights that He would give more light to him and me.

1. I believe, till I was about ten years old I had not sinned away that "washing of the Holy Ghost" which was given me in baptism, having

---

From *The Journal of John Wesley*, A.M., ed. Nehemiah Curnock (New York: Eaton & Mains, 1909), 1:465-78, with the annotation omitted.

been strictly educated and carefully taught that I could only be saved "by universal obedience, by keeping all the commandments of God"; in the meaning of which I was diligently instructed. And those instructions, so far as they respected outward duties and sins, I gladly received and often thought of. But all that was said to me of inward obedience or holiness I neither understood nor remembered. So that I was indeed as ignorant of the true meaning of the law as I was of the gospel of Christ.

2. The next six or seven years were spent at school; where, outward restraints being removed, I was much more negligent than before, even of outward duties, and almost continually guilty of outward sins, which I knew to be such, though they were not scandalous in the eye of the world. However, I still read the Scriptures, and said my prayers morning and evening. And what I now hoped to be saved by, was, (1) not being so bad as other people; (2) having still a kindness for religion; and (3) reading the Bible, going to church, and saying my prayers.

3. Being removed to the University for five years, I still said my prayers both in public and in private, and read, with the Scriptures, several other books of religion, especially comments on the New Testament. Yet I had not all this while so much as a notion of inward holiness; nay, went on habitually, and for the most part very contentedly, in some or other known sin: indeed, with some intermission and short struggles, especially before and after the Holy Communion, which I was obliged to receive thrice a year. I cannot well tell what I hoped to be saved by now, when I was continually sinning against that little light I had; unless by those transient fits of what many divines taught me to call repentance.

4. When I was about twenty-two, my father pressed me to enter into holy orders. At the same time, the providence of God directing me to Kempis's *Christian Pattern,* I began to see, that true religion was seated in the heart, and that God's law extended to all our thoughts as well as words and actions. I was, however, very angry at Kempis for being too strict; though I read him only in Dean Stanhope's translation. Yet I had frequently much sensible comfort in reading him, such as I was an utter stranger to before; and meeting likewise with a religious friend, which I never had till now, I began to alter the whole form of my conversation, and to set in earnest upon a new life. I set apart an hour or two a day for religious retirement. I communicated every week. I watched against all sin, whether in word or deed. I began to aim at, and pray for, inward ho-

liness. So that now, "doing so much, and living so good a life," I doubted not but I was a good Christian.

5. Removing soon after to another College, I executed a resolution which I was before convinced was of the utmost importance, — shaking off at once all my trifling acquaintance — I began to see more and more the value of time. I applied myself closer to study. I watched more carefully against actual sins; I advised others to be religious, according to that scheme of religion by which I modelled my own life. But meeting now with Mr. Law's *Christian Perfection* and *Serious Call,* although I was much offended at many parts of both, yet they convinced me more than ever of the exceeding height and breadth and depth of the law of God. The light flowed in so mightily upon my soul, that everything appeared in a new view. I cried to God for help, and resolved not to prolong the time of obeying Him as I had never done before. And by my continued endeavour to keep His whole law inward and outward, to the utmost of my power, I was persuaded that I should be accepted of Him, and that I was even then in a state of salvation.

6. In 1730 I began visiting the prisons; assisting the poor and sick in town; and doing what other good I could, by my presence or my little fortune, to the bodies and souls of all men. To this end I abridged myself of all superfluities, and many that are called necessaries of life. I soon became a by-word for so doing, and I rejoiced that my name was cast out as evil. The next spring I began observing the Wednesday and Friday Fasts, commonly observed in the ancient Church; tasting no food till three in the afternoon. And now I knew not how to go any further. I diligently strove against all sin. I omitted no sort of self-denial which I thought lawful; I carefully used, both in public and in private, all the means of grace at all opportunities. I omitted no occasion of doing good; I for that reason suffered evil. And all this I knew to be nothing, unless as it was directed toward inward holiness. Accordingly this, the image of God, was what I aimed at in all, by doing His will, not my own. Yet when, after continuing some years in this course, I apprehended myself to be near death, I could not find that all this gave me any comfort or any assurance of acceptance with God. At this I was then not a little surprised; not imagining I had been all this time building on the sand, nor considering that "other foundation can no man lay than that which is laid" by God, "even Christ Jesus."

7. Soon after, a contemplative man convinced me still more than I was convinced before, that outward works are nothing, being alone;

and in several conversations instructed me how to pursue inward holiness, or a union of the soul with God. But even of his instructions (though I then received them as the words of God) I cannot but now observe (1) that he spoke so incautiously against trusting in outward works, that he discouraged me from doing them at all; (2) that he recommended (as it were, to supply what was wanting in them) *mental prayer,* and the like exercises, as the most effectual means of purifying the soul and uniting it with God. Now these were, in truth, as much my own works as visiting the sick or clothing the naked; and the union with God thus pursued was as really my own righteousness as any I had before pursued under another name.

8. In this refined way of trusting to my own works and my own righteousness (so zealously inculcated by the Mystic writers), I dragged on heavily, finding no comfort or help therein till the time of my leaving England. On shipboard, however, I was again active in outward works; where it pleased God of His free mercy to give me twenty-six of the Moravian brethren for companions, who endeavoured to show me "a more excellent way." But I understood it not at first. I was too learned and too wise. So that it seemed foolishness unto me. And I continued preaching, and following after, and trusting in, that righteousness whereby no flesh can be justified.

9. All the time I was at Savannah I was thus beating the air. Being ignorant of the righteousness of Christ, which, by a living faith in Him, bringeth salvation "to every one that believeth," I sought to establish my own righteousness; and so laboured in the fire all my days. I was now properly "under the law"; I knew that "the law" of God was "spiritual; I consented to it that it was good." Yea, "I delighted in it, after the inner man." Yet was I "carnal, sold under sin." Every day was I constrained to cry out, "What I do, I allow not: for what I would, I do not; but what I hate, that I do. To will is" indeed "present with me: but how to perform that which is good, I find not. For the good which I would, I do not; but the evil which I would not, that I do. I find a law, that when I would do good, evil is present with me": even "the law in my members, warring against the law of my mind," and still "bringing me into captivity to the law of sin."

10. In this vile, abject state of bondage to sin, I was indeed fighting continually, but not conquering. Before, I had willingly served sin: now it was unwillingly; but still I served it. I fell, and rose, and fell again. Sometimes I was overcome, and in heaviness: sometimes I overcame,

and was in joy. For as in the former state I had some foretastes of the terrors of the law; so had I in this, of the comforts of the gospel. During this whole struggle between nature and grace, which had now continued above ten years, I had many remarkable returns to prayer, especially when I was in trouble; I had many sensible comforts, which are indeed no other than short anticipations of the life of faith. But I was still "under the law," not "under grace" (the state most who are called Christians are content to live and die in); for I was only striving with, not freed from, sin. Neither had I the witness of the Spirit with my spirit, and indeed could not; for I "sought it not by faith, but as it were by the works of the law."

11. In my return to England, January 1738, being in imminent danger of death, and very uneasy on that account, I was strongly convinced that the cause of that uneasiness was unbelief; and that the gaining a true, living faith was the "one thing needful" for me. But still I fixed not this faith on its right object: I meant only faith in God, not faith in or through Christ. Again, I knew not that I was wholly void of this faith; but only thought I had not enough of it. So that when Peter Böhler, whom God prepared for me as soon as I came to London, affirmed of true faith in Christ (which is but one) that it had those two fruits inseparably attending it, "dominion over sin and constant peace from a sense of forgiveness," I was quite amazed, and looked upon it as a new gospel. If this was so, it was clear I had not faith. But I was not willing to be convinced of this. Therefore I disputed with all my might, and laboured to prove that faith might be where these were not: for all the scriptures relating to this I had been long since taught to construe away; and to call all Presbyterians who spoke otherwise. Besides, I well saw no one could, in the nature of things, have such a sense of forgiveness, and not *feel* it. But I felt it not. If, then, there was no faith without this, all my pretensions to faith dropped at once.

12. When I met Peter Böhler again, he consented to put the dispute upon the issue which I desired, namely, Scripture and experience. I first consulted the Scripture. But when I set aside the glosses of men, and simply considered the words of God, comparing them together, endeavouring to illustrate the obscure by the plainer passages, I found they all made against me, and was forced to retreat to my last hold, "that experience would never agree with the *literal interpretation* of those scriptures. Nor could I therefore allow it to be true, till I found some living witnesses of it." He replied, he could show me such at any time; if I

desired it, the next day. And accordingly the next day he came again with three others, all of whom testified, of their own personal experience, that a true living faith in Christ is inseparable from a sense of pardon for all past and freedom from all present sins. They added with one mouth that this faith was the gift, the free gift of God; and that He would surely bestow it upon every soul who earnestly and perseveringly sought it. I was now thoroughly convinced; and, by the grace of God, I resolved to seek it unto the end, (1) By absolutely renouncing all dependence, in whole or in part, upon *my own* works or righteousness; on which I had really grounded my hope of salvation, though I knew it not, from my youth up; (2) by adding to the constant use of all the other means of grace, continual prayer for this very thing, justifying, saving faith, a full reliance on the blood of Christ shed for *me;* a trust in Him, as *my* Christ, as *my* sole justification, sanctification, and redemption.

13. I continued thus to seek it (though with strange indifference, dullness, and coldness, and unusually frequent relapses into sin) till *Wednesday,* May 24. I think it was about five this morning, that I opened my Testament on those words, Τὰ μέγιστα ἡμῖν χαὶ τίμια ἐπαγγέλματα δεδώρηται, ἵνα γένησθε θείας κοινωνοὶ φύσεως. "There are given unto us exceeding great and precious promises, even that ye should be partakers of the divine nature" (2 Pet. i. 4). Just as I went out, I opened it again on those words, "Thou art not far from the kingdom of God." In the afternoon I was asked to go to St. Paul's. The anthem was, "Out of the deep have I called unto Thee, O Lord: Lord, hear my voice. O let Thine ears consider well the voice of my complaint. If Thou, Lord, wilt be extreme to mark what is done amiss, O Lord, who may abide it? For there is mercy with Thee; therefore shalt Thou be feared. O Israel, trust in the Lord: for with the Lord there is mercy, and with Him is plenteous redemption. And He shall redeem Israel from all his sins."

14. In the evening I went very unwillingly to a society in Aldersgate Street, where one was reading Luther's preface to the *Epistle to the Romans*. About a quarter before nine, while he was describing the change which God works in the heart through faith in Christ, I felt my heart strangely warmed. I felt I did trust in Christ, Christ alone for salvation; and an assurance was given me that He had taken away *my* sins, even *mine,* and saved *me* from the law of sin and death.

15. I began to pray with all my might for those who had in a more especial manner despitefully used me and persecuted me. I then testified openly to all there what I now first felt in my heart. But it was not long

before the enemy suggested, "This cannot be faith; for where is thy joy?" Then was I taught that peace and victory over sin are essential to faith in the Captain of our salvation; but that, as to the transports of joy that usually attend the beginning of it, especially in those who have mourned deeply, God sometimes giveth, sometimes withholdeth them, according to the counsels of His own will.

16. After my return home, I was much buffeted with temptations; but cried out, and they fled away. They returned again and again. I as often lifted up my eyes, and He "sent me help from His holy place." And herein I found the difference between this and my former state chiefly consisted. I was striving, yea, fighting with all my might under the law, as well as under grace. But then I was sometimes, if not often, conquered; now, I was always conqueror.

17. *Thur. 25.* — The moment I awaked, "Jesus, Master," was in my heart and in my mouth; and I found all my strength lay in keeping my eye fixed upon Him, and my soul waiting on Him continually. Being again at St. Paul's in the afternoon, "My song shall be always of the loving-kindness of the Lord: with my mouth will I ever be showing forth Thy truth from one generation to another." Yet the enemy injected a fear, "If thou dost believe, why is there not a more sensible change?" I answered (yet not I), "That I know not. But this I know, I have 'now peace with God.' And I sin not to-day, and Jesus my Master has forbid me to take thought for the morrow."

18. "But is not any sort of fear," continued the tempter, "a proof that thou dost not believe?" I desired my Master to answer for me, and opened His Book upon those words of St. Paul, "Without were fightings, within were fears." Then, inferred I, well may fears be within me; but I must go on, and tread them under my feet.

Jonathan Edwards

(1703-1758)

Like John Wesley, Jonathan Edwards brought one age to a close as a very new and different era made ready to appear. Reared in the Calvinistic tradition of New England, Edwards was the last of the Puritans as he carried forward their vigorous intellectual life.

Regarded by many as the greatest American theologian, Edwards personified what has been called "the New England mind." Philosophically reflective and literately articulate, it was a perspective that viewed the whole created panorama under the premise of the sovereignty of God.

Educated at Yale, Edwards served in Northampton for nearly twenty-five years. During this time, the revivalistic movement known as the Great Awakening swept through the churches and created not only religious enthusiasm but divisive controversy among the clergy. Edwards sided with the new movement and wrote at length about it, praising the place of the emotions in religious experience. "Our people," he said, "do not so much need to have their heads stored, as to have their hearts touched."

Three significant documents written by Edwards were an outgrowth of this Great Awakening period: *A Faithful Narrative of the Surprising Work of God in the Conversion of Many Hundred Souls in Northampton and the Neighboring Towns and Villages* (1737); *Sinners in the Hands of an Angry God* (1741); and *A Treatise concerning Religious Affections* (1746). The first report circulated widely in England; the second was a hell-fire sermon, though not typical of Edwards's preaching; the third was a rational argument in favor of religious emotions.

After a dispute with his congregation over requirements for church membership, Edwards was forced to leave Northampton. He moved to Stockbridge in the unlikely role of missionary and teacher to a community of

Housatunnock Native Americans. It was during this period that he wrote his most significant and thoughtful books. *Freedom of the Will* (1754) was Edwards's most philosophical work. *The Nature of True Virtue* (1755) was his lucid essay on Christian ethics. Also written at this time but not published until 1758 was his greatest theological work, *Original Sin*. The same year he became president of the College of New Jersey (now Princeton University), but within five weeks he died of the newly developed inoculation for smallpox.

The relation between the emotional upheaval of the Great Awakening and his erudite theological works corresponds to two important sides of Edwards's life and personality. He could be rigid and demanding in thought, brilliant in debate, and verbally persuasive, and yet at the same time he often seemed inwardly self-conscious, quietly contemplative, and personally introspective.

Many of his sermons and letters reflect this inner side of the thinker, and his own more private writings reveal this clearly. In this latter category belong such items as his early nature essays on insects, colors, and the rainbow, as well as jottings in his diary and a carefully kept list of "resolutions" (which he reminded himself to read over "once a week"). Edwards also wrote (in 1739) an account of his own conversion experience. Known as the *Personal Narrative* or the *Narrative of His Conversion,* the document illustrates Edwards's facility in combining the personal and the theological.

∼

The first instance, that I remember, of that sort of inward, sweet delight in God and divine things, that I have lived much in since, was on reading those words, 1 Tim. i. 17. *Now unto the King eternal, immortal, invisible, the only wise God, be honour and glory for ever and ever, Amen.* As I read the words, there came into my soul, and was as it were diffused through it, a sense of the glory of the Divine Being; a new sense, quite different from any thing I ever experienced before. Never any words of Scripture seemed to me as these words did. I thought with myself, how excellent a Being that was, and how happy I should be, if I might enjoy that God, and be rapt up to him in heaven, and be as it were swallowed up in him for ever! I kept saying, and as it were singing, over these words of scripture to myself; and went to pray to God that I might enjoy him,

From *The Works of President Edwards,* vol. 1 (New York: S. Converse, 1829), 60-61, 65-66, 132, 133-34, 135.

and prayed in a manner quite different from what I used to do; with a new sort of affection. But it never came into my thought, that there was any thing spiritual, or of a saving nature in this.

From about that time, I began to have a new kind of apprehensions and ideas of Christ, and the work of redemption, and the glorious way of salvation by him. An inward, sweet sense of these things, at times, came into my heart; and my soul was led away in pleasant views and contemplations of them. And my mind was greatly engaged to spend my time in reading and meditating on Christ, on the beauty and excellency of his person, and the lovely way of salvation by free grace in him. . . .

On *January* 12, 1723, I made a solemn dedication of myself to God, and wrote it down; giving up myself, and all that I had to God; to be for the future, in no respect, my own; to act as one that had no right to himself, in any respect. And solemnly vowed, to take God for my whole portion and felicity; looking on nothing else, as any part of my happiness, nor acting as if it were; and his law for the constant rule of my obedience: engaging to fight, with all my might, against the world, the flesh, and the devil, to the end of my life. But I have reason to be infinitely humbled, when I consider, how much I have failed, of answering my obligation. . . .

I have loved the doctrines of the gospel; they have been to my soul like green pastures. The gospel has seemed to me the richest treasure; the treasure that I have most desired, and longed that it might dwell richly in me. The way of salvation by Christ, has appeared, in a general way, glorious and excellent, most pleasant and most beautiful. It has often seemed to me, that it would, in a great measure, spoil heaven, to receive it in any other way. That text has often been affecting and delightful to me, Isa. xxxii. 2, *A man shall be an hiding place from the wind, and a covert from the tempest, &c.*

It has often appeared to me delightful, to be united to Christ; to have him for my head, and to be a member of his body; also to have Christ for my teacher and prophet. I very often think with sweetness, and longings, and pantings of soul, of being a little child, taking hold of Christ, to be led by him through the wilderness of this world. That text, Matt. xviii. 3, has often been sweet to me, *Except ye be converted, and become as little children, &c.* I love to think of coming to Christ, to receive salvation of him, poor in spirit, and quite empty of self, humbly exalting him alone; cut off entirely from my own root, in order to grow into, and out of Christ: to have God in Christ to be all in all; and to live by faith on the Son of God, a life of humble, unfeigned confidence in him. . . .

Once, as I rode out into the woods for my health, in 1737, having alighted from my horse in a retired place, as my manner commonly has been, to walk for divine contemplation and prayer, I had a view, that for me was extraordinary, of the glory of the Son of God, as Mediator between God and man, and his wonderful, great, full, pure and sweet grace and love, and meek and gentle condescension. This grace that appeared so calm and sweet, appeared also great above the heavens. The person of Christ appeared ineffably excellent, with an excellency great enough to swallow up all thought and conception — which continued, as near as I can judge, about an hour; which kept me the greater part of the time, in a flood of tears, and weeping aloud. I felt an ardency of soul to be, what I know not otherwise how to express, emptied and annihilated; to lie in the dust, and to be full of Christ alone; to love him with a holy and pure love; to trust in him; to live upon him; to serve and follow him; and to be perfectly sanctified and made pure, with a divine and heavenly purity. I have, several other times, had views very much of the same nature, and which have had the same effects.

I have, many times, had a sense of the glory of the Third Person in the Trinity, in his office of Sanctifier; in his holy operations, communicating divine light and life to the soul. God in the communications of his holy spirit, has appeared as an infinite fountain of divine glory and sweetness; being full and sufficient to fill and satisfy the soul; pouring forth itself in sweet communications, like the sun in its glory, sweetly and pleasantly diffusing light and life. And I have sometimes had an affecting sense of the excellency of the word of God as a word of life; as the light of life; a sweet, excellent, life-giving word; accompanied with a thirsting after that word, that it might dwell richly in my heart. . . .

Though it seems to me, that in some respects, I was a far better Christian, for two or three years after my first conversion, than I am now; and lived in a more constant delight and pleasure; yet of late years, I have had a more full and constant sense of the absolute sovereignty of God, and a delight in that sovereignty; and have had more of a sense of the glory of Christ, as a Mediator revealed in the gospel. On one Saturday night, in particular, I had such a discovery of the excellency of the gospel above all other doctrines, that I could not but say to myself, "This is my chosen light, my chosen doctrine," and of Christ, "This is my chosen Prophet." It appeared sweet, beyond all expression, to follow Christ, and to be taught, and enlightened, and instructed by him; to learn of him, and live to him.

John Newton

(1725–1807)

It would be difficult to exaggerate the sheer drama of John Newton's life story. Son of an English sea captain, he himself went to sea at eleven years of age. Under sail on many voyages through the Mediterranean and to the West Indies, Newton became a slave-ship captain during the most dreadful years of that traffic in black humanity. Then he was converted, sought ordination, and served as a minister with distinction. During these years he wrote poems and hymns, and died at age eighty-three, full of grace and highly respected everywhere.

During his long and lonely sea voyages, Newton educated himself by mastering Euclid, learning Latin to read Virgil and Erasmus, studying the Bible (in Hebrew and Greek), and conducting Sunday worship for his crews. A friend of George Whitefield and John Wesley, he applied, after retiring from the sea, for ordination in the Church of England but was refused. In 1764, with the help of Lord Dartmouth, he was appointed to the more evangelical curacy of the church at Olney.

Newton soon became known as a preacher, and his little church added a gallery to accommodate the crowds who came to hear him. The poet William Cowper (1731-1800) moved to Olney and collaborated with Newton in the publishing of the "Olney Hymns." Newton contributed nearly three hundred hymns, including "How Sweet the Name of Jesus Sounds," "Glorious Things of Thee Are Spoken," and "Amazing Grace," which in our own time has become phenomenally popular with people from diverse religious backgrounds.

The anguish of his former slave-trade experience could not be forgotten, and, in later years, Newton became the motivating influence upon William Wilberforce (1759-1833) and the ultimate abolition of the slave trade in Britain. The emancipation of the slaves in America would not come until 1863, but in

1792 the College of New Jersey (now Princeton University) conferred an honorary degree upon John Newton. Two other recipients of honorary degrees at the same time were Alexander Hamilton and Thomas Jefferson.

The first verse of "Amazing Grace" (originally titled "Faith's Review and Expectation") sums up John Newton's religious experience.

> Amazing grace! (how sweet the sound!)
>   That saved a wretch like me;
> I once was lost, but now am found;
>   Was blind, but now I see.

Before he died, he prepared his own epitaph, which read, in part:

> John Newton, once an infidel and libertine, a servant of slaves in Africa, was, by the rich mercy of our Lord and Saviour, Jesus Christ, preserved, restored, pardoned, and appointed to preach the faith he had long laboured to destroy. . . .

~

I went to bed that night in my usual security and indifference, but was awakened from a sound sleep by the force of a violent sea, which broke on board us; so much of it came down below as filled the cabin I lay in with water. This alarm was followed by a cry from the deck, that the ship was going down or sinking. As soon as I could recover myself, I essayed to go upon deck: but was met upon the ladder by the captain, who desired me to bring a knife with me. While I returned for the knife, another person went up in my room, who was instantly washed overboard. We had no leisure to lament him, nor did we expect to survive him long; for we soon found the ship was filling with water very fast. The sea had torn away the upper timbers on one side, and made a mere wreck in a few minutes. I shall not affect to describe this disaster in marine dialect, which would be understood by few; and therefore I can give you but a very inadequate idea of it. Taking in all circumstances, it was astonishing, and almost miraculous, that any of us survived to relate the story. We had immediate recourse to the pumps; but the water in-

---

Excerpts from *The Works of the Rev. John Newton,* ed. Richard Cecil (New York: Robert Carter Co., 1844), 1:95-110.

creased against our efforts. Some of us were set to baling in another part of the vessel; that is, to lade it out with buckets and pails. We had but eleven or twelve people to sustain this service; and, notwithstanding all we could do, she was full, or very near it: and then, with a common cargo, she must have sunk of course; but we had a great quantity of bees' wax and wood on board, which were specifically lighter than the water; and as it pleased God that we received this shock in the very crisis of the gale, towards morning we were enabled to employ some means for our safety, which succeeded beyond hope. In about an hour's time, the day began to break, and the wind abated. We expended most of our clothes and bedding to stop the leaks (though the weather was exceedingly cold, especially to us, who had so lately left a hot climate); over these we nailed pieces of boards, and at last perceived the water abate. At the beginning of this hurry, I was little affected. I pumped hard, and endeavoured to animate myself and companions: I told one of them, that in a few days, this distress would serve us to talk of over a glass of wine; but he being a less hardened sinner than myself, replied, with tears, "No; it is too late now." About nine o'clock, being almost spent with cold and labour, I went to speak with the captain, who was busied elsewhere, and just as I was returning from him, I said almost without any meaning, "If this will not do the Lord have mercy upon us." This (though spoken with little reflection) was the first desire I had breathed for mercy for the space of many years. I was instantly struck with my own words; and, as Jehu said once, "what hast thou to do with peace!" so it directly occurred, "What mercy can there be for me!" I was obliged to return to the pump, and there I continued till noon, almost every passing wave breaking over my head; but we made ourselves fast with ropes, that we might not be washed away. Indeed, I expected that every time the vessel descended in the sea, she would rise no more; and though I dreaded death now, and my heart foreboded the worst, if the scriptures, which I had long since opposed, were indeed true; yet still I was but half convinced, and remained for a space of time in a sullen frame, a mixture of despair and impatience. I thought, if the Christian religion was true, I could not be forgiven; and was, therefore, expecting, and almost, at times, wishing, to know the worst of it. . . .

. . . For about the space of six years, the Lord was pleased to lead me in a secret way. I had learned something of the evil of my heart; I had read the Bible over and over, with several good books, and had a general view of gospel truths. But my conceptions were, in many respects, confused; not having, in all this time, met with one acquaintance who could assist my inquiries. But upon my arrival at St. Christopher's, this voyage, I found a captain of a ship from London, whose conversation was greatly helpful to me. He was, and is a member of Mr. B——r's church, a man of experience in the things of God, and of a lively, communicative turn. We discovered each other by some casual expressions in mixed company, and soon became (so far as business would permit) inseparable. For near a month, we spent every evening together, on board each other's ship alternately, and often prolonged our visits till towards day-break. I was all ears; and what was better, he not only informed my understanding, but his discourse inflamed my heart. He encouraged me to open my mouth in social prayer; he taught me the advantage of Christian converse; he put me upon an attempt to make my profession more public, and to venture to speak for God. From him, or rather from the Lord, by his means, I received an increase of knowledge; my conceptions became clearer and more evangelical, and I was delivered from a fear which had long troubled me, the fear of relapsing into my former apostasy. But now I began to understand the security of the covenant of grace, and to expect to be preserved, not by my own power and holiness, but by the mighty power and promise of God, through faith in an unchangeable Saviour. He likewise gave me a general view of the state of religion, with the errors and controversies of the times (things to which I had been entirely a stranger), and finally directed me where to apply in London for further instruction. With these newly acquired advantages, I left him, and my passage homewards gave me leisure to digest what I had received. I had much comfort and freedom during those seven weeks, and my sun was seldom clouded. I arrived safe in [Liverpool], August, 1754.

My stay at home was intended to be but short, and by the beginning of November, I was again ready for the sea: but the Lord saw fit to overrule my design. During the time I was engaged in the slave trade, I never had the least scruple as to its lawfulness. I was, upon the whole, satisfied with it, as the appointment Providence had marked out for me; yet it was, in many respects, far from eligible. It is, indeed, accounted a genteel employment, and is usually very profitable, though to me it did not prove so, the Lord seeing that a large increase of wealth could not be good for me. However, I considered myself as a sort of gaoler or turnkey; and I was sometimes shocked with an employment that was perpetually conversant with chains, bolts, and shackles. In this view I had often petitioned, in my prayers, that the Lord, in his own time, would be pleased to fix me in a more humane calling, and, if it might be, place me where I might have more frequent converse with his people and ordinances, and be freed from those long separations from home, which very often were hard to bear. My prayers were now answered, though in a way I little expected. I now experienced another sudden, unforeseen change of life. I was within two days of sailing, and, to all appearance, in good health as usual; but in the afternoon, as I was sitting with Mrs. [Newton], by ourselves, drinking tea, and talking over past events, I was in a moment seized with a fit which deprived me of sense and motion, and left me no other sign of life than that of breathing. I suppose it was of the apoplectic kind. It lasted about an hour, and when I recovered, it left a pain and dizziness in my head, which continued with such symptoms as induced the physicians to judge it would not be safe or prudent for me to proceed on the voyage. Accordingly, by the advice of my friend, to whom the ship belonged, I resigned the command the day before she sailed; and thus I was unexpectedly called from that service, and freed from a share of the future consequences of that voyage, which proved extremely calamitous. The person who went in my room, most of the officers, and many of the crew, died, and the vessel was brought home with great difficulty.

As I was now disengaged from business, I left [Liverpool], and spent most of the following year at London, and in Kent. But I entered upon a new trial. You will easily conceive that Mrs. [Newton] was not an unconcerned spectator, when I lay extended, and, as she thought, expiring upon the ground. In effect, the blow that struck me reached her in the same instant: she did not, indeed, immediately feel it, till her apprehensions on my account began to subside; but as I grew better, she became worse: her surprise threw her into a disorder, which no physicians could define, or medicines remove. Without any of the ordinary symptoms of a consumption, she decayed almost visibly, till she became so weak that she could hardly bear any one to walk across the room she was in. I was placed for about eleven months in what Dr. Young calls the

" — dreadful post of observation,
Darker every hour."

It was not till after my settlement in my present station, that the Lord was pleased to restore her by his own hand, when all hopes from ordinary means were at an end. But before this took place, I have some other particulars to mention. . . .

All this while I had two trials, more or less, upon my mind; the first and principal was Mrs. [Newton's] illness; she still grew worse, and I had daily more reason to fear that the hour of separation was at hand. When faith was in exercise, I was in some measure resigned to the Lord's will; but too often my heart rebelled, and I found it hard either to trust or to submit. I had likewise some care about my future settlement; the African trade was overdone that year, and my friends did not care to fit out another ship till mine returned. I was sometime in suspense. . . .

One word concerning my view to the ministry, and I have done. I have told you, that this was my dear mother's hope concerning me; but her death, and the scenes of life in which I afterwards engaged, seemed to cut off the probability. The first desires of this sort of my own mind, arose many years ago, from a reflection on Gal. i. 23, 24. I could not but wish for such a public opportunity to testify the riches of divine grace. I thought I was, above most living, a fit person to proclaim that faithful saying, "That Jesus Christ came into the world to save the chief of sinners," and as my life had been full of remarkable turns, and I seemed selected to show what the Lord could do, I was in some hopes that, perhaps, sooner or later, he might call me into his service.

Elizabeth Bayley Seton

(1774–1821)

The first American-born canonized saint of the Roman Catholic Church, Elizabeth Bayley Seton began to question her Episcopal background during a visit to Leghorn, Italy. Her father was a distinguished physician and professor of medicine at King's College, New York (now Columbia), and her mother's father was rector of St. Andrew's Episcopal Church, Staten Island.

When she was twenty years old, she married William M. Seton, a wealthy merchant who promptly lost his fortune and his health. With their five children, the Setons visited Italy in search of rest and physical restoration. William died, and Elizabeth was befriended by the Filicchi family in Leghorn where she came into direct contact with the Catholic faith.

Returning to New York, Mrs. Seton struggled with her religious commitment, and, mostly for reasons of historical priority, she joined the Catholic Church. It was, she wrote later, "where true faith first began." Deserted and ostracized by friends and family, she retreated to Canada until she was invited to Baltimore to found a new religious community.

It was a time of bitter animosity between Protestants and Catholics. The former were polemical and unfair in their criticism, and the latter became overly sensitive and defensive. For both Christian traditions, it marked an ebb tide for theology, biblical scholarship, and simple human tolerance.

In Baltimore, Mrs. Seton and a few like-minded associates established what came to be known as the Sisters of Charity. Dedicated to social work among the poor, the order also began new programs of education for Catholic children, a local effort credited with establishing the widespread and sometimes controversial Catholic parochial school system.

Against the formidable intolerance of the times, Mother Seton made her way without bluster or attack and in time received the respect not only of

Protestants but also of civic leaders. Many years later, Pope John XXIII became involved in the process that led to her canonization by Pope Paul VI in 1975.

~

The Catholic religion so fully satisfied my heart and soul in Italy, that had not my duty towards my children deterred me, I would have retired into a convent after my husband's death. In losing him, my father, and my sister Rebecca, all seems ended here on earth; for although my children are indeed a treasure, I dare not rest a hope of happiness on such frail young beings whose lives are so uncertain. When I arrived here from Leghorn, the clergy had much to say to me on the score of religion, and spoke of Antichrist, idolatry, and urged any number of objections, all of which, without altering the opinions I had formed, were quite enough to frighten me into irresolution as to what step I should take; and here now I am in God's hands, praying day and night for His heavenly direction, which alone can guide me straight. I instruct my children in the religion of Catholics as well as I can, without, however, taking any decided course, although my greatest comfort is found in imagining myself a member of their church. . . .

In desperation of heart I went last Sunday to St. George's [Episcopal] Church; the wants and necessities of my soul were so pressing, that I looked straight up to God, and I told Him since I can not see the way to please You, whom alone I wish to please, every thing is indifferent to me, and until You do show me the way You mean me to go, I will walk on in the path You suffered me to be placed on at my birth, and even go to the very sacrament where I once used to find you. So away I went, but if I left the house a Protestant, I returned to it a Catholic I think, since I determined to go no more to the Protestants, being much more troubled than ever I thought I could be. But so it was that at the bowing of my head before the bishop to receive his absolution, which is given publicly and universally to all in the church, I had not the least faith in his prayer, and looked for an apostolic loosing from my sins. . . .

Then, trembling, I went to communion, half dead with the inward struggles, when they said: "The body and blood of Christ." . . . I became

From *Memoir, Letters and Journal of Elizabeth Seton, Convert to the Catholic Faith and Sister of Charity,* ed. Robert Seton, Prothonotary Apostolic (New York: P. O'Shea, Publisher, 1869), 1:203-13.

half crazy, and for the first time could not bear the sweet caresses of my darlings or bless their little dinner. O my God! that day. But it finished calmly at last, abandoning all to God with a renewed confidence in the Blessed Virgin, whose mild and peaceful look reproached my bold excesses, and reminded me to fix my heart above with better hopes.

Now, my friends tell me to take care, that I am a mother, and must answer for my children at the judgment-seat, whatever faith I lead them to. That being so, I will go peaceably and firmly to the Catholic Church. For if faith is so important to our salvation, I will seek it where true faith first began, will seek it among those who received it from God Himself. The controversies on it I am quite incapable of deciding, and as the strictest Protestant allows salvation to a good Catholic, to the Catholics will I go, and try to be a good one. May God accept my good intention and pity me. As to supposing the word of our Lord has failed, and that He suffered His first foundation to be built on by Antichrist, I can not stop on that without stopping on every other word of our Lord, and being tempted to be no Christian at all. For if the chief church became Antichrist's, and the second holds her rights from it, then I should be afraid both might be antichristian, and I be lost by following either.

Charles G. Finney

(1792–1875)

American Protestantism has produced many revivalist preachers, but few can compare with Charles Grandison Finney. In a long and productive life, he transformed American evangelicalism and gave it most of its distinctive theological emphases and many of its evangelistic methods. In a democratic age, he made grace available to common people and reinterpreted theology for the understanding of ordinary individuals.

Finney's conversion, according to one biographer, "is one of the classics of American religious folklore." Nominally religious in his youth, he became a lawyer, and his work brought him to the study of the Mosaic law. This exposed him to more of the Bible, and eventually he decided, as he characteristically put it, "that I would settle the question of my soul's salvation at once." For Finney, the burden of salvation lay with the sinful individual, not in God's mysterious election of the saved, and his own powerful conversion experience served as the basis of his theology.

He became a lawyer in the pulpit, for as he told one of his clients immediately after his conversion, "I have a retainer from the Lord Jesus Christ to plead his cause, and I cannot plead yours." He convicted people of their sins, and then offered them the choice: plead innocent, and die in sin; or plead guilty, accept Jesus Christ, and be saved. Although his theology collided with the strict Calvinism of the Presbyterian Church, Finney sought ordination as a Presbyterian minister. His presbytery wanted him to go to Princeton Theological Seminary, but he coolly refused, saying he did not like the way Princeton influenced its graduates. He called the Westminster Confession "this wonderful theological fiction" and its doctrines "cannotism." Nevertheless, his presbytery ordained him, and he soon won fame as a revivalist in New York, leading a series of important evangelistic services throughout the state from 1821 to 1832.

His theology, he said, was based on his own reason and the Bible, and his methods were pragmatic. Revivals were not simply the work of God, he argued, but the right application of the right methods. He later published a "how-to-do-it" manual for preachers, *Lectures on Revivals of Religion* (1835), insisting that revivals were like planting grain: sow the seed and then reap the harvest. Finney also developed what were known as "new measures": the anxious bench (where potential converts were directly addressed by the preacher); protracted meetings that built up the intensity of the appeals to repent; allowing women to pray in public worship in the presence of men; and direct appeals by name to individuals in the congregation. Such practices were controversial, but for Finney they worked. His followers made them a staple of American revivalism.

Finney also believed that it was impossible for a person to be both holy and sinful at the same time, and this belief encouraged a tendency toward perfectionism. He was opposed to slavery but focused most of his attention on converting sinners. His influence was widespread, not only through his preaching but also through his association with Oberlin College, Ohio, where he served on the faculty from 1835 to 1875 and as president from 1851 to 1866.

Finney's conversion changed his life and dramatically influenced American Protestantism. He embodied the spirit of nineteenth-century America in its self-reliance and independence; and, by choosing salvation, Finney also opened the door for others.

On a Sabbath evening in the autumn of 1821, I made up my mind that I would settle the question of my soul's salvation at once, that if it were possible I would make my peace with God. But as I was very busy in the affairs of the office, I knew that without great firmness of purpose, I should never effectually attend to the subject. I therefore, then and there resolved, as far as possible, to avoid all business, and everything that would divert my attention, and to give myself wholly to the work of securing the salvation of my soul. I carried this resolution into execution as sternly and thoroughly as I could. I was, however, obliged to be a good deal in the office. But as the providence of God would have it, I was not much occupied either on Monday or Tuesday; and had opportunity to read my Bible and engage in prayer most of the time.

Excerpted from *Memoirs of Rev. Charles G. Finney* (New York, 1876), 12-23.

But I was very proud without knowing it. I had supposed that I had not much regard for the opinions of others, whether they thought this or that in regard to myself; and I had in fact been quite singular in attending prayer meetings, and in the degree of attention that I had paid to religion, while in Adams. In this respect I had been so singular as to lead the church at times to think that I must be an anxious inquirer. But I found, when I came to face the question, that I was very unwilling to have any one know that I was seeking the salvation of my soul. When I prayed I would only whisper my prayer, after having stopped the key-hole to the door, lest some one should discover that I was engaged in prayer. Before that time I had my Bible lying on the table with the law-books; and it never had occurred to me to be ashamed of being found reading it, any more than I should be ashamed of being found reading any of my other books.

But after I had addressed myself in earnest to the subject of my own salvation, I kept my Bible, as much as I could, out of sight. If I was reading it when anybody came in, I would throw my law-books upon it, to create the impression that I had not had it in my hand. Instead of being outspoken and willing to talk with anybody and everybody on the subject as before, I found myself unwilling to converse with anybody. I did not want to see my minister, because I did not want to let him know how I felt, and I had no confidence that he would understand my case, and give me the direction that I needed. For the same reasons I avoided conversation with the elders of the church, or with any of the Christian people. I was ashamed to let them know how I felt, on the one hand; and on the other, I was afraid they would misdirect me. I felt myself shut up to the Bible.

During Monday and Tuesday my convictions increased; but still it seemed as if my heart grew harder. I could not shed a tear; I could not pray. I had no opportunity to pray above my breath; and frequently I felt, that if I could be alone where I could use my voice and let myself out, I should find relief in prayer. I was shy, and avoided, as much as I could, speaking to anybody on any subject. I endeavored, however, to do this in a way that would excite no suspicion, in any mind, that I was seeking the salvation of my soul.

Tuesday night I had become very nervous; and in the night a strange feeling came over me as if I was about to die. I knew that if I did I should sink down to hell; but I quieted myself as best I could until morning.

At an early hour I started for the office. But just before I arrived at the office, something seemed to confront me with questions like these: indeed, it seemed as if the inquiry was within myself, as if an inward voice said to me, "What are you waiting for? Did you not promise to give your heart to God? And what are you trying to do? Are you endeavoring to work out a righteousness of your own?"

Just at this point the whole question of Gospel salvation opened to my mind in a manner most marvellous to me at the time. I think I then saw, as clearly as I ever have in my life, the reality and fullness of the atonement of Christ. I saw that his work was a finished work; and that instead of having, or needing, any righteousness of my own to recommend me to God, I had to submit myself to the righteousness of God through Christ. Gospel salvation seemed to me to be an offer of something to be accepted; and that it was full and complete; and that all that was necessary on my part, was to get my own consent to give up my sins, and accept Christ. Salvation, it seemed to me, instead of being a thing to be wrought out, by my own works, was a thing to be found entirely in the Lord Jesus Christ, who presented himself before me as my God and my Savior.

Without being distinctly aware of it, I had stopped in the street right where the inward voice seemed to arrest me. How long I remained in that position I cannot say. But after this distinct revelation had stood for some little time before my mind, the question seemed to be put, "Will you accept it now, to-day?" I replied, "Yes; I will accept it to-day, or I will die in the attempt."

North of the village, and over a hill, lay a piece of woods, in which I was in the almost daily habit of walking, more or less, when it was pleasant weather. It was now October, and the time was past for my frequent walks there. Nevertheless, instead of going to the office, I turned and bent my course toward the woods, feeling that I must be alone, and away from all human eyes and ears, so that I could pour out my prayer to God.

But still my pride must show itself. As I went over the hill, it occurred to me that some one might see me and suppose that I was going away to pray. Yet probably there was not a person on earth that would have suspected such a thing, had he seen me going. But so great was my pride, and so much was I possessed with the fear of man, that I recollect that I skulked along under the fence, till I got so far out of sight that no one from the village could see me. I then penetrated into the woods, I should think, a quarter of a mile, went over on the other side of the hill, and found a place where some large trees had fallen across each other, leaving an open place between. There I saw I could make a kind of closet. I crept into this place and knelt down for prayer. As I turned to go up into the woods, I recollect to have said, "I will give my heart to God, or I never will come down from there." I recollect repeating this as I went up — "I will give my heart to God before I ever come down again."

But when I attempted to pray I found that my heart would not pray. I had supposed that if I could only be where I could speak aloud, without being overheard, I could pray freely. But lo! when I came to try, I was dumb; that is, I had nothing to say to God; or at least I could say but a few words, and those without heart. In attempting to pray I would hear a rustling in the leaves, as I thought, and would stop and look up to see if somebody were not coming. This I did several times.

Finally I found myself verging fast to despair. I said to myself, "I cannot pray. My heart is dead to God, and will not pray." I then reproached myself for having promised to give my heart to God before I left the woods. When I came to try, I found I could not give my heart to God. My inward soul hung back, and there was no going out of my heart to God. I began to feel deeply that it was too late; that it must be that I was given up of God and was past hope.

The thought was pressing me of the rashness of my promise, that I would give my heart to God that day or die in the attempt. It seemed to me as if that was binding upon my soul; and yet I was going to break my vow. A great sinking and discouragement came over me, and I felt almost too weak to stand upon my knees.

Just at this moment I again thought I heard some one approach me, and I opened my eyes to see whether it were so. But right there the revelation of my pride of heart, as the great difficulty that stood in the way, was distinctly shown to me. An overwhelming sense of my wickedness in being ashamed to have a human being see me on my knees before God, took such powerful possession of me, that I cried at the top of my voice, and exclaimed that I would not leave that place if all the men on earth and all the devils in hell surrounded me. "What!" I said, "such a degraded sinner as I am, on my knees confessing my sins to the great and holy God; and ashamed to have any human being, and a sinner like myself, find me on my knees endeavoring to make my peace with my offended God!" The sin appeared awful, infinite. It broke me down before the Lord.

Just at that point this passage of Scripture seemed to drop into my mind with a flood of light: "Then shall ye go and pray unto me, and I will hearken unto you. Then shall ye seek me and find me, when ye shall search for me with all your heart." I instantly seized hold of this with my heart. I had intellectually believed the Bible before; but never had the truth been in my mind that faith was a voluntary trust instead of an intellectual state. I was as conscious as I was of my existence, of trusting at that moment in God's veracity. Somehow I knew that that was a passage of Scripture, though I do not think I had ever read it. I knew that it was God's word, and God's voice, as it were, that spoke to me. I cried to Him, "Lord, I take thee at thy word. Now thou knowest that I do search for thee with all my heart, and that I have come here to pray to thee; and thou hast promised to hear me."

That seemed to settle the question that I could then, that day, perform my vow. The Spirit seemed to lay stress upon that idea in the text, "When you search for me with all your heart." The question of when, that is of the present time, seemed to fall heavily into my heart. I told the Lord that I should take him at his word; that he could not lie; and that therefore I was sure that he heard my prayer, and that he would be found of me.

He then gave me many other promises, both from the Old and the New Testament, especially some most precious promises respecting our Lord Jesus Christ. I never can, in words, make any human being understand how precious and true those promises appeared to me. I took them one after the other as infallible truth, the assertions of God who could not lie. They did not seem so much to fall into my intellect as into my heart, to be put within the grasp of the voluntary powers of my mind; and I seized hold of them, appropriated them, and fastened upon them with the grasp of a drowning man.

I continued thus to pray, and to receive and appropriate promises for a long time, I know not how long. I prayed till my mind became so full that, before I was aware of it, I was on my feet and tripping up the ascent toward the road. The question of my being converted had not so much as arisen to my thought; but as I went up, brushing through the leaves and bushes, I recollect saying with great emphasis, "If I am ever converted, I will preach the Gospel."

I soon reached the road that led to the village, and began to reflect upon what had passed; and I found that my mind had become most wonderfully quiet and peaceful. I said to myself. "What is this? I must have grieved the Holy Ghost entirely away. I have lost all my conviction. I have not a particle of concern about my soul; and it must be that the Spirit has left me." "Why!" thought I, "I never was so far from being concerned about my own salvation in my life."

Then I remembered what I had said to God while I was on my knees — that I had said I would take him at his word; and indeed I recollected a good many things that I had said, and concluded that it was no wonder that the Spirit had left me; that for such a sinner as I was to take hold of God's word in that way, was presumption if not blasphemy. I concluded that in my excitement I had grieved the Holy Spirit, and perhaps committed the unpardonable sin.

I walked quietly toward the village; and so perfectly quiet was my mind that it seemed as if all nature listened. It was on the 10th of October, and a very pleasant day. I had gone into the woods immediately after an early breakfast; and when I returned to the village I found it was dinner time. Yet I had been wholly unconscious of the time that had passed; it appeared to me that I had been gone from the village but a short time.

But how was I to account for the quiet of my mind? I tried to recall my convictions, to get back again the load of sin under which I had been laboring. But all sense of sin, all consciousness of present sin or guilt, had departed from me. I said to myself, "What is this, that I cannot arouse any sense of guilt in my soul, as great a sinner as I am?" I tried in vain to make myself anxious about my present state. I was so quiet and peaceful that I tried to feel concerned about that, lest it should be a result of my having grieved the Spirit away. But take any view of it I would, I could not be anxious at all about my soul, and about my spiritual state. The repose of my mind was unspeakably great. I never can describe it in words. The thought of God was sweet to my mind, and the most profound spiritual tranquillity had taken full possession of me. This was a great mystery; but it did not distress or perplex me.

I went to my dinner, and found I had no appetite to eat. I then went to the office, and found that Squire W—— had gone to dinner. I took down my bass-viol, and, as I was accustomed to do, began to play and sing some pieces of sacred music. But as soon as I began to sing those sacred words, I began to weep. It seemed as if my heart was all liquid; and my feelings were in such a state that I could not hear my own voice in singing without causing my sensibility to overflow. I wondered at this, and tried to suppress my tears, but could not. After trying in vain to suppress my tears, I put up my instrument and stopped singing.

After dinner we were engaged in removing our books and furniture to another office. We were very busy in this, and had but little conversation all the afternoon. My mind, however, remained in that profoundly tranquil state. There was a great sweetness and tenderness in my thoughts and feelings. Everything appeared to be going right, and nothing seemed to ruffle or disturb me in the least.

Just before evening the thought took possession of my mind, that as soon as I was left alone in the new office, I would try to pray again — that I was not going to abandon the subject of religion and give it up, at any rate; and therefore, although I no longer had any concern about my soul, still I would continue to pray.

By evening we got the books and furniture adjusted; and I made up, in an open fire-place, a good fire, hoping to spend the evening alone. Just at dark Squire W——, seeing that everything was adjusted, bade me good night and went to his home. I had accompanied him to the door; and as I closed the door and turned around, my heart seemed to be liquid within me. All my feelings seemed to rise and flow out; and the utterance of my heart was, "I want to pour my whole soul out to God." The rising of my soul was so great that I rushed into the room back of the front office, to pray.

There was no fire, and no light, in the room; nevertheless it appeared to me as if it were perfectly light. As I went in and shut the door after me, it seemed as if I met the Lord Jesus Christ face to face. It did not occur to me then, nor did it for some time afterward, that it was wholly a mental state. On the contrary it seemed to me that I saw him as I would see any other man. He said nothing, but looked at me in such a manner as to break me right down at his feet. I have always since regarded this as a most remarkable state of mind; for it seemed to me a reality, that he stood before me, and I fell down at his feet and poured out my soul to him. I wept aloud like a child, and made such confessions as I could with my choked utterance. It seemed to me that I bathed his feet with my tears; and yet I had no distinct impression that I touched him, that I recollect.

I must have continued in this state for a good while; but my mind was too much absorbed with the interview to recollect anything that I said. But I know, as soon as my mind became calm enough to break off from the interview, I returned to the front office, and found that the fire that I had made of large wood was nearly burned out. But as I turned and was about to take a seat by the fire, I received a mighty baptism of the Holy Ghost. Without any expectation of it, without ever having the thought in my mind that there was any such thing for me, without any recollection that I had ever heard the thing mentioned by any person in the world, the Holy Spirit descended upon me in a manner that seemed to go through me, body and soul. I could feel the impression, like a wave of electricity, going through and through me. Indeed it seemed to come in waves and waves of liquid love; for I could not express it in any other way. It seemed like the very breath of God. I can recollect distinctly that it seemed to fan me, like immense wings.

No words can express the wonderful love that was shed abroad in my heart. I wept aloud with joy and love; and I do not know but I should say, I literally bellowed out the unutterable gushings of my heart. These waves came over me, and over me, and over me, one after the other, until I recollect I cried out, "I shall die if these waves continue to pass over me." I said, "Lord, I cannot bear any more"; yet I had no fear of death.

How long I continued in this state, with this baptism continuing to roll over me and go through me, I do not know. But I know it was late in the evening when a member of my choir — for I was the leader of the choir — came into the office to see me. He was a member of the church. He found me in this state of loud weeping, and said to me, "Mr. Finney, what ails you?" I could make him no answer for some time. He then said, "Are you in pain?" I gathered myself up as best I could, and replied, "No, but so happy that I cannot live."

He turned and left the office, and in a few minutes returned with one of the elders of the church, whose shop was nearly across the way from our office. This elder was a very serious man; and in my presence had been very watchful, and I had scarcely ever seen him laugh. When he came in, I was very much in the state in which I was when the young man went out to call him. He asked me how I felt, and I began to tell him. Instead of saying anything, he fell into a most spasmodic laughter. It seemed as if it was impossible for him to keep from laughing from the very bottom of his heart.

There was a young man in the neighborhood who was preparing for college, with whom I had been very intimate. Our minister, as I afterward learned, had repeatedly talked with him on the subject of religion, and warned him against being misled by me. He informed him that I was a very careless young man about religion; and he thought that if he associated much with me his mind would be diverted, and he would not be converted.

After I was converted, and this young man was converted, he told me that he had said to Mr. Gale several times, when he had admonished him about associating so much with me, that my conversations had often affected him more, religiously, than his preaching. I had, indeed, let out my feelings a good deal to this young man.

But just at the time when I was giving an account of my feelings to this elder of the church, and to the other member who was with him, this young man came into the office. I was sitting with my back toward the door, and barely observed that he came in. He listened with astonishment to what I was saying, and the first I knew he partly fell upon the floor, and cried out in the greatest agony of mind, "Do pray for me!" The elder of the church and the other member knelt down and began to pray for him; and when they had prayed, I prayed for him myself. Soon after this they all retired and left me alone.

The question then arose in my mind, "Why did Elder B—— laugh so? Did he not think that I was under a delusion, or crazy?" This suggestion brought a kind of darkness over my mind; and I began to query with myself whether it was proper for me — such a sinner as I had been — to pray for that young man. A cloud seemed to shut in over me; I had no hold upon anything in which I could rest; and after a little while I retired to bed, not distressed in mind, but still at a loss to know what to make of my present state. Notwithstanding the baptism I had received, this temptation so obscured my view that I went to bed without feeling sure that my peace was made with God.

I soon fell asleep, but almost as soon awoke again on account of the great flow of the love of God that was in my heart. I was so filled with love that I could not sleep. Soon I fell asleep again, and awoke in the same manner. When I awoke, this temptation would return upon me, and the love that seemed to be in my heart would abate; but as soon as I was asleep, it was so warm within me that I would immediately awake. Thus I continued till, late at night, I obtained some sound repose.

When I awoke in the morning the sun had risen, and was pouring a clear light into my room. Words cannot express the impression that this sunlight made upon me. Instantly the baptism that I had received the night before, returned upon me in the same manner. I arose upon my knees in the bed and wept aloud with joy, and remained for some time too much overwhelmed with the baptism of the Spirit to do anything but pour out my soul to God. It seemed as if this morning's baptism was accompanied with a gentle reproof, and the Spirit seemed to say to me,

"Will you doubt?" "Will you doubt?" I cried, "No! I will not doubt; I cannot doubt." He then cleared the subject up so much to my mind that it was in fact impossible for me to doubt that the Spirit of God had taken possession of my soul.

In this state I was taught the doctrine of justification by faith, as a present experience. That doctrine had never taken any such possession of my mind, that I had ever viewed it distinctly as a fundamental doctrine of the Gospel. Indeed, I did not know at all what it meant in the proper sense. But I could now see and understand what was meant by the passage, "Being justified by faith, we have peace with God through our Lord Jesus Christ." I could see that the moment I believed, while up in the woods all sense of condemnation had entirely dropped out of my mind; and that from that moment I could not feel a sense of guilt or condemnation by any effort that I could make. My sense of guilt was gone; my sins were gone; and I do not think I felt any more sense of guilt than if I never had sinned.

This was just the revelation that I needed. I felt myself justified by faith; and, so far as I could see, I was in a state in which I did not sin. Instead of feeling that I was sinning all the time, my heart was so full of love that it overflowed. My cup ran over with blessing and with love; and I could not feel that I was sinning against God. Nor could I recover the least sense of guilt for my past sins. Of this experience I said nothing that I recollect, at the time, to anybody; that is, of this experience of justification.

Sojourner Truth

(1797?–1883)

"Isabella" was born a slave in New York, the property of a wealthy Dutch land-owner, and for the rest of her life she spoke with a heavy Dutch accent. She served several masters and gave birth to five children; in 1827 she was emancipated by Isaac Van Wagener, one year before New York state outlawed slavery. She moved to New York City in 1829 where she became involved with a religious visionary, Elijah Pierson, but the Pierson sect dissolved in 1835 in a scandal over its sexual mores.

After her initial conversion, she had religious visions and mystical experiences, and in 1843, following one divine encounter, she changed her name to Sojourner Truth. Taking to the pulpit and the lecture platform, she traveled throughout New England, describing her religious experience and attracting huge crowds. After 1843, however, she was not content to confine herself to religious subjects, and she became a powerful voice opposing slavery. Like other abolitionists, she also moved to the point of likening black slavery to discrimination against women, and she spoke out forcefully for women's suffrage and women's rights.

During the Civil War she helped outfit volunteer black regiments, successfully campaigned to desegregate streetcars in Washington, D.C., and was received at the White House by Abraham Lincoln. After the war, she worked for the National Freedmen's Relief Association in Virginia, assisting in resettlement, health, and education programs.

In her faith and in her life, she held forth the promise of the freedom proclaimed by Paul in Galatians 3:28: "There is no longer Jew or Greek, there is no longer slave or free, there is no longer male and female; for all of you are one in Christ Jesus." She asked Americans to make that freedom a reality for all.

During her lifetime she was known as "the Libyan Sibyl," and fellow abolitionist leader Parker Pillsbury said of her, "The wondrous experiences of that most remarkable woman would make a library, if not indeed a literature, could they all be gathered and spread before the world."

Sojourner Truth, like many former slaves, dictated her autobiography to a white person, a friend named Olive Gilbert. "Isabella" is referred to, in the account, in the third person. Such slave narratives were extremely important in shaping antislavery sentiment in the North, and in 1850 Sojourner Truth distributed her own account at rallies and meetings.

~

When Isabella had been at Mr. Van Wagener's a few months, she saw in prospect one of the festivals approaching. She knows it by none but the Dutch name, Pingster, as she calls it — but I think it must have been Whitsuntide, in English. She says she "looked back into Egypt," and everything looked "so pleasant there," as she saw retrospectively all her former companions enjoying their freedom for at least a little space, as well as their wonted convivialities, and in her heart she longed to be with them. With this picture before her mind's eye, she contrasted the quiet, peaceful life she was living with the excellent people of Wahkendall, and it seemed so dull and void of incident, that the very contrast served but to heighten her desire to return, that, at least, she might enjoy with them, once more, the coming festivities. These feelings had occupied a secret corner of her breast for some time, when, one morning, she told Mrs. Van Wagener that her old master Dumont would come that day, and that she should go home with him on his return. They expressed some surprise, and asked her where she obtained her information. She replied, that no one had told her, but she felt that he would come.

It seemed to have been one of those "events that cast their shadows before"; for, before night, Mr. Dumont made his appearance. She informed him of her intention to accompany him home. He answered, with a smile, "I shall not take you back again; you ran away from me." Thinking his manner contradicted his words, she did not feel repulsed, but made herself and child ready; and when her former master had

---

Excerpt from the last revision of the autobiography, *Narrative of Sojourner Truth: A Bondswoman of Olden Time . . . Drawn from Her "Book of Life"* (Battle Creek, MI, 1878), 64-71.

seated himself in the open dearborn, she walked towards it, intending to place herself and child in the rear, and go with him. But, ere she reached the vehicle, she says that God revealed himself to her, with all the suddenness of a flash of lightning, showing her, "in the twinkling of an eye, that he was *all over*" — that he pervaded the universe — "and that there was no place where God was not." She became instantly conscious of her great sin in forgetting her almighty Friend and "ever-present help in time of trouble." All her unfulfilled promises arose before her, like a vexed sea whose waves run mountains high; and her soul, which seemed but one mass of lies, shrunk back aghast from the "awful look" of Him whom she had formerly talked to, as if He had been a being like herself; and she would now fain have hid herself in the bowels of the earth, to have escaped His dread presence. But she plainly saw there was no place, not even in hell, where He was not: and where could she flee? Another such "a look," as she expressed it, and she felt that she must be extinguished forever, even as one, with the breath of His mouth, "blows out a lamp," so that no spark remains.

A dire dread of annihilation now seized her, and she waited to see if, by "another look," she was to be stricken from existence, — swallowed up, even as the fire licketh up the oil with which it comes in contact.

When at last the second look came not, and her attention was once more called to outward things, she observed her master had left, and exclaiming aloud, "Oh, God, I did not know you were so big," walked into the house, and made an effort to resume her work. But the workings of the inward man were too absorbing to admit of much attention to her avocations. She desired to talk to God, but her vileness utterly forbade it, and she was not able to prefer a petition. "What!" said she, "shall I lie again to God? I have told him nothing but lies; and shall I speak again, and tell another lie to God?" She could not; and now she began to wish for some one to speak to God for her. Then a space seemed opening between her and God, and she felt that if some one, who was worthy in the sight of heaven, would but plead *for* her in their own name, and not let God know it came from *her*, who was so unworthy, God might grant it. At length a friend appeared to stand between herself and an insulted Deity; and she felt as sensibly refreshed as when, on a hot day, an umbrella had been interposed between her scorching head and a burning sun. But who was this friend? became the next inquiry. Was it Deencia, who had so often befriended her? She looked at her with her new power of sight — and, lo! she, too, seemed all "bruises and putrifying sores," like herself. No, it was some one very different from Deencia.

"Who *are* you?" she exclaimed, as the vision brightened into a form distinct, beaming with the beauty of holiness, and radiant with love. She then said, audibly addressing the mysterious visitant — "I *know* you, and I *don't* know you." Meaning, "You seem perfectly familiar; I feel that you not only love me, but that you always *have* loved me — yet I know you not — I cannot call you by name." When she said, "I know you," the subject of the vision remained distinct and quiet. When she said, "I don't know you," it moved restlessly about, like agitated waters. So while she repeated, without intermission, "I know you, I know you," that the vision might remain — "Who are you?" was the cry of her heart, and her whole soul was in one deep prayer that this heavenly personage might be revealed to her, and remain with her. At length, after bending both soul and body with the intensity of this desire, till breath and strength seemed failing, and she could maintain her position no longer, an answer came to her, saying distinctly, "It is Jesus." "Yes," she responded, "it is *Jesus.*"

Previous to these exercises of mind, she heard Jesus mentioned in reading or speaking, but had received from what she heard no impression that he was any other than an eminent man, like a Washington or a Lafayette. Now he appeared to her delighted mental vision as so mild, so good, and so every way lovely, and he loved her so much! And, how strange that he had always loved her, and she had never known it! And how great blessing he conferred, in that he should stand between her and God! And God was no longer a terror and a dread to her.

She stopped not to argue the point, even in her own mind, whether he had reconciled her to God, or God to herself (though she thinks the former now), being but too happy that God was no longer to her as a consuming fire, and Jesus was "altogether lovely." Her heart was now full of joy and gladness, as it had been of terror, and at one time of despair. In the light of her great happiness, the world was clad in new beauty, the very air sparkled as with diamonds, and was redolent of heaven. She contemplated the unapproachable barriers that existed between herself and the great of this world, as the world calls greatness, and made surprising comparisons between them, and the union existing between herself and Jesus, — Jesus, the transcendently lovely as well as great and powerful; for so he appeared to her, though he seemed but human; and she watched for his bodily appearance, feeling that she should know him, if she saw him; and when he came, she should go and dwell with him, as with a dear friend.

It was not given her to see that he loved any other; and she thought if others came to know and love him, as she did, she should be thrust aside and forgotten, being herself but a poor ignorant slave, with little to recommend her to his notice. And when she heard him spoken of, she said mentally — "What! others know Jesus! I thought no one knew Jesus but me!" and she felt a sort of jealousy, lest she should be robbed of her newly found treasure.

She conceived, one day, as she listened to reading, that she heard an intimation that Jesus was married, and hastily inquired if Jesus had a wife. "What!" said the reader, "*God* have a wife?" "Is Jesus *God?*" inquired Isabella. "Yes, to be sure he is," was the answer returned. From this time, her conceptions of Jesus became more elevated and spiritual; and she sometimes spoke of him as God, in accordance with the teaching she had received.

But when she was simply told, that the Christian world was much divided on the subject of Christ's nature — some believing him to be co-equal with the Father — to be God in and of himself, "very God, of very God"; — some, that he is the "well-beloved," "only begotten Son of God"; — and others, that he is, or was, rather, but a mere man — she said, "Of that I only know as I saw. I did not see him to be God; else, how could he stand between me and God? I saw him as a friend, standing between me and God, through whom, love flowed as from a fountain." Now, so far from expressing her views of Christ's character and office in accordance with any system of theology extant, she says she believes Jesus is the same spirit that was in our first parents, Adam and Eve, in the beginning, when they came from the hand of their Creator. When they sinned through disobedience, this pure spirit forsook them, and fled to heaven; that there it remained, until it returned again in the person of Jesus; and that, previous to a personal union with him, man is but a brute, possessing only the spirit of an animal.

She avers that, in her darkest hours, she had no fear of any worse hell than the one she then carried in her bosom; though it had ever been pictured to her in its deepest colors, and threatened her as a reward for all her misdemeanors. Her vileness and God's holiness and all-pervading presence, which filled immensity, and threatened her with instant annihilation, composed the burden of her vision of terror. Her faith in prayer is equal to her faith in the love of Jesus. Her language is,

"Let others say what they will of the efficacy of prayer, *I* believe in it, and *I* shall pray. Thank God! Yes, *I shall always pray,*" she exclaims, putting her hands together with the greatest enthusiasm.

For some time subsequent to the happy change we have spoken of, Isabella's prayers partook largely of their former character; and while, in deep affliction, she labored for the recovery of her son, she prayed with constancy and fervor; and the following may be taken as a specimen: — "Oh, God, you know how much I am distressed, for I have told you again and again. Now, God, help me get my son. If you were in trouble, as I am, and I could help you, as you can me, think I wouldn't do it? Yes, God, you *know* I would do it." "Oh, God, you know I have no money, but you can make the people do for me, and you must make the people do for me. I will never give you peace till you do, God." "Oh, God, make the people hear me — don't let them turn me off, without hearing and helping me." And she has not a particle of doubt, that God heard her, and especially disposed the hearts of thoughtless clerks, eminent lawyers, and grave judges and others — between whom and herself there seemed to her almost an infinite remove — to listen to her suit with patient and respectful attention, backing it up with all needed aid. The sense of her nothingness, in the eyes of those with whom she contended for her rights, sometimes fell on her like a heavy weight, which nothing but her unwavering confidence in an arm which she believed to be stronger than all others combined could have raised from her sinking spirit. "Oh! how little I did feel," she repeated, with a powerful emphasis. "Neither would you wonder, if you could have seen me, in my ignorance and destitution, trotting about the streets, meanly clad, bare-headed, and bare-footed! Oh, God only could have made such people hear me; and he did it in answer to my prayers." And this perfect trust, based on the rock of Deity, was a soul-protecting fortress, which, raising her above the battlements of fear, and shielding her from the machinations of the enemy, impelled her onward in the struggle, till the foe was vanquished, and the victory gained.

Phoebe Palmer

(1807–1874)

Phoebe Palmer was one of the most influential Protestant figures in nineteenth-century America. She played an enormously powerful role in American Methodism and in the Holiness movement in the United States and the Higher Life movement in the United Kingdom. In the twentieth century, she was ignored and forgotten until her significant theological and ecclesiastical contributions were recovered in the late twentieth century by women historians and other scholars.

Like so many evangelical Christians, Phoebe Palmer wrestled with a profound spiritual problem. She knew she was a Christian; she had a deep relationship with Christ. And yet, she agonized over the certainty of her salvation, the purity of her soul. For Palmer, this spiritual struggle was made even more acute by death and tragedy. She had married a New York physician, Walter C. Palmer, in 1827. Their first two children — both boys — died in infancy. Their third child — a girl — died when her crib caught on fire in 1836.

Almost exactly a year after her daughter's death, Phoebe Palmer had an experience of God that had been enigmatically described by Methodism's founder, John Wesley, as sanctification or Christian perfection. Phoebe Palmer and her husband called it "entire sanctification," and it electrified Methodism and helped lay the foundation for the Holiness movement and, later, Pentecostalism.

Phoebe Palmer began to enunciate her understanding of the Christian life, secured in God's gift of holiness and protected from sin and doubt, in a series of Tuesday meetings held in her home, which the Palmers shared with Phoebe Palmer's sister and her husband. The meetings were initiated by Phoebe Palmer's sister, but Palmer eventually took them over. The Tuesday Meeting for the Promotion of Holiness was initially designed for women only, but men were eventually allowed to attend. Methodist bishops came and listened and helped spread Palmer's ideas throughout the Methodist Church.

Her achievements were staggering, especially by comparison to her more well-known contemporaries. She wrote constantly, and *The Way of Holiness* (1843) went through many printings during her lifetime and beyond. According to theologian Thomas Oden, she should be considered the most significant woman theologian in Protestantism until the twentieth century. Her thinking was very influential in a number of denominations and movements in addition to Methodism, including the Salvation Army, the Wesleyan Church, the Church of the Nazarene, the Assemblies of God, and others. But her most enduring influence was felt in the holiness-Pentecostal movement that has transformed global Christianity in the twentieth century.

She and her sister helped found a journal, *Guide to Christian Perfection,* later *Guide to Holiness,* and Phoebe Palmer and her husband eventually took it over. It had one of the largest circulations (37,000) of any religious journal of its time. She influenced many significant leaders of her day — book publishers, journalists, editors, Methodist bishops, theologians, college presidents, etc.

She founded America's first inner-city mission — New York's Five Points Mission on the Bowery — and advocated for food relief, rent-free housing, the care of orphans and the poor, rehabilitation for alcoholics, and ministry to immigrants. She was an ardent advocate for lay ministry and a role model for women in ministry. She and her husband considered becoming missionaries; instead, they chose to be advocates for global missionary activity, and she is considered one of the founders of the Methodist missionary enterprise.

God entered Phoebe Palmer's life in the midst of grief and uncertainty and brought her an awareness that she had been blessed and sanctified for service. The rest of her life bore witness to the power of that experience of God's grace.

～

[My dear Mrs. W——,]

July 26. On the morning of this day, while with most grateful emotions remembering the way by which my heavenly Father had led me, my thoughts rested more especially upon the beloved one whom God

---

Excerpted from Phoebe Palmer, *Faith and Its Effects, Or, Fragments from My Portfolio* (1848), 68-74, reprinted with permission from the facsimile edition in *The Devotional Writings of Phoebe Palmer* (New York and London: Garland Publishing, 1985).

had given to be the partner of my life. How truly a gift from God, and how essentially connected with my spiritual, as also my temporal happiness, is this one dear object! I exclaimed.

Scarcely had these suggestions passed, when with keenness these inquiries were suggested: "Have you not professedly given up all for Christ? If he who now so truly absorbs your affections were required, would you not shrink from the demand?" I need not say that this one dear object, though often in name surrendered, was not in reality given up. My precious little ones, whom God had taken to himself, were then brought to my recollection, as if to admonish me relative to making the sacrifice. I thought how fondly I had idolized them. He who had said, "I the Lord your God am a jealous God," saw the idolatry of my heart, and took them to himself. The remembrance of how decidedly I had, by these repeated bereavements, been assured that He whose right it is to reign, would be the sole sovereign of my heart, assisted me in the resolve, that neither should this, the yet dearer object, be withheld.

The remainder of the day, until toward evening, was unexpectedly spent from home. The evening I had resolved to spend in supplication. So intense was my desire for the seal of the Spirit, that I made up my mind I would not cease to plead until it were given. Thoughts were presented as to risk of health, &c.; but my spirit surmounted every discouraging insinuation. Thus fixed in purpose, I, in the firmness of faith, entered as a suppliant into the presence of the Lord. As if preparatory to a long exercise, I thought, Let me begin just right; and though I have heretofore entered into covenant with God, let me now particularize, and enter into an *everlasting* covenant, which shall in all things be well ordered and sure. I imagined some extraordinary exercise, such as an unusual struggle, or a desperate venture of faith, &c., preparatory to the realization of my desire, saying in my heart, though hardly aware of it, that some great thing must surely be wrought. But how God works in order to hide pride from man, I will endeavor to show you in my next.

Yours in the bonds of love. . . .

My Dear Mrs. W——. I left you in my last endeavoring to lay hold on the terms of the covenant, — fixed in purpose, — surrendering myself in the bonds of an everlasting obligation to God.

I began to particularize. The thoughts and exercises of the morning occurred again with yet greater power. Can God be about to take from me this one dear object, for which life is principally desirable? thought

I. Looking into the future, I said, "What a blank!" Never before had I realized, that the very fibres of my existence were so closely interwoven with his. My impression was, that the Lord was about to take my precious husband from me. The inquiry with me was, whether it were possible that my heavenly Father could require me to make the surrender, when he had authorized my love, by making it my duty to be of one heart and soul with him. But grace interposed; and from more mature consideration, I was led to regard it as extraordinary condescension in God thus to apprise me of his designs, by way of preparing my heart for the surrender.

With Abraham I said, "I have lifted my hand to the Lord." In word, I had again and again made the sacrifice before, and said, "My husband and child I surrender to thee." I had not been insincere, but I now saw that I had not in fact done that which, in word, had often been named. Far, indeed, had I been from realizing the depth of obligation which, in word, I had taken upon myself.

Truth in the inward part I now in verity apprehended as God's requirement. Grace triumphed. In full view of the nature of the sacrifice, I said,

"Take life or friends away."

I could just as readily have said, "Take *life*," as I could have said, "Take friends"; for that which was just as dear, if not dearer, than life, had been required. And when I said, "Take him who is the supreme object of my earthly affections," I, from that moment, felt that I was fully set apart for God, and began to say, "Every tie that has bound me to earth is severed." I could now as easily have doubted of my existence as to have doubted that God was the supreme object of my affections. The language of my heart, and, as far as memory serves, the expressions of my lips, were, I live but to glorify thee. Let my spirit from henceforth ceaselessly return to the God that gave it. Let this body be actuated by the Spirit, as an instrument in thy hand for the performance of thy pleasure in all things. I am thine — wholly thine. Thou dost now reign in my heart unrivaled. Glory! Glory be to the Father, Son, and Holy Ghost, for ever!

While thus glorying in being enabled to feel and know that I was now altogether the Lord's, the question, accompanied with light, power, and unquestionable assurance, came to my mind, "What is this but the state of holiness which you have so long been seeking?" It was enough! I now felt that the seal of consecration had in verity been set. God, by the testimony of his Spirit, had proclaimed me wholly his! I said, and also felt, in such a peculiar sense as my spirit still most delightfully appreciates, "Henceforth I am not of earth; the prince of this world, though he may come, yet hath nothing in me. The Lord, my Redeemer, hath raised up a standard against him; *I am set apart for ever for thy service!"*

While thus exulting, the voice of the Spirit again appealingly applied to my understanding, "Is not this sanctification?" I could no longer hesitate; reason as well as grace forbade; and I rejoiced in the assurance that I was wholly sanctified — throughout *body, soul,* and *spirit.*

O with what triumph did my soul expatiate on the infinitude of the atonement! I saw its unbounded efficacy, as sufficient to cleanse a world of sinners, and present them faultless before the throne. I felt that I was enabled to plunge, and lose myself, in this ocean of purity — yes,

> "Plunged in the Godhead's deepest sea,
> And lost in love's immensity."

It was enough! My spirit returned consciously to its Source, and rested in the embrace of God. From my inmost soul I said, "Lord, it is enough!" I pause at the exclamation; for I hesitate what language to use, or what expression to make of my views of the condescension of my covenant-keeping God, relative to this eventful period of my Christian history. Ah! I have no doubt but, even after innumerable ages of eternity have past, the amazing condescension thus manifested for the establishment of one so fearful and unbelieving, will be by me exultingly rehearsed to a listening multitude of rejoicing angels, and cause a renewed burst of holy triumph from the adoring throng.

Every shade of objection, or thought of scruple, was thus by Omnipotence himself rebuked, or rather utterly silenced. What I mean by scruples should be mentioned. It is this: — Though I have ever been a firm believer in the doctrine of Christian holiness, embracing the entire sanctification of body, soul, and spirit, as taught from the Scriptures by the apostolic Wesleys, and their cotemporaries; yet the terms made use of, in speaking of this attainment, were objectionable to my mind, in a manner which I cannot now take time to explain. Though from early life

I had felt that I needed just the blessing comprehended, yet the terms made use of I seldom used. Now there seemed such a glorious propriety in the words "HOLINESS," "SANCTIFICATION," that I thought nothing less than infinite Wisdom could have devised words so infinitely proper.

What more reasonable, thought I, now that I have been enabled through grace to resolve on being wholly the Lord's, than that he should set the seal which proclaims me his; and still further, now that I have set myself apart exclusively for his service, that he should take cognizance of the act, and by the seal of the Spirit ratify the engagement? So clear was the work, and so apart from anything like extravagance in feeling or otherwise, that though I had fixed my calculations on the performance of some great thing, such as an amazing struggle — a desperate venture of faith — I was now ready to exclaim, "How simple and rational! and how precisely as might have been expected as the result of such exercises." It is all here; I, through the Spirit's influence, have given all for Christ, and now he hath revealed himself, and given himself to me, and become my all in ALL.

Your sister in Christ.

David Livingstone

(1813–1873)

Perhaps no figure has had a greater influence on Western attitudes toward Africa than David Livingstone, the missionary explorer. Through a combination of incredible physical endurance and evangelical zeal, he "opened" the continent of Africa, literally and figuratively, traveling widely through southern and central Africa, coast to coast. An imperialist as well as a forerunner of African nationalism and self-determination, Livingstone believed that the combination of Christianity and commerce would be the salvation of Africa, and yet he also urged that native-born Africans should carry out the task of evangelization. He was passionately committed to the abolition of African slavery, and his writings and speeches were influential in awakening Britain and the West to the horrors of the slave trade. But he was also an example of Victorian paternalism in his relationships with black people.

Born near Glasgow into a poor Scottish family, Livingstone was raised in the ethos of Scots Calvinism with its emphases on piety, self-discipline, hard work, education, and duty. At the age of ten he entered the cotton mill to help his family — and worked with a book before him, reading a sentence or two as the machine spun. In 1834 he responded to an appeal for medical missionaries in China, working part-time in the mill while he studied Greek, theology, and medicine for two years at the University of Glasgow. In 1838, he was accepted by the London Missionary Society, but his determination to go to China was frustrated by the Opium War. Then in London he met the South African missionary Robert Moffat, who convinced him to come to Africa.

In 1840, he was ordained as a missionary by the London Missionary Society, and took the first of his African journeys. He arrived in South Africa in 1841, and within a year had pushed farther north than any other white person. He married Moffat's daughter in 1845, and she and their children accompanied him on his journeys; however, one child died in infancy and his wife became gravely ill. For the sake of their health, security, and education, he sent them back to Britain in 1852 and confessed later that one of his chief regrets was that he had not taken an hour a day to play with his children.

Africa and destiny beckoned, and in 1853 he declared, "I shall open up a path into the interior, or perish." From 1853 to 1856, with a small band of Africans, he pushed deeper into the continent of Africa, finally discovering the mammoth waterfalls on the Zambezi River and naming them, with a burst of British patriotism, Victoria Falls. In 1857 he published his *Missionary Travels and Researches in South Africa,* which became a best seller and captured the imagination of the English-speaking world. Quietly severing his relationship with the London Missionary Society, Livingstone left on his Zambezi expedition (1858-1864) as a British consul, and in 1866 he departed again on his famous search for the origin of the Nile. It was on this journey that the explorer H. M. Stanley was commissioned by the *New York Herald* to discover whether Livingstone was alive or dead. Upon reaching him, Stanley greeted him with typical British propriety, "Dr. Livingstone, I presume." Stanley tried to persuade Livingstone to return with him, but he refused. On May 1, 1873, Livingstone was found dead, kneeling at his bedside, apparently in prayer.

A complex man of strong ego but also selfless determination to explore Africa, Livingstone possessed a fervent but understated faith. The following account of his conversion is tantalizingly brief and restrained, but one can glimpse his piety and his passion for discovery in a portion of his diary, written on his birthday and shortly before his death:

> 19 March 1872 — Birthday. My Jesus, my King, my life, my All; I again dedicate my whole self to Thee. Accept me and grant, O gracious Father, that ere this year is gone I may finish my task. In Jesus' name I ask it. Amen, so let it be. David Livingstone.

When he died, his African companions buried his heart and entrails in Africa and shipped his body back to England, where he was buried in Westminster Abbey.

~

Great pains had been taken by my parents to instill the doctrines of Christianity into my mind, and I had no difficulty in understanding the theory of our free salvation by the atonement of our Savior, but it was only about this time that I really began to feel the necessity and value of a personal application of the provisions of that atonement to my own case. The change was like what may be supposed would take place were it possible to cure a case of "color blindness." The perfect freeness with which the pardon of all our guilt is offered in God's book drew forth feelings of affectionate love to Him who bought us with His blood, and a sense of deep obligation to Him for His mercy has influenced, in some small measure, my conduct ever since. But I shall not again refer to the inner spiritual life which I believe then began, nor do I intend to specify with any prominence the evangelistic labors to which the love of Christ has since impelled me. This book will speak, not so much of what has been done, as of what still remains to be performed, before the Gospel can be said to be preached to all nations.

In the glow of love which Christianity inspires, I soon resolved to devote my life to the alleviation of human misery. Turning this idea over in my mind, I felt that to be a pioneer of Christianity in China might lead to the material benefit of some portions of that immense empire; and therefore set myself to obtain a medical education, in order to be qualified for that enterprise.

Excerpted from *Missionary Travels and Researches in South Africa* (New York, 1858), 4-5.

Fanny Crosby

(1820–1915)

Fanny Crosby was an inspiration to those who heard her and read her, but most of all to those who sang her hymns. There were more than 8,000 of them, making her one of the most prolific hymn writers in history. In fact, she ended up writing under dozens of pseudonyms because hymn publishers did not like to include too many hymns by the same author.

She was born into a poor family, and tragedy struck immediately. When she was six weeks old, she developed a cold, and her parents called upon a quack because the family doctor was unavailable. The erstwhile medical practitioner put mustard plasters on her eyes, and she became blind.

Remarkably, Fanny Crosby bore no ill will toward the medical quack. She wrote later in life, "I have not for a moment, in more than eighty-five years, felt a spark of resentment against him, for I have always believed from my youth up that the good Lord, in His infinite mercy, by this means consecrated me to the work that I am still permitted to do." In fact, she found joy in her blindness, for at age eight or nine, she composed the following lines:

> Oh, what a happy soul I am!
>   Although I cannot see,
> I am resolved that in this world
>   Contented I will be.

> How many blessings I enjoy
>   That other people don't!
> To weep and sigh because I'm blind
>   I cannot and I won't.

When she was only one year old, her father died, and so she was raised by her mother and grandmother in an atmosphere of evangelical Protestant piety, centered in the Bible. She developed a prodigious ability to remember large amounts of information — for example, committing to memory the first three books of the Bible. Her greatest fear was that she would receive no education, but when she was fourteen she was enrolled at the New York Institute for the Blind. There she remained for eight years as a student, learning how to play the piano and guitar and how to sing, as well as traditional subjects. After she finished her work, she remained for another fifteen years as a teacher. She also married another blind former student, Alexander Van Alstyne, who insisted that she retain her maiden name. She said of their marriage, "Our tastes are congenial and he composed the music of several of my hymns."

Fanny Crosby, because of the popularity of her hymns and her heroic achievement despite her blindness, was made for public lecture tours, which she conducted frequently, especially in the last decades of her life. She became a notable public figure, both because of her faith and because of her ability to win support for the cause of the blind. She became a speaker before Congress in behalf of people with vision impairments and won the friendship of several presidents of the United States.

Despite the piety of her home and upbringing, Fanny Crosby made "a complete surrender" to God during a revival at her Methodist church in 1850. The experience not only brought her into a more intimate relationship with God but also empowered her to speak and write about her faith. Though raised as a Christian as a child, she was converted as an adult. Because of her experience of God's grace, the blind Fanny Crosby could exclaim with conviction in her most famous hymn:

> Blessed assurance, Jesus is mine!
> Oh, what a foretaste of glory divine!
> Heir of salvation, purchase of God,
> Born of His Spirit, washed in His blood.
>
> This is my story, this is my song,
> Praising my Savior all the day long;
> This is my story, this is my song,
> Praising my Savior all the day long.

Now turn to the year 1839, and the class-meetings at the Eighteenth Street Methodist Church. Some of us used to go down there regularly, and on Thursday evening of each week a leader came from that church to conduct a class in the Institution. In those days I was timid, and never spoke in public when I could possibly avoid it; and I must confess that I had grown somewhat indifferent to the means of grace — so much so, in fact, that I attended the meetings and played for them on the condition that they should not call on me to speak.

But one evening the leader brought a young man with him who was destined to have an important influence on my life. He was Mr. Theodore Camp, a teacher in the city schools; and a man noted for his generous public spirit. From the beginning of our acquaintance I found him a true friend; and I used to consult him concerning all matters in which I was undetermined how to act. In 1845 he was placed in charge of our industrial department; and then we used to attend the class-meetings together, but he never urged me in religious matters. And yet I owe my conversion to that same friend, in so far as I owe it to any mortal. By a strange dream I was aroused from a comparative state of indifference — not that the dream had any particular effect, in itself, except as the means of setting me to thinking. It seemed that the sky had been cloudy for a number of days; and finally some one came to me and said that Mr. Camp desired to see me at once. Then I thought I entered the room and found him very ill.

"Fanny, can you give up our friendship?" he asked.

"No, I cannot," I replied; "you have been my adviser and friend, and what could I do without your aid?"

"But," said he, "why would you chain a spirit to earth when it longs to fly away and be at rest?"

"Well," I rejoined, "I cannot give you up of myself, but I will seek Divine assistance."

"But will you meet me in Heaven?"

"Yes, I will, God helping me," I replied; and I thought his last words were: "Remember, you promise a dying man!" Then the clouds seemed to roll from my spirit, and I awoke from the dream with a start. I could not forget those words, "Will you meet me in Heaven?" and although my friend was perfectly well I began to consider whether I

Excerpted from Fanny Crosby, *Memories of Eighty Years* (London: Hodder and Stoughton/Morgan and Scott, 1907), 30-33.

could really meet him or any other acquaintance in the Better Land, if called to do so.

The weeks sped on until the autumn of 1850, when Revival meetings were being held in the Thirtieth Street Methodist Church. Some of us went down every evening; on two occasions I sought peace, but did not find the joy I craved, until one evening, November 20, 1850, it seemed to me that the light must indeed come then or never; and so I arose and went forward alone. After prayer, the congregation began to sing the grand old consecration hymn: —

Alas, and did my Saviour bleed,
And did my Sovereign die?

And when they reached the third line of the fourth stanza,

Here, Lord, I give myself away,

my very soul was flooded with a celestial light. I sprang to my feet, shouting "Hallelujah!" and then for the first time I realized that I had been trying to hold the world in one hand and the Lord in the other.

But my growth in grace was very slow from the beginning. The next Thursday evening I gave a public testimony at our class-meeting; when I finished, the tempter said to me: "Well, Fanny, you made a good speech, didn't you?" and I realized at once that this was the old pride returning again to reign in my heart. For a few days I was greatly depressed until a kind friend suggested that I must "go back and do the first works quickly," which meant that I had not made a complete surrender of my will; and then I promised to do my duty whenever the dear Lord should make it plain to me.

Not many weeks later, Mr. Stephen Merritt asked me to close one of our class-meetings with a brief prayer. My first thought was, "I cannot"; then the voice of conscience said: "But your promise!" and from that hour, I believe I have never refused to pray or speak in a public service, with the result that I have been richly blessed.

Leo Tolstoy

(1828–1910)

Leo Tolstoy is one of the heroic figures in world literature, renowned primarily for his two powerful novels, *War and Peace* and *Anna Karenina*. He is also regarded as one of the most important religious and philosophical thinkers of the nineteenth century, and his understanding of history, human nature, and Christian discipleship had considerable influence during his lifetime and continues to affect people in the twenty-first century.

He was born into a family of Russian aristocracy. His mother died before he was two, and he spent his life trying to remember her and to bring back the love that he idealized in her. After a dissolute life at the university and in the army, he married in 1862 and settled down to manage his estate and raise a family that eventually numbered thirteen children. His writings won acclaim from critics, and he enjoyed affluence and comfort; yet he still struggled for meaning and purpose in life. Despairing of the counsel of philosophers, theologians, and scientists, he considered suicide, but in 1879 he was converted.

The results of his conversion were not adherence to traditional Christianity, for Tolstoy sought a return to what he believed was the primitive Christianity of the Gospels. "For me," he wrote, "religion comes from life, not life from religion." He sought "the religion of Christ, but divested of faith and mysteries, a practical religion, not promising eternal bliss but providing bliss here on earth." Denying the divinity of Christ, he celebrated instead his understanding of the essence of Christ's teachings: the suppression of anger and the imperative of pacifism; love of one's enemies; nonresistance to evil and a refusal to exert force of any kind over others; the taking of oaths as morally wrong; and the sinfulness of sex outside of marriage.

This was a form of Christian and political anarchism — a repudiation of the supernatural dimensions of Christianity, the authority of the church and its sacraments, and the legitimacy of the state. In 1901 Tolstoy was excommunicated by the Russian Orthodox Church, and his religious writings were suppressed. He spent his last years trying to live out the practical implications of his creed by taking on the dress and lifestyle of a peasant.

After his conversion, Tolstoy refused to write what he considered mere fiction and tried to communicate his faith through religious articles and in what he hoped would be seen as moral works of art. These have not been judged to be his best work, but Tolstoy did become a symbol of Christian radicalism. In contrast to communist philosophy, Tolstoy believed that the perfect society would not be achieved by economic materialism but by increasing the goodness of human nature. His aspiration for a Kingdom of God without war, poverty, and oppression was not realized, and a different version of an earthly kingdom was implemented in Russia; yet his vision of Christian discipleship still beckons.

~

My conviction of the error into which all knowledge based on reason must fall assisted me in freeing myself from the seductions of idle reasoning. The conviction that a knowledge of truth can be gained only by living, led me to doubt the justness of my own life; but I had only to get out of my own particular groove, and look around me, to observe the simple life of the real working-class, to understand that such a life was the only real one. I understood that, if I wished to understand life and its meaning, I must live, not the life of a parasite, but a real life; and, accepting the meaning given to it by the combined lives of those that really form the great human whole, submit it to a close examination.

At the time I am speaking of, the following was my position: —

During the whole of that year, when I was asking myself almost every minute whether I should or should not put an end to it all with a cord or a pistol, during the time my mind was occupied with the thoughts which I have described, my heart was oppressed by a tormenting feeling. This feeling I cannot describe otherwise than as a searching after God.

Excerpted from *My Confession, My Religion, The Gospel in Brief* (New York, 1899), 54-59, 72-75.

This search after a God was not an act of my reason, but a feeling, and I say this advisedly, because it was opposed to my way of thinking; it came from the heart. It was a feeling of dread, or orphanhood, of isolation amid things all apart from me, and of hope in a help I knew not from whom.

Though I was well convinced of the impossibility of proving the existence of God — Kant had shown me, and I had thoroughly grasped his reasoning, that this did not admit of proof — I still sought to find a God, still hoped to do so, and still, from the force of former habits, addressed myself to one in prayer, whom I sought, and did not find.

At times I went over in my mind the arguments of Kant and of Schopenhauer, showing the impossibility of proving the existence of the Deity; at times I began to test their arguments and refute them.

I would say to myself that causation is not in the same category of thought as space and time. If I am, there is a cause of my being, and that the cause of all causes. That cause of all things is what is called God; and I dwelt on this idea, and strove with all my being to reach a consciousness of the presence of this cause.

As soon as I became conscious that there is such a power over me, I felt a possibility of living. Then I asked myself: —

"What is this cause, this power? How am I to think of it? What is my relation to what I call God?"

And only the old familiar answer came into my mind, "He is the creator, the giver of all."

This answer did not satisfy me, and I felt that what was necessary for life was failing me, a great horror came over me, and I began to pray to Him whom I sought, that He would help me. But the more I prayed, the clearer it became that I was not heard, that there was no one to whom one could turn. With despair in my heart that there was no God, I cried: —

"Lord, have mercy on me, and save! O Lord, my God, teach me!"

But no one had mercy on me, and I felt that my life had come to a standstill.

But again and again, from various other directions, I came back to the same conviction that I could not have appeared on earth without any motive or meaning, — that I could not be such a fledgling dropped from a nest as I felt myself to be. What if I cry, as the fallen fledgling does on its back in the high grass? It is because I know that a mother bore me, cared for me, fed me, and loved me. Where is she, where is that mother? If I have been thrown out, then who threw me? I cannot help seeing that some one who loved me brought me into being. Who is that some one? Again the same answer — God. He knows and sees my search, my despair, my struggle. "He is," I said to myself. I had only to admit that for an instant to feel that life re-arose in me, to feel the possibility of existing and the joy of it.

Then, again, from the conviction of the existence of God, I passed to the consideration of our relation toward Him, and again I had before me the triune God, our Creator, who sent His Son, the Redeemer. Again, this God, apart from me and from the world, melted from before my eyes as ice melts; again there was nothing left, again the source of life dried up. I fell once more into despair, and felt that I had nothing to do but to kill myself, while, worst of all, I felt also that I should never do it.

Not twice, not three times, but tens, hundreds, of times did I pass through these alternations, — now of joy and excitement, now of despair and of consciousness of the impossibility of life.

I remember one day in the early springtime I was alone in the forest listening to the woodland sounds, and thinking only of one thing, the same of which I had constantly thought for two years — I was again seeking for a God.

I said to myself: —

"Very good, there is no God, there is none with a reality apart from my own imaginings, none as real as my own life — there is none such. Nothing, no miracles can prove there is, for miracles only exist in my own unreasonable imagination."

And then I asked myself: —

"But my idea of the God whom I seek, whence comes it?"

And again at this thought arose the joyous billows of life. All around me seemed to revive, to have a new meaning. My joy, though, did not last long. Reason continued its work: —

"The idea of a God is not God. The idea is what goes on within myself; the idea of God is an idea which I am able to rouse in my mind or not as I choose; it is not what I seek, something without which life could not be."

Then again all seemed to die around and within me, and again I wished to kill myself.

After this I began to retrace the process which had gone on within myself, the hundred times repeated discouragement and revival. I remembered that I had lived only when I believed in a God. As it was before, so it was now; I had only to know God, and I lived; I had only to forget Him, not to believe in Him, and I died.

What was this discouragement and revival? I do not live when I lose faith in the existence of God; I should long ago have killed myself, if I had not had a dim hope of finding Him. I really live only when I am conscious of Him and seek Him. "What more, then, do I seek?" A voice seemed to cry within me, "This is He, He without whom there is no life. To know God and to live are one. God is life."

Live to seek God, and life will not be without God. And stronger than ever rose up life within and around me, and the light that then shone never left me again.

Thus I was saved from self-murder. When and how this change in me took place I could not say. As gradually, imperceptibly as life had decayed in me, till I reached the impossibility of living, till life stood still, and I longed to kill myself, so gradually and imperceptibly I felt the glow and strength of life return to me.

And strangely enough this power of life which came back to me was not new; it was old enough, for I had been led away by it in the earlier part of my life.

I returned, as it were, to the past, to childhood and my youth. I returned to faith in that Will which brought me into being and which required something of me; I returned to the belief that the one single aim of life should be to become better, that is, to live in accordance with that Will; I returned to the idea that the expression of that Will was to be found in what, in the dim obscurity of the past, the great human unity had fashioned for its own guidance; in other words, I returned to a belief in God, in moral perfectibility, and in the tradition which gives a meaning to life. The difference was that formerly I had unconsciously accepted this, whereas now I knew that without it I could not live.

The state of mind in which I then was may be likened to the following: It was as if I had suddenly found myself sitting in a boat which has been pushed off from some shore unknown to me, had been shown the direction of the opposite shore, had had oars put into my inexperienced hands, and had been left alone. I had used the oars as best I could and rowed on; but the farther I went toward the center, the stronger became the current which carried me out of my course, and the oftener I met other navigators, like myself, carried away by the stream. There were here and there solitary navigators who had continued to row hard, there were others who had thrown down their oars, there were large boats, and enormous ships crowded with men; some struggled against the stream, others glided on with it. The farther I got, the more, as I watched the long line floating down the current, I forgot the course pointed out to me as my own.

In the very middle of the stream, amid the crowd of boats and vessels floating down, I had altogether lost the course and thrown down my oars. From all sides the joyful and exulting navigators, as they rowed or sailed down-stream, with one voice assured me and one another that there could be no other direction. And I believed them, and let myself go with them. I was carried far, so far that I heard the roar of the rapids in which I was bound to perish, and I already saw boats that had been broken up within them.

Then I came to myself. It was long before I clearly comprehended what had happened. I saw before me nothing but the destruction toward which I was hurrying, which I dreaded, and I saw no salvation and knew not what I was to do! But on looking back, I saw a countless multitude of boats engaged in a ceaseless struggle against the force of the torrent, and then I remembered all about the shore, the oars, and the course, and at once I began to row hard up the stream and again toward the shore.

That shore was God, that course was tradition, those oars were the free will given me to make for the shore to seek union with the Deity. . . .

The above was written by me three years ago.

The other day, on looking over this part again, on returning to the train of thought and to the feelings through which I had passed while writing it, I saw a dream.

This dream repeated for me in a condensed form all that I had lived through and described, and I therefore think that a description of it may, for those who have understood me, serve to render clearer, to refresh the remembrance of, and to collect into one whole, all that has been described at so much length in these pages. The dream was as follows.

I see myself lying in bed, and I feel neither particularly well and comfortable, nor the contrary. I am lying on my back. I begin to think whether it is well for me to lie, and something makes me feel uncomfortable in the legs; if the bed be too short or ill-made, I know not, but something is not right. I move my legs about, and at the same time begin to think how and on what I am lying, a thing which previously had never troubled me. I examine my bed, and see that I am lying on a network of cords fashioned to the sides of the bedstead. My heels lie on one of these cords, my legs on another, and this is uncomfortable. I am somehow aware that the cords can be moved, and with my legs I push the cords away, and it seems to me that thus it will be easier.

But I had pushed the cord too far; I tried to catch it with my legs, but this movement causes another cord to slip from under me, and my legs hang down. I move my body to get right again, convinced that it will be easy, but this movement causes other cords to slip and change their places beneath me, and I perceive that my position is altogether worse; my whole body sinks and hangs, without my legs touching the ground. I hold myself up only by the upper part of the back, and I feel now not only discomfort, but horror. I now begin to ask myself what I had not thought of before. I ask myself where I am, and on what I am lying. I begin to look round, and first I look below, to the place toward which my body sank, and where I feel it must soon fall. I look below, and I cannot believe my eyes.

I am on a height far above that of the highest tower or mountain, a height beyond all my previous powers of conception. I cannot even make out whether I see anything or not below me, in the depths of that bottomless abyss over which I am hanging, and into which I feel drawn. My heart ceases to beat, and horror fills my mind. To look down is horrible. I feel that if I look down I shall slip from the last cord, and perish. I stop looking, but not to look is still worse, for then I think of what will at once happen to me when the last cord breaks. I feel that I am losing, in my terror, the last remnant of my strength, and that my back is gradually sinking lower and lower. Another instant, and I shall fall.

Then all at once comes into my mind the thought that this cannot be true — it is a dream — I will awake.

I strive to wake myself, and cannot. "What can I do? what can I do?" I ask myself, and as I put the question I look above.

Above stretches another gulf. I look into this abyss of heaven, and try to forget the abyss below, and I do actually forget it. The infinite depth repels and horrifies me; the infinite height attracts and satisfies me. I still hang on the last cords which have not yet slipped from under me, over the abyss; I know that I am hanging thus, but I look only upwards, and my terror leaves me. As happens in dreams, I hear a voice saying, "Look well; it is there!" My eyes pierce farther and farther into the infinity above, and I feel that it calms me. I remember all that has happened, and I remember how it happened — how I moved my legs, how I was left hanging in air, how I was horrified, and how I was saved from my horror by looking above. I ask myself, "And now, am I not hanging still?" and I feel in all my limbs, without looking, the support by which I am held. I perceive that I no longer hang, and that I do not fall, but have a fast hold. I question myself how it is that I hold on. I touch myself, I look around, and I see that under the middle of my body there passes a stay, and on looking up I find that I am lying perfectly balanced, and that it was this stay alone that held me up before.

As happens in dreams, the mechanism by which I am supported appears perfectly natural to me, a thing to be easily understood, and not to be doubted, although this mechanism has no apparent sense when I am awake. In my sleep I was even astonished that I had not understood this before. At my bedside stands a pillar, the solidity of which is beyond doubt, though there is nothing for it to stand on. From this pillar runs a cord, somehow cunningly and at the same time simply fixed, and if I lie across this cord and look upward, there cannot be even a question of my falling. All this was clear to me, and I was glad and easy in my mind. It seemed as if some one said to me, "See that you remember!"

And I awoke.

Charles H. Spurgeon

(1834–1892)

It would be difficult to calculate the impact on his own day and on later generations of the so-called "Prince of Preachers." Forced to occupy ever-larger lecture halls to accommodate the thousands who crowded to hear him preach, Spurgeon seems, in retrospect, a pulpit phenomenon. His published sermons and other biblical volumes are still in print, years after his death.

Charles Haddon Spurgeon was born into the British Baptist tradition of John Bunyan. Without formal theological training, Spurgeon based his preaching on the Bible and the doctrines of sin and salvation. Independent and aggressive, he emphasized preaching and conversion in his ministry, rather than liturgy or sacraments.

Distrustful of the emerging biblical criticism, he stuck to the great Old Testament narratives and the simple gospel of Jesus. He appealed primarily through human emotions to the individual conscience of his hearers. An eloquent orator, Spurgeon expounded endlessly on the degradation of sin and the glory of salvation.

During the height of his preaching fame, and long before electronic amplification, Spurgeon spoke twice a week in the huge six-thousand-seat Metropolitan Tabernacle in London. He preached from a page of notes, and his sermons were taken down by hand, revised the next day by Spurgeon himself, and then published and distributed, as it was said, "literally by the ton." A later edition of his printed sermons in *The Tabernacle Pulpit* filled nearly fifty volumes. His extensive expositions on the Psalms were published in seven volumes as *The Treasury of David*.

Everything Spurgeon put his hand to seemed large as life. Even his autobiography runs to four big folio volumes. We are not surprised, therefore, to find his conversion (January 6, 1850) described on the grand scale. At the time, he considered it a simple surrender, but its subsequent influence on his life and especially on his preaching was clearly momentous.

~

In my conversion, the very point lay in making the discovery that I had nothing to do but to look to Christ, and I should be saved. I believe that I had been a very good, attentive hearer; my own impression about myself was that nobody ever listened much better than I did. For years, as a child, I tried to learn the way of salvation; and either I did not hear it set forth, which I think cannot quite have been the case, or else I was spiritually blind and deaf, and could not see it and could not hear it; but the good news that I was, as a sinner, to look away from myself to Christ, as much startled me, and came as fresh to me, as any news I ever heard in my life. Had I never read my Bible? Yes, and read it earnestly. Had I never been taught by Christian people? Yes, I had, by mother, and father, and others. Had I not heard the gospel? Yes, I think I had; and yet, somehow, it was like a new revelation to me that I was to "believe and live." I confess to have been tutored in piety, put into my cradle by prayerful hands, and lulled to sleep by songs concerning Jesus; but after having heard the gospel continually, with line upon line, precept upon precept, here much and there much, yet, when the Word of the Lord came to me with power, it was as new as if I had lived among the unvisited tribes of Central Africa, and had never heard the tidings of the cleansing fountain filled with blood, drawn from the Saviour's veins.

When, for the first time, I received the gospel to my soul's salvation, I thought that I had never really heard it before, and I began to think that the preachers to whom I had listened had not truly preached it. But, on looking back, I am inclined to believe that I had heard the gospel fully preached many hundreds of times before, and that this was the difference, — that I then heard it as though I heard it not; and when I did hear it, the message may not have been any more clear in itself than it had been at former times, but the power of the Holy Spirit was present to open my ear, and to guide the message to my heart. . . .

I sometimes think I might have been in darkness and despair until

From *The Autobiography of Charles H. Spurgeon,* compiled from his diary, letters, and records by his wife and his private secretary (New York: Fleming H. Revell Co., 1898), 1:102-13.

now had it not been for the goodness of God in sending a snowstorm, one Sunday morning, while I was going to a certain place of worship. When I could go no further, I turned down a side street, and came to a little Primitive Methodist Chapel. In that chapel there may have been a dozen or fifteen people. I had heard of the Primitive Methodists, how they sang so loudly that they made people's heads ache; but that did not matter to me. I wanted to know how I might be saved, and if they could tell me that, I did not care how much they made my head ache. The minister did not come that morning; he was snowed up, I suppose. At last, a very thin-looking man, a shoemaker, or tailor, or something of that sort, went up into the pulpit to preach. Now, it is well that preachers should be instructed; but this man was really stupid. He was obliged to stick to his text, for the simple reason that he had little else to say. The text was, —

"LOOK UNTO ME, AND BE YE SAVED, ALL THE ENDS OF THE EARTH."

He did not even pronounce the words rightly, but that did not matter. There was, I thought, a glimpse of hope for me in that text. The preacher began thus: — "My dear friends, this is a very simple text indeed. It says, 'Look.' Now lookin' don't take a deal of pains. It ain't liftin' your foot or your finger; it is just, 'Look.' Well, a man needn't go to College to learn to look. You may be the biggest fool, and yet you can look. A man needn't be worth a thousand a year to be able to look. Anyone can look; even a child can look. But then the text says, 'Look unto *Me*.' Ay!" said he, in broad Essex, "many on ye are lookin' to yourselves, but it's no use lookin' there. You'll never find any comfort in yourselves. Some look to God the Father. No, look to Him by-and-by. Jesus Christ says, 'Look unto *Me*.' Some on ye say, 'We must wait for the Spirit's workin'.' You have no business with that just now. Look to *Christ*. The text says, 'Look unto *Me*.'"

Then the good man followed up his text in this way: — "Look unto Me; I am sweatin' great drops of blood. Look unto Me; I am hangin' on the cross. Look unto Me; I am dead and buried. Look unto Me; I rise again. Look unto Me; I ascend to Heaven. Look unto Me; I am sittin' at the Father's right hand. O poor sinner, look unto Me! look unto Me!"

When he had gone to about that length, and managed to spin out ten minutes or so, he was at the end of his tether. Then he looked at me under the gallery, and I daresay, with so few present, he knew me to be a stranger. Just fixing his eyes on me, as if he knew all my heart, he said, "Young man, you look very miserable." Well, I did; but I had not been accustomed to have remarks made from the pulpit on my personal appearance before. However, it was a good blow, struck right home. He continued, "and you always will be miserable — miserable in life, and miserable in death, — if you don't obey my text; but if you obey now, this moment, you will be saved." Then, lifting up his hands, he shouted, as only a Primitive Methodist could do, "Young man, look to Jesus Christ. Look! Look! Look! You have nothin' to do but to look and live."

I saw at once the way of salvation. I know not what else he said, — I did not take much notice of it, — I was so possessed with that one thought. Like as when the brazen serpent was lifted up, the people only looked and were healed, so it was with me. I had been waiting to do fifty things, but when I heard that word, "Look!" what a charming word it seemed to me! Oh! I looked until I could almost have looked my eyes away. There and then the cloud was gone, the darkness had rolled away, and that moment I saw the sun; and I could have risen that instant, and sung with the most enthusiastic of them, of the precious blood of Christ, and the simple faith which looks alone to Him. Oh, that somebody had told me this before, "Trust Christ, and you shall be saved." . . .

It is not everyone who can remember the very day and hour of his deliverance; but, as Richard Knill[1] said, "At such a time of the day, clang went every harp in Heaven, for Richard Knill was born again," it was e'en so with me. The clock of mercy struck in Heaven the hour and moment of my emancipation, for the time had come. Between half-past ten o'clock, when I entered that chapel, and half-past twelve o'clock, when I was back again at home, what a change had taken place in me! I had passed from darkness into marvelous light, from death to life. Simply by looking to Jesus, I had been delivered from despair, and I was brought into such a joyous state of mind that, when they saw me at home, they said to me, "Something wonderful has happened to you"; and I was eager to tell them all about it. . . .

I have always considered, with Luther and Calvin, that the sum and substance of the gospel lies in that word *Substitution,* — Christ standing in the stead of man. If I understand the gospel, it is this: I deserve to be lost for ever; the only reason why I should not be damned is, that Christ

---

1. Richard Knill, 1787-1857, was a missionary contemporary.

was punished in my stead, and there is no need to execute a sentence twice for sin. On the other hand, I know I cannot enter Heaven unless I have a perfect righteousness; I am absolutely certain I shall never have one of my own, for I find I sin every day; but then Christ had a perfect righteousness, and He said, "There, poor sinner, take My garment, and put it on; you shall stand before God as if you were Christ, and I will stand before God as if I had been the sinner; I will suffer in the sinner's stead, and you shall be rewarded for works which you did not do, but which I did for you." I find it very convenient every day to come to Christ as a sinner, as I came at the first. "You are no saint," says the devil. Well, if I am not, I am a sinner, and Jesus Christ came into the world to save sinners. Sink or swim, I go to Him; other hope I have none. By looking to Him, I received all the faith which inspired me with confidence in His grace; and the word that first drew my soul — "Look unto Me," — still rings its clarion note in my ears. There I once found conversion, and there I shall ever find refreshing and renewal.

William Booth

(1829–1912)

The awesome urban poverty of nineteenth-century England spawned William Booth and his international revival and relief movement, the Salvation Army. Booth himself was born in poverty; fatherless by the age of thirteen, he was apprenticed to a pawnbroker, a position he detested. He later spoke repeatedly of his "blighted childhood." The wretched conditions of industrial cities in England made a profound impression on Booth, and he was particularly moved by the suffering of children. If it had not been for his conversion in 1844, he probably would have become a labor union leader in Britain.

Instead, he committed his life to the saving of souls and the alleviation of human misery. At the age of twenty, he went to London and worked as a pawnbroker, using all his free time for preaching and evangelistic work. In 1855, he met Catherine Mumford, a woman who redirected his life and focused his ministry. She persuaded him to become a full-time Methodist preacher, but soon Booth's violent tactics in the pulpit ran afoul of Methodist sensibilities. He organized the East London Revival Society in 1865, known as the Christian Mission, and in 1878 it became the Salvation Army with General William Booth in command. Catherine Booth became her husband's most valued ally, his most persistent critic, and the genius behind many of the Army's successes. She was largely responsible for guaranteeing equality for women in the Army, and her better education compensated for her husband's woeful lack of it.

In 1890, Catherine Booth died, and General Booth published *In Darkest England and the Way Out,* a manual for reform of English society in terms of evangelism and social relief. Booth never wavered from insisting that saving souls came first, but he did call for employment bureaus, vocational training programs, farm colonies for the poor, rehabilitation centers for "lost women," legal assistance and bank services for the poor, and other social programs.

His son Bramwell was the organizational force behind the Salvation Army in England, and his daughter Evangeline brought the Army to Canada and the United States, where it expanded rapidly during the early twentieth century. The striking Army uniforms, the stirring Army hymns, and the rich brass of the Army bands drew the curious, the scoffers, and the committed, and the Army reached out with a message of repentance and salvation as well as physical assistance.

Booth himself had practically no interest in theology. He said that people were responsible for their sins and God was responsible for their salvation. It was as simple as that, but behind it was also Christian compassion for the poor and a protest against the forces that degraded human life. "The first step in saving outcasts," Booth declared, "consists in making them feel that some decent human being cares enough for them to take an interest in the question of whether they are to rise or sink." To that end, the Salvation Army marched, a legacy of the man who vowed that "if I did go in for God I would do so with all my might."

When as a giddy youth of fifteen I was led to attend Wesley Chapel, Nottingham, I cannot recollect that any individual pressed me in the direction of personal surrender to God. I was wrought upon quite independently of human effort by the Holy Ghost, who created within me a great thirst for a new life.

I felt that I wanted, in place of the life of self-indulgence, to which I was yielding myself, a happy, conscious sense that I was pleasing God, living right, and spending all my powers to get others into such a life. I saw that all this ought to be, and I decided that it should be. It is wonderful that I should have reached this decision in view of all the influences then around me. My professedly Christian master never uttered a word to indicate that he believed in anything he could not see, and many of my companions were worldly and sensual, some of them even vicious.

Yet I had that instinctive belief in God which, in common with my fellow-creatures, I had brought into the world with me. I had no disposi-

Excerpted from G. S. Railton, *The Authoritative Life of General Booth: Founder of the Salvation Army* (New York, 1912), 9-12.

tion to deny my instincts, which told me that if there was a God His laws ought to have my obedience and His interests my service.

I felt that it was better to live right than to live wrong, and as to caring for the interests of others instead of my own, the condition of the suffering people around me, people with whom I had been so long familiar, and whose agony seemed to reach its climax about this time, undoubtedly affected me very deeply.

There were children crying for bread to parents whose own distress was little less terrible to witness.

One feeling specially forced itself upon me, and I can recollect it as distinctly as though it had transpired only yesterday, and that was the sense of the folly of spending my life in doing things for which I knew I must either repent or be punished in the days to come. In my anxiety to get into the right way, I joined the Methodist Church, and attended the Class Meetings, to sing and pray and speak with the rest. . . . But all the time the inward Light revealed to me that I must not only renounce everything I knew to be sinful, but make restitution, so far as I had the ability, for any wrong I had done to others before I could find peace with God.

The entrance to the Heavenly Kingdom was closed against me by an evil act of the past which required restitution. In a boyish trading affair I had managed to make a profit out of my companions, whilst giving them to suppose that what I did was all in the way of a generous fellowship. As a testimonial of their gratitude they had given me a silver pencil-case. Merely to return their gift would have been comparatively easy, but to confess the deception I had practised upon them was a humiliation to which for some days I could not bring myself.

I remember, as if it were but yesterday, the spot in the corner of a room under the chapel, the hour, the resolution to end the matter, the rising up and rushing forth, the finding of the young fellow I had chiefly wronged, the acknowledgment of my sin, the return of the pencil-case — the instant rolling away from my heart of the guilty burden, the peace that came in its place, and the going forth to serve my God and my generation from that hour.

It was in the open street that this great change passed over me, and if I could only have possessed the flagstone on which I stood at that happy moment, the sight of it occasionally might have been as useful to me as the stones carried up long ago from the bed of the Jordan were to the Israelites who had passed over them dry-shod.

Since that night, for it was near upon eleven o'clock when the happy change was realised, the business of my life has been not only to make a holy character but to live a life of loving activity in the service of God and man. I have ever felt that true religion consists not only in being holy myself, but in assisting my Crucified Lord in His work of saving men and women, making them into His Soldiers, keeping them faithful to death, and so getting them into Heaven.

I have had to encounter all sorts of difficulties as I have travelled along this road. The world has been against me, sometimes very intensely, and often very stupidly. I have had difficulties similar to those of other men, with my own bodily appetites, with my mental disposition, and with my natural unbelief.

Many people, both religious and irreligious, are apt to think that they are more unfavourably constituted than their comrades and neighbours, and that their circumstances and surroundings are peculiarly unfriendly to the discharge of the duties they owe to God and man.

I have been no exception in this matter. Many a time I have been tempted to say to myself, "There is no one fixed so awkwardly for holy living and faithful fighting as I am." But I have been encouraged to resist the delusion by remembering the words of the Apostle Paul: "There hath no temptation taken you but such as is common to man."

I am not pretending to say that I have worked harder, or practised more self-denial, or endured more hardships at any particular time of my life than have those around me; but I do want those who feel any interest in me to understand that faithfulness to God in the discharge of duty and the maintenance of a good conscience have cost me as severe a struggle as they can cost any Salvation Soldier in London, Berlin, Paris, New York, or Tokio to-day.

One reason for the victory I daily gained from the moment of my conversion was, no doubt, my complete and immediate separation from the godless world. I turned my back on it. I gave it up, having made up my mind beforehand that if I did go in for God I would do so with all my might. Rather than yearning for the world's pleasures, books, gains, or recreations, I found my new nature leading me to come away from it all. It had lost all charm for me. What were all the novels, even those of Sir Walter Scott or Fenimore Cooper, compared with the story of my Saviour? What were the choicest orators compared with Paul? What was the hope of money-earning, even with all my desire to help my poor mother and sisters, in comparison with the imperishable wealth of ingathered souls? I soon began to despise everything the world had to offer me.

In those days I felt, as I believe many Converts do, that I could willingly and joyfully travel to the ends of the earth for Jesus Christ, and suffer anything imaginable to help the souls of other men. Jesus Christ had baptised me, according to His eternal promise, with His Spirit and with Fire.

Yet the surroundings of my early life were all in opposition to this whole-hearted devotion. No one at first took me by the hand and urged me forward, or gave me any instruction or hint likely to help me in the difficulties I had at once to encounter in my consecration to this service.

Francis Thompson

(1859–1907)

Although he wrote many poems and essays on English literature, Francis Thompson today is known primarily for just one poem, "The Hound of Heaven." Written in a somewhat florid style, the poem's imagery shifts between the familiar and the strange. Yet there is no mistaking the meaning and the personal involvement of the poet himself.

The message of the lines reminds us that God seeks us out, even when we try to hide, and that the divine initiative cannot be ignored. As the psalmist expressed it — "Where can I go from your spirit? Or where can I flee from your presence?" (Ps. 139:7).

Speaking out of his disordered and often futile existence, Thompson's poem reveals to us not only his own inner spiritual experience but something of every person's struggle to find meaning. Born into a Catholic family that had been influenced by the conversion of John Henry Newman, Francis hoped to become an ordinand for the priesthood but was rejected. His physician father persuaded him to study medicine but he failed his exams.

Taking off for London to find a new life, Thompson was ill-suited physically and emotionally for life in the big city. His mind was full of images, pictures, and fantasies, some of which he transcribed as poems. But to live, he worked as a shoe-black, a match-seller, and a cab-caller. He neglected his health and became undernourished; and, following the example of Thomas De Quincey, whom he admired, Thompson became an opium addict.

At the depths of his depression, he was befriended by members of the literary and compassionate Meynell family. Restored to some degree of health, though never completely cured of his habit, he worked from time to time for one or more of the Meynell journals.

"The Hound of Heaven" was written in 1891, although not published until four years later. In the meantime, Thompson took up residence at the Francis-can monastery at Pantasaph in Wales. Here for a time he was at ease, reading and writing. But restless as ever, he returned to London, where he died alone and forlorn.

Speaking out of the depths of despair, Thompson's poem recalls the shepherd searching for the lost sheep. And near the close of the poem, we read the words: "Rise, clasp My hand, and come." Perhaps Francis Thompson was thinking of the gracious invitation of Jesus — "Come to me, all you that are weary and are carrying heavy burdens, and I will give you rest" (Matt. 11:28).

~

I fled Him, down the nights and down the days;
   I fled Him, down the arches of the years;
I fled Him, down the labyrinthine ways
   Of my own mind; and in the mist of tears
I hid from Him, and under running laughter.
      Up vistaed hopes, I sped;
      And shot, precipitated,
Adown Titanic glooms of chasméd fears,
  From those strong Feet that followed, followed after.
      But with unhurrying chase,
      And unperturbéd pace,
    Deliberate speed, majestic instancy,
      They beat — and a Voice beat
      More instant than the Feet —
  "All things betray thee, who betrayest Me."
      I pleaded, outlaw-wise,
By many a hearted casement, curtained red,
   Trellised with intertwining charities;
(For, though I knew His love Who followed,
      Yet was I sore adread
Lest, having Him, I must have naught beside)

The edition of the poem quoted here is *The Hound of Heaven*, with a Biographical Sketch and Notes, by Michael A. Kelly (Philadelphia: Peter Reilly, Publisher, 1916), 23-31.

But, if one little casement parted wide,
    The gust of His approach would clash it to.
    Fear wist not to evade as Love wist to pursue.
Across the margent of the world I fled,
    And troubled the gold gateways of the stars,
    Smiting for shelter on their clangéd bars;
        Fretted to dulcet jars
And silvern chatter the pale ports o' the moon.
I said to dawn: Be sudden; to eve: Be soon —
    With thy young skyey blossoms heap me over
        From this tremendous Lover!
Float thy vague veil about me, lest He see!
    I tempted all His servitors, but to find
My own betrayal in their constancy,
In faith to Him their fickleness to me,
    Their traitorous trueness, and their loyal deceit.
To all swift things for swiftness did I sue;
    Clung to the whistling mane of every wind.
        But whether they swept, smoothly fleet,
      The long savannahs of the blue;
        Or whether, Thunder-driven,
      They clanged His chariot 'thwart a heaven,
Plashy with flying lightnings round the spurn o'
        their feet: —
    Fear wist not to evade as Love wist to pursue.
        Still with unhurrying chase,
        And unperturbéd pace,
    Deliberate speed, majestic instancy,
        Came on the following Feet,
        And a Voice above their beat —
    "Naught shelters thee, who wilt not shelter Me."

I sought no more that, after which I strayed,
        In face of man or maid;
But still within the little children's eyes
      Seems something, something that replies,
They, at least, are for me, surely for me!
I turned me to them very wistfully;
But just as their young eyes grew sudden fair

With dawning answers there,
Their angel plucked them from me by the hair.
"Come then, ye other children, Nature's — share
With me" (said I) "your delicate fellowship;
    Let me greet you lip to lip,
    Let me twine with you caresses,
        Wantoning
    With our Lady-Mother's vagrant tresses,
        Banqueting
    With her in her wind-walled palace,
    Underneath her azured daïs,
    Quaffing, as your taintless way is,
        From a chalice
Lucent-weeping out of the dayspring."
        So it was done:
I, in their delicate fellowship was one —
Drew the bolt of Nature's secrecies.
    I knew all the swift importings
    On the wilful face of skies;
    I knew how the clouds arise,
    Spuméd of the wild sea-snortings;
        All that's born or dies
    Rose and drooped with; made them shapers
Of mine own moods, or wailful or divine —
    With them joyed and was bereaven.
    I was heavy with the even,
When she lit her glimmering tapers
    Round the day's dead sanctities.
    I laughed in the morning's eyes.
I triumphed and I saddened with all weather,
    Heaven and I wept together,
And its sweet tears were salt with mortal mine;
Against the red throb of its sunset-heart
        I laid my own to beat,
        And share commingling heat;
But not by that, by that, was eased my human smart.
In vain my tears were set on Heaven's grey cheek.
For ah! we know not what each other says,
    These things, and I; in sound *I* speak —

Their sound is but their stir, they speak in silences.
Nature, poor stepdame, cannot slake my drought;
    Let her, if she would owe me,
Drop yon blue bosom-veil of sky, and show me
    The breasts o' her tenderness:
Never did any milk of hers once bless
      My thirsting mouth.
      Nigh and nigh, draws the chase,
      With unperturbéd pace,
    Deliberate speed, majestic instancy,
      And past those noiséd Feet
      A Voice comes yet more fleet —
"Lo! naught contents thee, who content'st not Me."

Naked I wait Thy love's uplifted stroke!
My harness piece by piece Thou hast hewn from me,
      And smitten me to my knee;
      I am defenceless utterly.
      I slept, methinks, and woke,
And, slowly gazing, find me stripped in sleep.
In the rash lustihead of my young powers,
      I shook the pillaring hours
And pulled my life upon me; grimed with smears,
I stand amid the dust o' the mounded years —
My mangled youth lies dead beneath the heap.
My days have crackled and gone up in smoke,
Have puffed and burst as sun-starts on a stream.
    Yea, faileth now even dream
The dreamer, and the lute the lutanist;
Even the linked fantasies, in whose blossomy twist
I swung the earth a trinket at my wrist,
Are yielding; cords of all too weak account
For earth, with heavy griefs so overplussed.
    Ah! is Thy love indeed
A weed, albeit an amaranthine weed,
Suffering no flowers except its own to mount?
    Ah! must —
    Designer infinite! —
Ah! must Thou char the wood ere Thou canst limn with it?

My freshness spent its wavering shower i' the dust;
And now my heart is as a broken fount,
Wherein tear-drippings stagnate, spilt down ever
    From the dank thoughts that shiver
Upon the sighful branches of my mind.
     Such is; what is to be?
The pulp so bitter, how shall taste the rind?
I dimly guess what Time in mists confounds;
Yet ever and anon a trumpet sounds
From the hid battlements of Eternity,
Those shaken mists a space unsettle, then
Round the half-glimpséd turrets slowly wash again;
    But not ere Him Who summoneth
    I first have seen, enwound
With glooming robes purpureal, cypress-crowned;
His Name I know, and what His trumpet saith.
Whether man's heart or life it be which yields
    Thee harvest, must Thy harvest fields
    Be dunged with rotten death?
     Now of that long pursuit
     Comes on at hand the bruit;
That Voice is round me like a bursting sea:
    "And is thy earth so marred,
    Shattered in shard on shard?
   Lo, all things fly thee, for thou fliest Me!
   Strange, piteous, futile thing!
Wherefore should any set thee love apart?
Seeing none but I makes much of naught" (He said),
"And human love needs human meriting:
    How hast thou merited —
Of all man's clotted clay the dingiest clot?
    Alack, thou knowest not
How little worthy of any love thou art!
Whom wilt thou find to love ignoble thee,
    Save Me, save only Me?
All which I took from thee I did but take,
    Not for thy harms,
But just that thou might'st seek it in My arms.
    All which thy child's mistake

Fancies as lost, I have stored for thee at home:
    Rise, clasp My hand, and come."

    Halts by me that footfall;
    Is my gloom, after all,
Shade of His hand, outstretched caressingly?
    "Ah, fondest, blindest, weakest,
    I am He Whom thou seekest!
Thou dravest love from thee, who dravest Me."

Thérèse of Lisieux

(1873–1897)

St. Thérèse of Lisieux is another example of a very short life that left an enduring imprint on the Christian church. Through her autobiography, Thérèse captured the affection and admiration of people throughout the world for her simple faith and piety in everyday life. Early in her own life, she declared, "I want to be a saint," and to that goal she devoted all her energies. Pope Pius X described her as "the greatest saint of modern times."

She was born Marie Françoise Thérèse Martin, the youngest of nine children, in Alençon, France. Her father was a prosperous watchmaker, her mother a craftswoman. Thérèse's mother died when she was four, a devastating experience for the little girl, but she soon demonstrated a precocious religiosity, as did two of her sisters, Marie and Pauline, who became Carmelite nuns. Always a sickly child, at the age of ten Thérèse was stricken with a disease that included a combination of convulsions, hallucinations, and comas. After three months, she was cured by what Thérèse believed was a miraculous intervention of the Virgin Mary.

She called the period between the death of her mother and her conversion her "winter of trial," and her conversion marked a new level of religious and emotional maturity. She wanted to enter the Carmelite convent at Lisieux, but she was initially turned down because of her youth. After a pilgrimage to Rome with her father and after entreating the bishop, Thérèse was finally admitted to the convent in 1888, two years after her conversion; in 1889 she was admitted to the order and in 1893 became assistant to the mistress of novices. She was persuaded to write her autobiography *The Story of a Soul* in 1895, and after her death it became a worldwide best seller.

The Lisieux convent was badly divided during her lifetime, but Thérèse remained distant from the political disputes, practicing what she called her "little Way," a childlike submission to the will of God in all things. She suffered from tuberculosis but continued her monastic regimen until six months before her death. Hospitalized in the infirmary, she endured great pain and confessed, "I did not think it was possible to suffer so much." Her last words were, "My God, I love you."

In the wake of her tremendously popular autobiography, Thérèse became an especially revered figure among ordinary Catholics. Calling her growing fame "a hurricane of glory," Pius XI waived the traditional fifty-year waiting period and canonized her in 1925. As he paid tribute to her, the pope said that she had achieved sanctity "without going beyond the common order of things," and in this simple, direct, and practical piety lies the heart of Thérèse's appeal for today.

~

It was on December 25, 1886, that I received the grace of emerging from childhood — the grace of my complete conversion. We went to midnight Mass where I had the joy of receiving almighty God. When we got home again, I was excited at the thought of my shoes standing, full of presents, in the fireplace. When we were small children, this old custom gave us such delight that Céline [her sister] wanted to continue treating me like a baby as I was the youngest in the family. Daddy used to love to see my happiness and hear my cries of joy as I pulled out each surprise from the magic shoes, and the delight of my beloved King increased my own. But as Jesus wanted to free me from the faults of childhood, He also took away its innocent pleasures. He arranged matters so that Daddy was irritated at seeing my shoes in the fireplace and spoke about them in a way which hurt me very much: "Thank goodness it's the last time we shall have this kind of thing!" I went upstairs to take off my hat. Céline knew how sensitive I was. She said: "Thérèse, don't go downstairs again. Taking the presents out of your shoes will upset you too much." But Thérèse was not the same girl. Jesus had changed her. I suppressed my tears, ran downstairs, and picked up my shoes. I pulled out my presents with an air of great cheerfulness. Daddy laughed and

From *The Autobiography of St. Thérèse of Lisieux: The Story of a Soul,* by St. Thérèse of Lisieux, translation by John Beevers, translation copyright © 1957 by Doubleday, a division of Random House, Inc. Used by permission of Doubleday, a division of Random House, Inc.

Céline thought she was dreaming! But it was no dream. Thérèse had got back for good the strength of soul which she had lost when she was four and a half. On this glorious night the third period of my life began. It has been the loveliest of them all and the one richest with heavenly graces. Jesus, satisfied with my goodwill, accomplished in an instant what I had been unable to do in ten years. Like the apostles, we could say: "Master, I have toiled all the night, and caught nothing." Jesus was more merciful to me than to His disciples. He Himself took the net, cast it, and drew it up full of fishes. He made me a fisher of men. I longed to work for the conversion of sinners with a passion I'd never felt before. Love filled my heart, I forgot myself and henceforth I was happy.

One Sunday when I was looking at a picture of Our Lord on the Cross, I saw the Blood coming from one of His hands, and I felt terribly sad to think that It was falling to the earth and that no one was rushing forward to catch It. I determined to stay continually at the foot of the Cross and receive It. I knew that I should then have to spread It among other souls. The cry of Jesus on the Cross — "I am thirsty" — rang continually in my heart and set me burning with a new, intense longing. I wanted to quench the thirst of my Well-Beloved and I myself was consumed with a thirst for souls. I was concerned not with the souls of priests but with those of great sinners which I wanted to snatch from the flames of hell.

God showed me He was pleased with these longings of mine. I'd heard of a criminal who had just been condemned to death for some frightful murders. It seemed that he would die without repenting. I was determined at all costs to save him from hell. I used every means I could. I knew that by myself I could do nothing, so I offered God the infinite merits of Our Lord and the treasures of the Church. I was quite certain that my prayers would be answered, but to give me courage to go on praying for sinners I said to God: "I am sure You will forgive this wretched Pranzini. I shall believe You have done so even if he does not confess or give any other sign of repentance, for I have complete faith in the infinite mercy of Jesus. But I ask You for just one sign of his repentance to encourage me."

This prayer was answered. Daddy never allowed us to read any newspapers, but I thought I was justified in looking at the stories about Pranzini. On the day after his execution I eagerly opened *La Croix* and I had to rush away to hide my tears at what I read. Pranzini had mounted the scaffold without confessing and was ready to thrust his head beneath the guillotine's blade when he suddenly turned, seized the crucifix offered him by the priest, and thrice kissed the Sacred Wounds.

I had been given my sign, and it was typical of the graces Jesus has given me to make me eager to pray for sinners. It was at the sight of the Precious Blood flowing from the Wounds of Jesus that my thirst for souls had been born. I wanted to let them drink of this Immaculate Blood to cleanse them of their sins and the lips of my "first child" had pressed against the Sacred Wounds! What a wonderful reply to my prayers! After this striking favour my longing for souls grew greater every day. I seemed to hear Jesus say to me what He said to the Samaritan Woman: "Give me to drink." It was a real exchange of love: I gave souls the Blood of Jesus and offered Him these purified souls that His thirst might be quenched. The more I gave Him to drink, the more the thirst of my own poor soul increased, and He gave me this burning thirst to show His love for me.

In a short time God had lifted me out of the narrow circle in which I'd been going round and round, quite unable to escape from it. When I see the road He has made me tread, I am profoundly grateful, but it was essential that I should be fit for it, and though I'd made the first and greatest step along it, there still remained much for me to do. Now I was rid of my scruples and my excessive sensitiveness, my mind began to develop. All that was great and lovely had always appealed to me, but now I was gripped by an intense desire for learning. I wasn't satisfied with the lessons of Madame Papineau. I began working on my own at history and science. Other subjects didn't attract me at all, but I loved these two and I learnt more in a few months than in all the years before.

I was at the most dangerous time of life for young girls, but God did for me what Ezechiel recounts: Passing by me, Jesus saw that I was ripe for love. He plighted His troth to me and I became His. He threw His cloak about me, washed me with water and anointed me with oil, clothed me in fine linen and silk, and decked me with bracelets and priceless gems. He fed me on wheat and honey and oil and I had matchless beauty and He made me a great queen. Jesus did all that for me. I could go over every word of what I've just written and show how they applied to me, but the graces I've spoken about before are proof enough. All I'm going to write of now is the food Our Lord gave me so abundantly. For a long time I'd been fed on the wheat of *The Imitation*. It was the only book which did me any good, as I hadn't discovered the treasures of the Gospels. I knew every chapter by heart. I was never without this little book. My aunt often used to open it at random and I would recite whatever chapter appeared. When I was fourteen and had this passion for learning, God added honey and oil to the wheat of *The Imitation.* I found this honey and oil in Father Arminjon's book, *The End of This World and the Mysteries of the Future Life.* Reading it was one of the greatest graces I've known. All the great truths of religion and the secrets of eternity were there and filled my soul with a happiness not of this world. I saw already what God has in store for those who love Him. When I realised how trifling are the sacrifices of this life compared with the rewards of heaven, I wanted to love Jesus, to love Him passionately, and to give Him a thousand tokens of my love whilst I still could.

Céline shared my intimate thoughts. Since Christmas we understood each other perfectly. As Jesus wanted us to go forward together, He united us with bonds stronger than those of blood. He made us sisters in spirit, and we fulfilled those words of our Father, St. John of the Cross: "The young girls run gaily along the path in the track of Your footsteps. The touch of the spark and the spiced wine gives them longings for the Divine." We did indeed follow gaily in the footsteps of Jesus. The sparks of love He cast so generously into our souls and the strong, sweet wine He made us drink swept all the transient things of earth from our gaze and we breathed out words of love inspired by Him.

What wonderful talks we had every evening in our upstairs room! As we gazed out we saw the moon rise slowly above the trees and its silvery light pour over the sleeping world. The stars glittered in the dark blue of the sky and here and there a cloud drifted along blown by the night breeze. Everything drew our souls upwards to heaven. I think we were given many graces. As *The Imitation* says, God sometimes reveals Himself "in great light" or "appears veiled under signs and figures," and it was in this way that He disclosed Himself to us. But how light and transparent was the veil which hid Jesus from our eyes! Doubt wasn't possible and faith and hope were no longer needed, for love made us find on earth Him we sought: "When we were alone, He gave us His kiss, and now no one may despise us."

Such tremendous graces had to bear fruit and it was abundant. To be good became natural and pleasant for us. At first my face often betrayed the struggle I was having, but gradually spontaneous self-sacrifice came easily. Jesus said: "If ever a man is rich, gifts will be made to him, and his riches will abound." For every grace I made good use of, He gave me many more. He gave Himself to me in Holy Communion far oftener than I should have dared to hope. I had made it a rule to go very faithfully to every Communion allowed me by my confessor, but never to ask him to allow me more. In those days I hadn't the daring I have now, or I should have behaved quite differently, for I'm absolutely certain that people must tell their confessors of the longing they have to receive God. For He does not come down from heaven every day to lie in a golden ciborium: He comes to find another heaven which is infinitely dearer to Him — the heaven of our souls, created in His image, the living temples of the adorable Trinity!

Jesus, who saw what I wanted, moved my confessor to allow me to receive Holy Communion several times a week. I never said a word about what was going on in my soul. The path I trod was so bright and straight that I felt I needed no guide but Jesus. I considered spiritual directors were like mirrors which faithfully reflected the light of Jesus into souls, but I thought that God needed no intermediary where I was concerned. He dealt with me direct!

When a gardener takes trouble over fruit he wants to ripen early, it isn't because he wants to leave them hanging on the tree, but because he wants them to appear on a richly appointed table. It was the same reason that made Jesus shower His favours on His little flower. During His days on earth He exclaimed in a transport of joy: "I give thee praise that thou hast hidden all this from the wise and prudent, and revealed it to little children." As He wished to make His mercy evident through me and as I was small and weak, He stooped down to me and secretly taught me the secrets of His love. If scholars who had spent their lives in study had questioned me, I'm sure they'd have been amazed to come across a fourteen-year-old child who understood the secrets of perfection, secrets which all their learning couldn't reveal to them, for one has to be poor in spirit to understand them. As St. John of the Cross says: "I had neither guide nor light, except that which shone within my heart, and that guided me more surely than the midday sun to the place where He who knew me well awaited me." That place was Carmel, but before I could lie in the "shade cool to rest under" I had to go through many trials. Yet the divine call was so urgent that, if necessary, I'd have plunged through flames to follow Jesus.

Black Elk

(1863–1950)

In the late twentieth century, the name Black Elk became linked to a resurgence of interest in Native American history, culture, and spirituality. *Black Elk Speaks,* a version of his life by the poet John G. Neihardt, was first published in 1932, but it was reissued in paperback in 1961 and received vast attention and recognition from scholars and the general public as part of the resurgence of interest in Native American life.

Black Elk Speaks was based on Neihardt's interviews with this Sioux leader. Unfortunately, it was not good history. It was biased by Neihardt's own attachment to visions of Manifest Destiny for white settlers of North America and by his portrayal of Black Elk as a tragic figure, wistfully recalling his people's religious and folk ways of life. Apologists and advocates for the Native American way of life seized upon Black Elk as a symbol of a tradition that was lost but could be recovered and renewed.

Subsequent research has revealed a somewhat different version of Black Elk's life. In brief, as a young man Black Elk was regarded as a medicine man or holy man of the Oglala Lakota or Sioux. He was also a *heyoka* or "trickster" whose contrary ways of viewing the world fascinated others. However, when Black Elk was in his late thirties, he became a Christian through the work of Roman Catholic missionary priests. He spent much of the rest of his life as a lay catechist, traveling among his people as a teacher and exhorter of Christianity.

Considerable scholarly debate has erupted about the nature of Black Elk's conversion to Christianity — whether it was genuine and to what extent his adoption of Christianity represented a rejection of his Native American religious faith and practices. The debate is complicated by the fact that no first-hand account of his conversion exists; rather, the following account comes from his daughter. What does seem very clear is that, even though Black Elk probably did continue to practice some of the Native American traditions, he also became a respected Christian leader of his people.

One of his close friends and companions in his itinerant teaching was John Lone Goose, who is quoted in the latest and best book on this enigmatic leader by Michael F. Steltenkamp, *Nicholas Black Elk: Medicine Man, Missionary, Mystic* (2009):

> The priests gave him instructions in the faith and Nick said he wanted to teach God's word to the people. . . . [He] learned what the Bible meant, and that it was good. He said "I want to be a catechist the rest of my life. I want it that way from here on!" So he went around . . . all those districts. . . . Lots of people turned to the Catholic Church through Nick's work.
>
> He never talked about the old ways. All he talked about was the Bible and Christ. I was with him most of the time and I remember what he taught. He taught the name of Christ to Indians who didn't know it. The old people, the young people, the mixed blood, even the white man — everybody that comes to him, he teaches. . . .
>
> He was a pretty good speaker, and I think Our Lord gave him wisdom when he became a Christian. For even though he was kind of blind, his mind was not blind. And when he retired and was sick, he still taught God's word to the people. He turned Christian and took up catechist work. And he was still on it until he died. (pp. 102-103)

Black Elk's daughter Lucy flatly declared, "He sure was interested in that kind of life."

~

Beset with physical and emotional distress, Black Elk was spiritually restless in his role as a healer at the turn of the century. Respected elders came to his aid and provided counsel that offered the prospect of relief. Sam Kills Brave, especially, was instrumental in persuading Black Elk to reconsider what he was doing with his life.

Kills Brave was a principal leader of the reservation town of Manderson, South Dakota. He was a practicing Catholic, and the man who encouraged Black Elk to dispense with his yuwipi practice (the cer-

From Michael F. Steltenkamp, *Nicholas Black Elk: Medicine Man, Missionary, Mystic* (Norman, OK: University of Oklahoma Press, 2009), 90-91. Used with permission.

emony he performed in darkness, bound in a quilt, calling upon spirits). Kills Brave's advice was not taken lightly. It stayed with the medicine man as he answered a call one night in November of 1904 to doctor a young boy. In later years, Black Elk dramatically recounted what happened this night. Now regarded as his conversion experience, it is best understood as one incident in a process that had been ongoing for some time.

Family members found Black Elk's account both informative and amusing. For them, it was not a commentary on the confrontation of medicine men with missionary, but more the story of how their loved one became a catechist through the intervention of someone who became the family's respected friend — Father Joseph Lindebner (1845-1922). Black Elk's daughter, Lucy, provided the only account of her father's conversion experience, which occurred when he was in his late thirties:

> [He] walked over there carrying his medicine. . . . At that time, they walked those long trails if they didn't have a horse.
>
> When he got there, he found the sick boy lying in a tent. So right away, he prepared to doctor him. . . . My father was really singing away, beating his drum . . . when along came one of the black robes — Father Lindebner, Até Ptécela. . . .
>
> Father Lindebner had already baptized the boy and had come to give him the last rites. . . . He took whatever my father had prepared . . . and threw it all into the stove. . . . Then he took my father by the neck and said, "Satan, get out!" . . . Até Ptécela then administered the boy Communion and the last rites. He also cleaned up the tent and prayed with the boy.
>
> . . . He came out and saw my father sitting there looking downhearted and lonely — as though he lost all his powers. Next thing Father Lindebner said was "Come on and get in the buggy with me." My father was willing to go along, so he got in and the two of them went back to Holy Rosary Mission.
>
> Até Ptécela told the Jesuit brothers to clean him up, give him some clothes — underwear, shirt, suit, tie, shoes — and a hat to wear. . . . They fed him and gave him a bed to sleep in. My father never talked about that incident, but he felt it was Our Lord that appointed or selected him to do the work of the black robes. He wasn't bitter at all.

He stayed at Holy Rosary [the Catholic mission] two weeks preparing for baptism. . . . He gladly accepted the faith on December 6, 1904. . . . After he became a convert and started working for the missionaries, he put all his medicine practice away. He never took it up again.

. . . Black Elk's daughter told the conversion story as if reporting a humorous tale. She understood her father's encounter with Lindebner, whatever its particulars, as a special moment in her father's life. It marked the beginning of a vocation he wholeheartedly embraced.

Pandita Ramabai

(1858–1922)

Pandita Ramabai, born Ramabai Dongre, was born into poverty, suffering, and grief in Maharashtra, India. By the end of her enormously fruitful life, she was renowned as one of the singular Christians of India, a distinguished social reformer, a poet and scholar, and the first woman to translate the entire Bible.

Her father was a Brahmin priest, scholar, and reformer. A widower of forty-four, he married a girl who was only nine, and from this union came their daughter, Ramabai, another daughter, and a son. The family was very poor, for Ramabai's father was a pilgrim, devoted to a life of poverty. Yet, he was committed to educating his wife, a practice condemned by Hindus; and when Ramabai was born, she was taught as well. She was brilliant, and by the time she was twelve she had memorized 18,000 Sanskrit verses and their wisdom and had also mastered Marathi, into which she later translated the Bible. She eventually mastered eight other languages.

During the family pilgrimages, the family lived on what they could gain from charity. Ramabai encountered the awful suffering of child widows, women, and children in late nineteenth-century India. The practice of widow burning had been banned since 1828, but the plight of widows and children persisted. Her father — aged, infirm, and blind — died of starvation, followed by her mother and her sister. She and her brother continued on a pilgrimage, seeking spiritual peace. In 1878 in Calcutta, she attracted the attention of Bengali Brahmins, who were so impressed with her knowledge that they gave her the title of "Pandita," meaning "Learned." But during this pilgrimage, Ramabai became increasingly aware of the oppression of women and the way Hinduism contributed to their suffering.

As the following account makes clear, she was gradually introduced to

Christianity and acquired both a fervent faith in Christ and a clear vocation to relieve the plight of women, widows, and children in India. She published a widely read book in English, *The High Caste Hindu Woman,* and her royalties and her successful fund-raising in the United States made possible the founding of Mukti Mission (*mukti* means liberty, freedom, release, or salvation). Emblazoned on the mission's newsletter was the "Mukti Prayer Bell," with an engraving of the Liberty Bell in Philadelphia and the words, "Proclaim LIBERTY throughout all the Land unto all the inhabitants thereof — Lev. XXV, v. x."

Sometimes at the risk of her life, she traveled across India, rescuing impoverished women who were being forced into servitude and sexual oppression, and brought them to the Mukti Mission. There they received food, nurture, and education, and many went on to become accomplished women in India and around the world. Mukti was also the location of a revival in the burgeoning Pentecostal movement from 1905 to 1907, in which the women of Mukti had visions, fell into trances, and spoke in tongues. Ramabai defended this early manifestation of Pentecostalism as an expression of indigenous Indian Christianity, though she later backed off from her support.

Ramabai persisted in her work at Mukti, where it flourishes to the present day and provides housing, education, vocational training, and medical services for the poor, especially widows, orphans, and the blind. But during the last decades of her life, she began a translation of the Bible into Marathi. She first mastered Greek and Hebrew, and then worked on the texts and her translations wherever she went. Two years before her death, her own daughter, Manoramabai ("heart's joy") died. Ramabai became increasingly deaf, but she still pursued the Bible translation. The women of Mukti set the type for the Marathi translation, and she pored over the proofs. When she became gravely ill, she prayed to God for ten more days to finish the editorial work. Ten days later, she had completed her proofreading, and she died in her sleep on April 5, 1922.

Her name and reputation were suppressed in India because of her Christian faith, but in the late twentieth century her work and stature were raised up by Indian feminists. The government of India issued a commemorative postage stamp in 1989 to honor her.

Amritlal B. Shah categorically concludes, "Pandita Ramabai Sarawati was the greatest woman produced by Modern India and one of the greatest Indians in all of history. Her achievements as a champion of women's rights . . . remain unrivaled even after the lapse of . . . a century."

$\sim$

My father was a native of Mangalore District, but he chose a place in a dense forest on the top of a peak of the Western Ghats, on the borders of Mysore State, where he built a home for himself. This was done in order that he might carry on his educational work, and engage in devotion to the gods in a quiet place. He used to get his support from the rice fields and cocoanut plantations which he owned. The place he had selected for his home happened to be a sacred place of pilgrimage, where pilgrims came all the year round. He thought it was his duty to entertain them at his expense, as hospitality was a part of his religion. For thirteen years he stayed there and did his work quietly, but lost all his property because of the great expense he incurred in performing what he thought was his duty. So he was obliged to leave his home and lead a pilgrim's life.

My mother told me that I was only about six months old when they left their home. She placed me in a big box made of cane, and a man carried it on his head from the mountain top to the valley. Thus my pilgrim life began when I was a little baby. I was the youngest member of the family. My father, though a very orthodox Hindu and strictly adhering to caste and other religious rules, was yet a reformer in his own way. He could not see why women and people of Shudra caste should not learn to read and write the Sanskrit language and learn sacred literature, other than the Vedas. So he, at the risk of being excommunicated by the Brahmans, made up his mind to teach his wife, my mother, the Sanskrit language.

He found an apt pupil in my mother, who fell in line with his plan, and became an excellent Sanskrit scholar. She performed all her home duties, cooked, washed, and did all household work, took care of her children, attended to guests, and did all that was required of a good religious wife and mother. She devoted many hours of her time in the night to the regular study of the sacred Puranic literature and was able to store up a great deal of knowledge in her mind.

When I was about eight years old my mother began to teach me and continued to do so until I was about fifteen years of age. During these years she succeeded in training my mind so that I might be able to carry on my own education with very little aid from others. I did not know of any schools for girls and women existing then, where higher education

This account is excerpted from a pamphlet, *Pandita Ramabai: A Wonderful Life,* ed. J. J. Lucas (Madras and Allahabad: Christian Literature Society for India, 1926). The full text is still available as *A Testimony* or *My Testimony* in various editions.

was to be obtained. Ever since I remember anything, my father and mother were always travelling from one sacred place to another, staying in each place for some months bathing in the sacred river or tank, visiting temples, worshipping household gods and the images of gods in the temples, and reading Puranas in temples or in some convenient places.

The reading of the Puranas served a double purpose. The first and the foremost was that of getting rid of sin, and of earning merit in order to obtain Moksha (Salvation). The other purpose was to earn an honest living, without begging. My parents followed this vocation. We all read Puranas in public places. We never had to beg or work to earn our livelihood. We used to get all the money and food we needed, and more; what remained over after meeting all necessary expenses was spent in performing pilgrimages and giving alms to the Brahmans.

This sort of life went on until my father became too feeble to stand the exertion, when he was no longer able to direct the reading of the Puranas by us. Our parents had unbounded faith in what the sacred books said. They encouraged us to look to the gods to get our support. The sacred books declared that if people worshipped the gods in particular ways, gave alms to the Brahmans, repeated the names of certain gods and also some hymns in their honour, with fasting and performance of penance, the gods and goddesses would appear and talk to the worshippers, and give them whatever they desired.

We decided to take this course of meeting our temporal wants. For three years we did nothing but perform these religious acts. At last all the money which we had was spent, but the gods did not help us. We suffered from famine. The country too, *i.e.*, the Madras Presidency, where we lived at that particular time, had begun to feel the effects of famine. There was scarcity of food and water. People were starving all around, and we like the rest of the poor people, wandered from place to place. We were too proud to beg or to do menial work, and ignorant of any practical way of earning an honest living. Nothing but starvation was before us. My father, mother, and sister all died of starvation within a few months of each other. My brother and I survived and wandered about still visiting sacred places, bathing in rivers, and worshipping the gods and goddesses, in order to get our desire.

We had fulfilled all the conditions laid down in the sacred books and kept all the rules as far as our knowledge went, but the gods were not pleased with us, and did not appear to us. After years of fruitless service, we began to lose our faith in them and in the books which prescribed this course and held out the hope of a great reward to the worshippers of the gods.

We still continued to keep caste rules and worshipped gods and studied sacred literature as usual. We wandered from place to place, visiting many temples, bathing in many rivers, fasting and performing penance, worshipping gods, trees, animals, Brahmans, etc., for more than three years after the death of our parents and elder sister. We had walked more than four thousand miles on foot without any sort of comfort; sometimes eating what kind people gave us, and sometimes going without food, with poor coarse clothing, and finding but little shelter except in Dharma Shalas. We wandered from the south to the north as far as Cashmere, and then to the east, and went to Calcutta in 1878.

While staying in Calcutta we became acquainted with many learned Pandits. Some of them requested me to lecture to the Purdah women on the duties of women according to the Shastras. I had to study the subject well before I could lecture on it; so I bought the books of the Hindu law published in Calcutta. Besides reading them, I read other books which would help me in my work. While reading the Dharma Shastras I came to know many things which I never knew before. There were contradictory statements about almost everything. What one book said was most righteous, the other book declared as being unrighteous. While reading the *Mahābhārata* I found the following: "The Vedas differ from each other; Smritis, *i.e.,* books of sacred laws, do not agree with one another; the secret of religion is in some hidden place, the only way is that which is followed by great men."

This I found true of about everything, but there were two things on which all these books, the Dharma Shastras, the sacred epics, the Puranas and orthodox high caste men were agreed: that women of high and low caste, as a class, were bad, very bad, worse than demons, as unholy as untruth; and that they could not get Moksha as men. The only hope of their getting this much desired liberation from Karma and its results, *viz.,* countless millions of births and deaths and untold suffering, was the worship of their husbands. The woman has no right to study the Vedas and Vedanta, and without knowing them, no one can know the Brahma; without knowing Brahma no one can get liberation, *i.e.,* Moksha.

I had a vague idea of these doctrines of the Hindu religion from my childhood, but while studying the Dharma Shastras they presented themselves to my mind with great force. My eyes were being gradually opened, I was waking up to my own hopeless condition as a woman, and it was becoming clearer and clearer to me that I had no place anywhere as far as religious consolation was concerned. I became quite dissatisfied with myself, I wanted something more than the Shastras could give me, but I did not know what it was that I wanted.

One day my brother and I were invited by Keshab Chandra Sen to his house. He received us very kindly, took me to the inner part of the house, and introduced me to his wife and daughters. One of them was just married to the Maharaja of Cooch Behar, and the Brahmos and others were criticizing him for breaking the rule which was laid down for all Brahmos, *i.e.,* not to marry or give girls in marriage under fourteen years of age. He and his family showed great kindness to me, and when parting he gave me a copy of one of the Vedas. He asked if I had studied the Vedas. I answered in the negative, and said that women were not fit to read the Vedas and they were not allowed to do so. It would be breaking the rules of religion if I were to study the Vedas. He could not but smile at my declaration of this Hindu doctrine. He said nothing in answer, but advised me to study the Vedas and Upanishads.

New thoughts were awakening in my heart. I questioned myself why I should not study the Vedas and Vedanta. Soon I persuaded myself into the belief that it was not wrong for a woman to read the Vedas. So I began first to read the Upanishads, then the Vedanta, and the Veda.

I became more dissatisfied with myself. Having lost all faith in the religion of my ancestors, I married a Bengali gentleman of the Shudra caste.[1] My husband died of cholera within two years of our marriage, and I was left alone to face the world with one baby in my arms. I stayed in Bengal and Assam for four years in all and studied the Bengali language.

While living with my husband at Silchar, Assam, I had found a little pamphlet in my library. I do not know how it came there, but I picked it up and began to read it with great interest. It was St. Luke's Gospel in the Bengali language. As I had lost all faith in my former religion and my heart was hungering after something better, I eagerly learnt everything which I could about the Christian religion and declared my intention to become a Christian, if I were perfectly satisfied with this new religion. My husband, who had studied in a Mission School, was pretty well acquainted with the Bible, but did not like to be called a Christian.

---

1. Bepin Bihati Medhavi, M.A. See *Life of Pandita Ramabai* by Helen Dyer, p. 18.

Much less did he like the idea of his wife being publicly baptized and joining the despised Christian community.

I was desperately in need of some religion. The Hindu religion held out no hope for me: the Brahmo religion was not a very definite one. For it is nothing but what a man makes for himself. He chooses and gathers whatever seems good to him from all religions known to him, and prepares a sort of religion for his own use. The Brahmo religion has no other foundation than man's own natural light, and the sense of right and wrong which he possesses in common with all mankind. It could not and did not satisfy me: still I liked and believed a good deal of it that was better than what the orthodox Hindu religion taught.

After my husband's death, I left Silchar and came to Poona. Here I stayed for a year. The leaders of the reform party and the members of the Prarthana Samaj treated me with great kindness and gave me some help. Messrs. Ranade, Modak, Kelkar, and Dr. Bhandarkar were among the people who showed great kindness to me. Miss Hurford, then a missionary working in connexion with the High Church, used to come and teach me the New Testament in Marathi. I had at this time begun to study the English language, but did not know how to write or speak it. She used to teach me some lessons from the primary reading books, yet sometimes I was more interested in the study of the New Testament than in the reading books. The Rev. Father Goreh was another missionary who used to come and explain the difference between the Hindu and Christian religions. I profited much by their teaching.

I went to England early in 1883, in order to study and fit myself for my life work. When I first landed in England, I was met by the kind Sisters of Wantage, to one of whom I had been introduced by Miss Hurford at St. Mary's Home, in Poona. The sisters took me to their Home, and one of them, who became my spiritual mother, began to teach me both secular and religious subjects. I owe an everlasting debt of gratitude to her and to Miss Beale, the late Lady Principal of Cheltenham Ladies' College. Both of these ladies took great pains with me and taught me the subjects which would help me in my life. The instruction which I received from them was mostly spiritual. Their motherly kindness and deeply spiritual influence have greatly helped in building up my character. I praise and thank God for permitting me to be under the loving Christian care of these ladies.

The Mother Superior once sent me for a change to one of the branches of the Sisters' Home in London. The Sisters there took me to see the rescue work carried on by them. I met several of the women who had once been in their Rescue-Home, but who had so completely changed, and were so filled with the love of Christ and compassion for suffering humanity, that they had given their life for the service of the sick and infirm. Here for the first time in my life I came to know that something should be done to reclaim the so-called fallen women and that Christians, whom Hindus considered out-casts and cruel, were kind to these unfortunate women, degraded in the eyes of society.

I had never heard or seen anything of the kind done for this class of women by the Hindus in my own country. I had not heard anyone speaking kindly of them, nor seen anyone making any effort to turn them from the evil path they had chosen in their folly. The Hindu Shastras do not deal kindly with these women. The law commands that the king shall cause the fallen women to be eaten by dogs in the outskirts of the town. They are considered the greatest sinners, and not worthy of compassion.

After my visit to the Homes at Fulham, where I saw the work of mercy carried on by the Sisters of the Cross, I began to think that there was a real difference between Hinduism and Christianity. I asked the Sister who instructed me to tell me what it was that made the Christians care for and reclaim the "fallen" women. She read the story of Christ meeting the Samaritan woman, and His wonderful discourse on the nature of true worship, and explained it to me. She spoke of the Infinite Love of Christ for sinners. He did not despise them but came to save them. I had never read or heard anything like this in the religious books of the Hindus. I realized, after reading the fourth chapter of St. John's Gospel, that Christ was truly the Divine Saviour He claimed to be, and no one but He could transform and uplift the downtrodden womanhood of India, and of every land.

Thus my heart was drawn to the religion of Christ. I was intellectually convinced of its truth on reading a book written by Father Goreh and was baptized in the Church of England in the latter part of 1883 while living with the Sisters at Wantage. I was comparatively happy and felt a great joy in finding a new religion which was better than any other religion I had known before. I knew full well that it would displease my friends and my countrymen very much but I have never regretted having taken the step. I was hungry for something better than what the Hindu Shastras gave. I found it in the Christians' Bible and was satisfied.

Although I was quite contented with my newly-found religion, so far as I understood it, still I was labouring under great intellectual difficulties, and my heart longed for something better, which I had not found. I came to know after eight years from the time of my baptism that I had found the Christian *religion,* which was good enough for me; *but I had not found Christ who is the Life of the religion* and "the Light of every man that cometh into the world."

It was nobody's fault that I had not found Christ. He must have been preached to me from the beginning. My mind at that time had been too dull to grasp the teaching of the Holy Scriptures. The open Bible had been before me, but I had given much of my time to the study of other books about the Bible and had not studied the Bible itself as I should have done. Hence my ignorance of many important doctrines taught in it. I gave up the study of other books about the Bible after my return home from America and took to reading the Bible regularly. Following this course for about two years, I became very unhappy in my mind. I was dissatisfied with my spiritual condition. I took the Bible and read portions of it, meditating on the message which God gave me. There were so many things I did not understand intellectually. One thing I knew by this time, that I needed Christ, and not merely His religion.

There were some of the old ideas stamped on my brain: for instance, I thought that repentance of sin, and the determination to give it up, was what was necessary for forgiveness of sin; that the rite of baptism was the means of regeneration; that my sins were truly washed away when I was baptized in the name of Christ. These and such other ideas, which are akin to Hindu mode of religious thought, stuck to me. For some years after my baptism, I was comparatively happy to think that I had found a religion which gave its privileges equally to men and women; there was no distinction of caste, colour, or sex made in it. All this was very beautiful, no doubt. But I had failed to understand that we are "of God in Christ Jesus, who of God is made unto us wisdom, and righteousness, and sanctification and redemption." 1 Cor. i. 30.

I had failed to see the need of placing my implicit faith in Christ and His atonement in order to become a child of God by being born again of the Holy Spirit and justified by faith in the Son of God. My thoughts were not very clear on this and other points. I was desperate. I realized that I was not prepared to meet God, that sin had dominion over me, and I was not altogether led by the Spirit of God, and had not therefore received the Spirit of adoption, and had no witness of the Spirit that I was a child of God.

What was to be done? My thoughts could not and did not help me. I had at last come to an end of myself and unconditionally surrendered myself to the Saviour; and asked Him to be merciful to me, and to become my Righteousness and Redemption, and to take away all my sin. Only those who have been convicted of sin and have seen themselves as God sees them, under similar circumstances, can understand what one feels when a great and unbearable burden is rolled away from one's heart.

I shall not attempt to describe how and what I felt at the time when I made an unconditional surrender and knew I was accepted to be a child of God by adoption of Christ Jesus my Saviour. The Bible says that God does not wait for me to merit His love, but heaps it upon me without my deserving it. I looked to the blessed Son of God who was lifted up on the Cross and there suffered death, even the death of the Cross in my stead, that I might be made free from the bondage of sin and from the fear of death, and I received life. Oh the love, the unspeakable love of the Father for me, a lost sinner, who gave His Only Son to die for me! I have not merited this love, but that was the very reason why He showed it toward me. "Herein is love, not that we loved God, but that He loved us, and sent His Son to be the propitiation for our sins." 1 John iv. 9, 10.

What good news — for me a woman, a woman born in India, among Brahmans who hold out no hope for me and the like of me. The Bible declares that Christ did not reserve this great salvation for a particular caste or sex. No caste, no sex, no work, and no man was to be depended upon to get salvation, this everlasting life — but God gave it freely to any one and every one who believed on His Son Whom He sent to be the "propitiation for our sins."

And there was not a particle of doubt left as to whether this salvation was a present one or not. I had not to wait till after undergoing births and deaths for countless millions of times, when I should become a Brahman man, in order to get to know the Brahma. And then, was there any joy and happiness to be hoped for? No, there is nothing but to be amalgamated into Nothingless Shunya, Brahma.

The Holy Spirit made it clear to me from the Word of God that the salvation which God gives through Christ is present, and not something future. I believed it, I received it, and was filled with joy. I feel I must tell my fellow-creatures what great things the Lord Jesus has done for me, and I feel sure, as it was possible for Him to save such a great sinner as I am, He is quite able to save others. The only thing that must be done by me is to tell people of Him and of His love for sinners and His great power to save them.

Billy Sunday

(1862–1935)

Some thought he should have stuck to baseball or gone into the circus. But others, maybe as many as one hundred million, listened and watched with rapt attention as Billy Sunday belted out the gospel, punched sin in the nose, and thundered against the saloons.

In an age of famous revivalists and mass evangelism in tents and tabernacles, Billy Sunday developed his own distinctive style. Born into poverty in farmland Iowa, William Ashley Sunday joined the Chicago White Sox baseball team when he was about twenty and almost immediately seemed on his way to stardom. He excelled as a base runner, reportedly making the trip around the bases in fourteen seconds. He once won a game by stealing second, third, and home plate on three successive pitches. But Billy got religion, and his conversion changed not only his life but also his career. The baseball evangelist became an itinerant revivalist known all across the country. With his musical accompanist, Homer Rodeheaver, and his slide trombone, Billy Sunday tantalized enormous crowds, huddled together in hastily built wooden tabernacles. He was a born actor with an instinctive sense of the dramatic, a flair for local street-talk, and an uncanny ability to scare the daylights out of sinners. Lacking formal education, Billy Sunday invented his own down-to-earth preaching style, punctuated with lots of body language. "If the English language gets in my way," he said, "I tramp all over it." As for sin, he said, "I'll kick it as long as I've got a foot; and I'll fight it as long as I've got a fist. I'll butt it as long as I've got a head. I'll bite it as long as I've got a tooth."

There was a serious, no-nonsense side to Billy Sunday. He worked for the YMCA, was ordained a Presbyterian minister, made generous donations to charities, and advocated racial equality, women's suffrage, and sex education in the public schools.

Billy Sunday

A colorful figure, he made people laugh, and when they did, he said, he shoved the gospel down their throats when their mouths were open. If for some it seemed an unconventional method, for hundreds of others it worked.

~

Twenty-nine years ago I walked down a street in Chicago in company with some ball players who were famous in this world (some of them are dead now), and we went into a saloon.

It was Sunday afternoon and we got tanked up and then went and sat down on a corner. I never go by that street without thanking God for saving me. It was a vacant lot at that time.

We sat down on a curbing. Across the street a company of men and women were playing on instruments — horns, flutes and slide trombones — and the others were singing the gospel hymns that I used to hear my mother sing back in the old church, where I used to go to Sunday school.

And God painted on the canvas of my recollection and memory a vivid picture of the scenes of other days and other faces.

Many have long since turned to dust. I sobbed and sobbed, and a young man stepped out and said:

"We are going to the Pacific Garden Mission; won't you come down to the mission? I am sure you will enjoy it. You can hear drunkards tell how they have been saved and girls tell how they have been saved from the red light district."

I arose and said to the boys:

"I'm through. I am going to Jesus Christ. We've come to the parting of the ways," and I turned my back on them. Some of them laughed and some of them mocked me; one of them gave me encouragement, others never said a word.

Twenty-nine years ago I turned and left that little group on the corner of State and Madison streets and walked to the little mission and fell on my knees and staggered out of sin and into the arms of the Savior.

I went over to the West Side of Chicago, where I was keeping com-

---

This account of Billy Sunday's conversion is taken from a newspaper report of one of his sermons in *The Boston Herald*, December 4, 1916.

pany with a girl, now my wife, Nell. I married Nell. She was a Presbyterian, so I am a Presbyterian. If she had been a Catholic I would have been a Catholic — because I was hot on the trail of Nell.

The next day I had to go out to the ball park and practice. Every morning at 10 o'clock we had to be out there and practice. I never slept that night. I was afraid of the horse-laugh that gang would give me because I had taken my stand for Jesus Christ.

I walked down to the old ball grounds. I will never forget it. I slipped my key into the wicket gate and the first man to meet me after I got inside was Mike Kelley.

Up came Mike Kelley. He said, "Bill, I'm proud of you. Religion is not my long suit, but I'll help you all I can."

Up came Anson, the best ball player that ever played the game; Pfeffer, Clarkson, Flint, Jimmy McCormick, Burns, Williamson, and Dalrymple. There wasn't a fellow in the gang who knocked; every fellow had a word of encouragement for me.

That afternoon we played the old Detroit club. We were neck and neck for the championship. That club had Thompson, Richardson, Rowe, Dunlap, Hanlon, and Bennett, and they could play ball.

I was playing right field. Mike Kelley was catching and John G. Clarkson was pitching. He was as fine a pitcher as ever crawled into a uniform. There are some pitchers today — O'Toole, Bender, Wood, Mathewson, Johnson, Marquard — but I do not believe any one of them stood in the class with Clarkson. . . .

We had two men out and they had a man on second and one on third, and Bennett, their old catcher, was at bat. Charley had three balls and two strikes on him. Charley didn't hit a high ball. I don't mean a Scotch highball; but he could kill them when they went about his knee. I hollered to Clarkson and said: "One more and we got 'em."

You know every pitcher puts a hole in the ground where he puts his foot when he is pitching. John stuck his foot in the hole and he went clear to the ground.

Oh, he could make them dance. He could throw overhanded, and the ball would go down and up like that. He is the only man on earth I have seen do that. That ball would go by so fast that the batter could feel the thermometer drop two degrees as she whizzed by.

John went clear down, and as he went to throw the ball his right foot slipped and the ball went low instead of high.

I saw Charley swing hard and heard the bat hit the ball with a terrific boom. Bennett had smashed the ball on the nose. I saw the ball rise in the air and knew that it was going to clear over my head.

I could judge within 10 feet of where the ball would light. I turned my back to the ball and ran.

The field was crowded with people and I yelled: "Stand back!" and that crowd opened like the Red Sea opened for the rod of Moses.

I ran on and as I ran I made a prayer; it wasn't theological either, I tell you that. I said: "God, if you ever helped mortal man, help me to get that ball, and you haven't very much time to make up your mind, either."

I ran and jumped over the bench and stopped.

I thought I was close enough to catch it. I looked back and I saw it going over my head and I jumped and shoved out my left hand and the ball hit it and stuck.

At the rate I was going the momentum carried me on and I fell under the feet of a team of horses. I jumped up with the ball in my hand. Up came Tom Johnson. Tom used to be mayor of Cleveland.

"Here is $10, Bill. Buy yourself the best hat in Chicago. That catch won me $1500. Tomorrow go and buy yourself the best suit of clothes you can find in Chicago."

An old Methodist minister said to me a few years ago: "Why, William, you didn't take the $10 did you?"

I said: "You bet your life I did!"

Frank Flint, our old catcher, who caught for 19 years, drew $3200 a year on an average. He caught before they had chest protectors, masks and gloves.

I've seen old Frank Flint sleeping on a table in a stale beer joint, and I've turned my pockets inside out and said: "You're welcome to it, old pal."

He drank on and on and one day in winter he staggered out of a stale beer joint and stood on a corner, and was seized with a fit of coughing. The blood streamed out of his nose, mouth and eyes.

Down the street came a wealthy woman. She took one look and said: "My God, is it you, Frank?" and his wife came up and kissed him. "They telephoned me and I came." He said: "There's nothing in the life of years ago I care for now. I can hear the bleachers cheer when I make a hit that wins the game. But there is nothing that can help me out now; and if the umpire calls me out now won't you say a few words over me, Bill?"

Then he died.

He sat on the street corner with me drunk 29 years ago in Chicago, when I said: "Goodbye, boys, I'm through."

Men of Boston, did they win the game of life or did I?

Sun Chu Kil

(1869–1935)

The following is an edited and amended translation of Sun Chu Kil's life, taken from Deok Joo Rie, *Conversions of Korean Christians* (Institute for the History of Christianity in Korea, 2003). Our gratitude is owed to Professor Dae Young Ryu of Handong University who provided the text, and the Rev. Martin Han, pastor of the Korean Presbyterian Church of Louisville, Kentucky, who did the translation.

~

Sun Chu Kil is one of the foremost Christians in the first one hundred years of Korean Christian history. His life story — a dramatic conversion, the first graduate of the Presbyterian Seminary, the first ordained pastor, the champion of the Great Awakening in 1907 that set the character of the Korean church, one of the thirty-three members who signed the Declaration of Independence on March 1, 1919, and the leader of the nationwide revival from 1920 to 1930 based on his distinctive eschatological faith — is the story of the Korean church for a century. Indeed, Kil has often been called "the father of the Korean church."

Sun Chu Kil was born on March 15, 1869, the second son of a military officer's family in Anjoo, South Pyong Ahn Province. His parents were strict, and the mother was especially gifted in her knowledge of Chinese literature. He started learning Chinese characters and litera-

Adapted from Deok Joo Rhie, *Conversions of Korean Christians* (Institute for the History of Christianity in Korea, 2003). Used with permission.

ture from his mother when he was three. When he was seven, he entered a village schoolhouse to study classic Chinese books. He married when he was eleven, according to the tradition, and was hired by the local government at the age of thirteen.

Sun Chu Kil faced the first trial of his life when he was seventeen. Three brothers of a family who envied Kil's brother beat Kil instead half to death. Lawful resolution was almost impossible, because political power and bribes dominated at that time in Korea. His father was deeply upset and moved to Pyong Yang for revenge. Kil himself was deeply hurt by this injustice, and it threw his entire life off course. To make matters worse, he had to take care of his entire family. He began work at a store and owned one the following year. But he was not good at business. After running a store for a year, debt and a sense of failure overwhelmed him. Under the strain, his health deteriorated. This was the greatest trial of his life.

His wife rescued him from pessimism and his preoccupation with failure. He turned to the religious world since he was disillusioned with the present world. His wife suggested that he do a retreat at the Yongak Temple in Pyong Yang. There he first encountered Gwansung religion, which influenced a famous general in ancient China, and he began to see visions as he read its sacred book.

Sun Chu Kil met masters of Taoism and memorized some of its sacred books. He experienced peace in body and mind as he recited the sacred books. He decided to train himself in the rigors of Taoism. As he studied sacred books and prayed for a hundred days several times, he had a spiritual experience:

> As I trained myself with all my heart, I often heard the sound of a
> flute, which shook the room, or I was surprised by sounds, like a
> gun shooting. I was filled with joy that I found the truth through
> Zen training.

Kil continued to train himself with *Soo Cha Reok,* during which he drank seven cups of water at midnight to fill the water energy in the lower body, and *Yak Cha Reok,* which boosted energy with natural medicine. He also trained himself with many different exercises. As a result, he was able to jump over streams and break a log with his fist. He could even predict the short-term future. Eventually, he became known as the "Master Kil" in Pyong Yang. After ten years of training, he had what was regarded as some supernatural powers. However, Taoism did not fill his spiritual hunger.

Two events brought significant changes to Kil's life in 1895. One was meeting the American missionary Samuel A. Moffett, and the other was the tragedy of the Sino-Japanese War.

Moffett, based in Pyong Yang, began to evangelize Korean people in February 1893. The appearance of a Westerner became news among the people. Kil was curious about the Christian faith. He talked with Moffett and sent his close friend in Taoism, Jongsub Kim, to Moffett to find out about the new religion. Jongsub Kim himself became a Christian and tried to witness his faith to Sun Chu Kil, who was shocked. He was proud of Taoism, but his Taoist friend was converted. Kil feared the new religion, but at the same time he was deeply curious about Christianity. He began to read the Bible, but it didn't touch him at all. He decided to concentrate even more on the practice of Taoism.

Sun Chu Kil also experienced the Sino-Japanese War. The main battleground was Pyong Yang, where people suffered greatly. Korean people had to supply food for two foreign armies and were killed by their guns. Powerless people were plundered, evacuated, and killed by foreign soldiers. Kil was one of the refugees. He saw the predicament of ordinary people, and he couldn't do anything to change the situation even with his special powers from Taoist practice. He had recovered his health and found new supernatural power. People respected him. Some wanted to be his disciples. However, the truth that he found in Taoism could not protect the powerless and suffering people. After returning from being a refugee, he deeply felt his limitations in the ruins of Pyong Yang.

The Sino-Japanese War was a national trial for Koreans, but it was also a moment of progress in Christianity. Churches became refugee camps for the protection of people — their lives and their possessions. People came to the church for peace. When Kil returned to Pyong Yang, Jongsub Kim visited him more often to evangelize him. Jongsub Kim brought him a Christian newspaper and small booklets of Christian testimony, but Sun Chu Kil was not moved by them.

However, two of the books that Jongsub Kim gave to Sun Chu Kil made a significant impact on his conversion. They were *Pilgrim's Progress* and a catechism, translated by Moffett. These books increasingly opened his heart to Christianity. As Jongsub Kim gave him *Pilgrim's Progress,* he encouraged him to pray to God. Kil responded, "I already have *Sam Ryong Shin Kun* (the Three Spirits God King) in Taoism, and they are not much different from the God of Trinity in your faith. How can I pray to a different God?" Jongsub Kim said, "Then, pray to *Sam Ryong Shin Kun!*"

Sun Chu Kil prayed every day to *Sam Ryong Shin Kun,* "Let me know if Christianity is the truth or not." He also read *Pilgrim's Progress* and gradually developed a more positive attitude toward Christianity. One day Jongsub Kim visited him again.

> "How's your prayer to *Sam Ryong Shin Kun?*"
> "I am even more agonized."
> "Pray, then, to God the Father."
> "How can a human call God 'Father'?"
> "Forget the 'father,' then. Just pray to God!"

From then on, Kil prayed to God, instead of *Sam Ryong Shin Kun.* He asked God to let him know which one was the truth. This was what happened on the third day of his prayer.

> As I prayed in the dawn whether or not Jesus is the true Savior, I heard the clear sound of a flute, and the sound, like a loud gun shooting, which shook the room. And I heard from above, calling me three times, "Sun Chu Kil, Sun Chu Kil, Sun Chu Kil!" I trembled, and without lifting up my head, I said, "God the Father who loves me, forgive my sins and save me!" I cried out loud in tears. My body became hot, and I prayed fervently.

When Kil had a spiritual experience in Taoism, he had heard the sound of a flute and gun shot, but there were two significant differences. One is that he called to God as "Father," and the other is that he confessed his sins. As he called God "Father," he experienced God personally. In Taoism *Sam Ryong Shin Kun* were always absolute others and non-personal, neutral beings. But God in Christianity is the God who created human beings. God is related to and lives in humanity. Kil had asked, "How can a human call God 'Father'?," but in his conversion he called God "Father" and experienced the Spirit. This happened in the fall of 1896.

With Jongsub Kim, Kil went to Nuldarigol Church, which became Jangdaehyun Church or Central Presbyterian Church of Pyong Yang. He was baptized on August 15, 1896, by the missionary Graham Lee, and Kil eventually became the pastor of Central Presbyterian Church. He donated his land to the church, and a new building was constructed on the site.

After Sun Chu Kil's conversion, his life can be divided into two parts, and the dividing line is March 1, 1919. The first period from his conversion in 1896 to the March 1 movement in 1919 was the time when he devoted himself to forging a Christian faith with Korean traditions and forming the Korean nation in the Christian faith. After he was imprisoned and released in relation to the March 1 Independence Movement, however, he devoted himself to the revival movement based on his distinctive eschatological theology that focused on the imminent return of Christ.

During the first period, Sun Chu Kil was active both inside and outside of the church. After he was baptized, he traveled as an evangelist not only all over Pyong Yang but also in Pyong An Province and Hwang Hae Province. As a preaching elder, he also established the foundation of Jangdaehyun Church. He organized the women's group and was active in the liberation of women. He founded the Jesus School, which later became Soong Duk School, inside the church to teach nationalism based on the Christian faith. He started the practice of dawn prayer meetings, which became a seed of the Great Awakening in Korea. He became one of the first seven Korean graduates of the Presbyterian Seminary in 1907. He was ordained as a minister in the same year and became a founding member of Dok Presbytery of the Korean Presbyterian Church. His emphasis on mission and sending out missionaries from the Korean Presbyterian General Assembly left an enduring mark on the Korean Presbyterian Church and defined it as a missional church from its inception.

However, his most important activity was probably his role in the Great Awakening in 1907. It was initiated by missionaries in Pyong Yang, but the main actors were Korean Christians, including and most importantly Sun Chu Kil. His sermons quenched the spiritual thirst of the people and liberated them from moral bondage. The Awakening made the revival a central feature of Korean church life, and Kil was the premier revivalist.

Two distinctive features of the Great Awakening in 1907 were mass gatherings and Bible studies that called for confession of sins. Confession in the form of *Tongsung* prayer (all the people praying out loud) was an agonized expression of people crying out to God, and through such prayers they found great spiritual release. Bible studies inspired people to evangelize others, and churches grew rapidly.

The Great Awakening in 1907 was the turning point of Christianity in Korea. It was transformed from a Western religion to a religion deeply rooted in Korean tradition. Sun Chu Kil, the Taoist master turned Christian, was the core of that transformation.

Patterns of indigenous spiritual practice can be found in the Great Awakening. Dawn prayer meetings, which ignited the Great Awakening, are a traditional Korean spiritual practice, and they have since become one of the distinctive characteristics of Korean Christian piety. The *Tongsung* prayer is also unique in Korean churches. There were different types of offering in the Korean church in the early twentieth century. For instance, in the rice offering, women set aside a small amount of rice whenever they cooked rice. They gave the collected rice for an offering, instead of cash. There was also a day offering. Christians wrote a number of days on a piece of paper and gave it as an offering. On those promised days, they went out to evangelize. Such practices are unique in the Korean church, and they came out of the traditions of the Korean people.

Sun Chu Kil was a Christian not only for people but also for the nation. His most noticeable activity outside the church was to participate in creating the Pyong Yang branch of the Independence Club. On the opening day of the Independence Club, he urged national unity and renewal for the future of Korea. Although his spiritual passion was always greater than his concern for nationalism, his hope for the salvation of Korea as a nation was always his prayer concern.

In 1911 his brother was imprisoned and tortured by Japanese colonizers and died in 1918 in the aftermath of that torture. Through this incident Sun Chu Kil felt the evil power of Japan that took over Korea and oppressed powerless Korean people. His desire for national independence finally led him to join the thirty-three national delegates who signed the Declaration of Independence on March 1, 1919.

Sun Chu Kil's attitude toward indigenous Korean religions was expressed in his description of Taoism as "a rotten rope" and Christianity as "a new rope." However, his conversion may be less of a discontinuation and new start than a continuation and new transformation. Conversion is often interpreted as a total abandonment of a religion for a new beginning. However, conversion can be a continuation toward a new transformation and development, rather than discontinuation. Such a possibility can be found in Sun Chu Kil's conversion. He became a Christian, but he did not consider the old values and spirituality as meaningless. They were in him, and they continued to be reinterpreted in the light of Christianity. His old faiths — Confucianism, Taoism, and Buddhism — were illumined and reconstructed within the truth of Christianity. His early writings demonstrate this impulse that merged Korean traditions with Christian faith and practice.

His first Christian writing was *Indolence,* published in 1904. A small book of about 6,000 words, it was heavily influenced by *Pilgrim's Progress.* The story described people living in the castle of hope but eventually going to the land of eternity through the land of accomplishment. However, during the journey there is an animal called "Indolence" who interferes with each person's journey. The book has an element of enlightenment, and the narrative has the format of a traditional Korean storytelling book. In the last chapter of the book, Kil included saints of other religions among those who entered the land of accomplishment. This book was revised and enlarged with a new title, *All Things Well Accomplished,* in 1912. It became the basic structure of Kil's eschatology during his later years.

In summary, the early faith and theology of Sun Chu Kil were focused on the establishment of an indigenized Korean Christianity through Christian interpretation of Korean traditional faith and practices.

Kil's thinking underwent a significant shift after March 1, 1919. Although he was one of the thirty-three national delegates who signed the Declaration of Independence, his intention was not to declare independence but to appeal for it. There is some evidence that he was passive on the national independence issue. He excused himself from the March 1 declaration ceremony in Seoul because he was leading a revival. Unlike other national delegates who signed the Declaration of Independence, he spent only two years in prison and was eventually released and declared not guilty.

During his two years in prison, he is said to have read the book of Revelation eight hundred times and committed it to memory. It became the foundation of his eschatology and belief in the imminent second coming of Christ. He realized the limit of nonviolence and the peace movement of March 1. The national consciousness that sought peace and independence was mercilessly crushed by the force of Japanese imperialism. The Korean people's blood was shed, and they were powerless to overcome the massive power of evil. Right after he was re-leased from prison, he preached a sermon, "The Dawn of Peace." In it, he declared:

> World peace, it seems, does not exist for the weak. Ladies and gentlemen, do not let your heart be swayed, and from today on you must remember the words, "Peace kisses righteousness." One who fights on the foundation of justice should pray, "Open your hands from above and rule," so that the curtain of peace will open on the stage of righteousness.

He thought of the March 1 movement as an appeal to the Big Powers for the independence of Korea, but none showed their concern for such a small country. There was no peace for the powerless. Kil believed that the only way was for Christians to pray to God, "Reign over us from above to bring peace on earth." Divine intervention was the only way, and Kil saw that as the Second Coming of Jesus.

After Kil's release from prison, he traveled all over the country con-ducting revivals. He usually preached the passion of Christ at the dawn prayer service and eschatology in the afternoon. His extreme eschato-logical faith was his way of condemning the present world, and to a cer-tain extent it was escapism. The present age was evil and should be de-stroyed, and the New Jerusalem should be the only concern of faith. His theology was often criticized by young people who were influenced by socialism, and in 1926 there was even a movement by a group of young Christians to boycott him from the Jangdaehyun Church.

When Japan invaded Manchuria, Sun Chu Kil spoke out even louder about the Second Coming. He insisted that Christians move out of Pyong Yang, which was called "a Jerusalem in the orient," for Jerusa-lem would be destroyed. He even claimed, though he was not sure, that Jesus might come sometime in 1939 or in 2002.

Sun Chu Kil gave hope to the Korean people in their darkest hour with his preaching of "the New Jerusalem." Though partially blinded for nearly all his adult life, he provided a vision of a world to come that would be governed by God and not the forces of evil. While he was lead-ing a revival on November 25, 1935, he suffered a stroke and passed away the next day.

Evelyn Underhill

(1875-1941)

Behind the typical British reserve and formality in religion and theology, as in everything else, there has always been a mystical strain of inner spiritual questing.

Especially after the devastation of World War I, which decimated a whole British generation, there emerged here and there distinctive figures who looked for a peace that "passes understanding." Names like Dean Inge, Olive Wyon, Hywel Hughes, Baron Friedrich von Hügel, Charles Williams, and Evelyn Underhill became widely known among a select company of spiritual seekers.

Evelyn Underhill, "to the manor born" but with a nonreligious family background, came under the influence of the Austrian-born Baron Friedrich von Hügel. "The Baron," as she always referred to him, moved to England as a young boy and later was a recognized authority on the religious philosophy of spiritual experience. An ecumenical Catholic, he was eagerly read by Protestant theologians, and his major writings, such as *The Mystical Element of Religion* (2 vols., 1908; 1923), *Eternal Life* (1912), and *Philosophy of Religion* (1921; 1926), anticipated later theological trends. He insisted that the mystical, the institutional, and the intellectual spheres of religion be maintained in creative tension.

Under "the Baron's" gentle leading, Evelyn Underhill decided to profess her Christian faith by becoming a member of the Roman Catholic Church. She understood the formal ceremony to be an outward sign of her inner quest. But when, in 1907, Pope Pius X issued the decree against "Modernism" in the Catholic Church, she felt that her intelligence would be offended, and she joined the Church of England.

Through a series of intensely personal but scholarly volumes such as

Mysticism (1911) and *Worship* (1936), she became a leader, in spite of herself, of the spirituality movement both within and outside the churches. A self-contained person and something of a solitary contemplative, she was much in demand as a spiritual counselor and as a speaker at religious retreats.

The letters of Evelyn Underhill were edited after her death by the well-known writer Charles Williams. They reveal an alert mind at work and a sensitive spirit as critical of herself as of religious ideas. It is characteristic of her wry and witty side that among her "recreations" noted in the British *Who's Who* she listed "talking to cats."

~

General. I feel quite different from last year: but in ways rather difficult to define. Deeper in. More steady on my knees though not yet very steady on my *feet*. Not so rushing up and down between blankness and vehement consolations. Still much oscillation, but a kind of steady line persists instead of zigzags.

I have been trying all the time to shift the focus from feeling to will, but have not yet fully done it, and shall not feel safe till I have. The Christocentric side has become so much deeper and stronger — it nearly predominates. I never dreamed it was like this. It is just beginning to dawn on me what the Sacramental life really does involve: but it is only in flashes of miraculous penetration I can realise this. On the whole, in spite of blanks, times of wretched incapacity, and worse . . . I have never known such deep and real happiness, such a sense of at last having got my real permanent life, and being able to love without stint, where I am meant to love. It is as if one were suddenly liberated and able to expand all round. Such joy that it sometimes almost hurts. All this, humanly speaking, I owe entirely to you. Gratitude is a poor dry word for what I feel about it. I can't say anything.

The moral struggle is incessant, but there is a queer joy in it. I don't think I need bother much about that. Small renunciations are easier, but real ones still mean a fight. Nervous tension or exhaustion means a renewed attack of all my old temptations at full strength and

---

In June 1923, Evelyn Underhill wrote an extended letter to Baron Friedrich von Hügel, detailing the steps in her own spiritual pilgrimage. The letter is printed in the biography, *Evelyn Underhill,* by Margaret Cropper (London: Longmans, Green and Co., 1958), 105-10.

I feel invaded by hard, exasperated, critical, hostile, gloomy, and unloving inclinations.

Of course my will does not consent to these horrors: I do struggle with them: all the same they creep into my mind, and stick for days, another proof at bottom I am un-Christian still (for surely mere nervous tension should not mean these odious feelings?). And that lovely gentle suppleness and radiance I see in all my real Christian friends, and long for, I can't get. I don't think I have ever seen the deepest roots in myself of pride and self-love.

Many religious practices I still can't do, e.g. self-examination. I did make myself do a long written one at my retreat. . . . It looked horrid — but somehow I can't feel much interest in it, or that these curry combings matter much. So much more worth while and far more humbling, just to keep on trying to look at Christ. I know instantly by that when I do anything odious. Even before Holy Communion I don't do much else but, as it were, let that love flow over and obliterate everything. There is so little difference between one's best and worst. . . .

Last October, one day when I was praying, quite suddenly a Voice seemed to speak to me — with tremendous staccato sharpness and clearness. It only said one short thing, first in Latin and then in English! Please don't think I am going in for psychic automatisms or horrors of that sort. It has never happened again, and I don't want it to. Of course I know all about the psychological aspect and am not *hallucinated*. All the same, I simply cannot believe that there was not something deeper, more real, not me at all, behind. The effect was terrific. Sort of nailed me to the floor for half an hour, which went as a flash. I felt definitely called out and settled, once for all — that any falling back or leaving off, after that, will be an unpardonable treason. That sense has persisted — it marked a sort of turning point and the end of all the remorse and worry, and banging about. I feel now if all consolations went, it ought not to matter very much; though as a matter of fact derelictions are more painful and trying than they used to be, but have their purifying side. I feel a total, unconditioned dedication is what is asked, and it is so difficult. I shall never do it — one fails at every corner.

There have been other things since from time to time, but quite formless, and unspeakably sacred, penetrating, intimate, abasing. Now and then new lights, too, sort of intellectual intuitions, and quite clear of "sensible devotion"; but they are so quick and vast one can only retain about half. I would like to get away from the more vividly emotional feelings: I don't altogether trust them — but how can one help feeling pretty intensely. One has only one soul and body to do one's feelings with after all.

Prayer, at good times though still mixed, is more passive: a sort of inarticulate communion, or aspirations, often merely one word, over and over. Sometimes I wonder whether this is not too much taking the line of least resistance; but it is so wonderful, sweeps one along into a kind of warm inhabited darkness and blind joy — one lives in Eternity in that — can't keep at this pitch long, twenty minutes or so.

I do try to say a few psalms each day and do Intercessions, but one forgets everything then. Of course it's not always like this, often all distraction and difficulty.

As to Intercession, if I ask myself whether I would face complete spiritual deprivation for the good of another: e.g. to effect a conversion, I can't do that yet. So I have not got real Christian love: and the question is, can one intercede genuinely for anyone, unless ready to pay, if necessary, this price.

Special points (a) A terrible, overwhelming suspicion that after all, my whole "invisible experience" may be only subjective. There are times (of course when one has got it) when it seems incredible that these things could happen to me, considering what I have been. All the books say in unmortified beginners they are very suspicious, so what is one to think?

And further, there is the obvious fact that consolation and deprivation are somehow closely connected with the ups and downs of one's nervous and even bodily life. There is no real test: I may have deceived myself right through, and always studying these things, self-suggestion would be horribly easy. These doubts are absolute torture after what has happened. They paralyse one's life at the roots, once they lodge in the mind. I do not want to shirk *any* pain, but this does not seem a purifying kind. . . .

So far I have struggled through all right, generally by deliberate forced prayer — but this only shelves the problem, does not solve it — and it makes one feel horribly unsafe. The return to peace and certitude is wonderful; but how am I to know for certain this is not just some psychic mechanism? There are times when I wish I had never heard of psychology.

(b) Sometimes an even more terrifying visitation, when not *only* my own inner experience, but the whole spiritual scheme seems in ques-

tion. The universe seems cast iron and the deterministic view the obvious one. All the old difficulties come back: and especially that chasm between the universal and the historic experience of Christ. I see clearly that for me religious realism is the only thing that is any use. Generally I seem to have it with an increasingly vivid sense of real approach to, or communion with, God and Christ as objective facts, completely other than myself. I can't love on any other basis than this: even human love can't be spun from one's dreams, and this is far, far beyond that. But in these black times of doubt, it seems possible that one's hours of prayer and adoration simply react on oneself and produce the accompanying experiences. I have no guarantee of genuineness. It is not the awful moral struggle I knew I should have once I gave in; that has a sort of joy in it; those mental conflicts are just pure horror. . . .

Psycho-physical tangles. The parallels between nervous states and spiritual sensitiveness worry me: nerves and soul seem hopelessly mixed up; one thinks one is out of grace and finds it was only mental fatigue and impotence. Don't know how best to run my devotional life in nervous exhaustion. Often too stupefied to think, will, or love at all. I do keep my whole rule somehow — merely kneeling on a hard floor the proper time seems better than nothing — but the struggle to pray is fruitless then. This rule keeping tends to a sort of rigidity. I am restless and starved when my particular routine is upset. And during holidays, or when travelling, lecturing, etc., approximately a quarter of the year — I can't rely on keeping it. Often no privacy, no certain free time, safe from interruption: and the desperate struggle to get it at all costs induces a strain which is hostile to prayer. Lately, in fact, "holidays" have been periods of misery on this account. Of course, I never sacrifice Communions unless they are quite impossible — even these I cannot be sure of when we are yachting. What I want here is permission to be more flexible about the external rule and make up by taking every opportunity of quietude or of short aspirations, for any irregularity in long recollections. I believe I should do better like this and am sure it would not mean slackness. And there must be some way of super-naturalising one's active life when one can't have one's usual solitude and fixed adoration. After all it's not my choice that I have to be at other people's disposal the whole time. Could not one turn these conditions into something worth offering? . . .

Vocation. I feel great uncertainty as to what God chiefly wants of me. Selection has become inevitable. I can't meet more than half the demands made. I asked for more opportunity of personal service and have thoroughly been taken at my word! But there is almost no time or strength left now for study for its own sake; always giving or preparing addresses, advice, writing articles, trying to keep pace with work, going on committees and conferences — and with so little mental food I risk turning into a sort of fluid clergyman! More serious the conflict between family claims and duties and work is getting acute. My parents are getting old: they don't understand, and are a bit jealous of the claims on my life (especially as it's all unpaid work). I feel perhaps I ought to have more leisure for them, though I do see them nearly every day. But this could only be done by reducing what seems like direct work for God, or my poor people or something. I confess the work and the poor people are congenial: and idling about chatting and being amiable, when there is so much to be done, a most difficult discipline — so I can't judge the situation fairly. It is not a case of being needed in any practical sense: just of one's presence being liked, and one's duties slightly resented!

Albert Schweitzer

(1875–1965)

Early in his life, Albert Schweitzer realized that he had been graced much beyond his deserving. In fact, he did not yet know how gifted he was or how versatile his career would be. "From everyone to whom much has been given, much will be required" (Luke 12:48). Whether or not he had such a text in mind, Schweitzer's life was a deliberately dedicated payment of a debt as he tried to live his own version of the Christ-life.

Born in the Alsace region on the border between France and Germany, Schweitzer graduated from the University of Strasbourg, having specialized in philosophy and theology. He became principal of a theological college affiliated with the university and immediately plunged into several writing projects that were soon published.

The most important and controversial of all his works appeared in 1906 and was translated into English in 1910 as *The Quest of the Historical Jesus.* Upsetting the nineteenth-century liberal view of Jesus as a teacher of religious truths and a moral leader of humanitarian ideals, Schweitzer insisted on taking seriously the messianic eschatology of the Gospels.

For Schweitzer, the conclusion of the Christ story remained ambiguous. In giving himself, as the suffering servant, for the fulfillment of the kingdom, Jesus as the "One unknown" can only be known by those who respond to his invitation to "Follow me." Schweitzer was not given to work out a constructive Christology except in the one way that perhaps counts most, namely, by giving himself to serve others less fortunate.

In the meantime, Schweitzer was pursuing another career as a musicologist and an authority on J. S. Bach. He studied the organ in Paris and wrote a definitive edition on the music and religious meaning of Bach's chorales and cantatas.

In the same year, 1905, Schweitzer startled his friends and associates by announcing his intention to study medicine to become a missionary doctor in equatorial Africa. This decision emerged out of his early sense of gratitude and feeling of indebtedness. He was deeply disturbed by the radical difference between the gifts of civilization that the white peoples of the earth enjoyed and the abysmal poverty and disease of "the Black Continent."

The rest of the story is familiar, for it is one of the thrilling sagas of modern heroism and self-dedication. The hospital at Lambaréné, primitive but humane, became a symbol for all the world to see.

In 1928, Albert Schweitzer received the Goethe Prize, and in 1952 the Nobel Peace Prize. His last significant writing project involved a philosophy of civilization using "reverence for life" as his guiding principle.

Theologians and biblical scholars have continued to debate his views of the Christian gospel. The Paris Mission Society had doubts about his orthodoxy. But no one could question that this gifted and magnetic jungle doctor came closer than most to fulfilling the words of Jesus — "I was hungry and you gave me food, I was thirsty and you gave me something to drink, I was a stranger and you welcomed me, I was naked and you gave me clothing, I was sick and you took care of me" (Matt. 25:35-36).

On October 13th, 1905, a Friday, I dropped into a letter-box in the Avenue de la Grande Armée in Paris letters to my parents and to some of my most intimate acquaintances, telling them that at the beginning of the winter term I should enter myself as a medical student, in order to go later on to Equatorial Africa as a doctor. In one of them I sent in the resignation of my post as Principal of the Theological College of S. Thomas's, because of the claim on my time that my intended course of study would make.

The plan which I meant now to put into execution had been in my mind for a long time, having been conceived so long ago as my student days. It struck me as incomprehensible that I should be allowed to lead such a happy life, while I saw so many people around me wrestling with

---

The passage describing his decision to go to Africa comes from the chapter, "I Resolve to Become a Jungle Doctor," in his *Out of My Life and Thought: An Autobiography,* trans. C. T. Campion (New York: Henry Holt & Co., 1933), 102-18. Reprinted by permission.

care and suffering. Even at school I had felt stirred whenever I got a glimpse of the miserable home surroundings of some of my schoolfellows and compared them with the absolutely ideal conditions in which we children of the parsonage at Günsbach lived. While at the University and enjoying the happiness of being able to study and even to produce some results in science and art, I could not help thinking continually of others who were denied that happiness by their material circumstances or their health. Then one brilliant summer morning at Günsbach, during the Whitsuntide holidays — it was in 1896 — there came to me, as I awoke, the thought that I must not accept this happiness as a matter of course, but must give something in return for it. Proceeding to think the matter out at once with calm deliberation, while the birds were singing outside, I settled with myself before I got up, that I would consider myself justified in living till I was thirty for science and art, in order to devote myself from that time forward to the direct service of humanity. Many a time already had I tried to settle what meaning lay hidden for me in the saying of Jesus: "Whosoever would save his life shall lose it, and whosoever shall lose his life for My sake and the Gospel's shall save it." Now the answer was found. In addition to the outward, I now had inward happiness.

What would be the character of the activities thus planned for the future was not yet clear to me. I left it to circumstances to guide me. One thing only was certain, that it must be directly human service, however inconspicuous the sphere of it.

I naturally thought first of some activity in Europe. I formed a plan for taking charge of abandoned or neglected children and educating them, then making them pledge themselves to help later on in the same way children in similar positions. When in 1903, as Warden of the theological hostel, I moved into my roomy and sunny official quarters on the second floor of the College of S. Thomas, I was in a position to begin the experiment. I offered my help now here, now there, but always unsuccessfully. The constitutions of the organizations which looked after destitute and abandoned children made no provision for the acceptance of such voluntary co-operation. For example, when the Strassburg Orphanage was burnt down, I offered to take in a few boys, for the time being, but the Superintendent did not even allow me to finish what I had to say. Similar attempts which I made elsewhere were also failures. . . .

One morning in the autumn of 1904 I found on my writing-table in the College one of the green-covered magazines in which the Paris Missionary Society reported every month on its activities. A certain Miss Scherdlin used to put them there knowing that I was specially interested in this Society on account of the impression made on me by the letters of one of its earliest missionaries, Casalis by name, when my father read them aloud at his missionary services during my childhood. That evening, in the very act of putting it aside that I might go on with my work, I mechanically opened this magazine, which had been laid on my table during my absence. As I did so, my eye caught the title of an article: "Les besoins de la Mission du Congo" ("The needs of the Congo Mission").

It was by Alfred Boegner, the President of the Paris Missionary Society, an Alsatian, and contained a complaint that the Mission had not enough workers to carry on its work in the Gaboon, the northern province of the Congo Colony. The writer expressed his hope that his appeal would bring some of those "on whom the Master's eyes already rested" to a decision to offer themselves for this urgent work. The conclusion ran: "Men and women who can reply simply to the Master's call, 'Lord, I am coming,' those are the people whom the Church needs." The article finished, I quietly began my work. My search was over.

My thirtieth birthday a few months later I spent like the man in the parable who "desiring to build a tower, first counts the cost whether he have wherewith to complete it." The result was that I resolved to realize my plan of direct human service in Equatorial Africa.

With the exception of one trustworthy friend no one knew of my intention. When it became known through the letters I had sent from Paris, I had hard battles to fight with my relations and friends. Almost more than with my contemplated new start itself they reproached me with not having shown them so much confidence as to discuss it with them first. With this side issue they tormented me beyond measure during those difficult weeks. That theological friends should outdo the others in their protests struck me as all the more preposterous, because they had, no doubt, all preached a fine sermon — perhaps a very fine one — showing how S. Paul, as he has recorded in his letter to the Galatians, "conferred not with flesh and blood" beforehand about what he meant to do for Jesus.

My relatives and my friends all joined in expostulating with me on the folly of my enterprise. I was a man, they said, who was burying the talent entrusted to him and wanted to trade with false currency. Work among savages I ought to leave to those who would not thereby be compelled to leave gifts and acquirements in science and art unused. Widor, who loved me as if I were his son, scolded me as being like a general who wanted to go into the firing-line — there was no talk about trenches at that time — with a rifle. A lady who was filled with the modern spirit proved to me that I could do much more by lecturing on behalf of medical help for natives than I could by the action I contemplated. That saying from Goethe's *Faust* ("In the beginning was the Deed") was now out of date, she said. To-day propaganda was the mother of happenings.

In the many verbal duels which I had to fight, as a weary opponent, with people who passed for Christians, it moved me strangely to see them so far from perceiving that the effort to serve the love preached by Jesus may sweep a man into a new course of life, although they read in the New Testament that it can do so, and found it there quite in order. I had assumed as a matter of course that familiarity with the sayings of Jesus would produce a much better appreciation of what to popular logic is non-rational, than my own case allowed me to assert. Several times, indeed, it was my experience that my appeal to the act of obedience which Jesus' command of love may under special circumstances call for, brought upon me an accusation of conceit, although I had, in fact, been obliged to do violence to my feelings to employ this argument at all. In general, how much I suffered through so many people assuming a right to tear open all the doors and shutters of my inner self!

As a rule, too, it was of no use allowing them, in spite of my repugnance, to have a glimpse of the thoughts which had given birth to my resolution. They thought there must be something behind it all, and guessed at disappointment at the slow growth of my reputation. For this there was no ground at all, seeing that I had received, even as a young man, such recognition as others usually get only after a whole life of toil and struggle. Unfortunate love experiences were also alleged as the reason for my decision.

I felt as a real kindness the action of persons who made no attempt to dig their fists into my heart, but regarded me as a precocious young man, not quite right in his head, and treated me correspondingly with affectionate mockery.

I felt it to be, in itself, quite natural that relations and friends should put before me anything that told against the reasonableness of my plan. As one who demands that idealists shall be sober in their views, I was conscious that every start upon an untrodden path is a venture which only in unusual circumstances looks sensible and likely to be successful. In my own case I held the venture to be justified, because I had considered it for a long time and from every point of view, and credited myself with the possession of health, sound nerves, energy, practical common sense, toughness, prudence, very few wants, and everything else that might be found necessary by anyone wandering along the path of the idea. I believed myself, further, to wear the protective armour of a temperament quite capable of enduring an eventual failure of my plan. . . .

What seemed to my friends the most irrational thing in my plan was that I wanted to go to Africa, not as a missionary, but as a doctor, and thus when already thirty years of age burdened myself as a beginning with a long period of laborious study. And that this study would mean for me a tremendous effort, I had no manner of doubt. I did, in truth, look forward to the next few years with dread. But the reasons which determined me to follow the way of service I had chosen, as a doctor, weighed so heavily that other considerations were as dust in the balance.

I wanted to be a doctor that I might be able to work without having to talk. For years I had been giving myself out in words, and it was with joy that I had followed the calling of theological teacher and of preacher. But this new form of activity I could not represent to myself as being talking about the religion of love, but only as an actual putting it into practice. Medical knowledge made it possible for me to carry out my intention in the best and most complete way, wherever the path of service might lead me. In view of the plan for Equatorial Africa, the acquisition of such knowledge was especially indicated because in the district to which I thought of going a doctor was, according to the missionaries' reports, the most needed of all needed things. They were always complaining in their magazine that the natives who visited them in physical suffering could not be given the help they desired. To become one day the doctor whom these poor creatures needed, it was worth while, so I judged, to become a medical student. Whenever I was inclined to feel that the years I should have to sacrifice were too long, I reminded myself that Hamilcar and Hannibal had prepared for their march on Rome by their slow and tedious conquest of Spain.

There was still one more point of view from which I seemed directed to become a doctor. From what I knew of the Parisian Missionary Society, I could not but feel it to be very doubtful whether they would accept me as a missionary. . . .

The kindly Director of the Mission, Monsieur Boegner, was much moved at finding that someone had offered to join the Congo Mission in answer to his appeal, but at once confided to me that serious objections would be raised to my theological standpoint by members of the Committee, and that these would have to be cleared away first. My assurance that I wanted to come "merely as a doctor" lifted a heavy weight from his mind, but a little later he had to inform me that some members objected even to the acceptance of a mission-doctor, who had only correct Christian love, and did not, in their opinion, hold also the correct Christian belief. However, we both resolved not to worry about the matter too much so long beforehand, and relied on the fact that the objectors still had some years to wait during which they might be able to attain to a truly Christian reasonableness.

No doubt the more liberal Allgemeine Evangelische Missionsverein (General Union of Evangelical Missions) in Switzerland would have accepted me without hesitation either as missionary or doctor. But as I felt my call to Equatorial Africa had come to me through the article in the Paris Mission magazine, I felt I ought to try to join that Mission, if possible, in its activities in that colony. Further, I was tempted to persist in getting a decision on the question whether, face to face with the Gospel of Jesus, a missionary society could justifiably arrogate to itself the right to refuse to the suffering natives in their district the services of a doctor, because in their opinion he was not sufficiently orthodox.

But over and above all this, my daily work and daily worries, now that I was beginning my medical course, made such demands upon me, that I had neither time nor strength to concern myself about what was to happen afterwards.

E. Stanley Jones

(1884–1973)

A born evangelist, Stanley Jones was twice-born, and when he caught a vision of his missionary ministry, he was ever on the move.

Eli Stanley Jones began his evangelistic career with high castes in India. He developed the so-called Christian Ashram, a kind of discussion commune to which church leaders were invited to live together for a time of shared experiences. His Round Table Conference plan extended the format to include representatives of other religions, and his later interest in America in the "Federated" church proposal was still another attempt at innovative dialogue.

In 1925, he wrote *The Christ of the Indian Road,* a widely popular book that was translated into twenty languages and has sold over a million copies. Fiercely independent and somewhat of a loner in private, Jones made his own programs and was in constant demand as a speaker, especially to young people in college. Self-effacing and modest, he magnified Christ and always spoke with enthusiasm about the power of the gospel.

In later years, he became more involved in the social witness of Christianity, arranging in India for mobile dispensary trucks. He believed that Christianity was "the answer" to communism and wrote a much-read book called *Christ's Alternative to Communism* (1934). A pacifist and an advocate for home rule for India, Jones was often criticized by British government officials and even by American missionaries who felt uncomfortable with his free-wheeling methods. But his influence on behalf of a native and indigenous Indian Christianity was decisive and substantial at the time.

Surprised to be elected a Methodist bishop in 1928, Stanley Jones resigned in favor of his missionary vocation. Those who knew him felt he would make a good church administrator. But he thought otherwise, and the gospel was heard in many strange and unusual places because of his decision.

E. Stanley Jones

~

I am an ordinary man doing extraordinary things because I'm linked with the extraordinary. But apart from this I am very ordinary. And worse. A woman put it this way: "Apart from the Holy Spirit, Brother Stanley would be a mess." She was right. But with the Holy Spirit I am not a mess, but a message, for I have a message. This is not boasting. It is witnessing, witnessing to Another. To say anything else would be a false humility which is concealed pride.

How did it all begin? My first remembered contact with religion was when, as a little boy, I went to the Sunday school at Frederick Avenue Methodist Church, South, in Baltimore, dressed in a brand new suit. To call attention to my new suit, and me, I took a collection plate and began to pass it around before the grown-ups standing chatting. I didn't hope to get any money. I hoped to collect compliments for my new suit and incidentally for myself. Hardly an auspicious beginning with religion. And yet I had unwittingly run into the central problem in religion — the problem of the self-assertive self.

My second crisis contact with religion was when, about ten years later, at the age of fifteen, I was in the gallery of the Memorial Church, with a group of boys, mostly my chums. The speaker was an Englishman from John Bunyan's church in England. He was a man of God, and at the close of his address he pointed his finger to where we were seated and said, "Young men, Jesus said, 'He that is not with me is against me.'" It went straight to my heart. I knew I wasn't with him, but I didn't want to be against him. It shook me. I turned to my chum and said: "I'm going to give myself to Christ. Will you?" He replied: "No, I'm going to see life first." Then I saw that I would have to go alone, and did. I climbed over the young men, went down the steps and up the aisle to the altar, and took my place among the seekers. I felt undone and wept — wept because I was guilty and estranged. I fumbled for the latchstring of the Kingdom of God, missed it, for they didn't tell me the steps to find. I stood up at the close when they asked if it was all right with us. I wanted the Kingdom of God, wanted reconciliation with my heavenly Father, but took church membership as a substitute. My

---

From E. Stanley Jones, *A Song of Ascents: A Spiritual Autobiography* (Nashville: Abingdon Press, 1968), 26-33. Copyright © 1968 by Abingdon Press and used by permission.

mother came into my room next morning and silently kissed me before I got out of bed. Her son was a Christian. But I soon found I wasn't. I felt religious for a few weeks, and then it all faded out and I was back again exactly where I was before, the springs of my character and my habit formation unchanged. I had been horizontally converted, but not vertically. I was outwardly in, but not inwardly in. It was a sorry impasse. I could have lived out my life on that level the balance of my days, a cancelled-out person, neither here nor there.

But as I look back, I am not sorry I went through that half-conversion which was a whole failure. For the fact that I got out of that failure into the real thing may be used to encourage those who have settled down to a compromised stalemate, dull, listless, and with no note of victory. They, too, can get into the real things. So my failure can be used to help others to victory.

The real thing came two years later. An evangelist, Robert J. Bateman, came to Memorial Church. Through his rough exterior I saw there was reality within. He was a converted alcoholic, on fire with God's love. I said to myself, "I want what he has." This time I was deadly serious. I was not to be put off by catch phrases and slogans. I wanted the real thing or nothing. No halfway houses for me; I wanted my home. For three days I sought. During those three days I went to the altar twice. On one of those times my beloved teacher, Miss Nellie Logan, knelt alongside me and repeated John 3:16 this way: "God so loved Stanley Jones, that he gave his only begotten Son, that if Stanley Jones will believe on him he shall not perish, but have everlasting life." I repeated it after her, but no spark of assurance kindled my darkened heart. The third night came; before going to the meeting I knelt beside my bed and prayed the sincerest prayer I had prayed so far in my life. My whole life was behind that simple prayer: "O Jesus, save me tonight." And he did! A ray of light pierced my darkness. Hope sprang up in my heart. I found myself saying, "He's going to do it." I now believe he had done it, but I had been taught that you found him at an altar of prayer. So I felt I must get to the church to an altar of prayer. I found myself running the mile to the church. The eagerness of my soul got into my body. I was like Christian running from the City of Destruction to the Celestial City. I went into the church and took the front seat, a thing I had never done before. But I was all eagerness for the evangelist to stop speaking, so I could get to that altar of prayer. When he did stop, I was the first one there. I had scarcely bent my knees when Heaven broke into my spirit. I was enveloped by assurance, by acceptance, by reconciliation. I grabbed the man next to me by the shoulder and said: "I've got it." "Got it?" What did I mean? I see now it was not an "it": it was a him. I had him — Jesus — and he had me. We had each other. I belonged. My estrangement, my sense of orphanage were gone. I was reconciled. As I rose from my knees, I felt I wanted to put my arms around the world and share this with everybody. Little did I dream at that moment that I would spend the rest of my life literally trying to put my arms around the world to share this with everybody. But I have. This was a seed moment. The whole of my future was packed into it.

Crude? No, creative. Emotional? It took an emotional upheaval to carry me across from a self-preoccupied life to a Christ-preoccupied life. The center of being was changed from self to Savior. I didn't try by an act of will to give up my sins — they were gone. I looked into his face and was forever spoiled for anything that was unlike him. The whole me was converted. There was nothing the same except my name. It was the birthday of my soul. Life began there. Note I say "began" — the whole of my life has been an unfolding of what was infolded in that moment....

So a sense of the deepest gratitude a human is capable of knowing takes possession of me when I think of what I would have been had conversion not intervened and turned life into new channels. When the Memorial Church moved farther out the Frederick Road to a new site, they cut the altar rail where I knelt and was converted and made it into a prayer desk with an inscription on it: "At this spot Stanley Jones knelt and gave himself to Christ," and invited others to do the same. Tradition says that Zacchaeus used to go and water the sycamore tree in which he first met the Lord. I can understand that; I go periodically to that spot and water it with my tears of gratitude, for there "I first saw the light, and the burden of my heart rolled away."

He put a Song in my heart, for I had something to sing about. Many undertones and overtones have enriched that Song, but there I caught the standard note — "Jesus," a Savior — from what I didn't want to be to what I wanted to be. The United States Government strikes a standard note in Washington every day to let people tune their off-tune instruments again. From the day I was given the standard note to this day, sixty-six years later, I have been sounding that "note" through all the world. And I hope my last gasp will be, "I commend my Savior to you."

Toyohiko Kagawa

(1888–1960)

Japanese pacifist, Christian reformer, labor activist, novelist, and man of letters — Toyohiko Kagawa was, according to historian Richard Henry Drummond, "undoubtedly one of the greatest men of the twentieth century and one of the most creative persons in Japanese history in the area of social and political reform."

Born in Kobe, Kagawa's father was a highly successful businessman and an influential figure in Japanese politics. His mother was a concubine. Both of his parents died early in his life, so he was reared by his father's wife. The family suffered severe financial problems, and Kagawa was mistreated and shunned by other members of his erstwhile family. His own travail was traumatic and deep, and it gave him a life-long identification with the pain and suffering of others and a solidarity with the poor and outcast.

He was sent away to school, and there he was befriended by two Presbyterian missionaries, H. W. Myers and C. A. Logan, who opened their homes to him and provided him with the love he had yearned for in his childhood. Years later, in speaking of these missionary teachers, Kagawa wrote, "Two homes which have taught me what love means are the homes of Dr. Logan and Dr. Myers. It is not the Bible alone which has taught me what Christianity means but the love of these two homes. When tired of the battle and with no place to go, these two homes were open to me and a welcome always awaited me. These people brought me up as one of their own children."

The following narrative by Kagawa is a description of his pilgrimage from being a shunned child to a child of God and an advocate for the poor. What it does not cover is the rest of his remarkable life. He traveled to the United States and received two degrees — a B.D. from Princeton Theological Seminary and an M.A. from Princeton University. He shocked Japan with some of the earliest findings about the depths of Japanese poverty in his *Researches in the Psychology of the Poor*, including illicit prostitution, informal marriages, the selling of children, and infanticide. He became a Christian socialist and worked to unionize Japanese workers. He was a pacifist and a firm believer in the principle of nonviolence, which led him to oppose Japanese militarization and Japan's role in World War II. And all the while, he kept writing — more than 150 books — amid heavy criticism and occasional imprisonment by Japanese authorities.

He was twice nominated for the Nobel Prize in Literature and twice nominated for the Nobel Peace Prize. After he died, he was honored with the second highest tribute in Japan, induction into the Order of the Sacred Treasure.

Throughout his remarkable life, Kagawa insisted that he was primarily a Christian evangelist. All of his work for the laboring poor, for social justice, and for peace sprang from his fundamental commitment that this was the way of Christ. The core of his beliefs was the Sermon on the Mount, which Kagawa said "is the highest standard for human conduct; it is the highest example of human art. The inner room of all religion is there revealed. It is there that one discovers both the starting-point and the conclusion of all social conversion movements."

He agreed with Marxist social critiques, but as he said, "Communism's only power is to diagnose some of the ills of disordered society. It has no cure. It creates only an infantile paralysis of the social order."

The heart of Christianity, he declared, is life with the lost. "The Jesus religion is a sewage gatherer. We Christians must be refuse-gatherers, cleaning up the dirt left by others. If there are those among us who say they don't like to touch refuse, let them leave Christianity. Followers of Christ are those who must gather up the 'unclean.' This is called redemption — cleaning up the nasty dirty places — the Cross! Not knowing this, the Jesus-religion is often thought of as being very fine and fashionable — an 'elegant religion.' But it is not the least bit elegant to go out and gather the scum of the earth. Is there no one among us who would be willing to be Christ's refuse-gatherer?"

A Presbyterian minister tells the story of a meeting where Kagawa was a principal speaker. When it came time for Kagawa to address the gathering, he was nowhere to be seen. Leaders searched the building and finally found him — cleaning up the men's bathroom. Kagawa once said, "I read in a book that a man called Christ went about doing good. It is very disconcerting to me that I am so easily satisfied with just going about."

When I was a boy, Christianity was almost unknown in Japan. I was born in 1888, just sixteen years after freedom of faith had been declared. My father was one of the secretaries of the Privy Council of the Emperor. He had been made governor of two provinces and vice-president and governor over a third. In those days gentlemen could keep many wives, and I am sorry to say my father had two wives. My real mother was the concubine of my father. She was a *geisha* girl and she died when I was four. My father died just a few months before my mother's death, and as the first wife had no children I was adopted by her to inherit my father's estate. So I moved into the big house without any sort of love.

We had many rooms in the house and many servants. Our ancestors ruled over nineteen villages in the feudal system, and we were the wealthiest family in the village. We owned a factory and manufactured indigo, and we also manufactured some wine and had many fields.

My stepmother and her mother, who also lived with us, did not seem pleased to have me there. They always acted as if I were an intruder, an interloper. I lived in a big house without any love. So I always pretended I wasn't there. I would go out among the flowers and the bamboo trees in the garden, or out to the fields to work with the men, or into the storeroom to study all the relics — suits of armor and swords and shields — that my ancestors used in the feudal system. But I was very lonely as a child. I was put in school when I was four years and nine months of age. The regulations required six years of age, but because of my family an exception was made. All my schoolmates were older than I was, so even there I was considered an outsider.

The villagers had the terrible habit of gambling. I had to mix up with them so I became an expert gambler. I studied Buddhism and Confucianism and these said I should be a good boy. I tried to be a good boy, but I couldn't. When I was eleven I was sent away from home to a high school of the government. I lived there in the dormitory. Senior students of the upper class got drunk and went to bad places — to licensed quarters of public prostitution — but I attended biology classes instead. They told me there that the theory of evolution was true; that I was descended from a monkey. So then I discovered the reason why I was a bad boy: I was a descendant of the monkey!

Excerpted with permission from Emerson O. Bradshaw, *Unconquerable Kagawa* (St. Paul, MN: Macalester Park Publishing Co., 1952), 79-84.

I was dejected and I went around with my chin on my chest. One day I was walking down the street and there was a tent. Hymn singing was coming from the inside. It was a vacation Bible school. I went in. Dr. C. A. Logan, an American missionary from Virginia, was preaching. He was telling about love and the many sacrifices Christ made for all mankind, and it brought joy into my heart.

Dr. Logan introduced me to Dr. H. W. Myers, and I went to him to study English. He said to me: "Mr. Kagawa, I am willing to help you study English, but it will help if you memorize a few verses from the Sermon on the Mount." When I began to study these wonderful verses from the Sermon on the Mount I discovered that the creator of the universe is my Father in Heaven. Being an orphan, I discovered that God is my Father. Oh, I was happy!

"Consider the lilies of the field, how they grow!" These lines I could not forget; they kept repeating themselves over and over in my heart. "They toil not, neither do they spin; and yet I say unto you that even Solomon in all his glory was not arrayed like one of these. Wherefore, if God so clothe the grass of the field, which today is, and tomorrow is cast into the oven, shall he not much more clothe you, O, ye of little faith? Therefore, take no thought, saying, What shall we eat? or What shall we drink? or Wherewithal shall we be clothed? for your Heavenly Father knoweth that you have need of all these things. But seek ye first the kingdom of God, and His righteousness, and all these things shall be added unto you."

When I read these verses life took on new meaning, and the flowers everywhere seemed to blossom. I knew that what I read was true, so in secret I began to pray to God.

At that time I had gone to live with my uncle. He was president of a railroad company, also president of a steamship company. He hated Christianity because he knew the history of the Christian insurrection promoted by the Jesuit Order of Japan. He said to me: "Toyohiko, you may study English with that American missionary, but don't believe in Christianity. It is a bad religion. About three hundred years ago it tried to capture Japan. You must not believe in Christianity."

But I thought he was making a mistake, because Buddhism couldn't make me a good boy, nor Shintoism, nor Confucian teaching. But since I had begun to pray to the Father in Heaven in the name of Jesus Christ I felt new strength coming to my life. So I would retire to my bedroom, and putting the bedcovers over my head, I would simply pray: "O God, make me a good boy! Amen." I did not go to church. If I had gone to church I would have been kicked out of my house, which I wouldn't have liked. So I stayed away from church.

About eight months passed. I went to the American missionary to borrow some books. He asked me many questions: "Mr. Kagawa, do you believe in Christ?" "Yes sir." "Do you pray to God?" "Yes sir." "How do you pray to God?" I hesitated a minute, but then I answered, "Under the bedcovers, sir." He looked at me and said, "Why don't you come to church?" I told him if I would do so I should be kicked out of my house, which I wouldn't like. Then he said to me, "Mr. Kagawa, you are a timid and cowardly boy." Now all Japanese boys hate the word "coward." So I said, "You had better repeat the word 'coward' once more." "You are a timid and cowardly boy," he said. Then I told him that if he would keep on repeating the word "coward" I would go to church.

I did go to church, and on the third Sunday after I started, when I was fifteen years old, I was baptized. Oh, I was glad and happy! In appearance I was a monkey, but inside I was a son of God!

When I finished high school I determined to be a minister for Christ. I had to leave my house and I was disinherited because my uncle didn't like it, but Dr. Myers put me in the Presbyterian college in Tokyo. In college I tried to be a good boy, a Christian boy, but the other students didn't like it. I found a deserted dog and gave it a home in my dormitory room. The other boys protested, but I said, "Anyone will befriend a good-looking dog, but who will care for a mongrel like this unless I do it?" Then I found a beggar who had no place to live, and so I let him sleep in my room. The other boys didn't like that either. That was the time of the Russo-Japanese war. I could not believe in war and said so. They tried to teach the students to become soldiers. They gave us guns and started us to learning how to march. When they gave the order to march, I stood there. I did not believe in it, so I didn't move. This made the officer very angry. He came up to me and asked why I didn't march. I said, "Japan made a mistake to declare war on Russia." He was very much surprised. He couldn't believe a student would say that. He ordered me to get back in line and march. Instead I threw down the gun and went back to the dormitory. That night the students called me out to the playground. They called me a traitor, and they took turns beating me. I still wasn't convinced. I kept on preaching peace. After two years at college, when I was nineteen, I spent the summer preaching in the slums. There I preached continuously by myself on the streets every day for forty days.

On the fortieth day, at about nine o'clock in the evening, it began to rain while I was still preaching. For a week my voice had been getting weaker, and when the rain began falling my body was swaying to and fro. At one time I had difficulty in getting my breath. I began to feel horribly cold, but I determined, whatever happened, to finish my sermon.

"In conclusion," I cried, "I tell you God is love, and I will affirm God's love till I fall. Where there is love, God and life reveal themselves."

My fever was so high that I actually felt I would collapse. Somehow I stumbled back to where I was staying and went to bed. For two days I lay there coughing worse and worse, spitting up blood, but with no money to call a doctor.

At the end of the second day the pastor of the church did send for a doctor. He examined me. He told me that I had tubercular pneumonia, and there was no hope of my recovery.

On the third day my condition seemed completely hopeless. I could not cough anymore, nor even breathe without effort. For a week I lay there, just praying and waiting. Then the hemorrhages got worse and I got a very high fever. I thought that the time had come for me to die. The doctor said to notify my friends.

The sun was setting in the west. I could see its reflection on my pillow. For four hours I prayed, waiting for my last breath. Then there came a peculiar, mysterious experience — an ecstatic consciousness of God; a feeling that God was inside me and all around me. I felt a great ecstasy and joy. I coughed up a cupful of clotted blood. I could breathe again. The fever was reduced. I forgot to die. The doctor came back at nine-thirty. He was disappointed. He had written a certificate for my cremation and feared the people would call him a quack.

For a month I rested, praying and reading and meditating. Then I returned to school — this time to the Kobe Theological Seminary. I set forth at once to preach on the street corners of Shinkawa, the worst slum district in Japan. I was able to preach for a whole week before my strength gave out again.

This time the doctor seemed to think it was really serious, so Dr. Myers put me in a hospital for four months. I didn't want to bother him so much, so I left the hospital. I had only fifteen yen, but I rented a small fishing man's cottage for one yen a month. In your money that was only fifty cents. There was not much of anything in that cottage — no cot, no mattress — so I got some straw to make a bed on the floor and I lived in that house nearly a year.

I read very much and I preached to the fisherfolk, but I was very lonesome and I thought I was going to die. I wanted to say what Christ and death meant to me, so I wrote the first draft of a novel. I didn't have any paper, so I wrote it over the printed pages of old castaway magazines.

I collected animals to keep me company. I had many animals — one dog, one cat, one snake, and five spiders. But people didn't like to get close to me because of my terrible disease, so I was very lonesome. Then came Dr. Myers. He had taken his vacation and left his wife to come visit me. He stayed in that cottage about four days. We slept in the same bed. I asked if he wasn't afraid of me. "Your disease is contagious," he said, "but love is more contagious."

At that moment I realized more truly than ever what love really means: that love can have no fear; that love can have no limits; that love encompasses everything — the people sick like me, and the people sick in spirit and mind. I thought I must love everybody too — even the horrible people in the slums. I decided I must not be sick anymore. I told God that if He would let me live I would serve His children in the slums. Pretty soon I began to get well again.

Sadhu Sundar Singh

(1889–1929?)

During his brief life, Sadhu Sundar Singh won international acclaim and controversy for his role as missionary and mystic. One historian concludes that he "might well have stood model for the 'Oriental Christ' so beloved of the late nineteenth century; or at least for 'the Christ of the Indian Road.'"

He was born into an influential, wealthy Sikh family in northern India. Sikhs rejected both Hindu polytheism and Muslim intolerance, and they had secured an important presence in his birthplace. His mother introduced him to a Sadhu, an ascetic holy man, who lived in the jungle nearby, but she also sent him to Ewing Christian High School to learn English.

He was fourteen when his mother died, and in despair he responded with violence. He vented his resentment on the missionaries and persecuted Christian converts. It was in that state that Sundar Singh was converted on December 18, 1904.

After his conversion, he was baptized and began his itinerant life as a new Christian. He wore a turban and yellow robe, which was characteristic of a Hindu Sadhu. Like other Sadhu, he relied upon charity for his sustenance and meditated in jungles and other remote areas. But he also became an evangelist. "I am not worthy to follow in the steps of my Lord," he declared, "but like Him, I want no home, no possessions. Like Him, I will belong to the road, sharing the suffering of my people, eating with those who will give me shelter, and telling all men of the love of God."

His journeys took him far and wide — throughout India and to Kashmir, Afghanistan, Baluchistan, Tibet, Ceylon, Burma, China, Japan, and eventually Britain, the United States, and Australia. The reality of his suffering in his travels and his "visions" amid his travails earned him the title "the apostle with the bleeding feet" from his admirers and followers. At one point, he studied for the ministry at the Anglican college in Lahore, but his temperament and mysticism made him a poor candidate for ordination.

His simple, humble talks about Christ's love and God's compassion for the poor won him great praise from Christians and fascination from others. People frequently said, "He not only looks like Jesus; he talks like Jesus must have talked." His piety came from long and intense morning meditation, focused particularly on the Gospels. He was appalled at the materialism of Western culture during his trips to the English-speaking world. In 1929 he set off again for Tibet to preach and died somewhere en route.

Sundar Singh was controversial in his own day because of his mystical visions and somewhat eclectic form of Christian belief. He also encountered the writings of Emmanuel Swedenborg early in his ministry and claimed to have had visions of Swedenborg — all of which did not endear him to more conventional Christians.

The controversy about him continues among his biographers, some of whom are reverent and eager to endorse his life and ministry while others are deeply skeptical of his mystic visions throughout his life, even including the account of his own conversion.

Nevertheless, Sundar Singh is another example of the long tradition of Christian mysticism, and he stands today as one of the most important visionary leaders in Indian and world Christianity.

~

The story of [Sadhu Sundar Singh's] conversion, which occurred on December 18, 1904, is best given in his own words, quoted from one of the Kandy addresses. "Preachers and Christians in general had often come to me and I used to resist them and persecute them. When I was out in any town I got people to throw stones at Christian preachers. I would tear up the Bible and burn it when I had a chance. In the presence of my father I cut up the Bible and other Christian books and put kerosene oil upon them and burnt them. I thought this was a false religion and tried all I could to destroy it. I was faithful to my own religion, but I could not get any satisfaction or peace, though I performed all the ceremonies and rites of that religion. So I thought of leaving it all and committing suicide. Three days after I had burnt the Bible, I woke up about three

---

This account appears in B. H. Streeter and A. J. Appasamy, *Sadhu Sundar Singh: A Study in Mysticism on Practical Religion* (New York: Macmillan, 1921), 6-8.

o'clock in the morning, had my usual bath, and prayed, 'O God, if there is a God, wilt thou show me the right way or I will kill myself.' My intention was that, if I got no satisfaction, I would place my head upon the railway line when the 5 o'clock train passed by and kill myself. If I got no satisfaction in this life, I thought I would get it in the next. I was praying and praying but got no answer; and I prayed for half an hour longer hoping to get peace. At 4.30 A.M. I saw something of which I had no idea at all previously. In the room where I was praying I saw a great light. I thought the place was on fire. I looked round, but could find nothing. Then the thought came to me that this might be an answer that God had sent me. Then as I prayed and looked into the light, I saw the form of the Lord Jesus Christ. It had such an appearance of glory and love. If it had been some Hindu incarnation I would have prostrated myself before it. But it was the Lord Jesus Christ whom I had been insulting a few days before. I felt that a vision like this could not come out of my own imagination. I heard a voice saying in Hindustani, 'How long will you persecute me? I have come to save you; you were praying to know the right way. Why do you not take it?' The thought then came to me, 'Jesus Christ is not dead but living and it must be He Himself.' So I fell at His feet and got this wonderful Peace which I could not get anywhere else. This is the joy I was wishing to get. This was heaven itself. When I got up, the vision had all disappeared; but although the vision disappeared the Peace and Joy have remained with me ever since. I went off and told my father that I had become a Christian. He told me, 'Go and lie down and sleep; why, only the day before yesterday you burnt the Bible; and you say you are a Christian now.' I said, 'Well, I have discovered now that Jesus Christ is alive and have determined to be His follower. To-day I am His disciple and I am going to serve Him.'"

Samuel M. Shoemaker

(1893–1963)

Sam Shoemaker was one of a very few in his time who sensed the importance of the life of inner spirituality. Theologians, church leaders, and preachers tended not to be very personal or disclosive about their devotional life or conversion experience, if any. It was a blasé, aloof generation following World War I, and religion became perfunctory and formalized. Sam Shoemaker knew all about this first-hand as an undergraduate at Princeton University and later as the director of the Student Christian Association on campus.

After college, Shoemaker signed up for a "short term" missionary teaching stint at a Chinese boys' school sponsored by a group of interested Princeton alumni. This was a popular and adventuresome post-graduate option for those who felt some Christian or humanist concern for the peoples of Asia. While in Peking, as he tells the story, Shoemaker was himself re-converted in the process of trying to convert a Chinese friend. The experience stuck; it changed Shoemaker's life by providing direction and purpose for his future brilliant ministry.

Returning to New York, Shoemaker attended General Theological Seminary and became the assistant minister at Grace Episcopal Church. In 1925, he was appointed Rector of Calvary Episcopal Church, and in 1952 he moved to the Calvary Episcopal Church in Pittsburgh. He was a dynamic preacher, a compassionate pastor, and an intellectual and literary innovator. The author of a dozen popular books, he also edited a series of religious magazines, the best known of which, with a worldwide circulation, was *Faith at Work*. He also played an influential role in the origins and development of Alcoholics Anonymous.

While in Peking, Shoemaker met Frank Buchman, the founder of the so-called Oxford Group Movement, which later became known as Moral Re-Armament. He had launched his religious program at Princeton University with mixed and controversial results. Shoemaker was apparently deeply moved by the movement but never identified himself as a "Buchmanite."

Shoemaker took the best out of the Oxford Group and put it back into the full-time ministry of his mainline church. This meant a vigorous program of evangelism among all sorts of people, open and honest religious self-appraisal, cell groups and prayer fellowships of all kinds. The effect of this emphasis was to bring personal religious experience out into the open, unashamedly, for all to see. Sam Shoemaker, a no-nonsense, Ivy League, articulate Episcopalian rector, was just the man to do it — ahead of his time.

~

An experience in Peking . . . in January of 1918 changed the course of my life and ministry. It was war-time. I had gone out to China on short-term because I had agreed to go before the war began and was free to do so, having drawn a high number in the draft; but also because I had heard Dr. W. E. Orchard, then of King's Weigh House, London, say that "foreign missions are the one indisputably Christian flag flying at this moment."

Princeton University maintained then a business school where Chinese boys learned the rudiments of English and business methods. It was lodged in the Peking Christian Association.

Soon after my arrival, I was given a Bible class of young businessmen who were enquirers into the Christian faith. We gathered in my room around the stove. The first time there were about twenty, the next about fourteen, and the third about seven! I was aware that something was the matter with the Bible class, and with the methods I was using. But this was not all that was the matter. *God cannot use a channel that is not open.*

I had been brought up in a responsible, church-going Episcopalian family. I thank God for all those early associations and for what I learned. It had turned me towards religion and decided me on the ministry. But this is not enough. In China I found I did not have sufficient power to communicate my faith to other people. (I had learned that at home, too, but it was sharpened by the new experience.)

About that time a group of people came into the city who brought with them spiritual power. They seemed to know how to make faith live

---

From "The Turning Point," in Shoemaker's book *Faith at Work* (New York: Hawthorn Books, Inc., 1958), 80-84.

for other people, how to win them for Christ and set them on fire. Frank Buchman was the leader of this company, and I listened to what he told, and then went round to see him, asking him if he wouldn't help a young Chinese businessman who had been in my class, was not satisfied with Buddhism, and was seeking.

I have parted company with Frank Buchman for various reasons, but till my dying day I shall be thankful to him for what he did for me in those early times. He was the first, older religious leader who did not pat me on the back and say how fine it was I was going into the ministry. He said instead, "Why don't you win this man yourself?"

I replied that I had not been brought up in just that way and that we didn't do it quite that way in my Church. Then he said, "Now, what is the real reason?"

I countered by asking what he thought it was and he said, "Might be sin — resentment kept me from this kind of work for a whole year." He put before me "four absolutes" which Dr. Robert E. Speer distilled out as the essence of the Sermon on the Mount — absolute honesty, purity, unselfishness, and love. That night, when trying to say my prayers, everything jammed. I knew I was up against my Waterloo. Either I would or would not "let go."

Then I made my surrender to God's will so far as I could see it at the time. The crux of it was the willingness to stay in China for life if God willed it. Some of us have wills like a bar of iron, and it is hard to break them and let God's will come into their place. I faced as honestly as I could my sins and got down on my knees and gave them to God, and my will with them. I felt no emotion about this and saw no stars nor bright lights; but afterwards I felt light and at ease, as if life had slipped into its right groove at last.

Next morning I wakened with an uneasy sense that I must go and talk to my young Chinese business friend myself. That afternoon I got into a ricksha and drove over to the East City where he lived. I paced up and down outside his door, almost prayed he wouldn't be home, for I did not yet know what I would say to him. I don't know what would have happened if he had been out that day — but he wasn't!

Crossing his threshold I prayed God to tell me what to say. And it seemed to come to me, "Tell him what happened to you last night."

My Chinese friend asked me to sit down, and in a pair of creaky wicker chairs we began to talk.

"I believe you have been interested in my class," I began, "but not satisfied with it. The fault has been mine. May I tell you something that happened to me last night?" He listened to my story intently and when I had finished surprised me with, "I wish that could happen to me."

"It can if you will let God in completely."

And that day he made his decision and found Christ.

This is the way I began to be interested in one person at a time. After this I sought out individual after individual and asked each one to accept Christ and surrender himself to Him. Every day I would try to see one of the schoolboys after hours, and every evening a young man in business or government service.

I soon saw that there were four elements in the initial decision:

(1) *The break with conscious wrong.* Either sin controls us, or God controls us. And pride is the root sin — the pride that fundamentally wants to get on in its own way, even if one calls on God to help.

Many Christians do not make this step decisive enough and it accounts for their falling by the wayside later. Nothing can be tolerated that interferes with God's pouring His power into and through us.

(2) *Daily time for personal devotions.* I had struggled with the old "morning watch," and found prayer dry and the Bible like sawdust. Somehow my new experience made prayer live, for prayer became seeking God's will afresh, not trying to change it.

The Bible opened up as a living record of those who tried to live in obedience to God's will. I shall never forget how it helped me to read every reference I could find to Simon Peter; he had so many weaknesses, yet God greatly used him.

(3) *The need to put life's major decisions in God's hands.* It was not enough to have decided to be a minister; where did God want me, how must I serve Him, would I go anywhere if He said so? So many of us want to keep matters of vocation, and marriage, too, purely private, as our own choice and decision. But marriage also must be entered into in accordance with God's will, so far as we can find it. Christian marriage *is* a vocation.

(4) *The need to learn how to witness.* Most Christians are tongue-tied, and most Communists are articulate — that is the most serious fact in our world. If faith is real to us, we should be able to make it real to others.

Many of us cannot witness, because we have no real experience of conversion, of prayer, of experienced power, to witness to. We call it shyness, but it is really spiritual poverty. We can learn to make friends, to help people to talk about themselves, to bring Christ to bear upon the situations they reveal, to help them accept Him and begin living with Him, in Him, for Him.

We are not saved by our experiences; we are saved by the "mighty acts" of Christ for us — the Crucifixion and the Resurrection. But for many, these vast truths will only begin to be real as they come to see how He can help them with their immediate problems and situations.

These have been wonderful years. There have been bad failures and old Satan comes back always along familiar paths. But I would not take anything for the initial experience that launched me out in faith and flung me into the lives of individual persons, and taught me something of the small group wherein this new life is best conserved.

Thanks be to God Who giveth us the victory.

Bill W. (Wilson)

(1895–1971)

Bill Wilson had everything it took to make an alcoholic. It conspired to create not only a man enslaved by the illness of alcoholism but also a genius who found a way out of his disease and co-founded a movement — Alcoholics Anonymous — that became a blessing to millions of people suffering from the same disease.

His father was a heavy drinker and came from a long line of alcoholics. His mother was emotionally troubled, controlling, and abusive. Their marriage was fragile and finally collapsed when his father left home. His mother soon abandoned both her children to enter a career in osteopathic medicine. Maternal grandparents raised both Bill and his sister. When Bill turned seventeen, he experienced a deep depression when his first love died of complications following surgery.

Bill W., as he is called by those in AA, took his first drink in the Army after being mobilized to fight in World War I. "I had found the elixir of life," he later said. "Even that first evening I got thoroughly drunk, and within the next time or two I passed out completely. But as everyone drank hard, not too much was made of that."

He met his wife, Lois Burnham, in 1913, and they were married in 1918, just before he left to fight in World War I. After the war, the Wilsons settled in New York, where Bill W. studied law. He was a driven man, obsessed with success. But he never graduated from law school because he was too drunk to pick up his diploma. Instead, he turned to Wall Street, where he was initially successful. Eventually his voracious appetite for alcohol — coupled with the stock market crash in the 1920s — completely destroyed his career and his reputation. Nevertheless, Lois stayed with him.

By 1933, Bill W. was thoroughly shattered. He was hospitalized at the

Charles B. Towns Hospital for Drug and Alcohol Addictions in New York City, where the addiction pioneer Dr. William D. Silkworth treated him. Dr. Silkworth believed that alcoholism was an illness — a physical allergy and a mental obsession — and while Bill W. took some comfort in knowing that his problem was not primarily a moral failing, he continued to drink.

After polishing off four beers on the way, Bill W. entered Towns Hospital for the fourth time, where Dr. Silkworth administered belladonna, a psychedelic drug, for the first time. A former drinking buddy, Ebby Thacher, visited him again and gently explained how he had found sobriety from the insights of the Oxford Movement, a renewal movement popular in Protestant circles. Bill W. fervently believed in modern science and thought of himself as a rigorous rationalist, despite the irrationality of his life. He listened to Ebby Thacher, but after he left, Bill W.'s depression swept over him with renewed force.

He cried out: "If there be a God, let him show himself!" Then it happened. "Suddenly," he later wrote, "my room blazed with an indescribably white light. I was seized with an ecstasy beyond description. Every joy I had known was pale by comparison. . . . Then came the blazing thought, 'You are a free man.'"

And he was. Whether stimulated by a psychedelic drug or not, Wilson's encounter with God was the turning point in his life. When Lois Wilson visited him the next morning, she could see that he had changed and was sure he would never drink again. She was right. He never did.

In 1935, Bill W. and a fellow alcoholic, Dr. Bob Smith, founded Alcoholics Anonymous with an elementary discovery: one recovering alcoholic can help another alcoholic stay sober. This insight — that the sick can help the sick — lay at the foundation of Alcoholics Anonymous and the hundreds of mutual help associations it spawned. Indeed, Lois Wilson went on to found Alanon, an organization devoted to helping those affected but not afflicted by addiction.

Bill W. was the principal author of *Alcoholics Anonymous,* first published in 1939 with several subsequent editions, and known as "The Big Book" in AA. He also helped write the companion volume, *Twelve Steps and Twelve Traditions* (1953).

Although Bill W. found freedom from alcohol, he continued to struggle with crippling bouts of depression, womanizing, and chain-smoking. And yet, through his writings and occasional speeches, he explained and proclaimed the freedom from addiction he had found. He died in 1971 from emphysema and pneumonia. Through it all, Lois Wilson stayed at his side.

Time magazine identified Bill Wilson as one of the "100 most important people of the twentieth century." Aldous Huxley described him as "the greatest social architect of our century." Bill W. saw himself primarily as one who synthesized the ideas of others, and in one crucial respect he captured the heart of the spiritual life. As biographer Susan Cheever has written, "In Bill Wilson's story it is clear that alcohol is astonishingly powerful and that the only thing which can stop its course for an alcoholic is an experience of God, a spiritual awakening, a surrender of the rational mind."

⁓

The clearer I got, the more my spirits fell. I began to be frightfully depressed, and Lois came to see me each night after work, looking so sad and sick. The depression would become appalling after she left. I . . . collapsed. Maybe it would be a good thing if I died.

Cold sober now, the god Ebby [Thacher] had talked about seemed improbable, unreal. I could accept all his ideas save this. Briefly, I went on rebelling. My depression deepened, deepened. It gripped me in a living death.

One morning, the fourteenth of December, I think, Ebby appeared in the doorway of my room looking the picture of health and confidence. Sympathy and understanding mingled with his smile as he said, "Mighty sorry you had to land up here again. Thought I'd come up and say hello." As he started to talk, I felt better. What he said at this point I don't remember, but I did notice that he pointedly avoided the topics of alcohol and religion. He was just paying a friendly visit, asking for nothing. He wasn't going to try any evangelism on me after all.

This inspired me to start asking questions myself. Then he began to repeat his pat little formula for getting over drinking. Briefly and without ado he did so. Again he told how he found he couldn't run his own

---

The first excerpt is from *Bill W: My First Forty Years* (Center City, MN: Hazleden, 2000), 140-46. © 2000 Stepping Stones Foundation and used with permission. The second excerpt is from "Spiritual Experience," in *Alcoholics Anonymous,* 4th ed. (New York: Alcoholics Anonymous World Services, Inc., 2001), pp. 567-68. The excerpts from *Alcoholics Anonymous* are reprinted with permission of Alcoholics Anonymous World Services, Inc. ("AAWS"). Permission to reprint these excerpts does not mean that AAWS has reviewed or approved the contents of this publication, or that AAWS necessarily agrees with the views expressed therein. A.A. is a program of recovery from alcoholism only. Use of these excerpts in connection with programs and activities which are patterned after A.A., but which address other problems, or in any other non A.A. context, does not imply otherwise.

life, how he got honest with himself as never before. How he'd been making amends to the people he'd damaged. How he'd been trying to give of himself without putting a price tag on his efforts, and finally how he'd tried prayer just as an experiment and had found to his surprise that it worked.

Once more he emphasized the difference between being on the water wagon and his present state. He no longer had to fight the desire to drink. The desire had been lifted right out of him. It had simply vanished. He no longer sat on a powder keg. He was released. He was free. That was his simple story.

After I asked a few more questions he turned the talk to other matters. After a bit he left, promising to return soon again.

While Ebby talked I had almost surfaced from my depression, but the only conflict soon renewed itself. Had Ebby recovered through reality or by an illusion? Who or what was this god that so many people were so sure of? What made them so sure that this . . . sad and fathomless face among a million of suns was so darned important? The great forces of the cosmos responded to laws, some of which were known. But laws for what, or for whom? And did these laws have an author? That life on all levels was so cruelly competitive, so seemingly pointless. Men died and more were born. Cats ate birds, birds ate bugs, but dodo birds had gone extinct, and so had hundreds of other species, and all for what? Law here, chaos there. Sense here, nonsense there. . . . People talked about just loving a person. On the face of it that had to be nonsense. I simply couldn't go for it. I just wasn't capable of such an absurd illusion, even though it might save my life for a little while longer.

Depression caught me again. The undertow was remorseless and I sank.

One scene after another crossed through my mind as the depression grew. I thought of Lois, how magnificent, how devoted, how unwavering she had been. Fair weather or foul, it had always been the same. Never had she failed me. . . . Always, Lois was there, and even now she was beside me, hiding her hopelessness and waiting. Waiting for what? Well, we both knew. We were waiting for the end. All that mattered was past and gone. Shame and failure had replaced success, and fear had banished security. Of romance there would be none, for presently I would die or go mad. This was the finish, the jumping-off place.

The terrifying darkness had become complete. In agony of spirit, I again thought of the cancer of alcoholism which had now consumed me in mind and spirit, and soon the body. But what of the Great Physician? For a brief moment, I suppose, the last trace of my obstinacy was crushed out as the abyss yawned.

I remember saying to myself, "I'll do anything, anything at all. If there be a Great Physician, I'll call on him." Then, with neither faith nor hope I cried out, "If there be a God, let him show himself." The effect was instant, electric. Suddenly my room blazed with an indescribably white light. I was seized with an ecstasy beyond description. I have no words for this. Every joy I had known was pale by comparison. The light, the ecstasy. I was conscious of nothing else for a time.

Then, seen in the mind's eye, there was a mountain. I stood upon its summit where a great wind blew. A wind, not of air, but of spirit. In great, clean strength it blew right through me. Then came the blazing thought, "You are a free man." I know not at all how long I remained in this state, but finally the light and the ecstasy subsided. I again saw the wall of my room. As I became more quiet a great peace stole over me, and this was accompanied by a sensation difficult to describe. I became acutely conscious of a presence which seemed like a veritable sea of living spirit. I lay on the shores of a new world. "This," I thought, "must be the great reality. The God of the preachers."

Savoring my new world, I remained in this state for a long time. I seemed to be possessed by the absolute, and the curious conviction deepened that no matter how wrong things seemed to be, there would be no question of the ultimate rightness of God's universe. For the first time I felt that I really belonged. I knew that I was loved and could love in return. I thanked my God who had given me a glimpse of His absolute Self. Even though a pilgrim upon an uncertain highway, I need be concerned no more, for I had glimpsed the great beyond.

Save a brief hour of doubt next to come, these feelings and convictions, no matter what the vicissitude, have never deserted me since. For a reason that I cannot begin to comprehend, this great and sudden gift of grace has always been mine.

Bill W.'s own experience, plus the logic of the 12 Steps, involved alcoholics' acknowledgment of God's or a Higher Power's presence in order for them to find a solution to the alcohol over which they were powerless. This became known as "a spiritual awakening." Its importance for sobriety immediately raised the question of what "a spiritual awakening" might be, and so the second and all subsequent editions of the movement's basic text, *Alcoholics Anonymous,* contained the following appendix. Drawing on William James's *Varieties of Religious Experience,* the addition focuses on both the importance of a spiritual experience for sobriety and the various ways in which alcoholics might gain spiritual wisdom. It is perhaps one of the briefest and best descriptions of spiritual change, and it has inspired and guided millions to a new life.

~

The terms "spiritual experience" and "spiritual awakening" are used many times in this book which, upon careful reading, shows that the personality change sufficient to bring about recovery from alcoholism has manifested itself among us in many different forms.

Yet it is true that our first printing gave many readers the impression that these personality changes, or religious experiences, must be in the nature of sudden and spectacular upheavals. Happily for everyone, this conclusion is erroneous.

In the first few chapters a number of sudden revolutionary changes are described. Though it was not our intention to create such an impression, many alcoholics have nevertheless concluded that in order to recover they must acquire an immediate and overwhelming "God-consciousness" followed at once by a vast change in feeling and outlook.

Among our rapidly growing membership of thousands of alcoholics such transformations, though frequent, are by no means the rule. Most of our experiences are what the psychologist William James calls the "educational variety" because they develop slowly over a period of time. Quite often friends of the newcomer are aware of the difference long before he is himself. He finally realizes that he has undergone a profound alteration in his reaction to life; that such a change could hardly have been brought about by himself alone. What often takes place in a few months could seldom have been accomplished by years of self-discipline. With few exceptions our members find that they have tapped an unsuspected inner resource which they presently identify with their own conception of a Power greater than themselves.

Most of us think this awareness of a Power greater than ourselves is the essence of spiritual experience. Our more religious members call it "God-consciousness."

Most emphatically we wish to say that any alcoholic capable of honestly facing his problems in the light of our experience can recover, provided he does not close his mind to all spiritual concepts. He can only be defeated by an attitude of intolerance or belligerent denial.

We find that no one need have difficulty with the spirituality of the program. *Willingness, honesty and open mindedness are the essentials of recovery. But these are indispensable.*

"There is a principle which is a bar against all information, which is proof against all arguments and which cannot fail to keep a man in everlasting ignorance — that principle is contempt prior to investigation." (Herbert Spencer)

Dorothy Day

(1897–1980)

By her own admission, Dorothy Day was "different." Throughout her life, she combined an intense commitment to social justice with an unwavering allegiance to the Roman Catholic Church. With Peter Maurin, she became associated with the Catholic Worker Movement, and through its newspaper, *The Catholic Worker,* she spoke out tirelessly for renewed religious dedication and alleviation of the plight of the poor.

Political radicals considered Dorothy Day's religiosity odd, and fellow Catholics often questioned her politics. But she asked her own question: "Where are the saints to call the masses to God?" Her answer was that all must seek to be saints, for in that, she emphasized, "is the Revolution."

Day's beginnings did not point toward sainthood. In fact, her biographer, William Miller, observed, "If anyone, in the first twenty-five years of life, seemed headed for despair, it was she, yet she turned away from that fate and, having set her vision on eternity, she never looked back."

Coming from an ostensibly religious home, she was attracted to leftist politics and alienated intellectuals. Settling for a time in New York, she began nurse's training, endured an unhappy love affair, and entered upon a painful, short-lived marriage. Turning to writing, she published a novel and settled down to live with her common-law husband, Forster Batterham. In June 1926, she was overjoyed to find she was pregnant. But her desire that her daughter, Tamar, be baptized in the church conflicted with Batterham's disgust with all religion, and they separated.

The following account chronicles Day's struggle to become a Catholic and to have her baby baptized, and it concludes with her "postscript" on the purpose of the Catholic Worker Movement and her witness of "a harsh and dreadful love." The concern for baptism can be misinterpreted, for Dorothy Day was not seeking respectability or absolution for her "sin." Writing in her "notes," she said, "It was the glories of creation, the tender beauty of flowers and shells, the songs of birds, the smile of my baby, these things brought such exultation, such joy to my heart that I could not but cry out in praise of God."

Dorothy Day was haunted, as many have been, by Francis Thompson's poem "The Hound of Heaven," and eventually through a series of retreats she achieved serenity of purpose. "So I will not be afraid," she wrote, "and I will talk of love and write of love, and God will help me, I will suffer from it too — the humiliations, the degradations, the misunderstandings because 'what is it I love when I love my God?'"

She became the dominant and outstanding figure of the Catholic left, deeply influencing Thomas Merton, Daniel Berrigan, Michael Harrington, John Cogley, Cesar Chavez, and many others. She wrote constantly, traveled and spoke across the country, and when she returned "home," it was to the Catholic Worker soup kitchen on the lower East Side. She combined her radical politics for the poor with pacifism and a conservative, nonquestioning view of liturgy and the sacraments. The church was the center of her life; "she [the church] taught me the crowning love of the life of the Spirit."

Despite her dedication and devotion, Day felt that "we have scarcely begun to be Christian, to deserve the name Christian," and that sometimes one lived "on blind and naked faith." And yet "God sends intimations of immortality. We believe that if the will is right, God will take us by the hair of the head, as he did Habakkuk, who brought food to Daniel in the lions' den, and will restore us to the Way and no matter what our wandering, we can still say, 'All is Grace.'"

I was surprised that I found myself beginning to pray daily. I could not get down on my knees, but I could pray while I was walking. If I got down on my knees I thought, "Do I really believe? Whom am I praying to?" A terrible doubt came over me, and a sense of shame, and I wondered if I was praying because I was lonely, because I was unhappy.

Excerpted from *The Long Loneliness* by Dorothy Day. Illustrated by Fritz Eichenberg. Copyright © 1952 by Harper & Row, Publishers, Inc. Copyright renewed © 1980 by Tamar Hennessey. Introduction copyright © 1997 by Robert Coles. Reprinted by permission of HarperCollins, Publishers. The autobiography was reprinted in 1981 with an introduction by Daniel Berrigan.

But when I walked to the village for the mail, I found myself praying again, holding in my pocket the rosary that Mary Gordon gave me in New Orleans some years before. Maybe I did not say it correctly but I kept on saying it because it made me happy.

Then I thought suddenly, scornfully, "Here you are in a stupor of content. You are biological. Like a cow. Prayer with you is like the opiate of the people." And over and over again in my mind that phrase was repeated jeeringly, "Religion is the opiate of the people."

"But," I reasoned with myself, "I am praying because I am happy, not because I am unhappy. I did not turn to God in unhappiness, in grief, in despair — to get consolation, to get something from Him."

And encouraged that I was praying because I wanted to thank Him, I went on praying. No matter how dull the day, how long the walk seemed, if I felt sluggish at the beginning of the walk, the words I had been saying insinuated themselves into my heart before I had finished, so that on the trip back I neither prayed nor thought but was filled with exultation.

Along the beach I found it appropriate to say the *Te Deum.* When I worked about the house, I found myself addressing the Blessed Virgin and turning toward her statue.

It is so hard to say how this delight in prayer grew on me. The year before, I was saying as I planted seeds in the garden, "I *must* believe in these seeds, that they fall into the earth and grow into flowers and radishes and beans. It is a miracle to me because I do not understand it. Neither do naturalists understand it. The very fact that they use glib technical phrases does not make it any less of a miracle, and a miracle we all accept. Then why not accept God's mysteries?"

I began to go to Mass regularly on Sunday mornings. . . .

It was pleasant rowing about in the calm bay with Forster. The oyster boats were all out, and far on the horizon, off Sandy Hook, there was a four-masted vessel. I had the curious delusion that several huge holes had been stove in her side, through which you could see the blue sky. The other vessels seemed sailing in the air, quite indifferent to the horizon on which they should properly have been resting. Forster tried to explain to me scientific facts about mirages and atmospheric conditions, and, on the other hand, I pointed out to him how our senses lie to us.

But it was impossible to talk about religion or faith to him. A wall immediately separated us. The very love of nature, and the study of her secrets which was bringing me to faith, cut Forster off from religion.

I had known Forster a long time before we contracted our common-law relationship, and I have always felt that it was life with him that brought me natural happiness, that brought me to God.

His ardent love of creation brought me to the Creator of all things. But when I cried out to him, "How can there be no God, when there are all these beautiful things," he turned from me uneasily and complained that I was never satisfied. We loved each other so strongly that he wanted to remain in the love of the moment; he wanted me to rest in that love. He cried out against my attitude that there would be nothing left of that love without a faith.

I remembered the love story in Romain Rolland's *Jean Christophe,* the story of his friend and his engrossing marriage, and how those young people exhausted themselves in the intensity of their emotions.

I could not see that love between man and woman was incompatible with love of God. God is the Creator, and the very fact that we were begetting a child made me have a sense that we were made in the image and likeness of God, co-creators with him. I could not protest with Sasha about "that initial agony of having to live." Because I was grateful for love, I was grateful for life, and living with Forster made me appreciate it and even reverence it still more. He had introduced me to so much that was beautiful and good that I felt I owed to him too this renewed interest in the things of the spirit. . . .

Our child was born in March at the end of a harsh winter. In December I had come in from the country and taken an apartment in town. My sister came to stay with me, to help me over the last hard months. It was good to be there, close to friends, close to a church where I could pray. I read the *Imitation of Christ* a great deal during those months. I knew that I was going to have my child baptized, cost what it may. I knew that I was not going to have her floundering through many years as I had done, doubting and hesitating, undisciplined and amoral. I felt it was the greatest thing I could do for my child. For myself, I prayed for the gift of faith. I was sure, yet not sure. I postponed the day of decision.

A woman does not want to be alone at such a time. Even the most hardened, the most irreverent, is awed by the stupendous fact of creation. Becoming a Catholic would mean facing life alone and I clung to family life. It was hard to contemplate giving up a mate in order that my child and I could become members of the Church. Forster would have nothing to do with religion or with me if I embraced it. So I waited.

Those last months of waiting I was too happy to know the unrest of

225

indecision. The days were slow in passing, but week by week the time came nearer. I spent some time in writing, but for the most part I felt a great stillness. I was incapable of going to meetings, of seeing many people, of taking up the threads of my past life.

When the little one was born, my joy was so great that I sat up in bed in the hospital and wrote an article for the *New Masses* about my child, wanting to share my joy with the world. I was glad to write this joy for a workers' magazine because it was a joy all women knew, no matter what their grief at poverty, unemployment, and class war. The article so appealed to my Marxist friends that the account was reprinted all over the world in workers' papers. Diego Rivera, when I met him some four years afterward in Mexico, greeted me as the author of it. And Mike Gold, who was at that time editor of the *New Masses,* said it had been printed in many Soviet newspapers and that I had rubles awaiting me in Moscow. . . .

One of the disconcerting facts about the spiritual life is that God takes you at your word. Sooner or later one is given a chance to prove his love. The very word "diligo," the Latin word used for "love," means "I prefer." It was all very well to love God in His works, in the beauty of His creation which was crowned for me by the birth of my child. Forster had made the physical world come alive for me and had awakened in my heart a flood of gratitude. The final object of this love and gratitude was God. No human creature could receive or contain so vast a flood of love and joy as I often felt after the birth of my child. With this came the need to worship, to adore. I had heard many say that they wanted to worship God in their own way and did not need a Church in which to praise Him, nor a body of people with whom to associate themselves. But I did not agree to this. My very experience as a radical, my whole make-up, led me to want to associate myself with others, with the masses, in loving and praising God. Without even looking into the claims of the Catholic Church, I was willing to admit that for me she was the one true Church. She had come down through the centuries since the time of Peter, and far from being dead, she claimed and held the allegiance of the masses of people in all the cities where I had lived. They poured in and out of her doors on Sundays and holy days, for novenas and missions. What if they were compelled to come in by the law of the Church, which said they were guilty of mortal sin if they did not go to Mass every Sunday? They obeyed that law. They were given a chance to show their preference. They accepted the Church. It may have been an unthinking, unquestioning faith, and yet the chance certainly came, again and again, "Do I prefer the Church to my own will," even if it was only the small matter of sitting at home on a Sunday morning with the papers? And the choice was the Church. . . .

From the time Tamar Teresa was born I was intent on having her baptized. There had been that young Catholic girl in the bed next to me at the hospital who gave me a medal of St. Thérèse of Lisieux.

"I don't believe in these things," I told her, and it was another example of people saying what they do not mean.

"If you love someone you like to have something around which reminds you of them," she told me.

It was so obvious a truth that I was shamed. Reading William James' *Varieties of Religious Experience* had acquainted me with the saints, and I had read the life of St. Teresa of Ávila and fallen in love with her. She was a mystic and a practical woman, a recluse and a traveler, a cloistered nun and yet most active. She liked to read novels when she was a young girl, and she wore a bright red dress when she entered the convent. Once when she was traveling from one part of Spain to another with some other nuns and a priest to start a convent, and their way took them over a stream, she was thrown from her donkey. The story goes that our Lord said to her, "That is how I treat my friends." And she replied, "And that is why You have so few of them." She called life a "night spent at an uncomfortable inn." Once when she was trying to avoid that recreation hour which is set aside in convents for nuns to be together, the others insisted on her joining them, and she took castanets and danced. When some older nuns professed themselves shocked, she retorted, "One must do things sometimes to make life more bearable." After she was a superior she gave directions when the nuns became melancholy, "to feed them steak," and there were other delightful little touches to the story of her life which made me love her and feel close to her. I have since heard a priest friend of ours remark gloomily that one could go to hell imitating the imperfections of the saints, but these little incidents brought out in her biography made her delightfully near to me. So I decided to name my daughter after her. That is why my neighbor offered me a medal of St. Thérèse of Lisieux, who is called the little Teresa. . . .

"How can your daughter be brought up a Catholic unless you become one yourself?" Sister Aloysia kept saying to me. But she went resolutely ahead in making arrangements for the baptism of Tamar Teresa.

"You must be a Catholic yourself," she kept telling me. She had no reticence. She speculated rather volubly at times on the various reasons why she thought I was holding back. She brought me pious literature to read, saccharine stories of virtue, emasculated lives of saints young and old, back numbers of pious magazines. William James, agnostic as he was, was more help. He had introduced me to St. Teresa of Ávila and St. John of the Cross.

Isolated as I was in the country, knowing no Catholics except my neighbors, who seldom read anything except newspapers and secular magazines, there was not much chance of being introduced to the good Catholic literature of the present day. I was in a state of dull content — not in a state to be mentally stimulated. I was too happy with my child. What faith I had I held on to stubbornly. The need for patience emphasized in the writings of the saints consoled me on the slow road I was traveling. I would put all my affairs in the hands of God and wait.

Three times a week Sister Aloysia came to give me a catechism lesson, which I dutifully tried to learn. But she insisted that I recite word for word, with the repetition of the question that was in the book. If I had not learned my lesson, she rebuked me, "And you think you are intelligent!" she would say witheringly. "What is the definition of grace — actual grace and sanctifying grace? My fourth-grade pupils know more than you do!" ...

I had no particular joy in partaking of these three sacraments, Baptism, Penance and Holy Eucharist. I proceeded about my own active participation in them grimly, coldly, making acts of faith, and certainly with no consolation whatever. One part of my mind stood at one side and kept saying, "What are you doing? Are you sure of yourself? What kind of an affectation is this? What act is this you are going through? Are you trying to induce emotion, induce faith, partake of an opiate, the opiate of the people?" I felt like a hypocrite if I got down on my knees, and shuddered at the thought of anyone seeing me.

At my first communion I went up to the communion rail at the *Sanctus* bell instead of at the *Domine, non sum dignus,* and had to kneel there all alone through the consecration, through the *Pater Noster,* through the *Agnus Dei* — and I had thought I knew the Mass so well! But I felt it fitting that I be humiliated by this ignorance, by this precipitance.

I speak of the misery of leaving one love. But there was another love too, the life I had led in the radical movement. That very winter I was writing a series of articles, interviews with the workers, with the unemployed. I was working with the Anti-Imperialist League, a Communist affiliate, that was bringing aid and comfort to the enemy, General Sandino's forces in Nicaragua. I was just as much against capitalism and imperialism as ever, and here I was going over to the opposition, because of course the Church was lined up with property, with the wealthy, with the state, with capitalism, with all the forces of reaction. This I had been taught to think and this I still think to a great extent. "Too often," Cardinal Mundelein said, "has the Church lined up on the wrong side." "Christianity," Bakunin said, "is precisely the religion par excellence, because it exhibits, and manifests, to the fullest extent, the very nature and essence of every religious system, which is the impoverishment, enslavement, and annihilation of humanity for the benefit of divinity."

I certainly believed this, but I wanted to be poor, chaste, and obedient. I wanted to die in order to live, to put off the old man and put on Christ. I loved, in other words, and like all women in love, I wanted to be united to my love. Why should not Forster be jealous? Any man who did not participate in this love would, of course, realize my infidelity, my adultery. In the eyes of God, any turning toward creatures to the exclusion of Him is adultery and so it is termed over and over again in Scripture.

I loved the Church for Christ made visible. Not for itself, because it was so often a scandal to me. Romano Guardini said the Church is the Cross on which Christ was crucified; one could not separate Christ from His Cross, and one must live in a state of permanent dissatisfaction with the Church.

The scandal of businesslike priests, of collective wealth, the lack of a sense of responsibility for the poor, the worker, the Negro, the Mexican, the Filipino, and even the oppression of these, and the consenting to the oppression of them by our industrialist-capitalist order — these made me feel often that priests were more like Cain than Abel. "Am I my brother's keeper?" they seemed to say in respect to the social order. There was plenty of charity but too little justice. And yet the priests were the dispensers of the Sacraments, bringing Christ to men, all enabling us to put on Christ and to achieve more nearly in the world a sense of peace and unity. "The worst enemies would be those of our own household," Christ had warned us.

We could not root out the tares without rooting out the wheat also. With all the knowledge I have gained these twenty-one years I have been a Catholic, I could write many a story of priests who were poor, chaste, and obedient, who gave their lives daily for their fellows, but I am writing of how I felt at the time of my baptism.

Not long afterward a priest wanted me to write a story of my conversion, telling how the social teaching of the Church had led me to embrace Catholicism. But I knew nothing of the social teaching of the Church at that time. I had never heard of the encyclicals. I felt that the Church was the Church of the poor, that St. Patrick's had been built from the pennies of servant girls, that it cared for the emigrant, it established hospitals, orphanages, day nurseries, houses of the Good Shepherd, homes for the aged, but at the same time, I felt that it did not set its face against a social order which made so much charity in the present sense of the word necessary. I felt that charity was a word to choke over. Who wanted charity? And it was not just human pride but a strong sense of man's dignity and worth, and what was due to him in justice, that made me resent, rather than feel proud of so mighty a sum total of Catholic institutions. Besides, more and more they were taking help from the state, and in taking from the state, they had to render to the state. They came under the head of Community Chest and discriminatory charity, centralizing and departmentalizing, involving themselves with bureaus, building, red tape, legislation, at the expense of human values. By "they," I suppose one always means the bishops, but as Harry Bridges once pointed out to me, "they" also are victims of the system.

*   *   *

We were just sitting there talking when Peter Maurin came in.

We were just sitting there talking when lines of people began to form, saying, "We need bread." We could not say, "Go, be thou filled." If there were six small loaves and a few fishes, we had to divide them. There was always bread.

We were just sitting there talking and people moved in on us. Let those who can take it, take it. Some moved out and that made room for more. And somehow the walls expanded.

We were just sitting there talking and someone said, "Let's all go live on a farm."

It was as casual as all that, I often think. It just came about. It just happened.

I found myself, a barren woman, the joyful mother of children. It is not easy always to be joyful, to keep in mind the duty of delight.

The most significant thing about *The Catholic Worker* is poverty, some say.

The most significant thing is community, others say. We are not alone any more.

But the final word is love. At times it has been, in the words of Father Zossima, a harsh and dreadful thing, and our very faith in love has been tried through fire.

We cannot love God unless we love each other, and to love we must know each other. We know Him in the breaking of bread, and we know each other in the breaking of bread, and we are not alone any more. Heaven is a banquet and life is a banquet, too, even with a crust, where there is companionship.

C. S. Lewis

(1898–1963)

It is probably true that C. S. Lewis has in our time instructed more people in the reasonableness of Christian faith than all the theological faculties in the world. The curious thing is that he did this almost entirely through the written word, while he himself was content to remain mostly hidden and inconspicuous.

Like Thomas Aquinas, the "dumb ox" who roared like a lion, the quiet, scholarly Oxford and Cambridge professor, immersed in his books and his writing, became the foremost Christian apologist of the twentieth century.

Without pen and paper, we would likely not have heard of Clive Staples Lewis. Today there are many more books and articles about him than he himself produced. And his literary output was substantial, including poetry, literary criticism, allegory, science fiction, novels, children's books, as well as a whole series of volumes on theology and Christian doctrine.

The so-called space trilogy, which consists of *Out of the Silent Planet* (1938), *Perelandra* (1943), and *That Hideous Strength* (1946), predated the current immensely popular science fiction craze. The Chronicles of Narnia, a series of seven fantasy novels, is a classic in children's literature, having sold more than 100 million copies by the early twenty-first century and having been adapted for radio, stage, screen, and television. But Lewis's stories are parables as well as fantasies, and they are devoured by old as well as young readers. *The Screwtape Letters* (1942), best known and in some ways symbolic of his literary signature, combines all his talents for story-telling with a serious purpose.

The genius of Lewis's impact rests, no doubt, with the fact that he speaks to all kinds of people, the agnostic and the seeker, the child and the adult, the liberal and the conservative. Perhaps his classical training has something to do with his ability to convey meaning for us today out of the collective treasury of Greece and Rome and the whole of Western culture.

C. S. Lewis

C. S. Lewis has told of his conversion experience in his book entitled *Surprised by Joy* (1955). The word "Joy" is used by him in a special way and is not the same as happiness, gladness, or pleasure. In fact, for Lewis it includes a measure of agony and grief, but if once experienced it is eagerly sought for again and again. As would be expected, this personal account is closely reasoned, deliberate, and reflective. And it rings true.

~

The odd thing was that before God closed in on me, I was in fact offered what now appears a moment of wholly free choice. In a sense. I was going up Headington Hill on the top of a bus. Without words and (I think) almost without images, a fact about myself was somehow presented to me. I became aware that I was holding something at bay, or shutting something out. Or, if you like, that I was wearing some stiff clothing, like corsets, or even a suit of armour, as if I were a lobster. I felt myself being, there and then, given a free choice. I could open the door or keep it shut; I could unbuckle the armour or keep it on. Neither choice was presented as a duty; no threat or promise was attached to either, though I knew that to open the door or to take off the corslet meant the incalculable. The choice appeared to be momentous but it was also strangely unemotional. I was moved by no desires or fears. In a sense I was not moved by anything. I chose to open, to unbuckle, to loosen the rein. I say, "I chose," yet it did not really seem possible to do the opposite. On the other hand, I was aware of no motives. You could argue that I was not a free agent, but I am more inclined to think that this came nearer to being a perfectly free act than most that I have ever done. Necessity may not be the opposite of freedom, and perhaps a man is most free when, instead of producing motives, he could only say, "I am what I do." Then came the repercussion on the imaginative level. I felt as if I were a man of snow at long last beginning to melt. The melting was starting in my back — drip-drip and presently trickle-trickle. I rather disliked the feeling. . . .

Really, a young Atheist cannot guard his faith too carefully. Dangers lie in wait for him on every side. You must not do, you must not even try to do, the will of the Father unless you are prepared to "know of the doctrine." All my acts, desires, and thoughts were to be brought into harmony with universal Spirit. For the first time I examined myself with a seriously practical purpose. And there I found what appalled me; a zoo of lusts, a bedlam of ambitions, a nursery of fears, a harem of fondled hatreds. My name was legion.

Of course I could do nothing — I could not last out one hour — without continual conscious recourse to what I called Spirit. But the fine, philosophical distinction between this and what ordinary people call "prayer to God" breaks down as soon as you start doing it in earnest. Idealism can be talked, and even felt; it cannot be lived. It became patently absurd to go on thinking of "Spirit" as either ignorant of, or passive to, my approaches. Even if my own philosophy were true, how could the initiative lie on my side? My own analogy, as I now first perceived, suggested the opposite: if Shakespeare and Hamlet could ever meet, it must be Shakespeare's doing.[1] Hamlet could initiate nothing. Perhaps, even now, my Absolute Spirit still differed in some way from the God of religion. The real issue was not, or not yet, there. The real terror was that if you seriously believed in even such a "God" or "Spirit" as I admitted, a wholly new situation developed. As the dry bones shook and came together in that dreadful valley of Ezekiel's, so now a philosophical theorem, cerebrally entertained, began to stir and heave and throw off its gravecloths, and stood upright and became a living presence. I was to be allowed to play at philosophy no longer. It might, as I say, still be true that my "Spirit" differed in some way from "the God of popular religion." My Adversary waived the point. It sank into utter unimportance. He would not argue about it. He only said, "I am the Lord"; "I am that I am"; "I am."

People who are naturally religious find difficulty in understanding the horror of such a revelation. Amiable agnostics will talk cheerfully about "man's search for God." To me, as I then was, they might as well have talked about the mouse's search for the cat. The best image of my predicament is the meeting of Mime and Wotan in the first act of

1. I.e. Shakespeare could, in principle, make himself appear as Author within the play, and write a dialogue between Hamlet and himself. The "Shakespeare" within the play would of course be at once Shakespeare and one of Shakespeare's creatures. It would bear some analogy to Incarnation.

Siegfried; hier brauch' ich nicht Spärer noch Späher, Einsam will ich . . .
(I've no use for spies and snoopers. I would be private. . . .)

Remember, I had always wanted, above all things, not to be "interfered with." I had wanted (mad wish) "to call my soul my own." I had been far more anxious to avoid suffering than to achieve delight. I had always aimed at limited liabilities. The supernatural itself had been to me, first, an illicit dram, and then, as by a drunkard's reaction, nauseous. Even my recent attempt to live my philosophy had secretly (I now knew) been hedged round by all sorts of reservations. I had pretty well known that my ideal of virtue would never be allowed to lead me into anything intolerably painful; I would be "reasonable." But now what had been an ideal became a command; and what might not be expected of one? Doubtless, by definition, God was Reason itself. But would He also be "reasonable" in that other, more comfortable, sense? Not the slightest assurance on that score was offered me. Total surrender, the absolute leap in the dark, were demanded. The reality with which no treaty can be made was upon me. The demand was not even "All or nothing." . . .

You must picture me alone in that room in Magdalen, night after night, feeling, whenever my mind lifted even for a second from my work, the steady, unrelenting approach of Him whom I so earnestly desired not to meet. That which I greatly feared had at last come upon me. In the Trinity Term of 1929 I gave in, and admitted that God was God, and knelt and prayed: perhaps, that night, the most dejected and reluctant convert in all England. I did not then see what is now the most shining and obvious thing; the Divine humility which will accept a convert even on such terms. The Prodigal Son at least walked home on his own feet. But who can duly adore that Love which will open the high gates to a prodigal who is brought in kicking, struggling, resentful, and darting his eyes in every direction for a chance of escape? The words *compelle intrare,* compel them to come in, have been so abused by wicked men that we shudder at them; but, properly understood, they plumb the depth of the Divine mercy. The hardness of God is kinder than the softness of men, and His compulsion is our liberation. . . .

It must be understood that the conversion . . . was only to Theism, pure and simple, not to Christianity. I knew nothing yet about the Incarnation. The God to whom I surrendered was sheerly non-human.

It may be asked whether my terror was at all relieved by the thought that I was now approaching the source from which those arrows of Joy had been shot at me ever since childhood. Not in the least. No slightest hint was vouchsafed me that there ever had been or ever would be any connection between God and Joy. If anything, it was the reverse. I had hoped that the heart of reality might be of such a kind that we can best symbolise it as a place; instead, I found it to be a Person. For all I knew, the total rejection of what I called Joy might be one of the demands, might be the very first demand, He would make upon me. There was no strain of music from within, no smell of eternal orchards at the threshold, when I was dragged through the doorway. No kind of desire was present at all.

My conversion involved as yet no belief in a future life. I now number it among my greatest mercies that I was permitted for several months, perhaps for a year, to know God and to attempt obedience without even raising that question. . . .

The last stage in my story, the transition from mere Theism to Christianity, is the one on which I am now least informed. Since it is also the most recent, this ignorance may seem strange. I think there are two reasons. One is that as we grow older we remember the more distant past better than what is nearer. But the other is, I believe, that one of the first results of my Theistic conversion was a marked decrease (and high time, as all readers of this book will agree) in the fussy attentiveness which I had so long paid to the progress of my own opinions and the states of my own mind. For many healthy extroverts self-examination first begins with conversion. For me it was almost the other way round. Self-examination did of course continue. But it was (I suppose, for I cannot quite remember) at stated intervals, and for a practical purpose; a duty, a discipline, an uncomfortable thing, no longer a hobby or a habit. To believe and to pray were the beginning of extroversion. I had been, as they say, "taken out of myself." If Theism had done nothing else for me, I should still be thankful that it cured me of the time-wasting and foolish practice of keeping a diary. (Even for autobiographical purposes a diary is nothing like so useful as I had hoped. You put down each day what you think important; but of course you cannot each day see what will prove to have been important in the long run.[2])

2. The only real good I got from keeping a diary was that it taught me a just appreciation of Boswell's amazing genius. I tried very hard to reproduce conversations, in some of which very amusing and striking people had taken part. But none of these people came to life in the diary at all. Obviously something quite different from mere accurate reporting went into the presentation of Boswell's Langton, Beauclerk, Wilkes, and the rest.

As soon as I became a Theist I started attending my parish church on Sundays and my college chapel on weekdays; not because I believed in Christianity, nor because I thought the difference between it and simple Theism a small one, but because I thought one ought to "fly one's flag" by some unmistakable overt sign. I was acting in obedience to a (perhaps mistaken) sense of honour. The idea of churchmanship was to me wholly unattractive. I was not in the least anti-clerical, but I was deeply anti-ecclesiastical. . . .

But though I liked clergymen as I liked bears, I had as little wish to be in the Church as in the zoo. It was, to begin with, a kind of collective; a wearisome "get-together" affair. I couldn't yet see how a concern of that sort should have anything to do with one's spiritual life. To me, religion ought to have been a matter of good men praying alone and meeting by twos and threes to talk of spiritual matters. And then the fussy, time-wasting botheration of it all! the bells, the crowds, the umbrellas, the notices, the bustle, the perpetual arranging and organising. Hymns were (and are) extremely disagreeable to me. Of all musical instruments I liked (and like) the organ least. I have, too, a sort of spiritual *gaucherie* which makes me unapt to participate in any rite. . . .

I was by now too experienced in literary criticism to regard the Gospels as myths. They had not the mythical taste. And yet the very matter which they set down in their artless, historical fashion — those narrow, unattractive Jews, too blind to the mythical wealth of the Pagan world around them — was precisely the matter of the great myths. If ever a myth had become fact, had been incarnated, it would be just like this. And nothing else in all literature was just like this. Myths were like it in one way. Histories were like it in another. But nothing was simply like it. And no person was like the Person it depicted; as real, as recognisable, through all that depth of time, as Plato's Socrates or Boswell's Johnson (ten times more so than Eckermann's Goethe or Lockhart's Scott), yet also numinous, lit by a light from beyond the world, a god. But if a god — we are no longer polytheists — then not a god, but God. Here and here only in all time the myth must have become fact; the Word, flesh; God, Man. This is not "a religion," nor "a philosophy." It is the summing up and actuality of them all. . . .

I know very well when, but hardly how, the final step was taken. I was driven to Whipsnade one sunny morning. When we set out I did not believe that Jesus Christ is the Son of God, and when we reached the zoo I did. Yet I had not exactly spent the journey in thought. Nor in great emotion. "Emotional" is perhaps the last word we can apply to some of the most important events. It was more like when a man, after long sleep, still lying motionless in bed, becomes aware that he is now awake. . . .

Freedom, or necessity? Or do they differ at their maximum? At that maximum a man is what he does; there is nothing of him left over or outside the act. As for what we commonly call Will, and what we commonly call Emotion, I fancy these usually talk too loud, protest too much, to be quite believed, and we have a secret suspicion that the great passion or the iron resolution is partly a put-up job.

They have spoiled Whipsnade since then. Wallaby Wood, with the birds singing overhead and the bluebells underfoot and the Wallabies hopping all round one, was almost Eden come again.

But what, in conclusion, of Joy? for that, after all, is what the story has mainly been about. To tell you the truth, the subject has lost nearly all interest for me since I became a Christian. I cannot, indeed, complain, like Wordsworth, that the visionary gleam has passed away. I believe (if the thing were at all worth recording) that the old stab, the old bittersweet, has come to me as often and as sharply since my conversion as at any time of my life whatever. But I now know that the experience, considered as a state of my own mind, had never had the kind of importance I once gave it. It was valuable only as a pointer to something other and outer. While that other was in doubt, the pointer naturally loomed large in my thoughts. When we are lost in the woods the sight of a signpost is a great matter. He who first sees it cries, "Look!" The whole party gathers round and stares. But when we have found the road and are passing signposts every few miles, we shall not stop and stare. They will encourage us and we shall be grateful to the authority that set them up. But we shall not stop and stare, or not much; not on this road, though their pillars are of silver and their lettering of gold. "We would be at Jerusalem."

Howard Thurman

(1899–1981)

Howard Thurman was one of the most significant figures in American religious life during the twentieth century and beyond. His influence in African-American Christianity was profound, and his speaking and writing left a pervasive imprint on American Christianity during his lifetime and to the present day. He was first and foremost a pastor and preacher, but in his itinerant speaking at more than five hundred institutions and in his prolific publications of twenty books and numerous essays, he exerted a broad influence on American cultural life.

Like most black Protestants, Thurman was an evangelical — but with a mystical bent. Born into the segregated community of Daytona, Florida, and nurtured in the black Baptist church of his youth, Thurman was educated at Morehouse College (where he is reputed to have read every book in the library) and Rochester Theological Seminary. The Quaker mystic and philosopher Rufus Jones became his mentor at Haverford College, an influence that pervaded his later writing and speaking.

Thurman served as a professor at Morehouse College and then as professor and dean of the chapel at Howard University from 1932 to 1944, where he became known for his advocacy of interracial and intercultural relations through religious experience. He led the first "Negro Delegation of Friendship" to South Asia during this time, and his was the first African-American delegation to meet Gandhi. In 1944, Thurman cofounded the Church for the Fellowship of All Peoples in San Francisco, which was the first racially integrated, interreligious, and intercultural church in the United States.

He then became professor and dean of the chapel at Boston University from 1953 to 1965, the first African American to hold that position. While he was there, he influenced Martin Luther King Jr. and others who became prominent black leaders. During the latter years of his life he directed the Howard Thurman Educational Trust until his death.

Thurman himself always stressed the power of religious experience in understanding the Christian faith. He stayed away from political demonstrations and stressed "the inward journey," the title of one of his many books, but he was ardent in espousal of civil rights. Two of his books that have had an enduring effect on the understanding of African-American Christianity are *Deep River* (1945) and *The Negro Spiritual Speaks of Life and Death* (1947). *Life* magazine named him one of the "great preachers" of the twentieth century.

The following account of Thurman's conversion suggests what he reacted against in his own black church tradition as well as the powerful and formative influence of the black family and the black church in leading young people into faith.

[When my father died, we had] to find someone to preach the funeral. By chance — if there is such a thing — there was a traveling evangelist in town, a man named Sam Cromarte. I shall never forget him. He offered to preach Papa's funeral. He did not need to be persuaded. We sat on the front pew, the "mourners bench." I listened with wonderment, then anger, and finally mounting rage as Sam Cromarte preached my father into hell. This was his chance to illustrate what would happen to "sinners" who died "out of Christ," as my father had done. And he did not waste it. Under my breath I kept whispering to Mamma, "He didn't know Papa, did he? Did he?" Out of her own pain, conflict, and compassionate love, she reached over and gripped my bare knees with her hand, giving a gentle but firm, comforting squeeze. It was sufficient to restrain for the moment my bewildered and outraged spirit.

In the buggy, coming home from the cemetery, I sought some explanation. Why would Reverend Cromarte do this to Papa? Why would he say such things? Neither Mamma nor Grandma would answer my persistent query. Finally, almost to myself, I said, "One thing is sure. When I grow up and become a man, I will never have anything to do with the church."

Excerpt from *With Head and Heart: The Autobiography of Howard Thurman*, copyright © 1979 by Howard Thurman, reprinted by permission of Houghton Mifflin Harcourt Publishing Company.

I remembered those words years later, driving home in the darkening shadows of that day in Roanoke, when a man had died, his hand in mine, taking with him my urgent prayers for the peace of his soul. I remembered too the road over which I had come, and followed my spirit back to the beloved woods of my childhood.

When I was young, I found more companionship in nature than I did among people. The woods befriended me. In the long summer days, most of my time was divided between fishing in the Halifax River and exploring the woods, where I picked huckleberries and gathered orange blossoms from abandoned orange groves. The quiet, even the danger, of the woods provided my rather lonely spirit with a sense of belonging that did not depend on human relationships. I was usually with a group of boys as we explored the woods, but I tended to wander away to be alone for a time, for in that way I could sense the strength of the quiet and the aliveness of the woods. . . .

My mother loved her church. Whenever she had jobs that made it possible for her to be home with the family on Sundays, we all went to church, morning and evening. Most often she was free to go to church with us only on Sunday night because her work required her to serve Sunday dinner. Yet my mother did not talk about religion very much. She read the Bible constantly but kept her prayer life to herself. I discovered the key to her inner religious life at the weekly prayer meeting, which she was always able to attend because it did not conflict with her work. The first time I heard her pray aloud in a meeting, I did not even recognize her voice. It had an unfamiliar quality at first; then I knew it was she. She spread her life out before God, telling him of her anxieties and dreams for me and my sisters, and of her weariness. I learned what could not be *told* to me.

I grew up in Mount Bethel Baptist Church. The church itself was a wooden building consisting of a sanctuary, without partitions, formed in the shape of a cross. All church meetings were held here. Sunday School classes met in separate sections of the same large area. The classes were conducted simultaneously, which meant we had to be sensitive to the presence of the others, and this sense of sharing was dramatized when the separate periods were over and we met as a group to listen to the review of the day's lesson, conducted by one of the deacons or by a visiting minister. Sometimes it was held by "jackleg" preachers. This term was applied to preachers who usually supported their families by working at secular jobs, but who had been "called" to preach and often were ordained. They assisted and sometimes substituted for the minister in emergencies. They were permitted to read the Scripture lesson, occasionally to give the morning's formal prayer in the regular Sunday service, and often they preached on the fifth Sunday night of the month. Sometimes they were the butt of insensitive jokes, and on the whole, they and their families were not treated with the respect they deserved. However, they endured and kept alive the flickering flame of the spirit when the harsh winds blew and the oil was low in the vessel.

Immediately after Sunday School there was a prayer service. At its conclusion, the minister and the choir appeared and the morning service began. The preachers in my church were not "whoopers"; they were more thoughtful than emotional. They were above average in schooling. Two of them had been college-trained. They were called "manuscript preachers." At the core of their preaching was solid religious instruction and guidance which augmented rather than diminished the emotional intensity of their words. One of these men, Dr. S. A. Owen, would later preach my ordination sermon. Under his guidance I preached my trial sermon, earning from the church a "license" that recommended me to the pulpit of any Baptist Church to preach but not to perform the rites of baptism, communion, or marriage. I was a freshman in college when I preached my trial sermon. My text was from one of the Psalms: "I will instruct thee and teach thee the way thou shall go. I will guide thee with Mine own eye." When I finished and before the congregation voted, Reverend Owen said to me, "Brother Howard, I will pass on to you what was told me when I preached my trial sermon many years ago: 'When you get through, sit down.'" I never forgot this admonition, though at first it took some doing.

In the fellowship of the church, particularly in the experience of worship, there was a feeling of sharing in primary community. Not only did church membership seem to bear heavily upon one's ultimate destiny beyond death and the grave; more than all the other communal ties, it also undergirded one's sense of personal identity. It was summed up in the familiar phrase "If God is for you, who can prevail against you?"

The view that the traditional attitude of the religion of black people was, or is, otherworldly is superficial and misguided. "Take all the world but give me Jesus" is a false and simplistic characterization of our religion. A "saved soul," as symbolized by conversion and church membership, gave you a personal validation that transcended time and space, because its ultimate guarantor was God, through Jesus Christ. It was nevertheless of primary importance to the individual living in "real" time and "real" space, because membership in the "fellowship of believers" provided the communal experience of being part of a neighborhood and gave the member a fontal sense of worth that could not be destroyed by any of life's outrages.

Hence, the "sinner" was a unique isolate within the generally binding character of community. It was this ultimate isolation that made the sinner the object of such radical concern in the church of my childhood. In the case of my father, the tensions existing between the two were never resolved. I was twelve years old when I joined the church. It was the custom to present oneself to the deacons, which I did. They examined me, and I answered their questions. When they had finished, the chairman asked, "Howard, why do you come before us?" I said, "I want to be a Christian." Then the chairman said, "But you must come before us after you have been converted and have already become a Christian. Come back when you can tell us of your conversion."

I went straight home and told my grandmother that the deacons had refused to take me into the church. She took me by the hand — I can still see her rocking along beside me — and together we went back to the meeting, arriving before they adjourned. Addressing Mose Wright, who was the chairman, she said, "How dare you turn this boy down? He is a Christian and was one long before he came to you today. Maybe you did not understand his words, but shame on you if you do not know his heart. Now you take this boy into the church right now — before you close this meeting!" And they did. I was baptized in the Halifax River. On Sunday morning everybody met at the church after Sunday School. We did not hold the morning service in the church. Instead, a procession was formed outside. The candidates for baptism, in white robes, were led by the minister and the deacons, who were dressed in black waterproof clothing. At the rear of the procession were the members and all others who wished to witness the ceremony. Some rode ahead on bicycles to be at the riverbank when we arrived. This procession moved down the middle of the street led by old lady Wright, who "sang" us to the river. In full and glorious voice, she began:

"Oh, mourner, don't you want to go,
Oh, mourner, don't you want to go,
Oh, mourner, don't you want to go,
Let's go down to Jordan, Hallelu . . ."

Then the crowd picked it up:

> "Let's go down to Jordan,
> Let's go down to Jordan,
> Let's go down to Jordan,
> Halleluja . . ."

Verse after verse she sang all the way, until we turned the corner and the river lay before us.

The candidates were then grouped before two deacons. One deacon walked out into the water to stand near the stick that was put down to mark the spot where the ceremony would take place. The other led the candidates to this spot. The minister took each candidate and, facing the people on the shore, spoke the great words: "Upon the confession of your faith, my brother, I baptize you in the name of the Father, Son, and Holy Ghost." Then he dipped each one under the water. With the help of the assisting deacon we would be raised to our feet again as the minister said, "Amen." Then there was a chorus of Amens. This was repeated until all the candidates were baptized.

Once you had joined the church, the next step in your validation was to be placed under the tutelage of older members. Often there were two, a man and a woman, who were spiritual guides assigned to you. Every Tuesday afternoon, all the very young converts would attend a prayer meeting. We were taught how to raise a hymn, to pray in public, and to lead a prayer meeting. This took courage for a beginner, but Tuesday after Tuesday we rehearsed thoroughly, and slowly self-confidence developed. Finally, we were ready for the final test, which was to lead an adult prayer service in the company of our sponsors. This done, the process of joining the church was complete. With each learning step, your sense of your own worth as a Christian was heightened. Your sponsor reinforced this by reminding you of your confession of faith whenever your behavior warranted it. "Now that you are a Christian, you cannot behave that way. That was a part of your old life."

Unfortunately, I was soon tested and found wanting. Once or twice a week it was my regular routine to take orders for fish, catch them, and deliver them in time for supper. On the Monday after baptism, I was rowing my boat across the river to get to the pilings of the bridge closest to the channel where there was a plentiful supply of angelfish. Suddenly, a strong wind came up and it began to rain. I was pulling against the tide when the oar slipped, and I fell back, striking my head on the seat. I shouted a spectacular series of profanities; then I remembered that I had recently been baptized in those same waters. I cried all afternoon. "Let that be an object lesson to you," my sponsor said when I confessed to her. "Satan is always waiting to tempt you to make you turn your back on your Lord."

Looking back, it is clear to me that the watchful attention of my sponsors in the church served to enhance my consciousness that whatever I did with my life *mattered*. They added to the security given to me by the quiet insistence of my mother and especially my grandmother that their children's lives were a precious gift. Often, Grandma would sense this awareness beginning to flag in us. When this happened — even when we were not aware of it — she would gather us around and tell us a story that came from her life as a slave.

Once or twice a year, the slave master would permit a slave preacher from a neighboring plantation to come over to preach to his slaves. The slave preacher followed a long tradition, which has hovered over the style of certain black preachers even to the present time. It is to bring the sermon to a grand climax by a dramatization of the crucifixion and resurrection of Jesus. At such times, one would wait for the moment when the preacher would come to this grand, creative exposition. Sometimes he would begin in Gethsemane "with sweat like drops of blood running down . . ." or with Jesus hanging on the cross. But always there was the telling of the timeless story of the seven last words, the mother at the foot of the cross, the darkening sun, and the astonishment of the soldiers — all etched in language of stark reality. At the end, he would be exhausted, but his congregation would be uplifted and sustained with courage to withstand the difficulties of the week to come. When the slave preacher told the Calvary narrative to my grandmother and the other slaves, it had the same effect on them as it would later have on their descendants. But this preacher, when he had finished, would pause, his eyes scrutinizing every face in the congregation, and then he would tell them, "You are not niggers! You are not slaves! You are God's children!"

When my grandmother got to that part of her story, there would be a slight stiffening in her spine as we sucked in our breath. When she had finished, our spirits were restored.

Ethel Waters

(1900–1977)

"I never was a child. I never was coddled, or liked, or understood by my family. I never felt I belonged. I was always an outsider. I was born out of wedlock, but that had nothing to do with all this. To people like mine a thing like that just didn't mean much. Nobody brought me up."

This is the way Ethel Waters began her best-selling autobiography, the story of a black girl of the urban ghetto who rose to stardom and acclaim, not only on stage and in film, but also within the church. Born in Chester, Pennsylvania, Ethel Waters described herself as "a real dead-end kid": "I just ran wild as a little girl. I was bad, always a leader of the street gang in stealing and general hell-raising." She believed that her mixed blood was partly responsible; her maternal great-grandfather was a native of India, and her paternal grandmother was Dutch. She stole for food and earned $4.75 a week as a maid before she sought out the stage, first in Philadelphia, then in Baltimore, finally finding success in Harlem.

She became known for her renditions of "St. Louis Blues" and "Stormy Weather" in particular, but also for "Dinah," "Takin' a Chance on Love," "Cabin in the Sky," and "Am I Blue." For her the blues were her autobiography: "I sang them out of the depths of the private fire in which I was brought up," she said. "Only those who are being burned know what fire is like." Of her singing, the *New Yorker* wrote, "There is every reason (voice, technique, originality) to believe" that Ethel Waters "is the one truly great, compleat, popular singer this country has produced."

Her dramatic career began on Broadway in 1927 when she appeared in the all-black musical "Africana," and her last Broadway production was "Evening with Ethel Waters" in 1959. Her most famous role was Berenice Sadie Brown in "Member of the Wedding." In addition, she appeared in nine films and received an Academy Award nomination for her performance in "Pinky" in 1959.

She preferred acting to singing, and she regretted the "ungodly raw" songs that she had to sing in her youth; but, she said, "they didn't come up to Harlem to go to church. I wanted to sing decent things, but they wouldn't let me. They didn't even know I could." In the late 1950s, she joined the Billy Graham Crusade and sang at numerous Graham evangelistic meetings. She particularly loved to sing one black spiritual that she learned from her grandmother, and she made it the title of her autobiography, *His Eye Is on the Sparrow:*

Why should I feel discouraged
Why should the shadows come
Why should my heart be lonely
And long for heaven and home
When Jesus is my portion
My constant friend is He
His eye is on the sparrow
And I know He watches me.

Ethel Waters was never particular about her denominational affiliation, and late in life she stated her faith simply: "I don't say I'm a religious person. I say I'm a born-again Christian. And that is the most important thing in my life because I've found my living Savior."

Though dancing, being chased by the boys, and mysteries of human birth all fascinated me, my greatest interest, when I was eleven, lay in the Church. Though I was a Catholic, I recognized, as I said, that Louise's little Protestant churches had something. I'd watch the grownups praying and would get the same feeling they had of elation, exaltation, of being carried above and beyond oneself.

The beauty that came into the tired faces of the very old men and women excited me. All week long so many of them were confused and inarticulate. But on Sunday, in the church, they had no difficulty expressing themselves both in song and talk. The emotion that had invaded them was so much bigger than they. Some would rock. Some would cry. Some would talk with eloquence and fire, their confusions and doubts dispelled. And, oh, those hymns!

It began to dawn on me that if sordidness left a deep and lasting mark, so could the goodness in life. The big thing in my life was the feeling that I was getting close to God. Not that I could accept all the doctrine preached. My logic, my reasoning powers made me question much of the doctrine.

For example, as a little girl I was told to ask God to forgive my sins. But what sins could a little girl commit?

My search for God and my finding of Him were to begin in one of those Protestant churches where they were having a children's revival. It was there that I came truly to know and to reverence Christ, the Redeemer.

All my girl friends in the neighborhood were going to this children's revival. I went religiously, every day. When the preacher, the Reverend R. J. Williams, called those who wished to repent and be saved, all my gang would go up there to the mourners' bench and kneel down — but not for long. They would pop up quick as hot cakes and as though they had brand-new souls. But we stout hearts in the back knew they hadn't been cleansed of sin but were just trying to attract attention.

"Come up and shake my hand," the Reverend R. J. Williams would say in his booming voice. "Don't you want to be little soldiers of the Lord?"

Two or three times I did go up to shake his hand. Then I'd return to my seat. I wasn't sure I wanted to be saved. "What can I ask God?" I kept thinking. "What have I got to say to Him?"

One night there were only three of us youngsters still left unsaved in the whole congregation. All the rest had gone to the mourners' bench and been redeemed.

"Come!" cried the Reverend Williams, an inspired and fiery preacher. "Get down on your knees and pray to our Lord!"

So I thought, "I will get down on my knees and pray just to see what happens." I prayed, "O Lord! I don't know what to ask of You!"

I did this every night. Every night I was on my knees — and nothing happened. I didn't feel purged of sin or close to the Lord. I didn't feel what some of the others felt so sincerely. It was this way with me right through the last night of the children's revival meeting.

I was the only one left who was still unsaved, and the preacher looked at me. He looked at me and announced he would continue the revival, if necessary, for three more nights — just to save me. I like to think that the Reverend R. J. Williams saw something special and fervent in me, something deep and passionate struggling toward salvation and spiritual expression.

On the last of the three extra nights of the meeting I got down on the mourners' bench, down on my knees once more. And I told myself, "If nothing happens tonight, I'll not come back again."

Nobody had come that night to the meeting, nobody but the very old people who were always there. I was praying hard and hopefully, asking God, "What am I seeking here? What do I want of You? Help me! If nothing happens, I can't come back here any more!"

And then it happened! The peace of heart and of mind, the peace I had been seeking all my life.

I know that never again, so long as I live, can I experience that wonderful reaction I had that night in the little church. Love flooded my heart and I knew I had found God and that now and for always I would have an ally, a friend close by to strengthen me and cheer me on.

I don't know exactly what happened or when I got up. I don't even know whether I talked. But the people who were there that night were astounded. Afterward they told me that I was radiant and like one transfixed. They said that the light in my face electrified the whole church. And I did feel full of light and warmth.

The preacher, the Reverend R. J. Williams, had some compelling force in him that enabled him to contact people. Great actresses and statesmen and other popular idols have that same force, but great preachers most of all. He could soothe you and calm you and also stir you to the depths of your soul with what lay in his eyes, his voice, and his heart.

Somehow, after that, it seemed more quiet in the house. Or perhaps things did not trouble me so much. I was no longer alone and knew now that I could never be alone anywhere, no matter what I did.

I started to go to church every Sunday. Any church to me has always been the House of God, whatever the denomination. I was a Catholic, but I didn't think He would mind whether I went to that church, a Protestant church, a synagogue, or a Hindu temple.

I was not made more grave and solemn by what had happened. I remained the same as before. Everybody smiled and said, "It is wintertime religion that Ethel has. When summertime comes it will wear off."

I smiled back at them. I didn't have to answer. I knew it was not just wintertime religion with me and that my feeling of being watched over and protected would never leave me.

Clare Boothe Luce

(1903–1987)

A gifted and creative person in many areas, Clare Boothe Luce achieved acclaim as a journalist, editor, war correspondent, playwright, author, and congresswoman. She served in various editorial positions on magazines such as *Vanity Fair, Life,* and *Vogue.* She was elected to Congress for two terms and was appointed U.S. Ambassador to Italy.

A prolific author, Clare Boothe Luce wrote, among other things, three highly successful plays — *The Women* (1936), *Kiss the Boys Goodbye* (1938), and *Margin for Error* (1939). All three were Broadway successes, and all three were later made into films. She also wrote and lectured on religious and humanitarian issues, and in 1948 she spoke before large audiences all across the country on "Christianity in the Atomic Age."

In 1935, she married Henry R. Luce, the well-known editor and publisher of *Time* magazine. Mr. Luce, born of Protestant missionary parents, was a staunch Presbyterian, but in 1946 Clare Boothe Luce converted to the Roman Catholic Church. She prepared several articles for *McCall's Magazine* under the title "The Real Reason," explaining the steps and arguments that seemed persuasive to her at the time.

In another connection, she reported an early visionary experience that much later came back to her as confirmation of her decision to become a Catholic. Her later reflective reasons were mostly intellectual and theological, but her early conversion experience was on a very different level of awareness. A portion of that mystical illumination is reprinted here.

Let me give one example from my own experience of the honest diffi-culty in revealing all that seems important to a conversion.

It is an experience which occurred when I was perhaps sixteen or seventeen years old. I no longer remember where it took place, except that it was a summer day on an American beach. I seem to remember that it was early morning, and that I must have been standing on the sand for some time alone, for even now I distinctly remember that this experience was preceded by a sensation of utter aloneness. Not loneli-ness, but a sort of intense solitariness.

I remember that it was a cool, clean, fresh, calm, blue, radiant day, and that I stood by the shore, my feet not in the waves. And now — as then — I find it difficult to explain what did happen. I expect that the easiest thing is to say that suddenly SOMETHING WAS. My whole soul was cleft clean by it, as a silk veil slit by a shining sword. And I *knew.* I do not know what I knew. I remember, I didn't know even then. That is, I didn't *know* with any "faculty." It was not in my mind or heart or blood stream. But whatever it was I knew, it was something that made ENORMOUS SENSE. And it was final. And yet that word could not be used, for it meant *end,* and there was no end to *this* finality. Then joy abounded in all of me. Or rather, I abounded in joy. I seemed to have no nature, and yet my whole nature was adrift in this immense joy, as a speck of dust is seen to dance in a great golden shaft of sun-light.

I don't know how long this experience lasted. It was, I should think, closer to a second than to an hour — though it might have been either. The memory of it possessed me for several months afterward. At first I marvelled at it. Then I revelled in it. Then it began to obsess me and I tried to put it in some category of previous experience. I remember, I concluded that on that certain day the beauty of nature must have concorded with some unexpected flush of tremendous physical well-being. . . . Gradually I forgot it.

The memory of it never returned to me until one day several years after my conversion, during the first minute of the liturgy of the Mass, where the server says: *"Ad Deum qui laetificat juventutem meum . . ."*

My childhood had been an unusually unhappy and bitter one. I had

From *The Road to Damascus: The Spiritual Pilgrimage of Fifteen Converts to Catholi-cism,* edited by John A. O'Brien. Used by permission of Doubleday, a division of Ran-dom House, Inc.

brooded about it increasingly as I grew older. Indeed until the very day of my conversion, it was a source of deep melancholy and resentment.

"Unless the cup is clean, whatever you pour into it turns sour," said Plato. A conversion cleans the heart of much of its bitterness. Afterwards I seldom remembered my marred childhood, except at one strange moment: at the very beginning of the Mass, during the prayers at the foot of the altar. The priest says: "I will go in unto the altar of God." And generally a small altar boy responds in a clear, shy, thin, little voice: "Unto God who giveth joy to my youth." This phrase, unhappily, always awakened faint echoes of bitter youth, and I would think: *Why* didn't God give joy to my youth! Why was joy withheld from *my* innocence?

One day, long months after I had been a convert, as these words were said, the bitterness did not come. Instead there suddenly flooded into my mind the experience of which I speak, and my heart was gently suffused with an afterglow of that incredible joy.

Then I knew that this strange occurrence had had an enormous part in my conversion, although I had *seemed* to forget it completely. Long ago, in its tremendous purity and simplicity, and now, in its far fainter evocation, I knew it had been, somehow, the most real experience of my whole life.

But how exactly did this affect my conversion? Why had I forgotten it? Why had I remembered it? God only knows! And what use is it to recount it to anyone interested in "Why I Became a Catholic"?

I mention it here partly to elucidate the real difficulty of "telling all," and partly lest anyone think the convert is not aware of the mysterious movements of his own soul, and that much of a conversion may take place on subconscious levels.

Malcolm Muggeridge

(1903–1990)

A maverick with a quick wit, a nimble intellect, and a prophetic conscience, Malcolm Muggeridge enjoyed his self-appointed role as moral gadfly. A "vendor of words," as he called himself, he was associated all his long life with journalism, writing, editing, and publishing.

Most of the time he was moving from one place to another — from Cambridge to Cairo, back to the *Manchester Guardian,* then to Moscow as correspondent, to India, Africa, Italy, and France with the Intelligence Corps in World War II, later to Washington as a correspondent, and then to England as editor of *Punch*. During this incessant, fifty-year pilgrimage, he was in addition to his journalistic assignments also writing books on a variety of topics.

Two deepening experiences began to absorb Muggeridge's full attention. One was his growing disillusionment with the programs and politics of modern society, whether communist, capitalist, or socialist, to bring in a kingdom of heaven on earth. As his custom was, he stated it bluntly:

> I disbelieve in progress, the pursuit of happiness, and all the concomitant notions and projects for creating a society in which human beings find ever greater contentment by being given in ever greater abundance the means to satisfy their material and bodily hopes and desires. . . . The half century in which I have been consciously alive seems to me to have been quite exceptionally destructive, murderous, and brutal. More people have been killed and terrorized, more driven from their homes and native places, more of the past's heritage has been destroyed, more lies propagated and base persuasion engaged in, with less compensatory achievement in art, literature, and imaginative understanding, than in any comparable period of history.

But Muggeridge's second compelling idea, as if to redeem his gloomy analysis of modern society, embraced classical Christianity as the only support, comfort, and hope in a time such as ours. He disclaimed being a theologian or even a conventional church-goer. But he believed that the Christ figure enshrines the only sure and certain truth in an age of skepticism, shifting values, and gross materialism.

Muggeridge wrote several books growing out of his Christian convictions, but his conversion — as he tells it — was more in the nature of an intellectual self-persuasion than an emotional surrender before some dazzling light from heaven. In the excerpt reprinted here, Muggeridge allows us to relive with him his dawning awareness of the only alternative to ultimate despair. Addressed, as it were, to Jesus himself, he speaks informally yet with reverence of the Christ figure as "You."

It was padding about the streets of Moscow that the other dream — the kingdom of heaven on earth — dissolved for me, never to be revived. Those gray, anonymous figures, likewise padding about the streets, seemed infinitely remote, withdrawn, forever strangers, yet somehow near and dear. The gray streets were paradise, the eyeless buildings the many mansions of which heaven is composed. I caught another glimpse of paradise in Berlin after it had been liberated — there the mansions made of rubble, and the heavenly hosts, the glow of liberation still upon them, bartering cigarettes for tins of Spam, and love for both. (Later, this paradise was transformed by means of mirrors into a shining, glowing one, running with *schlag* and fat cigars, with bartered love still plentifully available, but for paper money, not Spam.) So many paradises springing up all over the place, all with many mansions, mansions of light and love; the most majestic of all, the master paradise on which all the others were based — on Manhattan Island! Oh, what marvelous mansions there reaching into the sky! What heavenly Muzak overflowing the streets and buildings, what brilliant lights spelling out

The text is taken from the chapter "Jesus Rediscovered," in his book with the same title (New York: Doubleday & Co., 1969), 48-51. Used with permission. The chapter originally appeared in *Esquire* magazine, June 1969, under the title "On Rediscovering Jesus." Muggeridge also published *Conversion: The Spiritual Journey of a Twentieth Century Pilgrim* (1988), in which his journey of faith is addressed.

what delectable hopes and desires, what heavenly hosts pursuing what happiness on magic screens in living color!

And You? I never caught even a glimpse of You in any paradise — unless You were an old, colored shoeshine man on a windy corner in Chicago one February morning, smiling from ear to ear; or a little man with a lame leg in the Immigration Department in New York, whose smiling patience as he listened to one Puerto Rican after another seemed to reach from there to eternity. Oh, and whoever painted the front of the little church in the woods at Kliasma near Moscow — painted it in blues as bright as the sky and whites that outshone the snow? That might have been You. Or again at Kiev, at an Easter service when the collectivization famine was in full swing, and Bernard Shaw and newspaper correspondents were telling the world of the bursting granaries and apple-cheeked dairymaids in the Ukraine. What a congregation that was, packed in tight, squeezed together like sardines! I myself was pressed against a stone pillar, and scarcely able to breathe. Not that I wanted to, particularly. So many gray, hungry faces, all luminous like an El Greco painting; and all singing. How they sang — about how there was no help except in You, nowhere to turn except to You; nothing, nothing that could possibly bring any comfort except You. I could have touched You then, You were so near — not up at the altar, of course, where the bearded priests, crowned and bowing and chanting, swung their censers — one of the gray faces, the grayest and most luminous of all.

It was strange in a way that I should thus have found myself nearest to You in the land where for half a century past the practice of the Christian religion has been most ruthlessly suppressed; where the very printing of the Gospels is forbidden, and You are derided by all the organs of an all-powerful state as once You were by ribald Roman soldiers when they decked you out as King of the Jews. Yet, on reflection, not so strange. How infinitely preferable it is to be abhorred, rather than embraced, by those in authority. Where the distinction between God and Caesar is so abundantly clear, no one in his senses — or out of them, for that matter — is likely to suggest that any good purpose would be served by arranging a dialogue between the two of them. In the Communist countries an unmistakable and unbridgeable abyss divides the kingdoms on earth in the Devil's gift and Your kingdom, with no crazed clerics gibbering and grimacing in the intervening no man's land. It provides the perfect circumstances for the Christian faith to bloom anew

— so uncannily like the circumstances in which it first bloomed at the beginning of the Christian era. I look eastwards, not westwards, for a new Star of Bethlehem.

It would be comforting to be able to say, Now I see! To recite with total satisfaction one of the Church's venerable creeds: "I believe in God, the Father Almighty. . . ." To point to such a moment of illumination when all became miraculously clear. To join with full identification in one of the varieties of Christian worship. Above all, to feel able to say to you, "Lord!" and confidently await Your command. Comforting — but, alas, it would not be true. The one thing above all others that You require of us is, surely, the truth. I have to confess, then, that I see only fitfully, believe no creed wholly, have had no all-sufficing moment of illumination.

And You? What do I know of You? A living presence in the world; the one who, of all the billions of our human family, came most immediately from God and went most immediately to God, while remaining most humanly and intimately here among us, today, as yesterday and tomorrow; for all time. Did You live and die and rise from the dead as they say? Who knows, or, for that matter, cares? History is for the dead, and You are alive. Similarly, all those churches raised and maintained in Your name, from the tiniest, weirdest conventicle to the great cathedrals rising so sublimely into the sky — they are for the dead, and must themselves die; are, indeed, dying fast. They belong to time, You to eternity. At the intersection of time and eternity — nailed there — You confront us; a perpetual reminder that living, we die, and dying, we live. An incarnation wonderful to contemplate; the light of the world, indeed.

Fiat lux! Let there be light! So everything began at God's majestic command; so it might have continued till the end of time — history unending — except that You intervened, shining another light into the innermost recesses of the human will, where the ego reigns and reaches out in tentacles of dark desire. Having seen this other light, I turn to it, striving and growing towards it as plants do towards the sun. The light of love, abolishing the darkness of hate; the light of peace, abolishing the darkness of strife and confusion; the light of life, abolishing the darkness of death; the light of creativity, abolishing the darkness of destruction. Though, in terms of history, the darkness falls, blacking out us and our world, You have overcome history. You came as light into the world in order that whoever believed in You should not remain in darkness. Your light shines in the darkness, and the darkness has not overcome it. Nor ever will.

Simone Weil

(1909–1943)

Simone Weil is one of the most provocative and yet perplexing thinkers of the twentieth century. She witnessed the horrors of Europe first-hand — the barbarism of industry, the rise of fascism, the brutality of war. From her experience emerged a philosophy that was never systematized but spoke eloquently of the sanctity of the human spirit.

Born into an affluent Jewish family in Paris, she was an extremely intelligent child, despite the fact that she felt inferior to her brilliant brother. She also demonstrated very early the sensitivity to human need that marked her entire life; at the age of five she refused to eat sugar when French soldiers at the front had none. After studying philosophy, classical philology, and science, she held a number of positions teaching philosophy, but her conflict with school boards made each appointment short-lived.

In 1934-1935 she began work in an auto factory to experience first-hand the oppression of workers, but her delicate health failed. In 1936 she joined an anarchist unit training for battle in the Spanish Civil War, but since she was a pacifist, she would not carry a gun. Instead, she served as a cook for the soldiers until she suffered severe burns from boiling oil.

Recovering in Portugal, she visited a monastery at Solesmes where she had a deep and powerful religious experience in which, she said, "Christ himself came down and took possession of me." Despite her Jewish background, she said that she was born and grew up "within the Christian inspiration." She studied the Gospels avidly, but her commitment to Christianity did not include membership in the church. She refused baptism, for she argued that her faith was inclusive, embodying the truths of non-Christian and even heretical traditions. She centered this claim on the incarnation of Christ, emphasizing that in becoming human Christ took on the flesh of all peoples and all cultures.

The persecution of European Jewry forced Weil's parents to escape from France to New York with their daughter. Simone pleaded for an opportunity to return to France, and finally she did go to London in 1942, where she worked for the Free French Movement. Refusing to eat more than the daily French ration, she became sick again and died of pleurisy.

After her death, her writings were published, including *Waiting for God* (1951), her spiritual autobiography, and it is from this volume that the following account is taken. It is a letter written in 1942, addressed to the Roman Catholic priest, J. M. Perrin. Her philosophy and theology were spelled out in other volumes, including *Gravity and Grace* (1952), *Oppression and Liberty* (1958), and *Notebooks* (1956). For Simone Weil as for Søren Kierkegaard, suffering lay at the heart of Christian discipleship, and she could not endure society's inhumanity without protesting and taking suffering on herself.

~

Father,

Before leaving I want to speak to you again, it may be the last time perhaps, for over there I shall probably send you only my news from time to time just so as to have yours.

I told you that I owed you an enormous debt. I want to try to tell you exactly what it consists of. I think that if you could really understand what my spiritual state is you would not be at all sorry that you did not lead me to baptism. But I do not know if it is possible for you to understand this.

You neither brought me the Christian inspiration nor did you bring me to Christ; for when I met you there was no longer any need; it had been done without the intervention of any human being. If it had been otherwise, if I had not already been won, not only implicitly but consciously, you would have given me nothing, because I should have received nothing from you. My friendship for you would have been a reason for me to refuse your message, for I should have been afraid of the possibilities of error and illusion which human influence in the divine order is likely to involve.

I may say that never at any moment in my life have I "sought for

---

God." For this reason, which is probably too subjective, I do not like this expression and it strikes me as false. As soon as I reached adolescence I saw the problem of God as a problem of which the data could not be obtained here below, and I decided that the only way of being sure not to reach a wrong solution, which seemed to me the greatest possible evil, was to leave it alone. So I left it alone. I neither affirmed nor denied anything. It seemed to me useless to solve the problem, for I thought that being in this world, our business was to adopt the best attitude with regard to the problems of this world, and that such an attitude did not depend upon the solution of the problem of God.

This held good as far as I was concerned at any rate, for I never hesitated in my choice of an attitude; I always adopted the Christian attitude as the only possible one. I might say that I was born, I grew up and I always remained within the Christian inspiration. Whilst the very name of God had no part in my thoughts, with regard to the problems of this world and this life I shared the Christian conception in an explicit and rigorous manner, with the most specific notions it involves. Some of these notions have been part of my outlook for as far back as I can remember. With others I know the time and manner of their coming and the form under which they imposed themselves upon me.

For instance I never allowed myself to think of a future state, but I always believed that the instant of death is the centre and object of life. I used to think that, for those who live as they should, it is the instant when, for an infinitesimal fraction of time, pure truth, naked, certain and eternal enters the soul. I may say that I never desired any other good for myself. I thought that the life which leads to this good is not only defined by a code of morals common to all, but that for each one it consists of a succession of acts and events which are strictly personal to him, and so essential that he who leaves them on one side never reaches the goal. The notion of vocation was like this for me. I saw the carrying out of a vocation differed from the actions dictated by reason or inclination in that it was due to an impulse of an essentially and manifestly different order; and not to follow such an impulse when it made itself felt, even if it demanded impossibilities, seemed to me the greatest of all ills. Hence my conception of obedience; and I put this conception to the test when I entered the factory and stayed on there, even when I was in that state of intense and uninterrupted misery about which I recently told you. The most beautiful life possible has always seemed to me to be one where everything is determined, either by the pressure of circumstances or by impulses such as I have just mentioned and where there is never any room for choice.

At fourteen I fell into one of those fits of bottomless despair which come with adolescence, and I seriously thought of dying because of the mediocrity of my natural faculties. The exceptional gifts of my brother, who had a childhood and youth comparable to those of Pascal, brought my own inferiority home to me. I did not mind having no visible successes, but what did grieve me was the idea of being excluded from that transcendent kingdom to which only the truly great have access and wherein truth abides. I preferred to die rather than live without that truth. After months of inward darkness, I suddenly had the everlasting conviction that no matter what human being, even though practically devoid of natural faculties, can penetrate to the kingdom of truth reserved for genius, if only he longs for truth and perpetually concentrates all his attention upon its attainment. He thus becomes a genius too, even though for lack of talent his genius cannot be visible from outside. Later on, when the strain of headaches caused the feeble faculties I possess to be invaded by a paralysis which I was quick to imagine was probably incurable, the same conviction led me to persevere for ten years in an effort of concentrated attention which was practically unsupported by any hope of results.

Under the name of truth I also included beauty, virtue, and every kind of goodness, so that for me it was a question of a conception of this relationship between grace and desire. The conviction which had come to me was that when one hungers for bread one does not receive stones. But at that time I had not read the Gospel.

Just as I was certain that desire has in itself an efficacy in the realm of spiritual goodness whatever its form, I thought it was also possible that it might not be effective in any other realm.

As for the spirit of poverty, I do not remember any moment when it was not in me, although only to that unhappily small extent which is compatible with my imperfection. I fell in love with Saint Francis of Assisi as soon as I came to know about him. I always believed and hoped that one day Fate would force upon me the condition of a vagabond and a beggar which he embraced freely. Actually I felt the same way about prison.

From my earliest childhood I always had also the Christian idea of love for one's neighbour, to which I gave the name of justice; a name it bears in many passages of the Gospel and which is so beautiful. You know that on this point I have failed seriously several times.

261

The duty of acceptance in all that concerns the will of God, whatever it may be, was impressed upon my mind as the first and most necessary of all duties from the time when I found it set down in Marcus Aurelius under the form of the *amor fati* of the Stoics. I saw it as a duty we cannot fail in without dishonouring ourselves.

The idea of purity, with all that this word can imply for a Christian, took possession of me at the age of sixteen, after a period of several months during which I had been going through the emotional unrest natural in adolescence. This idea came to me when I was contemplating a mountain landscape and little by little it was imposed upon me in an irresistible manner.

Of course I knew quite well that my conception of life was Christian. That is why it never occurred to me that I could enter the Christian community. I had the idea that I was born inside. But to add dogma to this conception of life, without being forced to do so by indisputable evidence, would have seemed to me like a lack of honesty. I should even have thought I was lacking in honesty had I considered the question of the truth of dogma as a problem for myself, or even had I simply desired to reach a conclusion on this subject. I have an extremely severe standard for intellectual honesty, so severe that I never met anyone who did not seem to fall short of it in more than one respect; and I am always afraid of failing in it myself.

Keeping away from dogma in this way, I was prevented by a sort of shame from going into churches, though all the same I like being in them. Nevertheless I had three contacts with Catholicism which really counted.

After my year in the factory, before going back to teaching, I had been taken by my parents to Portugal, and while there I left them to go alone to a little village. I was, as it were, in pieces, soul and body. That contact with affliction had killed my youth. Until then I had not had any experience of affliction, unless we count my own, which, as it was my own, seemed to me to have little importance, and which moreover was only a partial affliction, being biological and not social. I knew quite well that there was a great deal of affliction in the world. I was obsessed with the idea, but I had not had prolonged and first-hand experience of it. As I worked in the factory, indistinguishable to all eyes, including my own, from the anonymous mass, the affliction of others entered into my flesh and my soul. Nothing separated me from it, for I had really forgotten my past and I looked forward to no future, finding it difficult to imagine the possibility of surviving all the fatigue. What I went through there marked me in so lasting a manner that still today when any human being, whoever he may be and in whatever circumstances, speaks to me without brutality, I cannot help having the impression that there must be a mistake and that unfortunately the mistake will in all probability disappear. There I received for ever the mark of a slave, like the branding of the red-hot iron which the Romans put on the foreheads of their most despised slaves. Since then I have always regarded myself as a slave.

In this state of mind then, and in a wretched condition physically, I entered the little Portuguese village, which, alas, was very wretched too, on the very day of its patronal festival. I was alone. It was the evening and there was a full moon. It was by the sea. The wives of the fishermen were going in procession to make a tour of all the ships, carrying candles and singing what must certainly be very ancient hymns of a heart-rending sadness. Nothing can give any idea of it. I have never heard anything so poignant unless it were the song of the boatmen on the Volga. There the conviction was suddenly borne in upon me that Christianity is pre-eminently the religion of slaves, that slaves cannot help belonging to it, and I among others.

In 1937 I had two marvellous days at Assisi. There, alone in the little XIIth Century Romanesque chapel of Santa Maria degli Angeli, an incomparable marvel of purity where Saint Francis often used to pray, something stronger than I was compelled me for the first time in my life to go down on my knees.

In 1938 I spent ten days at Solesmes, from Palm Sunday to Easter Tuesday, following all the liturgical services. I was suffering from splitting headaches; each sound hurt me like a blow; by an extreme effort of concentration I was able to rise above this wretched flesh, to leave it to suffer by itself, heaped up in a corner, and to find a pure and perfect joy in the unimaginable beauty of the chanting and the words. This experience enabled me by analogy to get a better understanding of the possibility of loving divine love in the midst of affliction. It goes without saying that in the course of these services the thought of the Passion of Christ entered into my being once and for all. . . .

Christianity should contain all vocations without exception since it is catholic. In consequence the Church should also. But in my eyes Christianity is catholic by right but not in fact. So many things are outside it, so many things that I love and do not want to give up, so many things that God loves, otherwise they would not be in existence. All the immense stretches of past centuries, except the last twenty, are among them; all the countries inhabited by coloured races; all secular life in the white peoples' countries; in the history of these countries, all the traditions banned as heretical, those of the Manicheans, and Albigenses for instance; all those things resulting from the Renaissance, too often degraded but not quite without value.

Christianity being catholic by right but not in fact, I regard it as legitimate on my part to be a member of the Church by right but not in fact, not only for a time, but for my whole life if need be.

But it is not merely legitimate. So long as God does not give me the certainty that he is ordering me to do anything else, I think it is my duty.

I think, and so do you, that our obligation for the next two or three years, an obligation so strict that we can scarcely fail in it without treason, is to show the public the possibility of a truly incarnated Christianity. In all the history now known there has never been a period in which souls have been in such peril as they are today in every part of the globe. The bronze serpent must be lifted up again so that whoever raises his eyes to it may be saved.

But everything is so closely bound up together that Christianity cannot be really incarnated unless it is catholic in the sense that I have just defined. How could it circulate through the flesh of all the nations of Europe if it did not contain absolutely everything in itself? Except of course falsehood. But in everything that exists there is most of the time more truth than falsehood.

Having so intense and so painful a sense of this urgency, I should betray the truth, that is to say the aspect of truth that I see, if I left the point, where I have been since my birth, at the intersection of Christianity and everything that is not Christianity.

I have always remained at this exact point, on the threshold of the Church, without moving, quite still ἐν ὑπομένῃ (it is so much more beautiful a word than *patiential*); only now my heart has been transported, for ever, I hope, into the Blessed Sacrament exposed on the altar.

Mother Teresa

(1910–1997)

If and when Mother Teresa is made a saint by the Vatican, few will be surprised. Within a decade of her death, she was already beatified for her work with the poor of India and other nations — one step away from sainthood. This diminutive woman seized the moral imagination of the world in the late twentieth century, especially after the 1969 documentary by Malcolm Muggeridge, *Something Beautiful for God*. Muggeridge's experience in making the film and working with Mother Teresa proved instrumental in his own journey from unbelief to Christian faith. (See Muggeridge's account of his conversion in this volume.)

Mother Teresa was born Agnese Gonsche Bojaxhiu to a poor Albanian grocer and his wife. Her name means "rosebud" in Albanian. Her father died when she was eight, and she said his death brought her family closer together. She enjoyed reading about missionaries and their service, and by age twelve she thought she should become a nun. At eighteen, she left home to join the Sisters of Loreto and never saw her mother or sister again.

After briefly studying English in Ireland, Mother Teresa was sent to India to teach school children. Her first post was in Darjeeling, near the Himalayan mountains, and when she took her first vows as a nun in 1931, she adopted the name Teresa after Thérèse of Lisieux, the patron saint of missionaries. She was transferred to Calcutta, where she made her solemn vows as a nun in 1937. The squalid poverty of Calcutta roiled her conscience, and on September 10, 1946, Mother Teresa heard a voice from God — what she later termed "a call within the call." She would devote her life to alleviating the suffering of the poor.

One of the following excerpts gives what became her public explanation of the "call within the call." Following her death, the private side of Mother

Teresa became public in *Mother Teresa, Come Be My Light: The Private Writings of the "Saint of Calcutta"* (2007), edited by Brian Kolodiejchuk, M.C. In her letters, it becomes clear that "the call within the call" was rooted in her visions of and conversations with God and that Mother Teresa was a twentieth-century mystic. The second excerpt demonstrates this rich dimension of her faith and experience.

Come Be My Light also revealed what at first glance seems astonishing. Mother Teresa — beginning with her "call within the call" — lived a life of spiritual desolation and estrangement from God. As she acknowledged with agonized repetition to her archbishop, "There is so much contradiction in my soul. — Such deep longing for God — so deep that it is painful — a suffering continual — and yet not wanted by God — repulsed — empty — no faith — no love — no zeal." The absence of God in her life abated occasionally, but the fact is that this saint of compassion also lived in spiritual desolation. Perhaps this was owing to her identification with Jesus Christ, who cried, "My God, my God, why hast thou forsaken me?" But it also makes her life and witness all the more compelling to know that so much good came from a woman who felt her faith was so fragile.

Mother Teresa began her work in Calcutta in 1948. She shed the habit of her Loreto order and dressed in a white cotton sari with a blue border. She became an Indian citizen. But church recognition of her missionary work was gradual. The Vatican gave her permission in 1950 to create a diocesan congregation that eventually became the Missionaries of Charity; later it became an order directly responsible to the Pope.

When her order was launched, it had only thirteen members in Calcutta, but by 2007 it had grown exponentially to more than 5,000 sisters and an associated brotherhood of 450 members, with 610 missions in 123 countries. The order also received support from more than one million Co-Workers. It focused its attention on the "poorest of the poor," especially through hospices and homes for people with HIV/AIDS, leprosy, and tuberculosis; soup kitchens; children's and family counseling programs; personal helpers; orphanages; and schools.

Mother Teresa had her critics, including those who accused her of only treating poverty and not trying to eradicate its causes. The standards of hygiene and health care in her missions were described as inadequate. She was attacked for her stands on abortion and divorce, and some criticized her fundraising, saying it was focused excessively on expanding the work of the order, rather than improving the conditions of the people to whom the order ministered.

Nevertheless, she won steadily increasing recognition and fame as the benefactor and protector of the poor. As early as 1962, the Indian government gave her the Padma Shri, and other awards were showered upon her, including the Bharat Ratna, India's highest civilian award, in 1980. The Vatican gave her the first Pope John XXIII Peace Prize in 1971 and the Pacem in Terris Award in 1976. She was the first recipient of the Templeton Prize in Religion (1973), the Albert Schweitzer International Prize (1975), and the Nobel Peace Prize (1979), among other awards.

Her solace — and her inspiration for her work and her order — were the words of Jesus from the cross, "I thirst." "Why does Jesus say 'I thirst'? What does it mean?" she asked. "Something so hard to explain in words — . . . 'I thirst' is something much deeper than just Jesus saying 'I love you.' Until you know deep inside that Jesus thirsts for you — you can't begin to know who He wants to be for you. Or who He wants you to be for Him."

The thirsting Jesus gave the doubting Mother Teresa the strength and courage to move beyond her own fragile faith to offer hope and comfort to those who thirst — in India and throughout the world. It all started with "the call within the call."

I am Albanian by birth. Now I am a citizen of India. I am also a Catholic nun. In my work, I belong to the whole world. But in my heart, I belong to Christ.

The first time I said I wanted to devote my life to God, my mother opposed me. Then, she said, "All right, my daughter, you go. But be careful to be always of God and Christ, only." Not only God, but also she would have condemned me if I had not followed my vocation with faithfulness. She will ask me one day, "My daughter, have you lived only for God?"

I was still very young, no more than twelve years old, when, in the heart of my family, I first experienced the desire to belong completely to God.

First excerpt from *My Life for the Poor: Mother Teresa of Calcutta,* ed. Jose Luis Gonzalez-Balado and Janet N. Playfoot (South Yarmouth, MA: John Curley & Associates, Inc., 1985), 1-10. Used with permission. Second excerpt from letter from Mother Teresa to Archbishop Périer, published in *Mother Teresa, Come Be My Light: The Private Writings of the "Saint of Calcutta,"* ed. Brian Kolodiejchuk (New York: Doubleday, 2007). Copyright © 2007 by the Mother Teresa Center. Reprinted by permission of the Mother Teresa Center.

I thought and prayed about it for six years.

At times, I had the impression that my vocation did not exist. But finally I was convinced that God called me.

Our Lady of Letnice interceded for me and helped me to discover it.

In the moments when I was uncertain about my vocation, some advice of my mother's helped me a lot.

She often repeated to me, "When you accept a task, do it willingly. If not, don't accept it!"

Once I asked my confessor for advice about my vocation. I asked, "How can I know if God is calling me and for what he is calling me?"

He answered, "You will know by your happiness. If you are happy with the idea that God calls you to serve him and your neighbor, this will be proof of your vocation. Profound joy of the heart is like a magnet that indicates the path of life. One has to follow it, even though one enters into a way full of difficulties."

I often remember my mother and father praying together, every night, with the other members of the family.

Because of his work, my father was often absent from home. But even in those cases we came together every night around our mother to pray with her.

Our most frequent prayer in those cases was the holy rosary.

It was at the feet of our Lady of Letnice (in Skopje) where I first heard the divine call, convincing me to serve God and to devote myself to his service.

I remember the afternoon of her feast of the Assumption. I was praying with a lighted candle in my hands and singing in my heart, full of joy inside, when I took the decision to wholly devote myself to God through religious life.

I also remember that it was in the sanctuary of our Lady of Letnice in Skopje where I heard the voice of God calling me to be all his by consecrating myself to him and to the service of my neighbors.

For some time it had been a wish that I had carried hidden in my heart.

I still remember those beautiful times and some of the hymns that we sang to our Lady, especially the one entitled *Në Cëernagore kem nji Nanë* (In the Black Mountain we've a mother).

A few years ago, I was able to return to Skopje and to Letnice. I felt very happy kneeling again in front of the image of our Lady to pray to her. The habit of the image had changed but the eyes and her look continued to be the same after so many years. With my prayer I wanted to give thanks to God for the past years from the first time I had left Skopje. They were fruitful years, and if I had to begin again, I would leave Skopje to take the same path.

I found Skopje very changed, but it continued to be my Skopje, where I had spent my childhood with my family and where I was happy.

We opened a house of the Missionaries of Charity in Skopje. This filled me with happiness. Establishing a small community of Missionaries of Charity in the town where I was born showed my gratitude and that of the sisters of God and to my place of birth.

In my address to the people of Skopje I said, "The sisters are the present that I make to my village. I hope that Skopje gives more vocations to the church so that we can offer more sisters. I always carry in my heart the people of Skopje and Albania. I ask God that his peace descend over all the hearts of all their inhabitants and over those of all the world."

We were a very happy family.

We were very closely united, especially after my father's death.

We lived for each other and we made each other's lives very full and very happy.

I have never forgotten my mother.

She used to be very busy the whole day, but as soon as the evening came, she moved quickly to get ready to meet my father.

At the time, we didn't understand. We used to smile, we used to laugh, we used to tease her. Now, I remember what a tremendous, delicate love she had for him.

It didn't matter what happened: she was ready there with a smile to meet him.

My mother was a holy woman.

She imparted to all her children that love for God and that love for her neighbor.

She brought us up very closely, in the love of Jesus. She herself prepared us for our first communion, and so we learned to love God above all things from our mother.

I was only twelve years old, no more, and lived at home with my parents in Skopje (Yugoslavia) when I felt for the first time the desire to become a nun.

I went to a non-Catholic school but there were good priests who helped boys and girls to follow their vocation, according to God's will.

It was then that I realized that my vocation was towards the poor.

But between twelve and eighteen years of age I forgot this desire to become a nun.

I'll repeat: we were a very happy family.

At eighteen years, I decided again to leave home to become a missionary.

From then on, I have never had the least doubt of my decision.

It was the will of God: he made the choice.

Some Jesuit missionaries went to India while I was still at home.

They used to send word to us what they were doing for the people there.

They used to give us the most beautiful descriptions about the experiences they had with the people and especially with the children of India.

They made the contact for me with the Loreto Sisters who were working in India at that time.

Through these Jesuit missionaries, I came into contact with the Loreto Sisters and joined them in Rathfarnham, Dublin.

Following my vocation was a sacrifice which Christ asked [of] me and my people, since we were a very happy and united family.

But I didn't leave home until I was eighteen.

Even after so many years, I still remember when I went to the mother house of the Loreto Sisters in Rathfarnham.

A few months ago, I saw the places where I had been as a young postulant. I still remember the community room and chapel, everything.

I left Rathfarnham after only six weeks. I had joined in October 1928 and in January I went to India to do the novitiate in 1929.

I did my novitiate in Darjeeling and took the vows with the Loreto Sisters.

For twenty years, I was at work in education in the St. Mary's High School, which was mostly for middle-class children. (There were some of the better-class people also.) That was the only Catholic high school that we had in Calcutta at the time. (I can't say whether I was a good teacher. This my pupils would know better. But I loved teaching.)

In Loreto I was the happiest nun in the world.

To leave the work that I carried out there was a great sacrifice.

What I didn't leave was my condition of being a nun.

The change was only in the work.

My Sisters of Loreto were limited to teaching, which is an authentic apostolate for Christ.

It was a call within the call: something like a second vocation.

It was the inner command to renounce Loreto, where I was very happy, to go to serve the poor in the streets.

In 1946, while I was going by train to Darjeeling for my spiritual retreat, I again experienced a call to renounce everything and to follow Christ into the slums, to serve the poorest of the poor.

I understood that God wanted something from me.

In 1948, twenty years after I came to India, I actually decided upon this close contact with the poorest of the poor. It was for me a special vocation to give all to belong to Jesus.

I felt that God wanted from me something more. He wanted me to be poor with the poor and to love him in the distressing disguise of the poorest of the poor.

I had the blessing of obedience.

Once I represented the matter to my superiors and to the bishop of Calcutta, they felt that it was God's will, that God wanted it. I had their blessing, the blessing of obedience.

With that, there is no doubt or mistake. Maybe it looks a failure, but if it's a failure, only in the eyes of people, not in the eyes of God.

I didn't have to give up anything: vocation is belonging to Christ, and my belonging to him had not changed.

I was only changing the means to serve the poorest of the poor.

The work is only a way to put our love for Christ into action.

(The vocation itself, my belonging to Christ, didn't have to change. It had rather deepened.)

My love for Christ had deepened by making that big sacrifice. That's why I call it a simple *call within a call.*

My vocation was a continuation of my belonging to Christ and of my being only his.

At the same time, some of the girls whom I was teaching and who visited the poor in the slums and the sick in the hospital, expressed the desire of becoming nuns so that they could devote themselves fully to the apostolate among the very poor.

It was on the tenth of September 1946, in the train that took me to

Darjeeling, the hill station in the Himalayas, that I heard the call of God.

In quiet, intimate prayer with our Lord, I heard distinctly, a call within a call.

The message was quite clear: I was to leave the convent and help the poor whilst living among them. It was an order. I knew where I belonged, but I did not know how to get there.

I felt intensely that Jesus wanted me to serve him among the poorest of the poor, the uncared for, the slum dwellers, the abandoned, the homeless. Jesus invited me to serve him and follow him in actual poverty, to practise a kind of life that would make me similar to the needy in whom he was present, suffered and loved.

*   *   *

St. Mary's Convent
13th Jan. 47

Your Grace,

From last Sept. strange thoughts and desires have been filling my heart. They got stronger and clearer during the 8 days retreat I made in Darjeeling. On coming here I told Fr. Van Exem everything — I showed him the few notes I had written during the retreat. — He told me he thought it was God's inspiration — but to pray and remain silent over it. I kept on telling him whatever passed in my soul — in thoughts and desires — Then yesterday he wrote this "I cannot prevent you from talking or writing to His Grace. You will write to His Grace as a daughter to her father, in perfect trust and sincerity, without any fear or anxiety, telling him how it all went, adding that you talked to me and that now I think I cannot in conscience prevent you from exposing everything to him."

Before I begin I want to tell you that at one word that Your Grace would say I am ready never to consider again any of those strange thoughts which have been coming continually.

During the year very often I have been longing to be all for Jesus and to make other souls — especially Indian, come and love Him fervently — to identify myself with Indian girls completely, and so love Him as He has never been loved before. I thought [it] was one of my many mad desires. I read the life of St. M. Cabrini — She did so much for the Americans because she became one of them. Why can't I do for India what

272

she did for Amer? She did not wait for souls to come to her — She went to them with her zealous workers. Why can't I do the same for Him here? There are so many souls — pure — holy who are longing to give themselves only to God. European orders are too rich for them — They get more than they give. — *"Wouldst thou not help."* How can I? I have been and am very happy as a Loreto Nun. — To leave that what I love and expose myself to new labours and sufferings which will be great, to be the laughing stock of so many — especially religious — to cling and choose deliberately the hard things of an Indian life — to [cling and choose] loneliness and ignominy — uncertainty — and all because Jesus wants it — because something is calling me "to leave all and gather the few — to live His life — to do His work in India." These thoughts were a cause of much suffering — but the voice kept on saying *"Wilt thou refuse."* One day at Holy Com. [Communion] I heard the same voice very distinctly — *"I want Indian nuns, Victims of my love, who would be Mary & Martha. Who would be so very united to me as to radiate my love on souls. I want free nuns covered with my poverty of the cross — I want obedient nuns covered with my obedience of the Cross. I want full of love nuns covered with the Charity of the Cross. Wilt thou refuse to do this for me?"* On another day. *"You have become my Spouse for my Love — you have come to India for Me. The thirst you had for souls brought you so far. — Are you afraid to take one more step for your Spouse — for me — for souls? — Is your generosity grown cold — am I a second to you? You did not die for souls — that is why you don't care what happens to them. — Your heart was never drowned in sorrow as it was My Mother's. We both gave our all for souls — and you? You are afraid that you will lose your vocation — you will become secular — you will be wanting in perseverance. — Nay — your vocation is to love and suffer and save souls and by taking this step you will fulfil my Heart's desire for you — That is your vocation. — You will dress in simple Indian clothes or rather like My Mother dressed — simple and poor. — Your present habit is holy because it is my symbol — your sarie will become holy because it will be my symbol."* I tried to persuade Our Lord that I would try to become a very fervent holy Loreto Nun, a real Victim here in this vocation — but the answer came very clear again. *"I want Indian Missionary Sisters of Charity — who would be My fire of love amongst the very poor — the sick — the dying — the little street children — The poor I want you to bring to me — and the Sisters that would offer their lives as victims of my love — would bring these souls to Me. You are I know the most uncapable person, weak & sinful, but just because you are that I want to use you, for my*

Glory! Wilt thou refuse?" These words or rather this voice frightened me. The thought of eating, sleeping — living like the Indians filled me with fear. I prayed long — I prayed so much — I asked Our Mother Mary to ask Jesus to remove all this from me. The more I prayed — the clearer grew the voice in my heart and so I prayed that He would do with me whatever He wanted. He asked again and again. Then once more the voice was very clear — *"You have been always saying 'do with me what ever you wish' — Now I want to act — let me do it — my little Spouse — My own little one. — Do not fear — I shall be with you always. — You will suffer and you suffer now — but if you are my own little Spouse — the Spouse of the Crucified Jesus — you will have to bear these torments on your heart. — Let me act — Refuse me not — Trust me lovingly — trust me blindly."* *"Little one give me souls — give me the souls of the poor little street children — How it hurts — if you only knew — to see these poor children soiled with sin. I long for the purity of their love. — If you would only answer my call — and bring me these souls — draw them away from the hands of the evil one. — If you only knew how many little ones fall into sin everyday. There are convents with numbers of nuns caring for the rich and able to do people, but for my very poor there is absolutely none. For them I long — them I love — Wilt thou refuse?"* *"Ask His Grace to give me this in thanksgiving of the 25 years of grace I have given him."*

This is what went on between Him and me during the days of much prayer. — Now the whole thing stands clear before my eyes as follows —

To be an Indian — to live with them — like them — so as to get at the people's heart. The order would start outside Calcutta — Cossipore — open lonely place or St. John's Sealdah where the Sisters could have a real contemplative life in their novitiate — where they would complete one full year of true interior life — and one in action. The Sisters are to cling to perfect poverty — Poverty of the Cross — nothing but God. — So as not to have riches enter their heart, they would have nothing of the outside — but they will keep up themselves with the labour of their hands — Franciscan poverty — Benedict's labour.

In the order girls of any nationality should be taken — but they must become Indian-minded — dress in simple clothes. A long white long-sleeved habit, light blue sarie, and a white veil, sandals — no stockings — a crucifix — girdle and rosary.

The Sisters should get a very full knowledge of the interior life — from holy priests who would help them to become so united to God so as to radiate Him when they join the mission field. They should become true Victims — no words — but in every sense of the word, Indian victims for India. Love should be the word, the fire, that will make them live the life to its full. If the nuns are very poor they will be free to love only God — to serve Him only — to be only His. The two years in perfect solitude should make them think of the interior while they will be in the midst of the exterior.

So as to renew and keep up the spirit — the Sisters should spend one day in every week in the house — the Mother house of the city when they are in the mission.

The Sisters' work would be to go to the people. — No boarding schools — but plenty of schools — free — up to class II only. In each parish two sisters would go — one for the sick and the dying — one for the school. If the number requires the pairs can increase. The Sisters would teach the little ones — help them have pure recreations and so keep them from the street and sin. The school should be only in the very poor places of the parish, to get the children from the streets, to keep them for the poor parents who have to work. The one who will take care of the sick — she will assist the dying — do all the work for the sick — just as much if not more, what a person gets in a hospital — wash them and prepare the place for His coming. At the appointed time the sisters will all meet at the same place from the different parishes and go home — where they would have this complete separation from the world. — This in the cities where the number of the poor is great. — In the villages — the same thing — only there they could leave the said village — once their work of instruction and service ends. To move about with great ease and fast each nun should learn how to ride a bicycle, some how to drive a bus. This is a little too up to date — but souls are dying for want of care — for want of love. These Sisters — these true victims should do the work that is wanting in Christ's Apostolate in India. They should also have a hospital for little children with bad diseases. The Nuns of this order will be Missionaries of Charity or Missionary Sisters of Charity.

God is calling me — unworthy and sinful that I am. I am longing to give all for souls. They will all think me mad — after so many years — to begin a thing which will bring me for the most part only suffering — but He calls me also to join the few to start the work, to fight the devil and deprive him of the thousand little souls which he is destroying every day.

This is rather long — but I have told you everything as I would have told my Mother. — I long to be really only His — to burn myself completely for Him and souls. — I want Him to be loved tenderly by many. — So if you think, if you wish — I am ready to do His Will. Count not my feelings — count not the cost I would have to pay — I am ready — for I have already given my all to Him. And if you think all this a deception — that too I would accept — and sacrifice myself completely. — I am sending this through Fr. Van Exem. I have given him full permission to use anything I have told him which is in connection with me and Him in this work. — My change to Asansol seems to me a part of His plan — there I will have more time to pray and prepare myself for His coming. In this matter I leave myself completely in your hands.

Pray for me. That I would become a religious according to His heart.

Your devoted child in J. C. [Jesus Christ],
Mary Teresa.

Clarence Jordan

(1912–1969)

The pantheon of Christian social prophets in twentieth-century America includes at least four figures — Walter Rauschenbusch, Dorothy Day, Martin Luther King Jr., and Clarence Jordan. Jordan founded Koinonia Farm in Sumter County, Georgia, which became a model for Christian community based on economic and racial equality and inspired Millard Fuller, who created Habitat for Humanity. Jordan was an eloquent voice for social and racial justice in the mid-twentieth century and the author of a paraphrase of much of the New Testament, known as "The Cotton Patch" version.

Jordan was a son of the South and the Southern Baptist Church. But, almost from the beginning, he heard a different gospel and marched to a different drummer. A native of Georgia, he early on developed a keen sense of the disparity between white and black people. In his Sunday School, he learned to sing "red and yellow, black and white, they are precious in his sight. Jesus loves the little children of the world." Later he recalled,

> The question arose in my mind, "Were the little black children precious in God's sight just like the little white children?" The song said they were. Then why were they always so ragged, so dirty and hungry? Did God have favorite children?
>
> I could not figure out the answers to these puzzling questions, but I knew something was wrong. A little light came when I began to realize that perhaps it wasn't God's doings, but man's. God didn't turn them away from our churches — we did. God didn't pay them low wages — we did. God didn't make them live in another section of town and in miserable huts — we did. God didn't make ragged, hungry little boys pick rotten oranges and fruit out of the garbage can and eat them — we did. Maybe

they were just as precious in God's sight, but were they in ours? My environment told me that they were not very precious in anybody's sight. A nigger was a nigger and must be kept in his place — the place of servitude and inferiority. (Dallas Lee, *The Cotton Patch Evidence* [New York: Harper & Row, 1971], 7-8)*

When a black man delivered some cleaning to the front door of the large Jordan home, his father dressed him down for not using the back door. Jordan was embarrassed and told his father off.

Behind the Jordan home was the Talbot County jail where a chain gang of convicted prisoners were camped in the yard. Young Clarence liked to stop and observe and became friends with the cook, who gave him cornbread and fatback on his way home from school each afternoon. He saw that nearly all the men were black and saw "the stretcher" — to which the men were attached, arms and legs, and then pulled in agonizing pain.

"This made tremendous traumatic impressions on me," he declared.

It hit me the hardest a night or two after I joined the church during the August revival. I remember it was hot and I remember that the warden of the chain gang was singing bass in the choir. I'll never forget how carried away he got singing "Love Lifted Me" that night.

But the next night I was awakened by agonizing groans from the direction of the chain gang camp. I was sure I could recognize who it was, and I was sure I knew what was happening. Ed Russell was in the stretcher. I knew not only who was in the stretcher, I knew who was pulling the rope. The same man who only hours before was so carried away singing "Love Lifted Me" was now lifting that man's body on the stretcher. That nearly tore me to pieces. I identified totally with that man in the stretcher. His agony was my agony. I got really mad with God. If He was love and the warden was an example of it, I didn't want anything to do with Him. (Lee, *The Cotton Patch Evidence*, 9)

But escaping God and the church proved impossible, and his conversion to radical Christian faith had begun. At first, Jordan flirted with becoming a lawyer, but then he settled on becoming a farmer and earned his degree from the Georgia State College of Agriculture at the University of Georgia in

*Excerpts from *The Cotton Patch Evidence* are reprinted by permission of Koinonia Farm, www.koinoniapertners.org, 1324 GA Hwy 49 S, Americus, GA 31719, 229-924-0391. Visitors welcomed year round.

Athens. There he became involved with Reserve Officers' Training Corps (which he eventually rejected because he saw war as a conflict with Jesus' teachings) and the Baptist Student Union. Despite his positive experiences on campus, he was restless.

> The thing that just bowled me over was the realization that whites seemed to have the very things that I wanted blacks to have, and the whites were living in such a hell. Why should I feel that blacks would be in any less a hell if they had these things. There had to be something extra somewhere. I was driven in a desperate search for spiritual resources. (Lee, *The Cotton Patch Evidence*, 11)

He decided to enter the ministry and enrolled at Southern Baptist Theological Seminary, where he received his basic theological degree, earned a Ph.D. in New Testament, and met and married his wife.

When he presented himself for ordination to the First Baptist Church of Athens, Georgia, he was characteristically blunt and visionary:

> If, according to popular opinion, being called to the ministry means spending all night in prayer, fighting constantly that voice which persistently speaks, being borne on the floods of passion, or having an "experience" — I repeat — if it means all that, I doubt very much that I have been called. But if being called to the ministry means lending an attentive ear to a simple statement, "My child, I want you to preach for me," then most assuredly I have been called.
>
> While I admit that God may choose the former method of speaking to those whom He wishes to preach, nevertheless I contend that it is not necessary, nor is it the only method. Behold a tree. Does it not speak to us thusly: "Don't you see that God is not working Himself into a frenzy in me? I am calmly, quietly, silently pouring forth my life and bringing forth fruit. Do thou likewise."
>
> And so it was with me. No battle was fought. My heart and soul were not torn by doubt, for when His voice came I was sure of its source. My strength was never pitted against His. He spoke. I listened. I can still hear him just as vividly: "My child, I want you to preach for me." You wish my answer? Here it is: "Yes, Lord, whatever you say, just promise me that you'll go with me." "And lo, I am with thee always, even unto the end of the world." "Lead on, O Christ, I'll follow." And that's all there was to it. (Lee, *The Cotton Patch Evidence*, 14)

Not exactly, or not so simply. While at Louisville's Southern Baptist Seminary, Jordan became immersed in inner-city churches and taught at Simmons University, an African-American school, and deepened his understanding of the lock of poverty on the black community. In 1941, Jordan met a fellow Baptist missionary, Martin England, at a Fellowship of Reconciliation meeting in Louisville, and the two began to discuss the desperate state of blacks in the rural South, especially following the Great Depression.

Out of these discussions was born the idea of Koinonia Farm, and they focused on a bleak and exhausted 440-acre tract eight miles from Americus, Georgia. Twenty-four years later, Jordan recalled with laughter the absurdity of those early discussions:

> When we started that thing, we were supposed to pay the fellow twenty-five hundred dollars down. And Martin England, who was a missionary under the American Baptist Foreign Mission Society to Burma — he and I agreed on the common purse — we were going to pool everything — and I had the idea Martin was loaded. I don't know why I should think that — [he] being an American Baptist missionary. But he talked "Let's do this" and "Let's do that," and I said, "Yeah, let's do," and I thought he had the money.
>
> So when we finally pooled our common assets, we had fifty-seven dollars and thirteen cents — and both of us had resigned our jobs. But on the first day of November 1941, right on the button, we walked in that real estate office and put down that twenty-five hundred dollars. A fellow brought it to us, said the Lord had sent him with it. I didn't question him, where he'd been talking to the Lord or anything like that. We'd take it right quick, before the Lord changed his mind. (Joyce Hollyday, ed., *Clarence Jordan: Essential Writings* [Maryknoll, NY: Orbis Books, 2003], 19)

Koinonia Farm was based on four basic convictions: the equality of all persons, the rejection of violence, stewardship of the environment, and common ownership of all possessions. At first, these Christian radicals were ignored by their Georgia neighbors, but during the 1950s and 1960s, the symbolism and reality of Koinonia made it a target for a crippling economic boycott and violence. And yet, it endured and prospered, largely on crops of peanuts.

Jordan stayed away from protest demonstrations and marches, believing that how he and the residents of Koinonia lived was their witness. From his little writing shack came the "Cotton Patch" version of the New Testament. In its homey text, Jesus was born in Gainesville, Georgia, and Mary put him in an apple box because there was no room in the hospital. Rome was Washington, D.C.; Judea was Georgia; Jerusalem was Atlanta. The letter to the Ephesians became "The Letter to the Christians in Birmingham."

Outsiders thought Koinonia Farm was an experiment in communal living, thus earning them the sobriquet of "communists" among the other verbal attacks that Jordan and his followers endured. But Jordan and his fellow farmers were insistent that all they were doing is living out New Testament Christianity, especially the Sermon on the Mount, which Jordan called "the platform of the God Movement." The intersection between biblical faith and social idealism permeated everything that Koinonia did and every word that Jordan wrote. Here is a summary of his faith, shaped decisively by the Sermon on the Mount, whose purpose, he said, was "not to evoke inspiration but perspiration."

For unbelievers, Jesus had but one word: "REPENT." It's a tremendous word. We must examine it. The Greek word from which it is translated means "to change one's mind for the better, heartily to amend with abhorrence of one's past sins" *(Thayer's Lexicon)*. So when he called on people to repent, he really demanded that they change their way of thinking, abandon their false concepts, forsake their wrong methods, and enter upon a new way of life. Imagine what this meant to the Pharisees, whose "good behavior" and whose "trust in the Lord" assured them of the divine favor. Weren't they already saved, and just about the best people God had on earth? Yet Jesus felt that of all people, these had the greatest need of changing their ways. He also told the wealthy, aristocratic, unscrupulous Sadducees to change their way of living. He called on the superpatriotic, military-minded Zealots to change their attitudes. He faced all these folk, as he does their spiritual descendants today, with that one terrific word: *repent!*

No one has a right, however, to call on *others* to change their ways *unless he or she has a more excellent way to offer.* Forsaking the wrong way is only half of repentance; accepting the right way is the other half. The call to repentance, then, must always be accompanied by the glorious announcement, "for the kingdom of God is here!" Jesus proclaimed it as "the good news." For him, it was the way, the only way, for people to live. Only when they had accepted the kingdom could it be said that they had truly repented. To enter it was to be saved, to find eternal life. (See Luke 18:18, 24, 26 where finding eternal life, entering the kingdom, and being saved seem to refer to the same thing.)

It is with this kingdom that the Sermon on the Mount concerns itself. We shall be better prepared to understand this great discourse of the Master's if, before entering upon a study of it, we keep constantly before us certain things about the kingdom.

First, its foundation is the revelation that God is a Father, that Jesus Christ is his Son and the rightful Lord of the faithful, and that the Holy Spirit is the guide of all citizens of the kingdom. Believers, by identification with the Son, become children of the Father. The result is a community, or family, of those who so believe.

Second, in this new relationship one can have no conflicting loyalties. The kingdom takes precedence over everything else — occupation (Matthew 4:20), family ties (Matthew 4:22; Luke 14:26), and possessions (Luke 14:33). One should be fully warned of this before going in quest of the kingdom. It should be made clear, however, that while one might be called upon at any time to give up these lesser pearls, one will be the possessor of a pearl of infinitely greater value. To accept the kingdom means to put first things first.

Third, the kingdom is not a department of life set off to itself, but like blood in the body, it extends to *every* area of human life. It makes adequate provision for *all* human need, whether it be spiritual ("They brought to him the demon-possessed"), mental (". . . and the lunatics"), or physical (". . . and the paralytics"), and he healed them all (Matthew 4:24). That his concept of the kingdom included the whole person is also seen in his threefold ministry of preaching (spiritual), teaching (mental), and healing (physical). To him the kingdom of God was far more than a religious interest; it was *the way of life*.

Fourth, the doors of the kingdom are open to all without respect to race, class, caste, color, nationality, education, or wealth. The children of God are under divine compulsion to accept as kin anyone who repents and believes. Inside the kingdom there are no partitions. Those who would erect them thereby declare themselves to be on the outside.

Jordan summarized the heart of Christianity as follows: "Faith is not belief in spite of the evidence but a life in scorn of the consequences."

As he lived, he died, attacked by his critics and beloved by his family, friends, and supporters. Since the coroner wouldn't come to the farm, Millard Fuller took his body to town where it was placed in a simple wooden crate, usually used to ship ornate coffins. Jordan hated ostentation. When he visited a fancy house, he was reputed to have declared, "Nice piece of plunder you got here."

As Joyce Hollyday records, "A few weeks before he died, a reporter asked Clarence, 'When you get up to heaven and the Lord meets you and says, "Clarence, I wonder if you could tell me in the next five minutes what you did down on earth," what would you tell the Lord?' Without hesitation, Clarence replied, 'I'd tell the Lord to come back, when he had more time.'" Hollyday concludes: "One wonders if the report has ended yet" (*Clarence Jordan: Essential Writings*, 36).

Thomas Merton

(1915–1968)

Poet, novelist, mystic, and theologian, Thomas Merton became one of the most widely read Catholic authors of the twentieth century. He was equally knowledgeable of both Western and Eastern spirituality, and he immersed himself in medieval piety, struggling to use the resources of the monastic tradition to address the religious and social issues of the modern world. He entered one of the strictest Catholic orders, the Trappists, which requires a vow of silence. Fortunately, the abbot encouraged this silent monk to speak through writing. The words flowed from his pen — a synthesis of the ancient and the contemporary, East and West.

Born in France, Merton was given a fine education there, in Bermuda, and in the United States. Orphaned in his youth, he was left a generous trust fund by his parents, and he used it to live extravagantly. While studying in England, he fathered an illegitimate child, and his trustee arranged for a financial settlement with the mother. Both the mother and the child were killed in the bombing raids on London during World War II.

Migrating to America, Merton studied at Columbia University and received a master's degree in literature. He was invited to join the faculty, but his dissatisfaction with his life and the injustices of society immobilized him. He first turned to a young communist group, and he also served in a Catholic settlement house in Harlem. Devouring Catholic writings of all kinds, he came to the conclusion that he must be baptized and enter "at last into the supernatural life of the Church."

He set out to climb "the high, seven-circled mountain of a Purgatory steeper and more arduous than I was able to imagine," and climb it he did. In 1941, he entered the Trappist monastery of Gethsemani in Kentucky, and there he wrote his autobiography, *The Seven-Storey Mountain*, published in

284

1948 and an immediate best seller. More books followed, and people flocked to Gethsemani on pilgrimage to learn from this person who had tasted the best of Western culture, rejecting it for silent, quiet contemplation.

Merton became a strong advocate of civil rights during the 1950s and 1960s and was critical of American foreign policy. Fame and controversy came to him in almost equal measure. His visitors increased, and finally he withdrew to a hermitage on the abbey property so that he could be completely isolated. Yet even that extreme measure was unsuccessful, and he left the abbey to find peace and anonymity in Asia. Agreeing to attend a religious conference in Bangkok, he died in a hotel from a freak accident, apparently the victim of electrocution when a fan fell into his bathtub.

Merton believed that "the whole work of man in this life is to find God," and he sought this goal with discipline and self-sacrifice. He concluded his autobiography with his own epitaph, which he believed to be the words of God:

> And when you have been praised a little and loved a little, I will take away all your gifts and all your love and all your praise and you will be utterly forgotten and abandoned and you will be nothing, a dead thing, a rejection. And in that day you shall begin to possess the solitude you have so long desired.

My mind was taken up with this one thought: of getting baptized and entering at last into the supernatural life of the Church. In spite of all my studying and all my reading and all my talking, I was still infinitely poor and wretched in my appreciation of what was about to take place within me. I was about to set foot on the shore at the foot of the high, seven-circled mountain of a Purgatory steeper and more arduous than I was able to imagine, and I was not at all aware of the climbing I was about to have to do.

The essential thing was to begin the climb. Baptism was that beginning, and a most generous one, on the part of God. For, although I was baptized conditionally, I hope that His mercy swallowed up all the guilt and temporal punishment of my twenty-three black years of sin in the

---

waters of the font, and allowed me a new start. But my human nature, my weakness, and the cast of my evil habits still remained to be fought and overcome.

Towards the end of the first week in November, Father Moore told me I would be baptized on the sixteenth. I walked out of the rectory that evening happier and more contented than I had ever been in my life. I looked at a calendar to see what saint had that day for a feast, and it was marked for St. Gertrude.

It was only in the last days before being liberated from my slavery to death, that I had the grace to feel something of my own weakness and helplessness. It was not a very vivid light that was given to me on the subject: but I was really aware, at last, of what a poor and miserable thing I was. On the night of the fifteenth of November, the eve of my Baptism and First Communion, I lay in my bed awake and timorous for fear that something might go wrong the next day. And to humiliate me still further, as I lay there, fear came over me that I might not be able to keep the eucharistic fast. It only meant going from midnight to ten o'clock without drinking any water or taking any food, yet all of a sudden this little act of self-denial which amounts to no more, in reality, than a sort of an abstract token, a gesture of good-will, grew in my imagination until it seemed to be utterly beyond my strength — as if I were about to go without food and drink for ten days, instead of ten hours. I had enough sense left to realize that this was one of those curious psychological reactions with which our nature, not without help from the devil, tries to confuse us and avoid what reason and our will demand of it, and so I forgot about it all and went to sleep.

In the morning, when I got up, having forgotten to ask Father Moore if washing your teeth was against the eucharistic fast or not, I did not wash them, and, facing a similar problem about cigarettes, I resisted the temptation to smoke.

I went downstairs and out into the street to go to my happy execution and rebirth.

The sky was bright and cold. The river glittered like steel. There was a clean wind in the street. It was one of those fall days full of life and triumph, made for great beginnings, and yet I was not altogether exalted: for there were still in my mind these vague, half animal apprehensions about the externals of what was to happen in the church — would my mouth be so dry that I could not swallow the Host? If that happened, what would I do? I did not know.

[Robert] Gerdy joined me as I was turning in to Broadway. I do not remember whether Ed Rice caught up with us on Broadway or not. [Robert] Lax and Seymour [Freedgood] came after we were in church.

Ed Rice was my godfather. He was the only Catholic among us — the only Catholic among all my close friends. Lax, Seymour, and Gerdy were Jews. They were very quiet, and so was I. Rice was the only one who was not cowed or embarrassed or shy.

The whole thing was very simple. First of all, I knelt at the altar of Our Lady where Father Moore received my abjuration of heresy and schism. Then we went to the baptistery, in a little dark corner by the main door.

I stood at the threshold.

"Quid petis ab ecclesia Dei?" asked Father Moore.

"Fidem!"

"Fides quid tibi praestat?"

"Vitam eternam."

Then the young priest began to pray in Latin, looking earnestly and calmly at the page of the *Rituale* through the lenses of his glasses. And I, who was asking for eternal life, stood and watched him, catching a word of the Latin here and there.

He turned to me:

"Abrenuntias Satanae?"

In a triple vow I renounced Satan and his pomps and his works.

"Dost thou believe in God the Father almighty, Creator of heaven and earth?"

"Credo!"

"Dost thou believe in Jesus Christ His only Son, Who was born, and suffered?"

"Credo!"

"Dost thou believe in the Holy Spirit, in the Holy Catholic Church, the Communion of saints, the remission of sins, the resurrection of the body and eternal life?"

"Credo!"

What mountains were falling from my shoulders! What scales of dark night were peeling off my intellect, to let in the inward vision of God and His truth! But I was absorbed in the liturgy, and waiting for the next ceremony. It had been one of the things that had rather frightened me — or rather, which frightened the legion that had been living in me for twenty-three years.

Now the priest blew into my face. He said: *"Exi ab eo, spiritus immunde:* Depart from him, thou impure spirit, and give place to the Holy Spirit, the Paraclete."

It was the exorcism. I did not see them leaving, but there must have been more than seven of them. I had never been able to count them. Would they ever come back? Would that terrible threat of Christ be fulfilled, that threat about the man whose house was clean and garnished, only to be reoccupied by the first devil and many others worse than himself?

The priest, and Christ in him — for it was Christ that was doing these things through his visible ministry, in the Sacrament of my purification — breathed again into my face.

"Thomas, receive the good Spirit through this breathing, and receive the Blessing of God. Peace be with thee."

Then he began again to pray, and sign me with Crosses, and presently came the salt which he put on my tongue — the salt of wisdom, that I might have the savor of divine things, and finally he poured the water on my head, and named me Thomas, "if thou be not already baptized."

After that, I went into the confessional, where one of the other assistants was waiting for me. I knelt in the shadows. Through the dark, close-meshed wire of the grille between us, I saw Father McGough, his head bowed, and resting on his hand, inclining his ear towards me. "Poor man," I thought. He seemed very young and he had always looked so innocent to me that I wondered how he was going to identify and understand the things I was about to tell him.

But one by one, that is, species by species, as best I could, I tore out all those sins by their roots, like teeth. Some of them were hard, but I did it quickly, doing the best I could to approximate the number of times all these things had happened — there was no counting them, only guessing. I did not have any time to feel how relieved I was when I came stumbling out, as I had to go down to the front of the church where Father Moore would see me and come out to begin his — and my — Mass. But ever since that day, I have loved confessionals.

Now he was at the altar, in his white vestments, opening the book. I was kneeling right at the altar rail. The bright sanctuary was all mine. I could hear the murmur of the priest's voice, and the responses of the server, and it did not matter that I had no one to look at, so that I could tell when to stand up and kneel down again, for I was still not very sure of these ordinary ceremonies. But when the little bells were rung I knew what was happening. And I saw the raised Host — the silence and simplicity with which Christ once again triumphed, raised up, drawing all things to Himself — drawing me to Himself.

Presently the priest's voice was louder, saying the *Pater Noster.* Then, soon, the server was running through the *Confiteor* in a rapid murmur. That was for me. Father Moore turned around and made a big cross in absolution, and held up the little Host.

"Behold the Lamb of God: behold Him Who taketh away the sins of the world."

And my First Communion began to come towards me, down the steps. I was the only one at the altar rail. Heaven was entirely mine — that Heaven in which sharing makes no division or diminution. But this solitariness was a kind of reminder of the singleness with which this Christ, hidden in the small Host, was giving Himself for me, and to me, and, with Himself, the entire Godhead and Trinity — a great new increase of the power and grasp of their indwelling that had begun only a few minutes before at the font.

I left the altar rail and went back to the pew where the others were kneeling like four shadows, four unrealities, and I hid my face in my hands.

In the Temple of God that I had just become, the One Eternal and Pure Sacrifice was offered up to the God dwelling in me: the sacrifice of God to God, and me sacrificed together with God, incorporated in His Incarnation. Christ born in me, a new Bethlehem, and sacrificed in me, His new Calvary, and risen in me: offering me to the Father, in Himself, asking the Father, my Father and His, to receive me into His infinite and special love — not the love He has for all things that exist — for mere existence is a token of God's love, but the love of those creatures who are drawn to Him in and with the power of His own love for Himself.

For now I had entered into the everlasting movement of that gravitation which is the very life and spirit of God: God's own gravitation toward the depths of His own infinite nature, His goodness without end.

Billy Graham

(b. 1918)

Billy (William Franklin) Graham was the preeminent Protestant leader of the second half of the twentieth century. Always designated in lists of the "most admired" or "most respected" figures in America, Graham's influence was enormous — from the White House (where he consulted with numerous presidents) to other nations (through his personal visits and charisma and the media reach of his Billy Graham Evangelistic Association). Graham asserted, undoubtedly correctly, that he preached to more people than anyone else in history — 215 million people in more than 185 countries.

Perhaps one word can summarize Graham's evangelistic ministry: "decision." His weekly radio program was called "Hour of Decision." His association's official magazine was called *Decision*. His newspaper column was called "My Answer." Among his many books were *America's Hour of Decision, My Answer, Billy Graham Answers Your Questions, The Challenge*, and *How to Be Born Again*.

This emphasis on a personal commitment to Jesus Christ was the central theme in all his preaching, and it was rooted in his own pilgrimage to faith. Graham was born into a prosperous dairy farming family in North Carolina. His father was at one point diffident and then dedicated to the Christian faith, while his mother provided a nearly unswerving commitment to Christ. Although the Grahams were church-goers and Presbyterian by membership, they were also deeply affected by the currents of southern evangelicalism.

Billy Graham's own conversion was "a decision." Moved by the preaching of the evangelist Mordecai Ham, Graham examined his own life in God's light and found it wanting. He knew he wasn't a bad person, but he also found he did not have the personal relationship with Christ that Ham described as central to salvation. So, he turned his life over to God.

As his autobiography makes clear, there was little drama to his decision. In fact, in the days following, he wondered whether his life would be different. But his decision as a teenager to submit himself to God and to God's will began a process that produced the famous evangelist and preacher of God's forgiveness of sin. Graham's commitment to enter the ministry and his choice of an evangelistic ministry were made gradually, but his first decision for Christ was decisive. He never sought a theological education, though he later helped found *Christianity Today*, which became a widely circulated and highly respected magazine of Protestant evangelicalism. By experience and intention, he kept his message simple: You are living in a state of sin. If you make a decision to turn your life over to God, you will be saved by Jesus Christ.

Graham was criticized for his political involvement (especially his association with Richard Nixon, which he regretted), although he won acclaim for what he described as two more conversions: his commitment to racial equality and his advocacy of world peace. In the midst of the political tumult of post–World War II America, he tried to keep evangelism as his primary purpose and goal, while advocating the ethical implications of the gospel. "I'm for morality, but morality goes beyond sex to human freedom and social justice," he declared later in his career. "We as clergy know so very little to speak with authority on the Panama Canal or superiority of armaments. Evangelists cannot be closely identified with any particular party or person. We have to stand in the middle in order to preach to all people, right and left. I haven't been faithful to my own advice in the past. I will be in the future." He added, "A lot of things that I commented on years ago would not have been of the Lord, I'm sure, but I think you have some — like communism, or segregation, on which I think you have a responsibility to speak out."

Every Graham service ended with an opportunity for people to come forward — to decide to turn over their lives to Christ. As they came, the words of a hymn resounded through the tent, or the arena, or the open air. Graham used the hymn as the title of his autobiography, and in his account of his conversion — his decision for Christ — he portrays himself as the hymn proclaimed: "Just As I Am."

> Just as I am, without one plea,
> but that thy blood was shed for me,
> and that thou bidst me come to thee,
> O Lamb of God, I come, I come.

Just as I am, thy love unknown
hath broken every barrier down;
now, to be thine, yea thine alone,
O Lamb of God, I come, I come.

~

Father [decided] to support the Christian businessmen in Charlotte who wanted to hold one of their all-day prayer meetings in our pasture in May 1934. The group had held three similar meetings since they started praying together eighteen months earlier. My mother invited the ladies to the farmhouse for their own prayer meeting.

That afternoon, when I came back from school and went to pitch hay in the barn across the road with one of our hired hands, we heard singing.

"Who are those men over there in the woods making all that noise?" he asked me.

"I guess they're some fanatics that have talked Daddy into using the place," I replied.

Years later my father recalled a prayer that Vernon Patterson had prayed that day: that out of Charlotte the Lord would raise up someone to preach the Gospel to the ends of the earth.

At that time, in 1934, it certainly wasn't obvious that that someone might be me. My father knew that I went along with the family to church every week only "grudgingly, or of necessity," to use a biblical phrase. I believe he sincerely wanted me to experience what he had felt a quarter-century earlier. In fact, he privately hoped and prayed that his firstborn son might someday fulfill the old Methodist evangelist's prophecy by becoming a preacher in his stead.

The church outside Charlotte in which my mother had been reared (and in which my grandfather had been an elder) was Steele Creek Presbyterian, called the largest country church in America at that time. My parents' later membership in the Associate Reformed Presbyterian Church in Charlotte was a compromise between them, encouraged by her sisters, who attended there. (The ARP, as it was called, traced its roots back to a very strict group that had seceded from the Church of Scotland in the eighteenth century.) Later Mother also came into fellowship with some Plymouth Brethren neighbors, and under their influence she studied the Scriptures more deeply than before.

In addition, she read the writings of noted Bible teachers Arno C. Gaebelein, Harry A. Ironside of the Moody Memorial Church in Chicago, and Donald Grey Barnhouse, a renowned preacher who pastored Tenth Presbyterian Church in Philadelphia. I could see that she took their writings seriously, but whenever she talked to me about the things they said in their magazines, I thought it was nonsense.

A local minister told Mother she would go crazy reading the Book of Revelation, the last book in the New Testament, but it was while reading about the Second Coming of Christ that a sense of her own religious conversion became meaningful to her. All of this spiritual development was going on quietly in her life for about two years before the Ham meetings in Charlotte.

At the beginning of the Ham-Ramsay meetings, even my mother was somewhat skeptical. Yet she sincerely desired to hear the visiting evangelist for her own spiritual nurture, and she wanted to encourage my father in his search for certainty of salvation. They went, and both found what they were seeking. "My experience," Daddy said, "is that Dr. Ham's meetings opened my eyes to the truth."

He commented on the dissatisfaction he had felt previously in simply moving his membership from one church to another. The Gospel had a new reality for him that made a marked difference in his life from then on.

Mother, in her quietly pointed fashion, got to the nub of the issue: "I feel that Dr. Ham's meetings did more, especially for the Christians, than any other meetings we've had here."

Despite my parents' enthusiasm, I did not want anything to do with anyone called an evangelist — and particularly with such a colorful character as Dr. Ham. Just turning sixteen, I told my parents that I would not go to hear him.

One day a few weeks into his campaign, I read in the *Charlotte News* about his charge regarding immoral conditions at Central High School in Charlotte. Apparently, the evangelist knew what he was talking about. He claimed to have affidavits from certain students that a house across the street from the school, supposedly offering the boys and girls lunch during noon recess, actually gave them some additional pleasures.

When the scandalous story broke, rumors flew that a number of angry students, on a night yet to be determined, were going to march on the tabernacle and demonstrate right in front of the platform. Maybe they would even do some bodily harm to the preacher. That stirred up my curiosity, and I wanted to go just to see what would happen. But how could I save face after holding out for nearly a month? That was when Albert McMakin stepped in.

"Why don't you come out and hear our fighting preacher?" he suggested.

"Is he a *fighter*?" I asked. That put a little different slant on things. "I *like* a fighter."

Albert added the incentive of letting me drive his old vegetable truck into town for the meeting, loaded with as many folks, white and black, as he could get to go along. We all sat in the rear of the auditorium to see the show, with a few thousand other people — one of the largest crowds I had ever been in.

As soon as the evangelist started his sermon, he opened his Bible and talked straight from his text. He talked loudly, even though there was an amplifying system. I have no recollection of what he preached about, but I was spellbound. In some indefinable way, he was getting through to me. I was hearing another voice, as was often said of Dwight L. Moody when he preached: the voice of the Holy Spirit.

Bumping along in the truck on the way home, I was deep in thought. Later, after I stretched out on my back in bed, I stared out the window at a Carolina moon for a long time.

The next night, all my father's mules and horses could not have kept me from getting to that meeting. From then on, I was a faithful attendant, night after night, week after week.

The tabernacle was well filled all the time. One reason for the good attendance was Dr. Ham's choice of lively topics, like the Second Coming of Christ. Mother had read about the Second Coming in the Book of Revelation, of course, but I did not recall having heard of it. He also preached on subjects such as money, infidelity, the Sabbath, and drinking.

I had never heard a sermon on Hell, either, though I was familiar with some people's use of that term as a swear word. Certainly our clergyman, Dr. Lindsay, never mentioned that it was a real place, even though I know he believed there was a Hell. But Dr. Ham left no doubt about it in anybody's mind!

That was not to say Dr. Ham neglected or minimized the great love of God. He just put it against a background of sin and judgment and Hell in a novel way that fascinated me. His words, and his way with words, grabbed my mind, gripped my heart. What startled me was that the same preacher who warned us so dramatically about the horrible fate of the lost in the everlasting lake of fire and brimstone also had a tremendous sense of humor and could tell stories almost as good as my father's.

I became deeply convicted about my sinfulness and rebellion. And confused. How could this evangelist be talking to me, of all people? I had been baptized as a baby, had learned the Shorter Catechism word perfect, and had been confirmed in the Associate Reformed Presbyterian Church with the full approval of the pastor and elders. I had gotten into mischief once in a while, but I could hardly be called wicked. I resisted temptations to break the moral code my parents had so strictly instilled in me. I was a good milker in the dairy barn and never complained about any of the nasty work, such as shoveling manure. I was even the vice president of my youth group in our church (although, granted, it wasn't a particularly vital organization).

So why would the evangelist always be pointing his bony finger at *me?*

One thing that echoed in my mind was Dr. Ham's singing, right in the middle of his sermon, "The toils of the road will seem nothing, when I get to the end of the way."

He had an almost embarrassing way of describing sins and shortcomings, and of demanding, on pain of divine judgment, that we mend our ways. I was so sure he had singled me out one night that I actually ducked behind the wide-brimmed hat of the lady sitting in front of me. Yet, as uncomfortable as I was getting to be, I simply could not stay away. . . .

What was slowly dawning on me during those weeks was the miserable realization that I did not know Jesus Christ for myself. I could not depend on my parents' faith. Christian influence in the home could have a lasting impact on a child's life, but faith could not be passed on as an inheritance, like the family silver. It had to be exercised by each individual.

I could not depend on my church membership either. Saying "I believe" in the Apostles' Creed every Sunday, or taking the bread and wine of Communion, could so easily become nothing but rote and ritual, without power in themselves to make me any different.

Nor could I depend on my own resolution to do better. I constantly failed in my efforts at self-improvement. Nobody needed to tell me *that.*

As a teenager, what I needed to know for certain was that I was right with God. I could not help but admit to myself that I was purposeless and empty-hearted. Our family Bible reading, praying, psalm-singing, and churchgoing — all these had left me restless and resentful. I had even tried, guiltily, to think up ways of getting out of all those activities as much as I could. In a word, I was spiritually dead.

And then it happened, sometime around my sixteenth birthday. On that night, Dr. Ham finished preaching and gave the Invitation to accept Christ. After all his tirades against sin, he gave us a gentle reminder: "But God commendeth his love toward us, in that, while we were yet sinners, Christ died for us" (Romans 5:8, KJV). His song leader, Mr. Ramsay, led us all in "Just As I Am" — four verses. Then we started another song: "Almost Persuaded, Now to Believe."

On the last verse of that second song, I responded. I walked down to the front, feeling as if I had lead weights attached to my feet, and stood in the space before the platform. That same night, perhaps three or four hundred other people were there at the front making spiritual commitments. The next night, my cousin Crook Stafford made his decision for Christ.

My heart sank when I looked over at the lady standing next to me with tears running down her cheeks. I was not crying. I did not feel any special emotion of any kind just then. Maybe, I thought, I was not supposed to be there. Maybe my good intentions to be a real Christian wouldn't last. Wondering if I was just making a fool of myself, I almost turned around and went back to my seat.

As I stood in front of the platform, a tailor named J. D. Prevatt, who was a friend of our family with a deep love for souls, stepped up beside me, weeping. Putting his arms around me, he urged me to make my decision. At the same time, in his heavy European accent, he explained God's plan for my salvation in a simple way. That explanation was addressed to my own mental understanding. It did not necessarily answer every question I had at the moment — and it certainly did not anticipate every question that would come to me in the months and years ahead — but it set forth simply the facts I needed to know in order to become God's child.

My tailor friend helped me to understand what I had to do to become a genuine Christian. The key word was *do.* Those of us standing up front had to decide to *do* something about what we knew before it could take effect.

He prayed for me and guided *me* to pray. I had heard the message, and I had felt the inner compulsion to go forward. Now came the moment to commit myself to Christ. Intellectually, I accepted Christ to the extent that I acknowledged what I knew about Him to be true. That was mental assent. Emotionally, I felt that I wanted to love Him in return for His loving me. But the final issue was whether I would turn myself over to His rule in my life.

I checked "Recommitment" on the card I filled out. After all, I had been brought up to regard my baptism and confirmation as professions of faith too. The difference was that this time I was doing it on *purpose,* doing it with *intention.* For all my previous religious upbringing and church activity, I believe that that was the moment I made my real commitment to Jesus Christ.

No bells went off inside me. No signs flashed across the tabernacle ceiling. No physical palpitations made me tremble. I wondered again if I was a hypocrite, not to be weeping or something. I simply felt at peace. Quiet, not delirious. Happy and peaceful.

My father came to the front and put his arm around my shoulders, telling me how thankful he was. Later, back home, when we went to the kitchen, my mother put her arm around me and said, "Billy Frank, I'm so glad you took the stand you did tonight."

That was all.

I went upstairs to my room. Standing at the window, I looked out across one of the fields that was glowing in the moonlight.

Then I went over to my bed and for the first time in my life got down on my knees without being told to do so. I really wanted to talk to God. "Lord, I don't know what happened to me tonight," I prayed. "*You* know. And I thank You for the privilege I've had tonight."

It took a while to fall asleep. How could I face school tomorrow? Would this action spoil my relationships with friends who were not interested in spiritual mutters? Might Coach Eudy, who had publicly expressed his dislike of Dr. Ham, make fun of me? Perhaps. I felt pretty sure, though, that the school principal, Connor Hutchinson, whose history lessons I enjoyed, would be sympathetic.

But the hardest question of all remained to be answered: What, exactly, had happened to me?

All I knew was that the world looked different the next morning when I got up to do the milking, eat breakfast, and catch the schoolbus. There seemed to be a song in my heart. . . .

It would take some time before I understood what had happened to me well enough to explain it to anybody else. There were signs, though, that my thinking and direction had changed, that I had truly been converted. To my own surprise, church activities that had bored me before seemed interesting all of a sudden — even Dr. Lindsay's sermons (which I took notes on!). The choir sounded better to me. I actually wanted to go to church as often as possible.

The Bible, which had been familiar to me almost since infancy, drew me now to find out what it said besides the verses I had memorized through the years. I enjoyed the few minutes I could take when I was by myself each morning and evening for quiet talking to God in prayer. As one of Mr. Ramsay's former choir members, I was even singing hymns while I milked the cows!

Before my conversion, I tended to be touchy, oversensitive, envious of others, and irritable. Now I deliberately tried to be courteous and kind to everybody around me. I was experiencing what the Apostle Paul had described: "The old has gone, the new has come!" (2 Corinthians 5:17). Mother especially, but other family members too, thought there was a difference. Most remarkable of all — to me at least — was an uncharacteristic enthusiasm for my studies! (It was about this time that I read Gibbon's *Decline and Fall of the Roman Empire*.)

Looking back now, I'm sure I spent entirely too much time working on the farm and playing baseball during my boyhood, and not enough time with the books. But what good would school do for me if I was going to be a farmer?

Purpose was still missing from my outlook on life in general. Although I had been converted, I did not have much of a concept of my life coming under some kind of divine plan. In the remaining year and a half of high school, I had no inkling of what my life work was to be. The future was foggy at best. But I could tell from my changed interests and new satisfactions that spiritual growth was going on.

Oral Roberts

(1918–2009)

Oral Roberts was, according to historian Grant Wacker, "the world's most prominent Pentecostal leader" in the twentieth century. He was a uniquely American phenomenon, rising from grinding poverty to pioneer in televangelism and bringing the revolutionary teachings of the Pentecostal-charismatic movement to millions of people around the world. His ministry of faith-healing brought in millions of dollars, sometimes accompanied by anguished pleas for support. The money founded the Oral Roberts Evangelistic Association and Oral Roberts University, with a first-class basketball team and ironically, some would say, a reputable medical center.

Roberts was born into a Pentecostal family. His father, he said, was "even-tempered and dependable, loving and kind, but limited in ambition." He pastored churches, but when things were going well, he "would 'retire for a while.'" His mother was as committed to the Pentecostal faith as her husband and was frequently called upon to minister to the sick. When she was six months' pregnant with Oral, she was called out to provide healing for an infant who a doctor had said would not survive the night. Crossing a field, she caught her dress on a barbed-wire fence. Exhausted, she prayed, "Oh God, I want to make a vow. I ask you to heal my neighbor's child tonight, and when mine is born, I will give him to you."

She prayed over the baby, and the baby survived. "For Mama," Roberts said, "that sealed the matter. The baby she was carrying would be a boy and a minister." When her baby was born, she named him "Granville Oral" and declared that he would be called "Oral." That was "an ironic choice," Roberts declared, "for as I grew up I stuttered and stammered badly." Stuttering made his life difficult. It was even more agonizing for a preacher's son. Roberts was

299

teased and got into fights, but his mother assured him, "Oral, someday you will talk without stammering. God will loosen your tongue."

God did loosen Roberts's tongue, but not before he rebelled against his parents and his religious heritage. In his teen years, he contracted a virulent case of tuberculosis, and it was then that both his body and his speech were healed.

He dropped out of college to hit the sawdust trail as a Pentecostal preacher, offering forgiveness from sin and release from sickness in tent meetings that involved as many as 3,000 people. Through his evangelistic organization, he conducted revivals on six continents and laid his hands on more than 2 million people — sometimes without effect and people died. His evangelistic impact was second only to Billy Graham. When people called him a faith-healer, he bristled: "God heals — I don't."

Roberts had his inevitable critics who castigated his fundraising techniques, his financial stewardship, his emphasis upon material prosperity as a gift of the Spirit, and the idea of faith-healing itself. And yet, the Pentecostal-charismatic movement became one of the most powerful forms of Christianity during the twentieth century — a "third force" in Christendom that has transformed the faith, not only in the United States but in Asia, Africa, and Latin America as well. Roberts was its preeminent leader, and it all began with the simple assurance that God would heal him.

There was a cycle of poverty in our lives that kept gnawing away at me. As I began to approach my early teens I felt I had to get away. And so one day I simply announced to Mamma and Papa that I was going to leave home. They had the normal reactions and began to protest, and Mamma to cry and Papa to exhort and to threaten. He said, "Oral, I will send for you. I will put the police on your trail and I will bring you home."

I replied, "If you do, I will just run away again."

I had made up my mind. I was on a dead-end road, and I felt my dreams could not be realized. There was no future or hope for me as the son of a poor preacher.

As I was leaving, Mamma and Papa asked me to kneel down and let

From *The Call: An Autobiography* by Oral Roberts, copyright © 1971 by Oral Roberts. Used by permission of Doubleday, a division of Random House, Inc.

them pray with me. That was kind of hard on me. We'd had a lot of prayer all my life. In fact, when I was small I felt quite sure that Jesus lived with us because Mamma and Papa talked to Him so much.

When we had knelt down, Mamma began to pray and to ask the Lord to take care of me and told Him they were committing me into His hands. As I was getting ready to go, she made me kneel down again and with tears coursing down her cheeks, she said, "Oral, you will never be able to go farther than our prayers. We will pray and ask God to send you home, and He will."

I must admit that almost made me back out. They had appealed to the side of me that deeply respected them, their prayers and their dedicated lives. But my rebellious youth conquered. I walked out of the house and out of their lives, never really intending to return. I felt I had to get into the mainstream.

I left home in Ada and went to Atoka, Oklahoma, and found lodging in a judge's home where I was allowed to have access to his law books. I began to study these with all the hunger of a young animal searching for food, and to dream of becoming a lawyer and being governor of Oklahoma.

To support myself I followed a demanding schedule. I served as a handyman in the judge's home, had a job in a grocery store on Saturdays, threw a paper route, and wrote a column and served as a reporter for my hometown paper, the *Ada Evening News.*

My rising time was 4 A.M. when I would build the fires. I went to bed around midnight after I'd finished the day's classes, practiced ball, thrown my paper route, written my column, and maybe even had a date. At school I carried a full load. I was an A student and loved to study. I had left home to make something of myself and I worked hard at it. I was elected president of my class and made the starting basketball team, but I began to push myself beyond what I was physically able to take.

I began to have small pains in my chest and to wake up at night in deep sweats. I tired easily. Many times after a basketball game I felt my lungs would burst. Every now and then I'd cough and spit up blood, but I thought nothing of it. I was excited by what was going on, fascinated by life, and supremely confident. I felt I had my future before me and nothing could stop me.

Then it all ended one night during a basketball game. It was the final game in the Oklahoma Seven Basketball Tournament. I had the ball and was dribbling down the court driving in for a layup as hard and fast as I could when suddenly everything began to blur before my eyes. I stumbled and collapsed on the gymnasium floor. Blood began to spurt from my mouth. I lost consciousness briefly and began hemorrhaging with every breath.

My coach, Mr. Hamilton, rushed over and soon he and others picked me up and carried me to his car and laid me on the back seat. He said, "Oral, you're going home."

As I lay there looking out at the night, it seemed the world began to fall down around me. I didn't know what was wrong but whatever it was I knew it was bad. Now I was heading back to poverty, back to a religion I had never accepted, back to my parents' discipline, and it tore me up inside.

When Mr. Hamilton got to my house, he went up to the front door and knocked. Papa came to the door and Mr. Hamilton said, "Reverend Roberts?"

My father answered, "Yes. Is something wrong?"

He said, "Reverend Roberts, I've brought your son home. Can you help me carry him in?"

When Mamma saw my coach and Papa carrying me in she screamed, "Oh God, I didn't know he would come home like this."

They put me in bed and although most Pentecostals in that day were strong on divine healing and had little to do with medical doctors, my dad was an exception. The doctors were called in and began to make their examinations. I had a terrible pain in my lungs. I would get to coughing and hemorrhaging at night so much that the wallpaper next to my bed had to be removed and new wallpaper put on.

One day my father came into my bedroom after the doctor had left and he started to say something to me. Tears began to well up in his eyes. I said, "Papa, what's wrong?"

He said, "Son, you're going to be all right."

I said, "Well, if I'm going to be all right, why are you crying?"

He said, "You're going to be all right, son."

I said, "Papa, tell me what's wrong. Why do my lungs hurt? Why do I cough up blood? Why don't I want to eat any more?"

Finally he told me. When he did, the world came crashing in on me. He said, "Oral, you have tuberculosis in both lungs."

I could not believe it, but he assured me it was true. I had tuberculosis and I was to be sent either to the state tubercular sanatorium at Talihina in the mountains of eastern Oklahoma or to a quiet place in the country.

This was 1934. In those days to have tuberculosis at age sixteen was a much greater threat than it would be today. There was no penicillin, no miracle drugs. I had had relatives who had died with tuberculosis. My oldest sister Velma had died at nineteen of pneumonia. Now suddenly death was staring me in the face.

When my brother Vaden found out he came in crying, and flung himself across the bed, asking God to let him have the tuberculosis instead of me. I finally pushed him off and reached over to a little table near the bed and picked up all the medicine. I said, "Here, Papa, take this."

Papa replied, "What do you mean, Oral?"

I said, "Papa, they can't cure tuberculosis. This medicine isn't going to do any good. I'm going to die."

Mamma came into the room and took my hand and began to talk to me. I finally stopped her and said, "Mamma, what did your daddy die of?"

She looked down and didn't answer.

I said, "Mamma, tell me. What did your daddy die of?"

Finally she answered, "Of tuberculosis."

This only confirmed my fears that I, too, was going to die. Day after day I lay there questioning and crying out at my fate. Mamma, however, was convinced that God would heal me and she urged my father to write everyone we knew to pray to and believe in God for my healing. Several times groups of these friends would come to stay with us a day or two to pray for me. It all seemed like a dream. I looked at them through eyes that didn't really see and heard through ears that didn't hear.

I talked often with my mother about my future, about being a lawyer. She would smooth my pillow, put a hand on me or lean over and kiss my brow and say, "We'll see, son, we'll see."

I would look at her and remember the many times she'd told me that someday my tongue would be released and someday I would be a preacher. Then I would begin to grow bitter that my lungs were bursting inside, that I was coughing day and night, that I had fever nearly all the time, and that when I tried to stand and walk, I was so weak that I stumbled and fell and had to have them pick me up and lay me back on the bed.

Papa finally accepted an appointment at a small church in Stratford, Oklahoma, so he could be home with me all the time. People came and went. They came to see the preacher's son who lay dying with tuberculosis.

When Papa and the coach had put me in bed, I weighed 160 pounds on a 6-foot 1½ -inch frame. After lying bedfast for 163 days, I was down to 120 pounds. Friends no longer recognized me. In fact, when they came to visit me they could hardly stand to look at me.

Food tasted like wood. Sharp pains were constantly in my chest clear through to my shoulder blades. Night sweats were constant and the bloody coughing was always there. I began to curse the day I was born.

I took a lot of medicines prescribed by the doctors and several homemade remedies given by well-meaning friends. Constant prayers were said over me, predictions were made from time to time that the end was near. I lived in a state of unreality except for the suffering in my body. My mind was in a shadow and it felt as if I was away off from normal things.

I didn't respond to my parents' entreaties to pray or to be converted. A stupor engulfed me and at last it was as if I didn't see or hear anyone. I refused to take any more medicine, saying, "If I'm going to die anyway, why take that bitter-tasting stuff." I kept wondering, "Why has this happened to me? What have I done to deserve it?"

My pastor at the Methodist Church came to visit me. I had joined the Methodist Church quite a while back even though my father was a Pentecostal Holiness minister. Most of my friends were Methodist, also. I had enjoyed my church relationship very much. But now, as my pastor started to leave, he said, "Oral, you've just got to be patient."

I had never been patient even when well, and now I certainly was not interested in patiently waiting for death. I thought, "Brother, if that's all you've got to offer, I don't want it."

I was equally repelled by my parents' religion. They and the people of the church were concerned about my dying and going to hell. They would talk to me about getting saved and going to Heaven. They found it difficult to appreciate my response: "I'm not interested in dying and going to Heaven or dying and going to hell. I'm interested in living. I want to be well."

Then one day something happened that changed my attitude. My sister, Jewell, who lived seventeen miles away had an urge to come to our house. She came into my bedroom and looked down and said, "Oral, God is going to heal you."

It was as though she had turned on a light in my soul. All at once I awakened and I became aware of Jesus. Sermons had never reached me, the beautiful songs had never touched me. But with those seven little words, my sister identified Jesus as being part of my life, part of my future and my existence. He knew my name. He knew I existed. I was a person, a human being worth saving. I had a life worth living. And He was concerned about me.

My lungs were being torn up, I stammered and stuttered, I'd run away from home, gone my own way, but God cared. He was going to heal me and He had known about me all the time.

Not too long after this my brother Elmer came to our house. Elmer was no more religious than I was, but he had attended a tent revival where an evangelist was praying for the sick. What he had seen there had convinced him that his little brother could be helped. He borrowed a car, bought gas with the last thirty-five cents he had, and drove over to get me. He came straight into my bedroom and said, "Oral, get up. God is going to heal you."

Since I had never heard him talk about religion much, I said, "Elmer, what do you mean?"

He said, "I'm taking you to a tent meeting they're having in Ada. God is going to heal you. Now get up and let's go."

I said, "Elmer, I can't get up."

He said, "Well, then, I'll carry you."

About this time Mamma and Papa came in the room. When Elmer told them what he was doing they immediately pitched in to help. Though none of my clothes would fit me now, they put an old suit on me. They couldn't afford an ambulance so they took my mattress and put it in the backseat of the car and then carried me out.

As the little car slowly made its way to Ada, I suddenly knew God was going to heal me. It was one thing for Jesus to know it. . . . I had to come into a knowing myself. The promise that my mother had made to God before I was born now became a reality for me. God spoke to my heart promising to heal me and He called me to take His healing power to my generation. His words rang clear to me: "Son, I am going to heal you and you are to take the message of my healing power to your generation."

Though I didn't have any idea what that meant, I did know that now my life was in His hands. I have never ceased to believe it.

When we arrived at the tent, they put me in a rocking chair with pillows on both sides, and when the evangelist finished preaching, they carried me up to him. He put his hands on my head and said a short prayer, "Thou foul disease! I command you in the name of Jesus Christ to come out of this boy's lungs! Loose him and let him go!"

The next thing I knew I was racing back and forth on the platform shouting at the top of my voice, "I am healed! I am healed! I am healed!"

The preacher came over and took hold of me. He led me to the microphone and said, "Son, tell the people what the Lord has done for you."

All my life I had been a stutterer. I had been scared of crowds. I would freeze on the spot. But I took the microphone from his hands and spoke to that crowd as if I had spent half of my life on a platform. My tongue was loose, and I could talk. I could breathe all the way down without burning pain and coughing and hemorrhaging. I walked up and down the platform proclaiming what Jesus of Nazareth had done for me.

Later my parents took me to the Sugg Clinic in Ada, Oklahoma. There I had my lungs fluoroscoped. Dr. Morry found them absolutely perfect. He came into my room after the fluoroscopy and said, "Son, just forget you ever had TB. Your lungs are as sound as a dollar."

From poverty, to a runaway, to deathbed, and healing — it all combined to make me a preacher. Within two months of my healing I delivered my first sermon. It was a little sermon but it was a start.

Aleksandr Solzhenitsyn

(1918–2008)

Solzhenitsyn was a twentieth-century prophet. With his long beard, he looked the part. But much more importantly, his moral outrage at totalitarianism — what was and is perhaps the greatest threat to human welfare in the modern world — made him a voice heard round the world during his lifetime and beyond.

Though he was very critical of Western materialism, he arrested the attention of his own Russian people and the moral awareness of other nations by his stinging indictment of the network of labor camps and prisons that made Soviet rule so ruthless and so cruel. His condemnation came first in a short work, *One Day in the Life of Ivan Denisovich* (1962), and most exhaustively in the three-volume work, *The Gulag Archipelago* (1973-1978).

He never knew his father, who was killed in a hunting accident just before Solzhenitsyn was born. He was raised by his mother, who educated him in the Russian Orthodox Church's traditions. Nevertheless, by the time he reached his university years, he was a Marxist and a believer in the communist ideology of the Soviet Union. During World War II, he was decorated twice for his service as an officer in the Red Army, but it was then that he began having doubts about the Soviet state and its political ideology. In 1945, after being arrested for writing negative comments about Stalin and his regime, he was sentenced to an eight-year term in a labor camp — the standard penalty.

Solzhenitsyn was shuttled from one labor camp to another, and in 1953, when his term expired, he was sentenced to internal exile for life. He contracted cancer, but the malignancy gradually eased into remission. Finally, when Nikita Khrushchev delivered his famous denunciation of Stalinism in 1956, Solzhenitsyn was released. He had a tenuous existence in Russia following his return from the labor camps — never knowing exactly how much he could say and yet burning with a desire to expose the brutality of the camps.

Alternatively permitted to publish and then imprisoned and/or banned, Solzhenitsyn was deported from Russia in 1974 and lived in Germany and the United States until 1994, when he returned to Russia. He won the Nobel Prize for Literature in 1970 and died of heart failure in Moscow in 2008 at the age of eighty-nine.

Unlike his works of fiction and poetry, *The Gulag Archipelago* is a historical work, linking the origins of the Soviet prison system to Lenin himself. It chronicles the system of state-sponsored terror and executions that killed an estimated 60 to 70 million prisoners from 1918 to 1959. Solzhenitsyn interviewed 256 former prisoners in addition to conducting his own research. His conclusion was "that nowhere on the planet, nowhere in history, was there a regime more vicious, more bloodthirsty, and at the same time more cunning and ingenious than the Bolshevik, the self-styled Soviet regime. That no other regime on earth could compare with it either in the number of those it had done to death, in hardiness, in the range of its ambitions, in its thoroughgoing and unmitigated totalitarianism — no, not even the regime of its pupil Hitler, which at that time blinded Western eyes to all else" (*Gulag Archipelago,* III, 28).

The Gulag Archipelago, written in nearly numbing detail, seized the attention of the Soviet authorities (which eventually led to his expulsion from Russia) and inspired the support of the West. The work eventually sold more than 30 million copies and was translated into thirty-five languages. No other work in the twentieth century had such a profound political impact.

Late in his imprisonment, Solzhenitsyn experienced what might be called the turning point in a process of conversion from Marxism to Christianity, and he narrates the event in his massive work. The moment is compelling, and it had vast consequences for him and the moral foundation of politics in the modern world. But the question that plagued Solzhenitsyn and the moral sensibility of the twentieth century was: How could this have happened? Here is Solzhenitsyn's conclusion:

> *Over a century ago, while I was still a child, I recall hearing a number of old people offer the following explanation for the great disasters that had befallen Russia: "Men have forgotten God; that's why all this has happened." Since* then I have spent well-nigh 50 years working on the history of our revolution; in the process I have read hundreds of books, collected hundreds of personal testimonies, and have already contributed eight volumes of my

own toward the effort of clearing away the rubble left by that upheaval. But if I were asked today to formulate as concisely as possible the main cause of the ruinous revolution that swallowed up some 60 million of our people, I could not put it more accurately than to repeat: "Men have forgotten God; that's why all this has happened." (Edward E. Ericson, "Solzhenitsyn — Voice from the Gulag," *Eternity*, October 1985, 23, 24)

Solzhenitsyn ultimately exclaimed:

God of the Universe! I believe again!
Though I renounced You, You were with me!

And, like a Hebrew prophet, his message became: Do not forget the Lord your God.

~

Following an operation, I am lying in the surgical ward of a camp hospital. I cannot move. I am hot and feverish, but nonetheless my thoughts do not dissolve into delirium — and I am grateful to Dr. Boris Nikolayevich Kornfeld, who is sitting beside my cot and talking to me all evening. The light has been turned out — so it will not hurt my eyes. He and I — and there is no one else in the ward.

Fervently he tells me the long story of his conversion from Judaism to Christianity. This conversion was accomplished by an educated, cultivated person, one of his cellmates, some good-natured old fellow like Platon Karatayev. I am astonished at the conviction of the new convert, at the ardor of his words.

We know each other very slightly, and he was not the one responsible for my treatment, but there was simply no one here with whom he could share his feelings. He was a gentle and well-mannered person. I could see nothing bad in him nor did I know anything bad about him. However, I was on guard because Kornfeld had now been living for two months in the hospital barracks without going outside, because he had shut himself up in here, at his place of work, and avoided moving around camp at all.

This meant . . . he was afraid of having his throat cut. In our camp it had recently become fashionable — to cut the throats of stool pigeons. This has an effect. But who could guarantee that only stoolies were getting their throats cut? One prisoner had had his throat cut in a clear case of settling a sordid grudge. And therefore . . . the self-imprisonment of Kornfeld in the hospital did not yet prove at all that he was a stool pigeon.

It is already late. All the hospital is asleep. Kornfeld is ending up his story thus:

"And on the whole, do you know, I have become convinced that there is no punishment that comes to us in this life on earth which is undeserved. Superficially it can have nothing to do with what we are guilty of in actual fact, but if you go over your life with a fine-tooth comb and ponder it deeply, you will always be able to hunt down that transgression of yours for which you have now received this blow."

I cannot see his face. Through the window come only the scattered reflections of the lights of the perimeter outside. And the door from the corridor gleams in a yellow electrical glow. But there is such mystical knowledge in his voice that I shudder.

These were the last words of Boris Kornfeld. Noiselessly he went out into the nighttime corridor and into one of the nearby wards and there lay down to sleep. Everyone slept. And there was no one with whom he could speak even one word. And I went off to sleep myself.

And I was wakened in the morning by running about and tramping in the corridor; the orderlies were carrying Kornfeld's body to the operating room. He had been dealt eight blows on the skull with a plasterer's mallet while he still slept. (In our camp it was the custom to kill immediately after rising time, when the barracks were all unlocked and open and when no one yet had got up, when no one was stirring.) And he died on the operating table, without regaining consciousness.

And so it happened that Kornfeld's prophetic words were his last words on earth. And, directed to me, they lay upon me as an inheritance. You cannot brush off that kind of inheritance by shrugging your shoulders.

But by that time I myself had matured to similar thoughts.

I would have been inclined to endow his words with the significance of a universal law of life. However, one can get all tangled up that way. One would have to admit that on that basis those who had been punished even more cruelly than with prison — those shot, burned at the stake — were some sort of super-evildoers. (And yet . . . the innocent are those who get punished most zealously of all.) And what would one then have to say about our so evident torturers: Why does not fate punish *them?* Why do they prosper?

(And the only solution to this would be that the meaning of earthly existence lies not, as we have grown used to thinking, in prospering, but . . . in the development of the soul. From *that* point of view our torturers have been punished most horribly of all: they are turning into swine, they are departing downward from humanity. From that point of view punishment is inflicted on those whose development . . . *holds out hope.*)

But there was something in Kornfeld's last words that touched a sensitive chord, and that I accept quite completely *for myself.* And many will accept the same for themselves.

In the seventh year of my imprisonment I had gone over and re-examined my life quite enough and had come to understand why everything had happened to me: both prison and, as an additional piece of ballast, my malignant tumor. And I would not have murmured even if all that punishment had been considered inadequate.

Punishment? But . . . whose?

Well, just think about that — *whose?*

I lay there a long time in that recovery room from which Kornfeld had gone forth to his death, and all alone during sleepless nights I pondered with astonishment my own life and the turns it had taken. In accordance with my established camp custom I set down my thoughts in rhymed verses — so as to remember them. And the most accurate thing is to cite them here — just as they came from the pillow of a hospital patient, when the hard-labor camp was still shuddering outside the windows in the wake of a revolt.

> When was it that I completely
> Scattered the good seeds, one and all?
> For after all I spent my boyhood
> In the bright singing of Thy temples.
>
> Bookish subtleties sparkled brightly,
> Piercing my arrogant brain,

311

The secrets of the world were . . . in my grasp,
Life's destiny . . . as pliable as wax.

Blood seethed — and every swirl
Gleamed iridescently before me,
Without a rumble the building of my faith
Quietly crumbled within my heart.

But passing here between being and nothingness,
Stumbling and clutching at the edge,
I look behind me with a grateful tremor
Upon the life that I have lived.

Not with good judgment nor with desire
Are its twists and turns illumined.
But with the even glow of the Higher Meaning
Which became apparent to me only later on.

And now with measuring cup returned to me,
Scooping up the living water,
God of the Universe! I believe again!
Though I renounced You, You were with me!

Looking back, I saw that for my whole conscious life I had not understood either myself or my strivings. What had seemed for so long to be beneficial now turned out in actuality to be fatal, and I had been striving to go in the opposite direction to that which was truly necessary to me. But just as the waves of the sea knock the inexperienced swimmer off his feet and keep tossing him back onto the shore, so also was I painfully tossed back on dry land by the blows of misfortune. And it was only because of this that I was able to travel the path which I had always really wanted to travel.

It was granted me to carry away from my prison years on my bent back, which nearly broke beneath its load, this essential experience: *how* a human being becomes evil and *how* good. In the intoxication of youthful successes I had felt myself to be infallible, and I was therefore cruel. In the surfeit of power I was a murderer, and an oppressor. In my most evil moments I was convinced that I was doing good, and I was well supplied with systematic arguments. And it was only when I lay there on rotting prison straw that I sensed within myself the first stirrings of good. Gradually it was disclosed to me that the line separating good and evil passes not through states, nor between classes, nor between political parties either — but right through every human heart — and through all human hearts. This line shifts. Inside us, it oscillates with the years. And even within hearts overwhelmed by evil, one small bridgehead of good is retained. And even in the best of all hearts, there remains . . . an unuprooted small corner of evil.

Since then I have come to understand the truth of all the religions of the world: They struggle with the *evil inside a human being* (inside every human being). It is impossible to expel evil from the world in its entirety, but it is possible to constrict it within each person.

And since that time I have come to understand the falsehood of all the revolutions in history: They destroy only *those carriers* of evil contemporary with them (and also fail, out of haste, to discriminate the carriers of good as well). And they then take to themselves as their heritage the actual evil itself, magnified still more.

The Nuremberg Trials have to be regarded as one of the special achievements of the twentieth century: they killed the very idea of evil, though they killed very few of the people who had been infected with it. (Of course, Stalin deserves no credit here. He would have preferred to explain less and shoot more.) And if by the twenty-first century humanity has not yet blown itself up and has not suffocated itself — perhaps it is this direction that will triumph?

Yes, and if it does not triumph — then all humanity's history will have turned out to be an empty exercise in marking time, without the tiniest mite of meaning! Whither and to what end will we otherwise be moving? To beat the enemy over the head with a club — even cavemen knew that.

"Know thyself!" There is nothing that so aids and assists the awakening of omniscience within us as insistent thoughts about one's own transgressions, errors, mistakes. After the difficult cycles of such ponderings over many years, whenever I mentioned the heartlessness of our highest-ranking bureaucrats, the cruelty of our executioners, I remember myself in my captain's shoulder boards and the forward march of my battery through East Prussia, enshrouded in fire, and I say: "So were *we* any better?"

When people express vexation, in my presence, over the West's tendency to crumble, its political shortsightedness, its divisiveness, its confusion — I recall too: "Were we, before passing through the Archipelago, more steadfast? Firmer in our thoughts?"

And that is why I turn back to the years of my imprisonment and say, sometimes to the astonishment of those about me: *"Bless you, prison!"*

Lev Tolstoi was right when he *dreamed* of being put in prison. At a certain moment that giant began to dry up. He actually needed prison as a drought needs a shower of rain!

All the writers who wrote about prison but who did not themselves serve time there considered it their duty to express sympathy for prisoners and to curse prison. I . . . have served enough time there. I nourished my soul there, and I say without hesitation:

"Bless you, prison, for having been in my life!"

(And from beyond the grave come replies: It is very well for you to say that — when you came out of it alive!)

Festo Kivengere

(1919–1988)

Festo Kivengere was the "Billy Graham of Africa" who preached the gospel to millions throughout Africa and the Western world.

He was born into a royal family in a rural setting of southwest Uganda, where he spent much of his early years as a cattle herder. His own family was not Christian in his youth, but as he cared for the beloved cows, he read children's books about Jesus. When he was about ten, he was enrolled in a mission school in his village and then sent away for additional education. At nineteen, he returned to his village as a hard-living, convinced agnostic and an inspiring, charismatic teacher, and he taught young children in the same mission school in which he was reared.

His village and eventually much of East Africa had been affected by the *balokole* ("saved ones") movement. Because his parents had died, Kivengere became erstwhile guardian for some of his relatives, who had been converted to Christianity during the revival. They began praying for Kivengere's salvation from the dissolute life he was leading. As the following account makes clear, he was eventually led to Christ in the midst of the evangelistic meetings. In his subsequent ministry, Kivengere became a major leader of the East African Revival, which started in the 1930s and constitutes one of the most remarkable and long-lasting movements in the history of Christian evangelism.

Kivengere was ordained as a deacon in the United States, ordained as a priest in the Anglican church in Uganda in 1967, and consecrated as a bishop in Uganda in 1972. In 1977 he and his wife were forced to leave Uganda because of the oppressive rule of Idi Amin, sometimes called "Africa's Hitler," who was responsible for the murder of his colleague Bishop Janani Luwum and the oppression of the churches. Kivengere returned to Uganda when

Amin was deposed in 1979, but he also continued to travel and preach widely in Africa and throughout the West. In 1988 he published *I Love Idi Amin: The Story of Triumph under Fire in the Midst of Suffering and Persecution in Uganda* — a testimony to the power of forgiveness in the face of evil and oppression. In it, he wrote, "On the cross, Jesus said, 'Father, forgive them, because they don't know what they are doing.' As evil as Idi Amin was, how can I do less toward him?"

Kivengere founded the African Evangelistic Enterprise, a pan-African movement that brought an indigenized Christianity to the African continent. He also forged a close friendship with Billy Graham, who asked him to preach at several of his own revival meetings. When Kivengere was working on translating some of Graham's sermons, Graham reportedly told him, "Don't bother to translate literally. You know what I mean, get that across."

Kivengere was critical of his own Church of Uganda for allowing the government to exacerbate divisions between Catholics and Protestants; and shortly before his death from leukemia, he ordained three women as priests in his own diocese. He received the International Freedom Prize in 1977 in Norway for his defense of freedom and rights in Africa, and the St. Augustine Cross from the Archbishop of Canterbury for his ministry to the church around the world.

He was renowned as a great storyteller for children — of all ages. One of his favorite stories goes as follows: "One day a little girl sat watching her mother working in the kitchen. She asked her mummy, 'What does God do all day long?' For a while her mother was stumped, but then she said, 'Darling, I'll tell you what God does all day long. He spends his whole day mending broken things.'"

~

We were a cattle people. To my tribe, cows were what made life worth living. By the time I was three, I knew the name of every one of my father's 120 cows, bulls and calves. Some men I knew thought more of their cattle than of their children. So there were many things that happened that were incredible.

For instance, one day the chief was holding court and his elders were

Excerpted from Bishop Festo Kivengere with Dorothy Smoker, *Revolutionary Love* (Fort Washington, PA: Christian Literature Crusade, 1983), 12-17. Copyright © African Enterprise and used with permission.

listening to his wisdom when a man arrived who was well known to be a pagan and wealthy in cattle. His servants had eight fine cows they were driving along. All the elders turned to look at them appreciatively.

The cattle baron greeted everyone, and then said, "Your Honor, I have come for a purpose."

The chief answered, "Fine. What are these cows for?"

"Sir, they are yours. I have brought them back to you."

"What do you mean, they are mine?"

"Well, sir, when I was looking after your cattle, I stole four of them when I told you we had been raided. These four are now eight. I have brought them to you."

"Who discovered this theft?"

"Jesus did, sir. He has given me peace and told me to bring them."

There was dead silence and no laughter. It was quite a shock. My uncle could see that this man was rejoicing, and all knew that what he had done was impossible for a man of our tribe.

"You can put me in prison, sir, or have me beaten. I deserve it. But I am at peace and a free man for the first time."

"Humph!" said my uncle. "If God has done that for you, who am I to put you in prison? Leave the cattle and go home."

A day or two later, when I saw my uncle, I said, "I hear you got eight good cows free."

"Yes, it's true."

"You must be happy."

"Forget it! Since that man came, I can't sleep. If I wanted the peace he has, I would have to return a hundred cows!" For the time being, however, he went right on resisting, and so did I. Nevertheless, we admitted that some power we had not seen before was at work in our tribe, and we tried to think up some good explanations.

I was hating God because the awareness of Him embarrassed me continually. I was running away from "churchianity," from the Bible and from clergy. I wanted to escape this business of being "holy." I simply wanted to be my own manager.

My life was turning round itself like a spinning top. A top has a big head and a thin base, so it can't stand up unless it is spinning round and round. If it slows down, it topples over. It depends on spinning to keep going.

My spinning cycle was work-play-eat-drink-sleep-work-play-eat-drink, and so on, round and round. The more humdrum it became, the speedier I got. I thought that the faster I went, the livelier life would be. But I was finding out that a directionless life is difficult to live.

Though I pushed them back, my sins were dark against me and threatening. Guilt pursued me like a hunting dog after its prey. I was a man ill at ease — young, but fragmented inside, a victim of perpetual civil war.

Of course, I was running headlong into self-destruction. At the age of nineteen I considered ending my life. It was not because I didn't have health or work or party friends; it was because the things I did lacked meaning. There was a hollowness inside and life seemed lonely and undependable. There was a haunting sense of uncertainty. Perhaps what happened then was because I had come to the end of hope and was looking at suicide. In a way, I felt I was drowning. It was rather like my first attempt to swim.

Near the first boarding school I went to was a deep river. Most of the boys knew how to swim but I never learned. I watched them as they jumped into the river, both short and tall boys, shouting and having great fun.

I grumbled, "Some of these kids are not even as tall as I am, and they are enjoying the river. They can keep their heads above water, so why can't I? I have arms like theirs, and legs. Why not try?" So I took off my shirt and jumped into the pool.

I don't have to tell you what happened next. I went down like a stone. My arms were thrashing and my feet wouldn't respond. Again I went down, came up, and swallowed a lot of water doing it.

Boys being boys, those watching on the shore were clapping and laughing and having a good time seeing this new fellow sink. They did nothing while I was struggling, but watched until my strength was gone. Then a big boy jumped in and came swimming toward me. By the time he reached me, I was utterly unable to help myself. Now I was rescuable. The boy reached out, grabbed me, and swam to the shore.

Perhaps the One from whom I was running so fast saw that I was now rescuable, and He had arranged an encounter for me on a certain day. He also had some people praying.

My sister, who was twelve years old, and my niece, fourteen, were staying with me and attending the girls' school. They were concerned that I was a "lost" teacher, and I could sometimes hear them praying for me. I didn't make it easy for them either, because I was careless and full of myself.

One Sunday morning I went to church and the service was full of "fire." After the first song, young people were giving their testimonies and people were being converted even before the preacher began to preach. As usual, I sat at the back near the door just in case things got hotter as the service went on.

Then, who should ask permission to speak but my niece! She said, "I want you to praise God. The devil has been making me afraid of telling you what the Lord has done for us. On Friday night the Lord assured us that our prayers for Festo are answered. And Festo is sitting in the corner right there, and we know that he is going to come back to the Lord today."

So I got up and went outside, absolutely in a rage. I spent that day drinking hard at my uncle's place, planning to come back and make things difficult for this girl who was foolish enough to take the liberty of speaking about me in public like that.

Late that afternoon I was cycling home, somewhat wobbly, when I saw a good friend of mine riding his bicycle toward me on the dusty road, with a look on his face as if he were flying. He was a teacher, like me, and I knew very well that he did not ordinarily have a glow on his face. I was surprised.

My friend pulled up beside me and said, breathlessly, "Festo! Three hours ago Jesus became a living reality to me. I know my sins are forgiven!"

He had never before spoken with any enthusiasm about Jesus. Then with complete sincerity, he said, "Please, I want you to forgive me, friend, . . ." and he named three specific things for which he wanted forgiveness, related to some questionable things we had done together. "I am sorry, Festo. I will no longer live like that. Jesus has given me something much better. So long!"

Off he went, whistling exuberantly, leaving me with my mouth open there on the road. If only he had stayed to let me argue . . . but he did not.

His joy overwhelmed me. His words, and the way he said them, shook me to the core. I felt like a shadow, having seen in my friend the reality I had missed. I cycled home utterly miserable and empty.

When I reached my room, I knelt by my bed, struggling for words to the One in whom I no longer believed. Finally I cried, "God! If You happen to be there, as my friend says, I am miserable. If You can do anything for me, then please do it now. If I'm not too far gone . . . HELP!"

Then what happened in that room! Heaven opened, and in front of me was Jesus. He was there real and crucified for me. His broken body was hanging on the cross, and suddenly I knew that it was my badness that did this to the King of Life. It shook me. In tears, I thought I was going to Hell. If He had said, "Go!" I would not have complained. Somehow I thought that would be His duty, as all the wretchedness of my life came out.

But then I saw His eyes of infinite love which were looking into mine. Could it be He who was clearly saying, "This is how much I love you, Festo!"

I shook my head, because I knew that couldn't be possible, and said, "No, I am Your enemy. I am rebellious. I have been hating Your people. *How can You love me like that?*"

Even today, I do not know the answer to that question. There is no reason in me for His love.

But that day I discovered myself clasped in the Father's arms. I was tattered and afraid, just like the younger son who went into the far country and then came to the end of himself. But *why* should the Father, who is holy, come running to hold *me* to His heart? I was dirty and desperate and had said and done much against Him.

That love was wholly unexpected, but it filled my room, and I was convinced. He is the only One who loves the unlovable and embraces the unembraceable. In spite of what I was, I knew I was accepted, was a son of the Father, and that whatever Jesus did on the cross, it was for me.

Ever since that day, the cross has been central in my thinking, and the Lord Jesus my Enabler for living near to it. I want to share some of what He is doing for me and what He will do for you by His Calvary love.

Martin Luther King Jr.

(1929–1968)

During the brief thirty-nine years of his life, Martin Luther King Jr. left a profound impact on American society — perhaps greater than any other person in the twentieth century. Never elected to a political office, he remained a minister until his death. Yet, through his speeches and activities, he galvanized the nation to confront the racism of its attitudes and institutions and inspired the effort to establish civil rights for its African-American citizens. The liberty and justice he sought for his fellow African Americans proved to be contagious, and since his death his vision of a more just and equal society and world has spread to other groups and other nations.

King was born into a relatively well-off minister's family in Atlanta. His father, Martin Luther King Sr., was the long-time pastor of the Ebenezer Baptist Church, and he (and his son) were both named "Michael" until the family visited Germany in 1934. After the trip, both father and son had their first names changed to "Martin Luther," the eloquent theologian of Christian liberty.

Despite the material comfort of his childhood, Martin Luther King Jr. witnessed first-hand the segregation of Atlanta, the discrimination in American society, and black poverty. At the same time, he also experienced the enduring affirmation of his parents and their assurance of his self-worth, and he came to know the power of the Christian gospel of God's love that made people worthy and imparted dignity to every person.

King attended Morehouse College, where he was deeply influenced by its president, Dr. Benjamin Mays, a distinguished African-American minister and religious thinker. Initially King considered medicine and the law, but eventually chose the ministry as his vocation, attending Crozer Theological Seminary and then Boston University, where he received his Ph.D. "Of course I was religious," King recalled. "I grew up in the church. My father is a preacher, my grandfather was a preacher, my great-grandfather was a preacher, my only brother is a preacher, my daddy's brother is a preacher. So I didn't have much choice."

He married Coretta Scott in 1953, and they had four children. A year after his marriage, King became pastor of the Dexter Avenue Baptist Church in Montgomery, Alabama, at the age of twenty-five. A year later, espousing non-violent protest, he was catapulted into public attention as one of the leaders of the Montgomery bus boycott. Fame bred violence, and during the boycott his house was bombed. His family was safe; the boycott was successful in removing segregation from Montgomery's buses; but the reality of violence remained for the rest of his life.

In 1957, King and other civil rights ministers founded the Southern Christian Leadership Conference, which King led until his death. King was heavily influenced by the thought and tactics of Gandhi, as taught by the theologian Howard Thurman, and from this and other sources King developed his strategy of nonviolent resistance. This political approach to segregation prompted demonstrations throughout the South and eventually the North. These met with violence from police and white demonstrators, which in turn only increased publicity for the movement and garnered sympathy with its goals.

In 1960, King joined his father as a pastor of Ebenezer Baptist Church in Atlanta, and from that base he continued his civil rights activities. The year 1963 brought forth his two most famous declarations: the "Letter from the Birmingham City Jail" (focusing on the Christian's and the individual's duty to disobey immoral laws) and the "I Have a Dream Speech" in Washington, D.C. (often described as one of the finest speeches in American history). A year later, at age thirty-five, he was awarded the Nobel Peace Prize, the youngest recipient in the award's history.

King's influence and the power of the civil rights movement were crucial in the passage of the historic Civil Rights Act of 1964 and the Voting Rights Act of 1965. Yet, even in its moment of victory, the civil rights movement fragmented. King's nonviolence was attacked by more militant African-American leaders. His opposition to the Vietnam War was criticized by still others. In a move to address economic injustice and spread its influence to northern cities, King found more obstacles and greater challenges. His opponents persisted in their critiques and attacks.

In 1968, King traveled to Memphis to lend support to the municipal garbage workers' strike. In his sermons, books, and speeches, he had long drawn on the Bible, especially the story of the Exodus, the moral injunctions of the Hebrew prophets, and the teaching of Jesus. In his last public words, he eloquently imparted a biblical vision and legacy to both his followers and his nation:

> I don't know what will happen now. We've got some difficult days ahead. But it doesn't matter now. Because I've been to the mountaintop. And I don't mind. Like anybody, I would like to live a long life. Longevity has its place. But I'm not concerned about that now. I just want to do God's will. And He's allowed me to go up to the mountain. And I've looked over. And I've seen the promised land. I may not get there with you. But I want you to know tonight, that we, as a people, will get to the promised land. And I'm happy, tonight. I'm not worried about anything. I'm not fearing any man. Mine eyes have seen the glory of the coming of the Lord!

Hours later, he was felled by an assassin's bullet.

~

I was born in the late twenties on the verge of the Great Depression, which was to spread its disastrous arms into every corner of this nation for over a decade. I was much too young to remember the beginning of this depression, but I do recall, when I was about five years of age, how I questioned my parents about the numerous people standing in breadlines. I can see the effects of this early childhood experience on my anticapitalistic feelings. . . .

The community in which I was born was quite ordinary in terms of social status. No one in our community had attained any great wealth. Most of the Negroes in my hometown who had attained wealth lived in a section of town known as "Hunter Hills." The community was characterized with a sort of unsophisticated simplicity. No one was in the extremely poor class. It is probably fair to class the people of this community as those of average income. It was a wholesome community,

---

King's autobiography is scattered throughout his writings and personal papers. The following is excerpted from *The Autobiography of Martin Luther King,* compiled and edited by Clayborne Carson (New York: Grand Central Publishing, 1998), 1-33. Passages in italics come from King's own writings. Reprinted by arrangement with The Heirs to the Estate of Martin Luther King Jr., c/o Writers House as agent for the proprietor, New York, NY. Copyright 1963 Dr. Martin Luther King Jr.; copyright renewed 1991 Coretta Scott King.

notwithstanding the fact that none of us were ever considered members of the "upper-upper class." Crime was at a minimum, and most of our neighbors were deeply religious.

From the very beginning I was an extraordinarily healthy child. It is said that at my birth the doctors pronounced me a one hundred percent perfect child, from a physical point of view. I hardly know how an ill moment feels. I guess the same thing would apply to my mental life. I have always been somewhat precocious, both physically and mentally. So it seems that from a hereditary point of view, nature was very kind to me.

My home situation was very congenial. I have a marvelous mother and father. I can hardly remember a time that they ever argued (my father happens to be the kind who just won't argue) or had any great falling out. These factors were highly significant in determining my religious attitudes. It is quite easy for me to think of a God of love mainly because I grew up in a family where love was central and where lovely relationships were ever present. It is quite easy for me to think of the universe as basically friendly mainly because of my uplifting hereditary and environmental circumstances. It is quite easy for me to lean more toward optimism than pessimism about human nature mainly because of my childhood experiences.

In my own life and in the life of a person who is seeking to be strong, you combine in your character antitheses strongly marked. You are both militant and moderate; you are both idealistic and realistic. And I think that my strong determination for justice comes from the very strong, dynamic personality of my father, and I would hope that the gentle aspect comes from a mother who is very gentle and sweet. . . .

My mother confronted the age-old problem of the Negro parent in America: how to explain discrimination and segregation to a small child. She taught me that I should feel a sense of "somebodiness" but that on the other hand I had to go out and face a system that stared me in the face every day saying you are "less than," you are "not equal to." She told me about slavery and how it ended with the Civil War. She tried to explain the divided system of the South — the segregated schools, restaurants, theaters, housing; the white and colored signs on drinking fountains, waiting rooms, lavatories — as a social condition rather than a natural order. She made it clear that she opposed this system and that I must never allow it to make me feel inferior. Then she said the words that almost every Negro hears before he can yet understand the injustice that makes them necessary: "You are as good as anyone." At this time Mother had no idea that the little boy in her arms would years later be involved in a struggle against the system she was speaking of.

Martin Luther King, Sr., is as strong in his will as he is in his body. He has a dynamic personality, and his very physical presence (weighing about 220 pounds) commands attention. He has always been a very strong and self-confident person. I have rarely ever met a person more fearless and courageous than my father, notwithstanding the fact that he feared for me. He never feared the autocratic and brutal person in the white community. If they said something to him that was insulting, he made it clear in no uncertain terms that he didn't like it. . . .

The thing that I admire most about my dad is his genuine Christian character. He is a man of real integrity, deeply committed to moral and ethical principles. He is conscientious in all of his undertakings. Even the person who disagrees with his frankness has to admit that his motives and actions are sincere. He never hesitates to tell the truth and speak his mind, however cutting it may be. This quality of frankness has often caused people to actually fear him. I have had young and old alike say to me, "I'm scared to death of your dad." Indeed, he is stern at many points.

My father has always had quite an interest in civil rights. He has been president of the NAACP in Atlanta, and he always stood out in social reform. From before I was born, he had refused to ride the city buses after witnessing a brutal attack on a load of Negro passengers. He led the fight in Atlanta to equalize teachers' salaries and was instrumental in the elimination of Jim Crow elevators in the courthouse.

As pastor of the Ebenezer Baptist Church, my father wielded great influence in the Negro community and perhaps won the grudging respect of the whites. At any rate, they never attacked him physically, a fact that filled my brother and sister and me with wonder as we grew up in this tension-packed atmosphere. With this heritage, it is not surprising that I also learned to abhor segregation, considering it both rationally inexplicable and morally unjustifiable. . . .

I joined the church at the age of five. I well remember how this event occurred. Our church was in the midst of the spring revival, and a guest evangelist had come down from Virginia. On Sunday morning the evangelist came into our Sunday school to talk to us about salvation, and after a short talk on this point he extended an invitation to any of us who wanted to join the church. My sister was the first one to join the church that morning, and after seeing her join I decided that I would not let her get ahead of me, so I was the next. I had never given this matter a thought, and even at the time of my baptism I was unaware of what was taking place. From this it seems quite clear that I joined the church not out of any dynamic conviction, but out of a childhood desire to keep up with my sister.

The church has always been a second home for me. As far back as I can remember I was in church every Sunday. My best friends were in Sunday school, and it was the Sunday school that helped me to build the capacity for getting along with people. I guess this was inevitable since my father was the pastor of my church, but I never regretted going to church until I passed through a state of skepticism in my second year of college.

The lessons which I was taught in Sunday school were quite in the fundamentalist line. None of my teachers ever doubted the infallibility of the Scriptures. Most of them were unlettered and had never heard of biblical criticism. Naturally, I accepted the teachings as they were being given to me. I never felt any need to doubt them — at least at that time I didn't. I guess I accepted biblical studies uncritically until I was about twelve years old. But this uncritical attitude could not last long, for it was contrary to the very nature of my being. I had always been the questioning and precocious type. At the age of thirteen, I shocked my Sunday school class by denying the bodily resurrection of Jesus. Doubts began to spring forth unrelentingly.

Two incidents happened in my late childhood and early adolescence that had a tremendous effect on my development. The first was the death of my grandmother. She was very dear to each of us, but especially to me. I sometimes think I was her favorite grandchild. I was particularly hurt by her death mainly because of the extreme love I had for her. She assisted greatly in raising all of us. It was after this incident that for the first time I talked at any length on the doctrine of immortality. My parents attempted to explain it to me, and I was assured that somehow my grandmother still lived. I guess this is why today I am such a strong believer in personal immortality.

The second incident happened when I was about six years of age. From the age of three I had a white playmate who was about my age. We always felt free to play our childhood games together. He did not live in our community, but he was usually around every day; his father owned a store across the street from our home. At the age of six we both entered school — separate schools, of course. I remember how our friendship began to break as soon as we entered school; this was not my desire but his. The climax came when he told me one day that his father had demanded that he would play with me no more. I never will forget what a great shock this was to me. I immediately asked my parents about the motive behind such a statement.

We were at the dinner table when the situation was discussed, and here for the first time I was made aware of the existence of a race problem. I had never been conscious of it before. As my parents discussed some of the tragedies that had resulted from this problem and some of the insults they themselves had confronted on account of it, I was greatly shocked, and from that moment on I was determined to hate every white person. As I grew older and older this feeling continued to grow.

My parents would always tell me that I should not hate the white man, but that it was my duty as a Christian to love him. The question arose in my mind: How could I love a race of people who hated me and who had been responsible for breaking me up with one of my best childhood friends? This was a great question in my mind for a number of years. . . .

When I was fourteen, I traveled from Atlanta to Dublin, Georgia, with a dear teacher of mine, Mrs. Bradley. I participated in an oratorical contest there and I succeeded in winning the contest. My subject, ironically enough, was "The Negro and the Constitution."

We cannot have an enlightened democracy with one great group living in ignorance. We cannot have a healthy nation with one-tenth of the people ill-nourished, sick, harboring germs of disease which recognize no color lines — obey no Jim Crow laws. We cannot have a nation orderly and sound with one group so ground down and thwarted that it is almost forced into unsocial attitudes and crime. We cannot be truly Christian people so long as we flout the central teachings of Jesus: brotherly love and the Golden Rule. We cannot come to full prosperity with one great group so ill-delayed that it cannot buy goods. So as we gird ourselves to defend democracy from foreign attack, let us see to it that increasingly at home we give fair play and free opportunity for all people.

Today thirteen million black sons and daughters of our forefathers continue the fight for the translation of the Thirteenth, Fourteenth, and Fifteenth Amendments from writing on the printed page to an actuality. We believe with them that "if freedom is good for any it is good for all," that we may conquer Southern armies by the sword, but it is another thing to conquer Southern hate, that if the franchise is given to Negroes, they will be vigilant and defend, even with their arms, the ark of federal liberty from treason and destruction by her enemies.

That night, Mrs. Bradley and I were on a bus returning to Atlanta. Along the way, some white passengers boarded the bus, and the white driver ordered us to get up and give the whites our seats. We didn't move quickly enough to suit him, so he began cursing us. I intended to stay right in that seat, but Mrs. Bradley urged me up, saying we had to obey the law. We stood up in the aisle for ninety miles to Atlanta. That night will never leave my memory. It was the angriest I have ever been in my life. . . .

Just before going to college I went to Simsbury, Connecticut, and worked for a whole summer on a tobacco farm to earn a little school money to supplement what my parents were doing. One Sunday, we went to church in Simsbury, and we were the only Negroes there. On Sunday mornings I was the religious leader and spoke on any text I wanted to 107 boys. I had never thought that a person of my race could eat anywhere, but we ate in one of the finest restaurants in Hartford.

After that summer in Connecticut, it was a bitter feeling going back to segregation. It was hard to understand why I could ride wherever I pleased on the train from New York to Washington and then had to change to a Jim Crow car at the nation's capital in order to continue the trip to Atlanta. The first time that I was seated behind a curtain in a dining car, I felt as if the curtain had been dropped on my selfhood. I could never adjust to the separate waiting rooms, separate eating places, separate rest rooms, partly because the separate was always unequal, and partly because the very idea of separation did something to my sense of dignity and self-respect. . . .

When I went to Morehouse as a freshman in 1944, my concern for racial and economic justice was already substantial. During my student days I read Henry David Thoreau's essay "On Civil Disobedience" for the first time. Here, in this courageous New Englander's refusal to pay his taxes and his choice of jail rather than support a war that would spread slavery's territory into Mexico, I made my first contact with the theory of nonviolent resistance. Fascinated by the idea of refusing to cooperate with an evil system, I was so deeply moved that I reread the work several times.

I became convinced that noncooperation with evil is as much a moral obligation as is cooperation with good. No other person has been more eloquent and passionate in getting this idea across than Henry David Thoreau. As a result of his writings and personal witness, we are the heirs of a legacy of creative protest. The teachings of Thoreau came alive in our civil rights movement; indeed, they are more alive than ever before. Whether expressed in a sit-in at lunch counters, a freedom ride into Mississippi, a peaceful protest in Albany, Georgia, a bus boycott in Montgomery, Alabama, these are outgrowths of Thoreau's insistence that evil must be resisted and that no moral man can patiently adjust to injustice. . . .

Because of the influence of my mother and father, I guess I always had a deep urge to serve humanity, but I didn't start out with an interest to enter the ministry. I thought I could probably do it better as a lawyer or doctor. One of my closest friends at Morehouse, Walter McCall, was clear about his intention of going into the ministry, but I was slow to make up my mind. I did serve as assistant to my father for six months.

As stated above, my college training, especially the first two years, brought many doubts into my mind. It was then that the shackles of fundamentalism were removed from my body. More and more I could see a gap between what I had learned in Sunday school and what I was learning in college. My studies had made me skeptical, and I could not see how many of the facts of science could be squared with religion.

I revolted, too, against the emotionalism of much Negro religion, the shouting and stamping. I didn't understand it, and it embarrassed me. I often say that if we, as a people, had as much religion in our hearts and souls as we have in our legs and feet, we could change the world.

I had seen that most Negro ministers were unlettered, not trained in seminaries, and that gave me pause. I had been brought up in the church and knew about religion, but I wondered whether it could serve as a vehicle to modern thinking, whether religion could be intellectually respectable as well as emotionally satisfying.

This conflict continued until I studied a course in Bible in which I came to see that behind the legends and myths of the Book were many profound truths which one could not escape. Two men — Dr. [Benjamin] Mays, president of Morehouse College and one of the great influences in my life, and Dr. George Kelsey, a professor of philosophy and religion — made me stop and think. Both were ministers, both deeply religious, and yet both were learned men, aware of all the trends of modern thinking. I could see in their lives the ideal of what I wanted a minister to be.

It was in my senior year of college that I entered the ministry. I had felt the urge to enter the ministry from my high school days, but accumulated doubts had somewhat blocked the urge. Now it appeared again with an inescapable drive. I felt a sense of responsibility which I could not escape.

I guess the influence of my father had a great deal to do with my going into the ministry. This is not to say that he ever spoke to me in terms of being a minister but that my admiration for him was the great moving factor. He set forth a noble example that I didn't mind following. I still feel the effects of the noble moral and ethical ideals that I grew up under. They have been real and precious to me, and even in moments of theological doubt I could never turn away from them. . . .

It has been my conviction ever since reading Rauschenbusch that any religion that professes concern for the souls of men and is not equally concerned about the slums that damn them, the economic conditions that strangle them, and the social conditions that cripple them is a spiritually moribund religion only waiting for the day to be buried. It well has been said: "A religion that ends with the individual, ends."

I feel that preaching is one of the most vital needs of our society, if it is used correctly. There is a great paradox in preaching: on the one hand it may be very helpful and on the other it may be very pernicious. It is my opinion that sincerity is not enough for the preaching ministry. The minister must be both sincere and intelligent. . . . I also think that the minister should possess profundity of conviction. We have too many ministers in the pulpit who are great spellbinders and too few who possess spiritual power. It is my profound conviction that I, as an aspirant for the ministry, should possess these powers.

I think that preaching should grow out of the experiences of the people. Therefore, I, as a minister, must know the problems of the people that I am pastoring. Too often do educated ministers leave the people lost in the fog of theological abstraction, rather than presenting that theology in the light of the people's experiences. It is my conviction that the minister must somehow take profound theological and philosophical views and place them in a concrete framework. I must forever make the complex the simple.

Above all, I see the preaching ministry as a dual process. On the one hand I must attempt to change the soul of individuals so that their societies may be changed. On the other I must attempt to change the societies so that the individual soul will have a change. Therefore, I must be concerned about unemployment, slums, and economic insecurity. I am a profound advocate of the social gospel. . . .

During this period [in seminary] I had about despaired of the power of love in solving social problems. I thought the only way we could solve our problem of segregation was an armed revolt. I felt that the Christian ethic of love was confined to individual relationships. I could not see how it could work in social conflict. . . .

Then one Sunday afternoon I traveled to Philadelphia to hear a sermon by Dr. Mordecai Johnson, president of Howard University. He was there to preach for the Fellowship House of Philadelphia. Dr. Johnson had just returned from a trip to India, and, to my great interest, he spoke of the life and teachings of Mahatma Gandhi. His message was so profound and electrifying that I left the meeting and bought a half-dozen books on Gandhi's life and works.

Like most people, I had heard of Gandhi, but I had never studied him seriously. As I read I became deeply fascinated by his campaigns of nonviolent resistance. I was particularly moved by his Salt March to the Sea and his numerous fasts. The whole concept of *Satyagraha* (*Satya* is truth which equals love, and *agraha* is force; *Satyagraha,* therefore, means truth force or love force) was profoundly significant to me. As I delved deeper into the philosophy of Gandhi, my skepticism concerning the power of love gradually diminished, and I came to see for the first time its potency in the area of social reform. Prior to reading Gandhi, I had about concluded that the ethics of Jesus were only effective in individual relationships. The "turn the other cheek" philosophy and the "love your enemies" philosophy were only valid, I felt, when individuals were in conflict with other individuals; when racial groups and nations were in conflict a more realistic approach seemed necessary. But after reading Gandhi, I saw how utterly mistaken I was.

Gandhi was probably the first person in history to lift the love ethic of Jesus above mere interaction between individuals to a powerful and effective social force on a large scale. Love for Gandhi was a potent instrument for social and collective transformation. It was in this Gandhian emphasis on love and nonviolence that I discovered the method for social reform that I had been seeking. The intellectual and moral satisfaction that I failed to gain from the utilitarianism of Bentham and Mill, the revolutionary methods of Marx and Lenin, the social contracts theory of Hobbes, the "back to nature" optimism of Rousseau, the superman philosophy of Nietzsche, I found in the nonviolent resistance philosophy of Gandhi.

But my intellectual odyssey to nonviolence did not end here. During my senior year in theological seminary, I engaged in the exciting reading of various theological theories. Having been raised in a rather strict fundamentalist tradition, I was occasionally shocked when my intellectual journey carried me through new and sometimes complex doctrinal lands, but the pilgrimage was always stimulating; it gave me a new appreciation for objective appraisal and critical analysis, and knocked me out of my dogmatic slumber.

When I came to Crozer, I could accept the liberal interpretation of Christianity with relative ease. Liberalism provided me with an intellectual satisfaction that I had never found in fundamentalism. I became so enamored of the insights of liberalism that I almost fell into the trap of accepting uncritically everything that came under its name. I was absolutely convinced of the natural goodness of man and the natural power of human reason.

The basic change in my thinking came when I began to question the liberal doctrine of man. My thinking went through a state of transition. At one time I found myself leaning toward a mild neo-orthodox view of man, and at other times I found myself leaning toward a liberal view of man. The former leaning may root back to certain experiences that I had in the South, with its vicious race problem, that made it very difficult for me to believe in the essential goodness of man. The more I observed the tragedies of history and man's shameful inclination to choose the low road, the more I came to see the depths and strength of sin. Liberalism's superficial optimism concerning human nature caused it to overlook the fact that reason is darkened by sin. The more I thought about human nature, the more I saw how our tragic inclination for sin causes us to use our minds to rationalize our actions. Liberalism failed to see that reason by itself is little more than an instrument to justify man's defensive ways of thinking. Moreover, I came to recognize the complexity of man's social involvement and the glaring reality of collective evil. I came to feel that liberalism had been all too sentimental concerning human nature and that it leaned toward a false idealism. Reason, devoid of the purifying power of faith, can never free itself from distortions and rationalizations.

On the other hand, part of my liberal leaning had its source in another branch of the same root. In noticing the gradual improvements of this same race problem, I came to see some noble possibilities in human nature. Also my liberal leaning may have rooted back to the great imprint that many liberal theologians have left upon me and to my ever-present desire to be optimistic about human nature. Of course there is one phase of liberalism that I hope to cherish always: its devotion to the search for truth, its insistence on an open and analytical mind, its refusal to abandon the best light of reason. Its contribution to the philological-historical criticism of biblical literature has been of immeasurable value.

During my last year in theological school, I began to read the works of Reinhold Niebuhr. The prophetic and realistic elements in Niebuhr's passionate style and profound thought were appealing to me, and made me aware of the complexity of human motives and the reality of sin on every level of man's existence. I became so enamored of his social ethics that I almost fell into the trap of accepting uncritically everything he wrote. . . .

At first, Niebuhr's critique of pacifism left me in a state of confusion. As I continued to read, however, I came to see more and more the shortcomings of his position. For instance, many of his statements revealed that he interpreted pacifism as a sort of passive non-resistance to evil expressing naive trust in the power of love. But this was a serious distortion. My study of Gandhi convinced me that true pacifism is not nonresistance to evil, but nonviolent resistance to evil. Between the two positions, there is a world of difference. Gandhi resisted evil with as much vigor and power as the violent resister, but he resisted with love instead of hate. True pacifism is not unrealistic submission to evil power, as Niebuhr contends. It is rather a courageous confrontation of evil by the power of love, in the faith that it is better to be the recipient of violence than the inflicter of it, since the latter only multiplies the existence of violence and bitterness in the universe, while the former may develop a sense of shame in the opponent, and thereby bring about a transformation and change of heart.

In spite of the fact that I found many things to be desired in Niebuhr's philosophy, there were several points at which he constructively influenced my thinking. Niebuhr's great contribution to theology is that he has refuted the false optimism characteristic of a great segment of Protestant liberalism. Moreover, Niebuhr has extraordinary insight into human nature, especially the behavior of nations and social groups. He is keenly aware of the complexity of human motives and of the relation between morality and power. His theology is a persistent reminder of the reality of sin on every level of man's existence. These elements in Niebuhr's thinking helped me to recognize the illusions of a superficial optimism concerning human nature and the dangers of a false idealism. While I still believed in man's potential for good, Niebuhr made me realize his potential for evil as well. Moreover, Niebuhr helped me to recognize the complexity of man's social involvement and the glaring reality of collective evil.

Many pacifists, I felt, failed to see this. All too many had an unwarranted optimism concerning man and leaned unconsciously toward self-righteousness. After reading Niebuhr, I tried to arrive at a realistic pacifism. In other words, I came to see the pacifist position not as sinless but as the lesser evil in the circumstances. I do not claim to be free from the moral dilemmas that the Christian non-pacifist confronts, but I am convinced that the church cannot be silent while mankind faces the threat of nuclear annihilation. I felt that the pacifist would have a greater appeal if he did not claim to be free from the moral dilemmas that the Christian non-pacifist confronts.

The thing that we need in the world today, is a group of men and women who will stand up for right and be opposed to wrong, wherever it is. A group of people who have come to see that some things are wrong, whether they're never caught up with. Some things are right, whether nobody sees you doing them or not.

All I'm trying to say is, our world hinges on moral foundations. God has made it so! God has made the universe to be based on a moral law. . . .

This universe hinges on moral foundations. There is something in this universe that justifies Carlyle in saying,

"No lie can live forever."

There is something in this universe that justifies William Cullen Bryant in saying,

"Truth, crushed to earth, will rise again."

There is something in this universe that justifies James Russell Lowell in saying,

"Truth forever on the scaffold,
Wrong forever on the throne.
With that scaffold sways the future.
Behind the dim unknown stands God,
Within the shadow keeping watch above his own."

There is something in this universe that justifies the biblical writer in saying,

"You shall reap what you sow."

As a young man with most of my life ahead of me, I decided early to give my life to something eternal and absolute. Not to these little gods that are here today and gone tomorrow. But to God who is the same yesterday, to-day, and forever.

I'm not going to put my ultimate faith in the little gods that can be de-stroyed in an atomic age, but the God who has been our help in ages past, and our hope for years to come, and our shelter in the time of storm, and our eternal home. That's the God that I'm putting my ultimate faith in. . . . The God that I'm talking about this morning is the God of the universe and the God that will last through the ages. If we are to go forward this morning, we've got to go back and find that God. That is the God that demands and commands our ultimate allegiance.

If we are to go forward, we must go back and rediscover these precious values — that all reality hinges on moral foundations and that all reality has spiritual control.

Charles W. Colson

(1931–2012)

Known as the "hatchet man" for Richard Nixon, Charles Colson was implicated in the Watergate scandal in 1974. As Special Assistant to the President, he was at the top and in the center of the political intrigues during that famous and frenetic period of time. Sentenced to prison, Colson served a seven-month term until his release, January 31, 1975.

Two years earlier, in 1973, Colson made public his conversion, saying that he had "accepted Jesus Christ." His account of that experience, in the context of the political events of the time, is graphically set forth in his book *Born Again* (1976). Though not described in theological or doctrinal language, his conversion has the authentic mark of sincerity and honesty.

After his prison release, Colson became increasingly involved in helping prison inmates. With the encouragement of good friends in Washington, such as Harold Hughes, former senator from Iowa, himself a twice-born Christian, and several interested wardens, he established what became known as the Prison Fellowship. Colson wrote about his work with this Christian evangelistic movement in a lively book entitled *Life Sentence* (1979).

Although some have questioned the genuineness of Colson's conversion, others, such as Billy Graham and Catharine Marshall, have testified in his favor, and many have been moved and inspired by his innovative and practical prison ministry. By the time of his death, Colson had become a major voice in American evangelicalism.

As so often happens in conversion experiences, someone stands by to help and encourage. In Colson's case, it was his friend Tom Phillips, president of the Raytheon Company, who gave him a copy of C. S. Lewis's *Mere Christianity*.

~

It was an unusually hot night for New England, the humidity like a heavy blanket wrapped around me. At Tom's insistence, first the dark gray business-suit jacket, then my tie came off. He pulled a wrought-iron ottoman close to the comfortable outdoor settee I sat on.

"Tell me, Chuck," he began, "are you okay?" It was the same question he had asked in March.

As the President's confidant and so-called big-shot Washington lawyer I was still keeping my guard up. "I'm not doing too badly, I guess. All of this Watergate business, all the accusations — I suppose it's wearing me down some. But I'd rather talk about you, Tom. You've changed and I'd like to know what happened."

Tom drank from his glass and sat back reflectively. Briefly he reviewed his past, the rapid rise to power at Raytheon: executive vice-president at thirty-seven, president when he was only forty. He had done it with hard work, day and night, nonstop.

"The success came, all right, but something was missing," he mused. "I felt a terrible emptiness. Sometimes I would get up in the middle of the night and pace the floor of my bedroom or stare out into the darkness for hours at a time."

"I don't understand it," I interrupted. "I knew you in those days, Tom. You were a straight arrow, good family life, successful, everything in fact going your way."

"All that may be true, Chuck, but my life wasn't complete. I would go to the office each day and do my job, striving all the time to make the company succeed, but there was a big hole in my life. I began to read the Scriptures, looking for answers. Something made me realize I needed a personal relationship with God, forced me to search."

A prickly feeling ran down my spine. Maybe what I had gone through in the past several months wasn't so unusual after all — except I had not sought spiritual answers. I had not even been aware that finding a personal relationship with God was possible. I pressed him to explain the apparent contradiction between the emptiness inside while seeming to enjoy the affluent life.

"It may be hard to understand," Tom chuckled. "But I didn't seem

---

to have anything that mattered. It was all on the surface. All the material things in life are meaningless if a man hasn't discovered what's underneath them."

We were both silent for a while as I groped for understanding. Outside, the first fireflies punctuated the mauve dusk. Tom got up and switched on two small lamps on end tables in the corners of the porch.

"One night I was in New York on business and noticed that Billy Graham was having a Crusade in Madison Square Garden," Tom continued. "I went — curious, I guess — hoping maybe I'd find some answers. What Graham said that night put it all into place for me. I saw what was missing, the personal relationship with Jesus Christ, the fact that I hadn't ever asked Him into my life, hadn't turned my life over to Him. So I did it — that very night at the Crusade."

Tom's tall, gangling frame leaned toward me, silhouetted by the yellow light behind him. Though his face was shaded, I could see his eyes begin to glisten and his voice became softer. "I asked Christ to come into my life and I could feel His presence with me, His peace within me. I could sense His Spirit there with me. Then I went out for a walk alone on the streets of New York. I never liked New York before, but this night it was beautiful. I walked for blocks and blocks, I guess. Everything seemed different to me. It was raining softly and the city lights created a golden glow. Something had happened to me and I knew it."

"That's what you mean by accepting Christ — you just ask?" I was more puzzled than ever.

"That's it, as simple as that," Tom replied. "Of course, you have to want Jesus in your life, really want Him. That's the way it starts. And let me tell you, things then begin to change. Since then I have found a satisfaction and a joy about living that I simply never knew was possible."

To me Jesus had always been an historical figure, but Tom explained that you could hardly invite Him into your life if you didn't believe that He is alive today and that His Spirit is a part of today's scene. I was moved by Tom's story even though I couldn't imagine how such a miraculous change could take place in such a simple way. Yet the excitement in Tom's voice as he described his experience was convincing and Tom was indeed different. More alive.

Then Tom turned the conversation again to my plight. I described some of the agonies of Watergate, the pressures I was under, how unfairly I thought the press was treating me. I was being defensive and when I ran out of explanations, Tom spoke gently but firmly.

"You know that I supported Nixon in this past election, but you guys made a serious mistake. You would have won the election without any of the hanky-panky. Watergate and the dirty tricks were so unnecessary. And it was wrong, just plain wrong. You didn't have to do it."

Tom was leaning forward, elbows on his knees, his hands stretched forward almost as if he was trying to reach out for me. There was an urgent appeal in his eyes. "Don't you understand that?" he asked with such genuine feeling that I couldn't take offense.

"If only you had believed in the rightness of your cause, none of this would have been necessary. None of this would have happened. The problem with all of you, including you, Chuck — you simply had to go for the other guy's jugular. You had to try to destroy your enemies. You had to destroy them because you couldn't trust in yourselves."

The heat at that moment seemed unbearable as I wiped away drops of perspiration over my lip. The iced tea was soothing as I sipped it, although with Tom's points hitting home so painfully, I longed for a Scotch and soda. To myself I admitted that Tom was on target: the world of *us* against *them* as we saw it from our insulated White House enclave — the Nixon White House against the world. Insecure about our cause, our overkill approach was a way to play it safe. And yet. . . .

"Tom, one thing you don't understand. In politics it's dog-eat-dog; you simply can't survive otherwise. I've been in the political business for twenty years, including several campaigns right here in Massachusetts. I know how things are done. Politics is like war. If you don't keep the enemy on the defensive, you'll be on the defensive yourself. Tom, this man Nixon has been under constant attack all of his life. The only way he could make it was to fight back. Look at the criticism he took over Vietnam. Yet he was right. We never would have made it if we hadn't fought the way we did, hitting our critics, never letting them get the best of us. We didn't have any choice."

Even as I talked, the words sounded more and more empty to me. Tired old lines, I realized. I was describing the ways of the political world, all right, while suddenly wondering if there could be a better way.

Tom believed so, anyway. He was so gentle I couldn't resent what he said as he cut right through it all: "Chuck, I hate to say this, but you guys brought it on yourselves. If you had put your faith in God, and if your cause were just, He would have guided you. And His help would have been a thousand times more powerful than all your phony ads and shady schemes put together."

With any other man the notion of relying on God would have seemed to me pure Pollyanna. Yet I had to be impressed with the way this man ran his company in the equally competitive world of business: ignoring his enemies, trying to follow God's ways. Since his conversion Raytheon had never done better, sales and profits soaring. Maybe there was something to it; anyway it's tough to argue with success.

"Chuck, I don't think you will understand what I'm saying about God until you are willing to face yourself honestly and squarely. This is the first step." Tom reached to the corner table and picked up a small paperback book. I read the title: *Mere Christianity* by C. S. Lewis.

"I suggest you take this with you and read it while you are on vacation." Tom started to hand it to me, then paused. "Let me read you one chapter."

I leaned back, still on the defensive, my mind and emotions whirling.

There is one vice of which no man in the world is free; which every one in the world loathes when he sees it in someone else; and of which hardly any people, except Christians, ever imagine that they are guilty themselves. I have heard people admit that they are bad-tempered, or that they cannot keep their heads about girls or drink, or even that they are cowards. I do not think I have ever heard anyone who was not a Christian accuse himself of this vice.... There is no fault ... which we are more unconscious of in ourselves. And the more we have it ourselves, the more we dislike it in others.

The vice I am talking of is Pride or Self-Conceit.... Pride leads to every other vice: it is the complete anti-God state of mind.

As he read, I could feel a flush coming into my face and a curious burning sensation that made the night seem even warmer. Lewis's words seemed to pound straight at me.

... it is Pride which has been the chief cause of misery in every nation and every family since the world began. Other vices may sometimes bring people together: you may find good fellowship and jokes and friendliness among drunken people or unchaste people. But Pride always means enmity — it *is* enmity. And not only enmity between man and man, but enmity to God.

In God you come up against something which is in every respect immeasurably superior to yourself. Unless you know God as that — and, therefore, know yourself as nothing in comparison — you do not know God at all. As long as you are proud you cannot know God. A proud man is always looking down on things and people: and, of course, as long as you are looking down, you cannot see something that is above you.

Suddenly I felt naked and unclean, my bravado defenses gone. I was exposed, unprotected, for Lewis's words were describing me. As he continued, one passage in particular seemed to sum up what had happened to all of us at the White House:

For Pride is spiritual cancer: it eats up the very possibility of love, or contentment, or even common sense.

Just as a man about to die is supposed to see flash before him, sequence by sequence, the high points of his life, so, as Tom's voice read on that August evening, key events in my life paraded before me as if projected on a screen. Things I hadn't thought about in years — my graduation speech at prep school — being "good enough" for the Marines — my first marriage, into the "right" family — sitting on the Jaycees' dais while civic leader after civic leader praised me as the outstanding young man of Boston — then to the White House — the clawing and straining for status and position — "Mr. Colson, the President is calling — Mr. Colson, the President wants to see you right away."

For some reason I thought of an incident after the 1972 election when a reporter, an old Nixon nemesis, came by my office and contritely asked what he could do to get in the good graces of the White House. I suggested that he try "slashing his wrists." I meant it as a joke, of course, but also to make him squirm. It was the arrogance of the victor over an enemy brought to submission.

Now, sitting there on the dimly lit porch, my self-centered past was washing over me in waves. It was painful. Agony. Desperately I tried to defend myself. What about my sacrifices for government service, the giving up of a big income, putting my stocks into a blind trust? The truth, I saw in an instant, was that I'd wanted the position in the White House more than I'd wanted money. There was no sacrifice. And the more I had talked about my own sacrifices, the more I was really trying to build myself up in the eyes of others. I would eagerly have given up everything I'd ever earned to prove myself at the mountaintop of government. It was pride — Lewis's "great sin" — that had propelled me through life.

Tom finished the chapter on pride and shut the book. I mumbled something noncommittal to the effect that "I'll look forward to reading that." But Lewis's torpedo had hit me amidships. I think Phillips knew it as he stared into my eyes. That one chapter ripped through the protective armor in which I had unknowingly encased myself for forty-two years. Of course, I had not known God. *How could I?* I had been concerned with myself. *I* had done this and that, *I* had achieved, *I* had succeeded and *I* had given God none of the credit, never once thanking Him for any of His gifts to me. I had never thought of anything being "immeasurably superior" to myself, or if I had in fleeting moments thought about the infinite power of God, I had not related Him to my life. In those brief moments while Tom read, I saw myself as I never had before. And the picture was ugly.

"How about it, Chuck?" Tom's question jarred me out of my trance. I knew precisely what he meant. Was I ready to make the leap of faith as he had in New York, to "accept" Christ?

"Tom, you've shaken me up. I'll admit that. That chapter describes me. But I can't tell you I'm ready to make the kind of commitment you did. I've got to be certain. I've got to learn a lot more, be sure all my reservations are satisfied. I've got a lot of intellectual hang-ups to get past."

For a moment Tom looked disappointed, then he smiled. "I understand, I understand."

"You see," I continued, "I saw men turn to God in the Marine Corps; I did once myself. Then afterwards it's all forgotten and everything is back to normal. Foxhole religion is just a way of using God. How can I make a commitment now? My whole world is crashing down around me. How can I be sure I'm not just running for shelter and that when the crisis is over I'll forget it? I've got to answer all the intellectual arguments first and if I can do that, I'll be sure."

"I understand," Tom repeated quietly.

I was relieved he did, yet deep inside of me something wanted to tell Tom to press on. He was making so much sense, the first time anyone ever had in talking about God.

But Tom did not press on. He handed me his copy of *Mere Christianity*. "Once you've read this, you might want to read the Book of John in the Bible." I scribbled notes on the key passages he quoted. "Also there's a man in Washington you should meet," he continued, "name of Doug Coe. He gets people together for Christian fellowship — prayer breakfasts and things like that. I'll ask him to contact you."

Tom then reached for his Bible and read a few of his favorite psalms. The comforting words were like a cold soothing ointment. For the first time in my life, familiar verses I'd heard chanted lifelessly in church came alive. "Trust in the Lord," I remember Tom reading, and I wanted to, right that moment I wanted to — if only I knew how, if only I could be sure.

"Would you like to pray together, Chuck?" Tom asked, closing his Bible and putting it on the table beside him.

Startled, I emerged from my deep thoughts. "Sure — I guess I would — Fine." I'd never prayed with anyone before except when someone said grace before a meal. Tom bowed his head, folded his hands, and leaned forward on the edge of his seat. "Lord," he began, "we pray for Chuck and his family, that You might open his heart and show him the light and the way. . . ."

As Tom prayed, something began to flow into me — a kind of energy. Then came a wave of emotion which nearly brought tears. I fought them back. It sounded as if Tom were speaking directly and personally to God, almost as if He were sitting beside us. The only prayers I'd ever heard were formal and stereotyped, sprinkled with *Thees* and *Thous.*

When he finished, there was a long silence. I knew he expected me to pray but I didn't know what to say and was too self-conscious to try. We walked to the kitchen together where Gert was still at the big table, reading. I thanked her and Tom for their hospitality.

"Come back, won't you?" she said. Her smile convinced me she meant it.

"Take care of yourself, Chuck, and let me know what you think of that book, will you?" With that, Tom put his hand on my shoulder and grinned. "I'll see you soon."

I didn't say much; I was afraid my voice would crack, but I had the strong feeling that I *would* see him soon. And I couldn't wait to read his little book.

Outside in the darkness, the iron grip I'd kept on my emotions began to relax. Tears welled up in my eyes as I groped in the darkness for the right key to start my car. Angrily I brushed them away and started the engine. "What kind of weakness is this?" I said to nobody.

The tears spilled over and suddenly I knew I had to go back into the house and pray with Tom. I turned off the motor, got out of the car. As I did, the kitchen light went out, then the light in the dining room. Through the hall window I saw Tom stand aside as Gert started up the stairs ahead of him. Now the hall was in darkness. It was too late. I stood for a moment staring at the darkened house, only one light burning now in an upstairs bedroom. Why hadn't I prayed when he gave me the chance? I wanted to so badly. Now I was alone, really alone.

As I drove out of Tom's driveway, the tears were flowing uncontrollably. There were no streetlights, no moonlight. The car headlights were flooding illumination before my eyes, but I was crying so hard it was like trying to swim underwater. I pulled to the side of the road not more than a hundred yards from the entrance to Tom's driveway, the tires sinking into soft mounds of pine needles.

I remember hoping that Tom and Gert wouldn't hear my sobbing, the only sound other than the chirping of crickets that penetrated the still of the night. With my face cupped in my hands, head leaning forward against the wheel, I forgot about machismo, about pretenses, about fears of being weak. And as I did, I began to experience a wonderful feeling of being released. Then came the strange sensation that water was not only running down my cheeks, but surging through my whole body as well, cleansing and cooling as it went. They weren't tears of sadness and remorse, nor of joy — but somehow, tears of relief.

And then I prayed my first real prayer. "God, I don't know how to find You, but I'm going to try! I'm not much the way I am now, but somehow I want to give myself to You." I didn't know how to say more, so I repeated over and over the words: *Take me.*

I had not "accepted" Christ — I still didn't know who He was. My mind told me it was important to find that out first, to be sure that I knew what I was doing, that I meant it and would stay with it. Only, that night, something inside me was urging me to surrender — to what or to whom I did not know.

I stayed there in the car, wet-eyed, praying, thinking, for perhaps half an hour, perhaps longer, alone in the quiet of the dark night. Yet for the first time in my life I was not alone at all.

Alvin Plantinga

(b. 1932)

Throughout the ages, and especially since the eighteenth century, waves of atheism have swept across Western culture. The late twentieth and early twenty-first centuries saw a renewal of philosophical and popular interest in the intellectual rejection of God.

In the midst of this attack upon belief stood Alvin Plantinga, who has been regarded by some as the leading philosopher of God in the English-speaking world. In his teaching and published works, Plantinga has argued for the viability of belief in God as being just as valid as the belief that other minds exist. He has also tackled the perennial and agonizing question of belief in a God of goodness in a world of evil, arguing that there is no logical contradiction between these two assertions.

Plantinga spent most of his academic career at Calvin College in Michigan and at Notre Dame University. His works include *God and Other Minds* (1967), *The Nature of Necessity* (1974), and *Warranted Christian Belief* (2000). He delivered the renowned Gifford Lectures at the University of Edinburgh three times and received several honorary degrees from, among others, the University of Glasgow and the Free University of Amsterdam.

Plantinga was praised in 1980 by *Time* magazine as "America's leading orthodox Protestant philosopher of God," and during his career he addressed both Christian and agnostic or atheist audiences with a rigorous defense of the rationality of belief in God. He has won respect and acclaim across schools of philosophical and theological thought for the clarity and cogency of his thinking.

The following excerpt is taken from an essay in spiritual autobiography. The essay makes clear the deep resources of religious nurture and religious

experience that formed the mind and rationality of America's most distinguished philosopher of religion in the late twentieth century.

~

When Kelly Clark asked me to write a spiritual autobiography, my first
impulse was to decline. That was also my second impulse, and my third.
For I have at least three good reasons not to do such a thing. First, I have
already written something called an "intellectual autobiography"; the
rule "At most one to a customer" seems to me an excellent one for auto-
biographies — more than one is unseemly. Second, my spiritual life and
its history isn't striking or of general interest: no dramatic conversions,
no spiritual heroism, no internal life of great depth and power, not
much spiritual sophistication or subtlety, little grasp of the various
depths and nuances and shading and peculiar unexplored corners of
the spiritual life. It is very much an ordinary meat-and-potatoes kind of
life. (It is also, I regret to say, a life that hasn't progressed nearly as
much as, by my age and given my opportunities, it should have.)

Third, writing any kind of autobiography has its perils; but writing a
spiritual autobiography is particularly perilous. The main problem has
to do with truthfulness and honesty: there are powerful temptations toward self-deception and hypocrisy. According to Psalm 51, the Lord desires truth in our innermost being; but according to Jeremiah, "the human heart is deceitful above all things; it is desperately sick; who can
understand it?" Truth in our innermost being is not easy to achieve. It is
hard to see what the truth *is;* it is also hard to *tell* the truth, to say what
you see without imposing some kind of self-justificatory and distorting
framework. (For example, you find good or at least coherent motives
where in fact there was really no discernible motive at all, or perhaps a
confusing welter of motives you can't really sort out, or don't *want* to
sort out; or maybe you subtly slant and shift things for no better reason
than that it makes a better tale.)

Still further, there are elements of my life before the Lord that
might be of interest and of use to others, and where I might even be able
both to see and to say what is at least fairly close to the truth, that I don't

---

propose to make public. For most of us, I'd guess, the whole truth about ourselves would be (from one perspective, anyway) a sorry spectacle we wouldn't want completely known even by our best friends — who in any event wouldn't particularly want to know. (Jeremiah is right, even if there is more to the story.) For most of us also, I suspect, there are sides of our lives with respect to which complete and public candor would cause others considerable pain. This is certainly so with me. . . .

I was born November 15, 1932, in Ann Arbor, Michigan, where my father, Cornelius A. Plantinga, was then a graduate student in philosophy at the University of Michigan. My mother, Lettie Plantinga (née Bossenbroek), was born near Alto, Wisconsin. On her mother's side her family had come to the United States about the time of the Civil War; her father's family came some twenty years later. Both groups came from the villages of Elspeet and Nunspeet in the province of Gelderland in the Netherlands, then distinguished for prosperous dairy farms and now also for the Kröller-Muller Museum. My father was born in Garijp, a small village in Friesland. The Dutch think of Friesland as their northwesternmost province. Frisians, however, know better. Friesland has its own culture, its own flag, and its own language closer to Old English than to Dutch (in fact, of all the Germanic languages, Frisian is closest to English).

Both sets of my grandparents — Andrew and Tietje Plantinga and Christian and Lena Bossenbroek — were reared in Calvinist churches originating in the so-called Afscheiding or secession of 1834. During the 1830s there was a religious reawakening ("The Reveille") in the Netherlands, as in much of the rest of Europe. Thoroughly disgusted with the theological liberalism, empty formalism and absence of genuine piety in the Dutch state church (the Hervormde Kerk), many congregations seceded from it to create the Gereformeerde Kerken, dedicated to the practice of historic Calvinism. The Seceders underwent a good deal of punishment and persecution at the hands of the established authorities; they were ready to risk their livelihoods and even their freedom for what they believed to be right worship of God.

Participating in the life of the seceding churches was a strenuous matter. The idea that religion is relevant just to one's private life or to what one does on Sunday was foreign to these people. For them religion was the central reality of life; all aspects of life, they thought, should be lived in the light of Christianity. They also held (rightly, I think) that *ed-*

ucation is essentially religious; there is such a thing as *secular* education but no such thing as an education that is both reasonably full-orbed and religiously *neutral.* They therefore established separate grade schools and high schools that were explicitly Christian, schools in which the bearing of Christianity on the various disciplines could be carefully and explicitly spelled out. Later, under the leadership of the great theologian and statesman Abraham Kuyper (premier of the Netherlands from 1901 to 1905), they established a Calvinist university in Amsterdam: the Free University — so called not, as one might expect, because it is free from the state, but because it is free from ecclesiastical control.

My mother's parents owned a farm in Wisconsin, between Waupun and Alto, and as a small boy I spent most of my summers there. Going to church, of course, was an extremely important part of life; there were two services on Sunday, one in the morning and one in the afternoon, and in those days the afternoon service was in Dutch. Some of my earliest memories are of long, hot Sunday afternoons in church, dressed in my sweltering Sunday best, listening to the minister drone on in a language I could barely understand, counting the tiles in the ceiling, while all along the cicadas outside were setting up their characteristic summertime din. As I saw it then, just getting outside would have been heaven enough. After church, the main topic was often the minister's sermon; and woe unto the preacher who got his doctrine wrong or was guilty of a "wrong emphasis"! Although most of the members of the church were rural folk who hadn't had the benefit of much formal education (my grandfather was lucky to finish the sixth grade), there was an astonishing amount of theological sophistication about. Many had read their Kuyper and Bavinck, and a few were considerably better at theology than some of the ministers in charge of the church.

What was preached, of course, was historic Calvinism. When I was eight or nine I began to understand and think seriously about some of the so-called five points of Calvinism enshrined in the TULIP acronym: Total depravity, Unconditional election, Limited atonement, Irresistible grace and the Perseverance of the saints. I remember wondering in particular about total depravity. I do indeed subscribe to that doctrine, which, as I understand it, quite properly points out that for most or all of us, every important area of our lives is distorted and compromised by sin. When I first began to think about it, however, I took it to mean that everyone was completely wicked, wholly bad, no better than a Hitler or a Judas. That seemed to me a bit confusing and hard to credit; was my grandmother (in fact a saintly woman) really completely wicked? Was there nothing good about her at all? That seemed a bit too much. True, I had heard her say "Shit" a couple of times: once when someone came stomping into the kitchen, causing three cakes in the oven to drop, and once when I threw a string of firecrackers into the fifty-gallon drum in which she was curing dried beef (they began exploding in rapid-fire succession just as she came to look into the drum). But was that really enough to make her a moral monster, particularly when so much else about her pointed in the opposite direction? I spent a good deal of time as a child thinking about these doctrines, and a couple of years later, when I was ten or eleven or so, I got involved in many very enthusiastic but undirected discussions of human freedom, determinism (theological or otherwise), divine foreknowledge, predestination and allied topics.

During junior-high and high-school days we lived in Jamestown, North Dakota, where my father was a professor of philosophy, psychology, Latin and Greek (with an occasional foray into sociology and religion) at Jamestown College. We attended the Presbyterian church in Jamestown; but I heard about as many sermons from my father as from the minister of the church we belonged to. He often preached in churches in nearby villages that were without a minister, and I often accompanied him. I went to church, Sunday school, a weekly catechism class my father organized, and weekly "Young People's" meetings. I also remember a series of midweek Lenten services that were deeply moving and were for me a source of spiritual awakening. In addition, we young people also went to summer Bible camps sponsored by the church. I'm sure these were spiritually useful for many and perhaps for me; and we were certainly stirred up emotionally. By and large, however, I found the girls more interesting than the sermons, and for me (and others) the stimulation was by no means exclusively spiritual. As I remember those camps, there was a sort of fervid, febrile atmosphere, shimmering and throbbing with energy and excitement that was as much sexual as spiritual.

Apart from my parents, perhaps the most important influence in high school was my association with Robert McKenzie (now a Presbyterian minister in the San Francisco Bay area). Bob was a couple of years my senior, and we spent an enormous amount of time together. One summer we spent twelve hours a day, six days a week (and eight hours on Sunday), working for a construction company, putting in a city water line in Westhope, North Dakota, a tiny village six miles or so from the Canadian border. Bob was (and is) enormously full of enthusiasm, idealism and energy; he laughed often, infectiously and loudly; he and I hatched a whole series of adolescent fantasies about how he would be a minister and I a professor in the same town and what great things we would accomplish. (At the same time we were also planning to run a construction company in the Colorado mountains; how this was supposed to mesh with our ministerial and professorial jobs is no longer clear to me.)

In the fall of 1949, a couple of months before my seventeenth birthday, I enrolled in Jamestown College. During that semester my father was invited to join the psychology department at Calvin College; he accepted the offer and took up his duties there in January of 1950. I reluctantly went along, having no desire at all to leave Jamestown and Jamestown College, where I had very strong attachments. During my first semester at Calvin I applied, just for the fun of it, for a scholarship at Harvard. To my considerable surprise I was awarded a nice fat scholarship; in the fall of 1950, therefore, I showed up in Cambridge.

I found Harvard enormously impressive and very much to my liking. I took an introductory philosophy course from Raphael Demos in the fall and a course in Plato from him in the spring. I still remember the sense of wonder with which I read *Gorgias* — its graceful language, absorbing argumentative intricacy and serious moral tone relieved now and then by gentle, almost rueful witticisms at the expense of the Sophists. I also took a splendid course from the classicist I. M. Finley, and in a large social science course (as it was called) my section leader was Bernard Bailyn, now a distinguished Harvard historian. I attended a Methodist church where the Sunday-school class for people my age was conducted by Peter Bertocci, the philosopher from Boston University. (He was the last of the series of three great Boston personalists whose names began with B: Edgar Sheffield Brightman, Bordon Parker Bowne and Bertocci.)

At Harvard I encountered serious non-Christian thought for the first time — for the first time in the flesh, that is; I had read animadversions on Christianity and theism by Bertrand Russell *(Why I Am Not a Christian)* and others. I was struck by the enormous variety of intellectual and spiritual opinion at Harvard, and spent a great deal of time arguing about whether there was such a person as God, whether Christianity as opposed to Judaism (my roommate Herbert Jacobs was the son of a St. Louis rabbi) was right and so on. I began to wonder whether what I had always believed could really be true. At Harvard, after all, there was such an enormous diversity of opinions about these matters, some of them held by highly intelligent and accomplished people who had little but contempt for what I believed. My attitude gradually became one of a mixture of doubt and bravado. On the one hand I began to think it questionable that what I had been taught and had always believed could be right, given that there were all these others who thought so differently (and were so much more intellectually accomplished than I). On the other hand, I thought to myself, what really is so great about these people? Why should I believe *them?* True, they know much more than I and have thought much longer: but what, precisely, is the *substance* of their objections to Christianity? Or to theism? Do these objections really *have* much by way of substance? And if, as I strongly suspected, *not,* why should their taking the views they did be relevant to what *I* thought? The doubts (in that form anyway) didn't last long, but something like the bravado, I suppose, has remained.

The two events that resolved these doubts and ambivalences for me occurred during my second semester. One gloomy evening (in January, perhaps) I was returning from dinner, walking past Widenar Library to my fifth-floor room in Thayer Middle (there weren't any elevators, and scholarship boys occupied the cheaper rooms at the top of the building). It was dark, windy, raining, nasty. But suddenly it was as if the heavens opened; I heard, so it seemed, music of overwhelming power and grandeur and sweetness; there was light of unimaginable splendor and beauty; it seemed I could see into heaven itself; and I suddenly saw or perhaps felt with great clarity and persuasion and conviction that the Lord was really there and was all I had thought. The effects of this experience lingered for a long time; I was still caught up in arguments about the existence of God, but they often seemed to me merely academic, of little existential concern, as if one were to argue about whether there has really been a past, for example, or whether there really were other people, as opposed to cleverly constructed robots.

Such events have not been common subsequently, and there has been only one other occasion on which I felt the presence of God with as much immediacy and strength. That was when I once foolishly went hiking alone off-trail in really rugged country south of Mt. Shuksan in the North Cascades, getting lost when rain, snow and fog obscured all the peaks and landmarks. That night, while shivering under a stunted tree in a cold mixture of snow and rain, I felt as close to God as I ever have, before or since. I wasn't clear as to his intentions for me, and I wasn't sure I approved of what I thought his intentions might be (the statistics on people lost alone in that area were not at all encouraging), but I felt very close to him; his presence was enormously palpable.

On many other occasions I have felt the presence of God, sometimes very powerfully: in the mountains (the overwhelming grandeur of the night sky from a slope at thirteen thousand feet), at prayer, in church, when reading the Bible, listening to music, seeing the beauty of the sunshine on the leaves of a tree or on a blade of grass, being in the woods on a snowy night, and on other kinds of occasions. In particular I have often been overwhelmed with a sense of *gratitude* — sometimes for something specific like a glorious morning, but often with no particular focus. What I *ought* to be most grateful for — the life and death and resurrection of Christ, with the accompanying offer of eternal life — is harder, simply because of its stupendous and incomprehensible magnitude. You can say "Thank you" for a glorious morning, and even for your children's turning out well; what do you say in response to the suffering and death and resurrection of the Son of God? Or to the offer of redemption from sin, and eternal life?

The second event that semester at Harvard was as follows. During spring recess I returned to Grand Rapids to visit my parents; since Calvin's spring recess did not coincide with Harvard's, I had the opportunity to attend some classes at Calvin. I had often heard my father speak of William Harry Jellema, who had been his philosophy professor at Calvin in the late twenties and early thirties. Accordingly I attended three of Jellema's classes that week — it was a course in ethics, I believe. That was a fateful week for me.

Jellema was obviously in dead earnest about Christianity; he was also a magnificently thoughtful and reflective Christian. He was lecturing about modernity: its various departures from historic Christianity, the sorts of substitutes it proposes, how these substitutes are related to the real thing and the like. Clearly he was profoundly familiar with the doubts and objections and alternative ways of thought cast up by modernity; indeed, he seemed to me to understand them better than those who offered them. But (and this is what I found enormously impressive) he was totally unawed. What especially struck me then in what he said (partly because it put into words something I felt at Harvard but couldn't articulate) was the thought that much of the intellectual opposition to

Christianity and theism was really a sort of intellectual imperialism with little real basis. We are told that humankind come of age has got beyond such primitive ways of thinking, that they are outmoded, or incompatible with a scientific mind-set, or have been shown wanting by modern science, or made irrelevant by the march of history or maybe by something else lurking in the neighborhood. (In this age of the wireless, Bultmann quaintly asks, who can accept them?) But why should a Christian believe any of these things? Are they more than mere claims?

I found Jellema deeply impressive — so impressive that I decided then and there to leave Harvard, return to Calvin and study philosophy with him. That was as important a decision, and as good a decision, as I've ever made. Calvin College has been for me an enormously powerful spiritual influence and in some ways the center and focus of my intellectual life. Had I not returned to Calvin from Harvard, I doubt (humanly speaking, anyway) that I would have remained a Christian at all; certainly Christianity or theism would not have been the focal point of my adult intellectual life.

Millard Fuller

(1935–2009)

Millard Fuller was a genius at selling things. He started early. When he was six, his father gave him a pig, which he fed and fattened and sold for $11. Eventually he was raising and selling more pigs, rabbits, and chickens and even selling worms and minnows to fishermen. After his father bought a 400-acre farm, Millard Fuller helped his father repair a shack for an elderly couple, and the memory of the joy of the couple was burned indelibly into his mind.

He graduated from Auburn University and then entered the University of Alabama School of Law. There he met Morris S. Dees Jr., and the two law students formed a partnership based on selling things to raise capital to buy rental real estate. It didn't really matter what was sold. They tried selling mistletoe and cypress knees (unsuccessfully), but also holly wreaths, Christmas decorations, rubber doormats, and student directories (successfully).

After graduation, the two partners opened a law office but quickly discovered they were better at selling than at litigating. They sold tractor cushions as fundraisers to the Future Farmers of America and could not produce enough to meet the demand. They became the largest publisher of cookbooks in the nation, including one title, *My Favorite Recipes,* which, as Fuller said, "sold thousands — and there was nothing in it but chapter headings and blank pages to be filled in by the owner!" And more. If it could be sold, they sold it.

Fuller and Dees had a goal: "to make a pile of money." They met their goal. Fuller and his wife Linda gradually moved from a vehicle with only one seat (she sat on an apple crate) to a Chevrolet, then a Buick, and then a Lincoln Continental. They moved from a two-room student apartment into a series of homes and then elegance, including "a barn and pasture for saddle horses, and of course a swimming pool."

"Everything has a price," Fuller later realized. He became "estranged" from his church. He compromised his "personal morality and integrity" in business and in racial matters. His marriage suffered and almost died when his wife Linda threatened to leave him because he was never around and neglected her.

Then Fuller "came to himself" and reconciled with Linda. They decided to rebuild their marriage and their lives on Christian principles. They sold their cars, their home, and their boat and went off to consult with Clarence Jordan, the leader of Koinonia Farm, a Christian community in Georgia. First they built homes near Koinonia Farm and then in Zaire; in 1976 they organized Habitat for Humanity in a chicken barn at Koinonia Farm.

Fuller moved from selling things to inspiring people, this time with the idea of building housing for low-income people. At the very first meeting of Habitat, he and his colleagues resolved to build houses for a million people, and they reached their goal in 2005. At the time of Fuller's death in 2009, Habitat had built more than 300,000 homes worldwide. His most famous carpenter and funder was former president Jimmy Carter.

In 2004 Fuller and his wife were fired by the board of Habitat over issues about the future of the organization and never-proven charges of sexual harassment by Fuller. He founded the Fuller Center for Housing in 2005 and became a tireless advocate for housing for the poor.

In 1996, President Bill Clinton awarded Fuller the Presidential Medal of Honor, the highest honor awarded to a civilian. In presenting the award, President Clinton said, "Millard Fuller has done as much to make the dream of homeownership a reality in our country and throughout the world as any living person. I don't think it's an exaggeration to say that Millard Fuller has literally revolutionized the concept of philanthropy."

~

In November of 1965, Linda brought the whole matter to the crisis point when she suddenly and firmly announced one evening that she had decided to go to New York to think about the future of our marriage. When she had gone, leaving me with our two young children, Chris and Kim, the rumbling thunderstorm within me began to roil. I was in agony. Never before or since have I suffered as I did during those days. Everything else — business, sales, profits, prestige, everything which had seemed so important — paled into total meaninglessness.

From Millard Fuller, *Bokotola* (New York: Association Press, 1977), 6-9.

I began to examine my life and to ask what it was all about. An image came into my mind of the day I would stand before the Judge of History and have Him ask me what I had done with my life. I could hear myself squeaking, "Lord, I sold a hell of a lot of cookbooks." In the presence of God that sounded so ridiculous I could only cringe.

After a week of misery I could sit still no longer. I asked a pilot in our company to arrange for an airplane to go on a trip.

"Where to?" he inquired.

"I think I'll go to Niagara Falls," I replied.

"But why?"

"Because I've never been there!"

"Okay. It's your money!"

As we were coming into the Niagara Falls airport in the early evening, we went into a cloud bank. We lost radio contact with the tower, and the wings were icing up. The plane began to lose altitude. Just at that moment the radio crackled and we heard the tower yelling, "Look out! Look out! Plane coming right under you!"

We thought we were done for. Suddenly we broke out of the cloud and saw the lights of the city of Niagara Falls spread out like a fairyland below us. We sailed in for a smooth, uneventful landing, but the whole episode was not exactly soothing to my already shaken psyche.

We took a taxi and drove to the Canadian side to find a hotel for the night. As we dressed for dinner in our room, Jim, the pilot, flipped on the television set. The program, just starting, featured a young woman who had gone to China as a missionary. After a few years there she fell in love with a young Chinese military officer. He loved her and wanted to marry her, but he knew it would probably mean the end of his military career. He went to an old village leader — a mandarin — to ask for advice. The old man thought for a moment, and then replied, "A planned life can only be *endured*."

Those words penetrated my innermost being. "A planned life." That's what I'm living, I thought. And I'm enduring it and suffering. My plan was simply to get richer and richer, to make the company bigger and bigger, to acquire more and more things. Finally I would be buried in the rich section of the Montgomery cemetery.

"A planned life can only be *endured*."

With those words ringing in my ears, I phoned Linda and persuaded her to let me come to New York to talk to her. The following day Jim flew me to Watervliet, New York, to see one of our suppliers of tooth brushes, and from there to La Guardia airport in New York City. Jim then took the plane back to Montgomery, leaving me to go to Linda.

She had been counseling with Dr. Lawrence Durgin, pastor of the Broadway United Church of Christ. We had both met Dr. Durgin a couple of years earlier when we had lived briefly in New York City. Linda had been impressed with him and had decided to seek his advice rather than that of someone in our home area. As we talked, Linda described her counseling sessions, but confessed that she had not arrived at a decision about our marriage.

That evening we decided to go to Radio City Music Hall. The movie was entitled "Never Too Late." What a prophetic title, I thought! It is never too late to come back from a wrong turn, to correct a broken relationship with another person, or with God. But how?

After the movie (which was, incidentally, a very funny comedy about a woman who got pregnant after she thought it was too late!), we went downstairs for refreshments while we waited for the stage show. As we were sipping orange juice, Linda suddenly broke down and began crying. I couldn't get her to stop. Finally, in exasperation, I grabbed our coats and we stumbled out into the cold November night, leaving the stage show, the orange juice, and an umbrella!

We walked around for a while just holding on to each other while Linda's sobs subsided. We sat down on the front steps of St. Patrick's Cathedral and talked. Then we walked some more, eventually ending up in the doorway of a shop just off Fifth Avenue. There it happened. Linda faced me and bared her soul. She confessed the ways in which she had betrayed our relationship. I poured out my own agony and regret for ways I had betrayed her. The wall was broken down, and love rushed in like a mighty flood. We grabbed each other and held on as the tears flowed down our cheeks.

After a long while we took a taxi and returned to our hotel. We stayed up all night talking, singing, and praying. The song that came to us was "We're Marching to Zion." That tune absolutely filled my heart and soul. I couldn't stop singing it. (We were still singing it three days later, on the plane to Montgomery, cheerfully ignoring the stares of our fellow passengers!)

> We're marching to Zion,
> Beautiful, beautiful Zion;

We're marching upward to Zion,
The beautiful city of God.

Come, we that love the Lord,
And let our joys be known,
Join in a song with sweet accord,
Join in a song with sweet accord,

And thus surround the throne.
And thus surround the throne.

We both felt a strong sense of God's presence as we talked about the future. We felt that God was calling us out of this situation to a new life, a new way of walking. To prepare for this new thing — whatever it was — we felt it necessary to leave the business, sell our interest in it, and give away all the proceeds.

The following morning we left our room and went downstairs to go somewhere — I've forgotten where. I hailed a taxi, and we crawled in. But the driver didn't drive off. Instead, he turned around to us with a big smile on his face.

"Congratulations!"

"Congratulations? For what?" I asked.

"This is a brand-new taxi. You are my first passengers!"

I turned to Linda. She was already crying.

"Driver," I said, "take us on a drive through Central Park. I've got a story to tell you."

As we wound our way through the park I leaned my arms on the back of the driver's seat and shared with him what we had experienced the night before and how we had decided to change our lives and serve God. He was deeply moved, and felt, as we did, that his picking us up that morning was a sign from God that we had made the right decision.

Francis S. Collins

(b. 1950)

Francis S. Collins is one of America's leading scientists in the twenty-first century. He is renowned for his leadership of the Human Genome Project and is widely considered a pioneer in the field of human genetics. He is also an articulate Christian, who is eloquent in his argument not only for the existence of God but also for the compatibility between science and religion.

During the presidency of Barack Obama, Dr. Collins was appointed as the Director of the National Institutes of Health, one of the premier positions in American science and public health. This prestigious appointment came after he pioneered in the study of how DNA affects diseases such as heart disease, cancer, and mental illness. Dr. Collins's appointment was confirmed unanimously by the U.S. Senate, but not before others charged that his outspoken Christian views made him unqualified to lead the NIH.

Dr. Collins was born in rural North Carolina and was home-schooled by his mother until the fourth grade. Early on, he was attracted to science, especially chemistry, but not biology. He attended the University of Virginia, where he received his bachelor's degree, and Yale University, where he earned a Ph.D. in chemistry. At Yale he realized the enormous new findings emerging in the molecules that shape the nature of life — DNA and RNA. He changed fields and entered the medical school at the University of North Carolina at Chapel Hill, where he received an M.D. in 1977.

His spiritual pilgrimage ranged from a nominally Christian home to agnosticism and ultimately atheism during his graduate education. During his medical education, conversations with patients persuaded him that he did not have answers to the deepest questions of life and death. Like so many others, he was heavily influenced by C. S. Lewis's writings, especially *Mere Christianity*, which prompted him to explore the existence of God and ultimately to make a commitment to faith. Later he had an experience that led him to devotion to Jesus Christ.

Dr. Collins's faith has included a steadfast commitment to the basic truths of science without giving up belief in God. For example, he steadfastly rejects the ideas of creationism and intelligent design, a position that has alienated him from some forms of conservative Christianity. Instead, he argues for the fundamental compatibility of a religious view of reality that does not negate science and affirms the divine presence and power behind all of life and creation itself. He is a strong voice in the field of bioethics, defending the confidentiality of genetic testing. Based on his experience as a volunteer medical doctor in Africa, he is also an eloquent voice in arguing for the extension of scientific advance throughout the developing world.

In the midst of a scientific discussion that frequently rejects and even ridicules the affirmations of religious faith, Dr. Collins is a notable and exceptional advocate not only for the compatibility of science and religion but also for the role of Christian faith in answering the deepest questions of human existence. His pilgrimage and his manifesto for Christian belief and scientific truth were presented in his book, *The Language of God: A Scientist Presents Evidence for Belief,* from which this narrative of his conversion is excerpted.

~

My early life was unconventional in many ways, but as the son of freethinkers, I had an upbringing that was quite conventionally modern in its attitude toward faith — it just wasn't very important. . . .

Faith was not an important part of my childhood. I was vaguely aware of the concept of God, but my own interactions with Him were limited to occasional childish moments of bargaining about something that I really wanted Him to do for me. For instance, I remember making a contract with God (at about age nine) that if He would prevent the rainout of a Saturday night theater performance and music party that I was particularly excited about, then I would promise never to smoke cigarettes. Sure enough, the rains held off, and I never took up the habit. Earlier, when I was five, my parents decided to send me and my next oldest brother to become members of the boys choir at the local

Episcopal church. They made it clear that it would be a great way to learn music, but that the theology should not be taken too seriously. I followed those instructions, learning the glories of harmony and counterpoint but letting the theological concepts being preached from the pulpit wash over me without leaving any discernible residue. . . .

Though I did not know the term at the time, I became an agnostic, a term coined by the nineteenth-century scientist T. H. Huxley to indicate someone who simply does not know whether or not God exists. There are all kinds of agnostics; some arrive at this position after intense analysis of the evidence, but many others simply find it to be a comfortable position that allows them to avoid considering arguments they find discomforting on either side. I was definitely in the latter category. In fact, my assertion of "I don't know" was really more along the lines of "I don't want to know." As a young man growing up in a world full of temptations, it was convenient to ignore the need to be answerable to any higher spiritual authority. I practiced a thought and behavior pattern referred to as "willful blindness" by the noted scholar and writer C. S. Lewis. . . .

At the same time, now only twenty-two but married with a bright and inquisitive daughter, I was becoming more social. I had often preferred to be alone when I was younger. Now, human interaction and a desire to contribute something to humanity seemed ever more important. . . . I questioned everything about my previous choices, including whether I was really cut out to do science or carry out independent research. I was just about to complete my Ph.D., yet after much soul-searching, I applied for admission to medical school. With a carefully practiced speech, I attempted to convince admissions committees that this turn of events was actually a natural pathway for the training of one of our nation's future doctors. Inside I was not so sure. After all, wasn't I the guy who had hated biology because you had to memorize things? Could any field of study require more memorization than medicine? But something was different now; this was about humanity, not crayfish; there were principles underlying the details; and this could ultimately make a difference in the lives of real people. . . .

This path also led me by the third year of medical school into intense experiences involving the care of patients. As physicians in training, medical students are thrust into some of the most intimate relationships imaginable with individuals who had been complete strangers until their experience of illness. Cultural taboos that normally prevent the exchange of intensely private information come tumbling down along with the sensitive physical contact of a doctor and his patients. It is all part of the long-standing and venerated contract between the ill person and the healer. I found the relationships that developed with sick and dying patients almost overwhelming, and I struggled to maintain the professional distance and lack of emotional involvement that many of my teachers advocated.

What struck me profoundly about my bedside conversations with these good North Carolina people was the spiritual aspect of what many of them were going through. I witnessed numerous cases of individuals whose faith provided them with a strong reassurance of ultimate peace, be it in this world or the next, despite terrible suffering that in most instances they had done nothing to bring on themselves. If faith was a psychological crutch, I concluded, it must be a very powerful one. If it was nothing more than a veneer of cultural tradition, why were these people not shaking their fists at God and demanding that their friends and family stop all this talk about a loving and benevolent supernatural power?

My most awkward moment came when an older woman, suffering daily from severe unbeatable angina, asked me what I believed. It was a fair question; we had discussed many other important issues of life and death, and she had shared her own strong Christian beliefs with me. I felt my face flush as I stammered out the words "I'm not really sure." Her obvious surprise brought into sharp relief a predicament that I had been running away from for nearly all of my twenty-six years: I had never really seriously considered the evidence for and against belief.

That moment haunted me for several days. Did I not consider myself a scientist? Does a scientist draw conclusions without considering the data? Could there be a more important question in all of human existence than "Is there a God?" And yet there I found myself, with a combination of willful blindness and something that could only be properly described as arrogance, having avoided any serious consideration that God might be a real possibility. Suddenly all my arguments seemed very thin, and I had the sensation that the ice under my feet was cracking.

This realization was a thoroughly terrifying experience. After all, if I could no longer rely on the robustness of my atheistic position, would I have to take responsibility for actions that I would prefer to keep unscrutinized? Was I answerable to someone other than myself? The question was now too pressing to avoid.

At first, I was confident that a full investigation of the rational basis for faith would deny the merits of belief, and reaffirm my atheism. But I determined to have a look at the facts, no matter what the outcome. Thus began a quick and confusing survey through the major religions of the world. Much of what I found in the CliffsNotes versions of different religions (I found reading the actual sacred texts much too difficult) left me thoroughly mystified, and I found little reason to be drawn to one or the other of the many possibilities. I doubted that there was any rational basis for spiritual belief undergirding any of these faiths. However, that soon changed. I went to visit a Methodist minister who lived down the street to ask him whether faith made any logical sense. He listened patiently to my confused (and probably blasphemous) ramblings, and then took a small book off his shelf and suggested I read it.

The book was *Mere Christianity* by C. S. Lewis. In the next few days, as I turned its pages, struggling to absorb the breadth and depth of the intellectual arguments laid down by this legendary Oxford scholar, I realized that all of my own constructs against the plausibility of faith were those of a schoolboy. Clearly I would need to start with a clean slate to consider this most important of all human questions. Lewis seemed to know all of my objections, sometimes even before I had quite formulated them. He invariably addressed them within a page or two. When I learned subsequently that Lewis had himself been an atheist, who had set out to disprove faith on the basis of logical argument, I recognized how he could be so insightful about my path. It had been his path as well.

The argument that most caught my attention, and most rocked my ideas about science and spirit down to their foundation, was right there in the title of Book One: "Right and Wrong as a Clue to the Meaning of the Universe." While in many ways the "Moral Law" that Lewis described was a universal feature of human existence, in other ways it was as if I was recognizing it for the first time. . . .

What we have here is very peculiar: the concept of right and wrong appears to be universal among all members of the human species (though its application may result in wildly different outcomes). It thus seems to be a phenomenon approaching that of a law, like the law of gravitation or of special relativity. Yet in this instance, it is a law that, if we are honest with ourselves, is broken with astounding regularity.

As best as I can tell, this law appears to apply peculiarly to human beings. Though other animals may at times appear to show glimmerings of a moral sense, they are certainly not widespread, and in many instances other species' behavior seems to be in dramatic contrast to any sense of universal rightness. It is the awareness of right and wrong, along with the development of language, awareness of self, and the ability to imagine the future, to which scientists generally refer when trying to enumerate the special qualities of *Homo sapiens*. . . .

Encountering this argument at age twenty-six, I was stunned by its logic. Here, hiding in my own heart as familiar as anything in daily experience, but now emerging for the first time as a clarifying principle, this Moral Law shone its bright white light into the recesses of my childish atheism, and demanded a serious consideration of its origin. Was this God looking back at me?

And if that were so, what kind of God would this be? Would this be a deist God, who invented physics and mathematics and started the universe in motion about 14 billion years ago, then wandered off to deal with other, more important matters, as Einstein thought? No, this God, if I was perceiving Him at all, must be a theist God, who desires some kind of relationship with those special creatures called human beings, and has therefore instilled this special glimpse of Himself into each one of us. This might be the God of Abraham, but it was certainly not the God of Einstein.

There was another consequence to this growing sense of God's nature, if in fact He was real. Judging by the incredibly high standards of the Moral Law, one that I had to admit I was in the practice of regularly violating, this was a God who was holy and righteous. He would have to be the embodiment of goodness. He would have to hate evil. And there was no reason to suspect that this God would be kindly or indulgent. The gradual dawning of my realization of God's plausible existence brought conflicted feelings: comfort at the breadth and depth of the existence of such a Mind, and yet profound dismay at the realization of my own imperfections when viewed in His light.

I had started this journey of intellectual exploration to confirm my atheism. That now lay in ruins as the argument from the Moral Law (and many other issues) forced me to admit the plausibility of the God hypothesis. Agnosticism, which had seemed like a safe second-place haven, now loomed like the great cop-out it often is. Faith in God now seemed more rational than disbelief.

It also became clear to me that science, despite its unquestioned powers in unraveling the mysteries of the natural world, would get me no further in resolving the question of God. If God exists, then He must be outside the natural world, and therefore the tools of science are not the right ones to learn about Him. Instead, as I was beginning to understand from looking into my own heart, the evidence of God's existence would have to come from other directions, and the ultimate decision would be based on faith, not proof. Still beset by roiling uncertainties of what path I had started down, I had to admit that I had reached the threshold of accepting the possibility of a spiritual worldview, including the existence of God.

It seemed impossible either to go forward or to turn back. Years later, I encountered a sonnet by Sheldon Vanauken that precisely described my dilemma. Its concluding lines:

> Between the probable and proved there yawns
> A gap. Afraid to jump, we stand absurd.
> Then see *behind* us sink the ground and, worse,
> Our very standpoint crumbling. Desperate dawns
> Our only hope: to leap into the Word
> That opens up the shuttered universe.

For a long time I stood trembling on the edge of this yawning gap. Finally, seeing no escape, I leapt. . . .

Lewis was right. I had to make a choice. A full year had passed since I decided to believe in some sort of God, and now I was being called to account. On a beautiful fall day, as I was hiking in the Cascade Mountains during my first trip west of the Mississippi, the majesty and beauty of God's creation overwhelmed my resistance. As I rounded a corner and saw a beautiful and unexpected frozen waterfall, hundreds of feet high, I knew the search was over. The next morning, I knelt in the dewy grass as the sun rose and surrendered to Jesus Christ. . . .

Seekers, there are answers to these questions. There is joy and peace to be found in the harmony of God's creation. In the upstairs hall of my home hangs a beautifully decorated pair of scripture verses, illuminated in many colors by the hand of my daughter. I come back to those verses many times when I am struggling for answers, and they never fail to remind me of the nature of true wisdom: "But if any of you lacks wisdom, let him ask of God, who gives to all men generously and without reproach, and it will be given him" (James 1:5). "The wisdom from above is first pure, then peaceable, gentle, reasonable, full of mercy and good fruits, unwavering, without hypocrisy" (James 3:17).

My prayer for our hurting world is that we would together, with love, understanding, and compassion, seek and find that kind of wisdom.

It is time to call a truce in the escalating war between science and spirit. The war was never really necessary. Like so many earthly wars, this one has been initiated and intensified by extremists on both sides, sounding alarms that predict imminent ruin unless the other side is vanquished. Science is not threatened by God; it is enhanced. God is most certainly not threatened by science; He made it all possible. So let us together seek to reclaim the solid ground of an intellectually and spiritually satisfying synthesis of *all* great truths. That ancient mother-land of reason and worship was never in danger of crumbling. It never will be. It beckons all sincere seekers of truth to come and take up residence there. Answer that call. Abandon the battlements. Our hopes, joys, and the future of our world depend on it.

Pat Day

(b. 1953)

Pat Day is a winner. As a jockey, his record is phenomenal. In twenty-one years of racing, he won 8,804 races (fourth on the all-time list). His winnings totaled nearly $298 million — a North American record at the time of his retirement in 2005. In 1989, he set another North American record at Arlington Park when he was victorious in eight of nine races — in one day.

He entered the Kentucky Derby every year for twenty-one years and won it once in 1999. His home is in Louisville, Kentucky, and he dominated racing at Kentucky's two most famous tracks — Churchill Downs and the Keeneland Race Course. Bettors used to complain at the Downs that Day's presence in a race made the odds on his horses go down. Day is the only jockey to ride at least one horse in each of the first twenty Breeders' Cup races; he won twelve of those.

As hard as it is to ride a thoroughbred, Day's biggest race was with alcohol and drugs — until he found God.

He never started racing until two years after he graduated from high school. As he immodestly but accurately says, "I started doing very good almost immediately." The highs from winning turned into highs from drugs and alcohol — a problem endemic in the horse-racing profession.

Finally, one night in a Miami hotel room, Day heard TV evangelist Jimmy Swaggart preach and issue a call to commitment. Day turned off the TV, fell on his knees, began to pray, and "wept and cried and invited Jesus Christ" into his life.

And that was the end of his drinking. Unlike so many in his situation, Day never went to rehab or had a relapse. Confronting Christ on January 27, 1984, was enough. God's grace was sufficient for him.

He continued to race and endured the pressure to use drugs and alcohol.

He had been delivered from his addiction. In following Christ, he gradually realized he needed to resist the temptation to use coarse language in the locker room. He literally cleaned up his act. In 1991, seven years after his conversion and fourteen years before he retired, he was inducted into the National Museum of Racing and Hall of Fame.

Since his retirement in 2005, Day has thrown himself into the mission work of the Race Track Chaplaincy of America and, with his wife, does social service work in Louisville.

One of the most memorable images of Day's racing is his raising of his crop as he crossed the Kentucky Derby finish line — victoriously — in 1999. He had won the race that was set before him, but he had won a deeper spiritual race as well. He was sober. His life belonged to Christ.

$\sim$

I was raised in Eagle, Colorado, in a great environment. My mother and father weren't opposed to having a drink on occasion, but they were not drinkers. My father was home every night. He wasn't an alcoholic that we had to pull out of the bars; he was probably the most responsible man I've known. If my father told you something, you could bank on it. He was a person of integrity, and the environment in which I was raised was opposed to over-abuse of anything.

I didn't have my first drink till I was a junior in high school. I started drinking a little bit of beer with kids on the weekends and didn't foresee it being a problem. After I graduated, it slowly became a problem, an every-night thing.

Two years after I graduated high school, I got introduced to the racing profession. In Arizona I went through the trenches, so to speak, and in July of 1973, I began riding races. I started doing very good almost immediately. My life-style at the time was going to the bar as soon as the races were over, partying until all hours of the night, and then getting up and going to work in the morning, going to the races in the afternoon, and starting right over again. It didn't seem to have a real negative effect in that I was able to do what I was doing and do it with tremendous success.

From Gary Stromberg and Jane Merrill, eds., *The Harder They Fall: Celebrities Tell Their Real-Life Stories of Addiction and Recovery* (Center City, MN: Hazelden, 2005), 209-16. Reprinted with permission.

Pat Day

After I'd been riding for about a year, drugs started becoming readily available. I went from drinking daily to messing with drugs. I began smoking dope and using little speed pills known as "white crosses" or "bennies." The next winter I was riding down in New Orleans, which is a pretty wild town, and the partying continued. In the spring of 1975, in Chicago, I had drug paraphernalia and some drugs in my car. I was searched and they were found. I was suspended for fifteen days and put on probation for six months. You'd have thought that would have been a wake-up call of some kind, but it wasn't. Success, especially in the sporting arena, can lead you to believe you're above the law. You can get out of a lot of jackpots, which just perpetuates the problem.

By the grace of God, I was able to regroup after that. I got my business back together and started doing good again. Then cocaine became my drug of choice. As time wore on and I continued to do well, the thrill of victory on the racetrack and the success I was having didn't seem to satisfy me. That gave me a good excuse for drinking and doing drugs. I told myself, "I'm in a high-stress environment, and I need this to unwind." When you want to do something bad enough, you can make some pretty good excuses why you could or should do that. That's what I was doing at the time.

Doing coke made me feel I was bigger and better. I remember going into the jocks' room with coke on me, but determined I wasn't going to use that day. I would go out and ride two or three races and wouldn't do good. So then I would succumb to the temptation. I'd do some coke, and it seemed like the next horse would win. Which further convinced me that "Yeah, that's my go-to medication. That's what I need." There again it's a lie right out of the pits of hell because it takes you down the road to destruction.

I've ridden considerably better without the drugs than with them, but while I did cocaine and rode, I had myself believing I was much superior when I indulged. It was a false sense of bravado. Eventually I phased out the drugs, but I was drinking every night. I was a blackout drinker.

I failed to tell you that I was raised in a Christian home. I was confirmed in the Lutheran faith. We went to church. I wasn't living a Christian life-style yet considered myself a believer — there was never any doubt on my part of that. In 1982 I was the leading rider in the country, but as time wore on, that success didn't hold the meaning or feeling that I thought it would. That sent me searching for answers and asking some serious questions: "Exactly what am I here for?" "What is life all

369

about?" "What is my purpose in all of this?" I remember vividly going out at night and looking up at the sky, at the immense heavens, and saying, "Where do I fit into this picture? There's got to be more to life than what I'm doing."

I think probably in large part due to the fact that I'd been raised in a Christian home, taking that upbringing for granted, ultimately that would be the last place I would look. I thought I was a Christian, and that didn't seem to be the answer I was looking for. Sort of like in that old country western song — "looking for love in all the wrong places" — only I was doing that for the meaning of life. I was looking behind every bush and under every rock, figuratively speaking. Yet I think God had been working on me ever since I'd gone to church, that I was raised the right way, but during the early years when I made a name for myself in racing, I kept patting myself on the back. The fame and the abuse had developed a horribly destructive mind-set. My ego had got more and more out of hand, and I was not listening.

Where cocaine gave me a false sense of superiority, I never drank and rode. I've come to realize that drugs of any kind are mind-altering merely in that they send you in the direction you're already going. People think if you drink it will lift your spirits. I believe it plays as a catalyst. For example, if you are down and depressed, alcohol drives you farther down. Now if you go out for an evening and are having a great time and have a couple of drinks to loosen up, it could enhance your evening. But I wouldn't recommend that, you see; I'd recommend instead you just go natural and enjoy it, just have fun and try to live each moment to the fullest.

There was a cartoon some years ago captioned "The Power of the Martini." The first frame depicted a bar with a man at one end and a woman at the other, both not very handsome or attractive, not blessed in the area of looks. And it shows one martini and they've changed and are looking better. Two, and they look a lot better. Then three. By the fourth martini, they're glamorous — you'd think it was some god and goddess sitting there. The power of the martini to change your perceptions: I've thought about it often, how drugs and alcohol mess with our perception of people, places, and situations.

In 1983 I was the leading rider again, but by now I knew that it was going to be a short-term satisfaction for a long-term problem. It was not going to be the joy, peace, and contentment that I was seeking. But we got the title, and then in late January while vacationing with my family in Colorado, my brother and his wife and my wife and I all tied one on.

We continued to mix it up pretty good, drinking beer, wine, and I don't know what all. In the aftermath I got quite sick, so I didn't drink anything. On January 27 I flew from Colorado to Miami, where I was scheduled to ride in a race on the twenty-eighth at Hialeah Race Track. I arrived in late evening. I was traveling by myself and checked into the hotel near the Miami International Airport.

When I got into the room, I turned on the TV set, as is a habit of mine, oftentimes just for company or noise, and went about getting ready for bed. I went about hanging up my clothes, when I noticed that I had tuned into a televised crusade of Jimmy Swaggart, the evangelist. Because I felt that I was a Christian, I didn't think what he had to offer was what I was looking for. I certainly wasn't going to sit and listen to some Bible-thumper preacher. Really at that point in time, I thought that to be vocal about your faith was for women, children, and wimps! It was a sign of weakness in my opinion. You had to "be a man," to have a go-it-alone kind of attitude.

So I flipped through the channels and nothing got my attention. I turned the TV set off and went to bed, and when my head hit the pillow, I went sound asleep. This was highly unusual — without several drinks as a sedative, it would ordinarily have been a difficult chore — because that evening I was probably as sober as I'd been in a long time. It was an incredibly deep sleep, and when I awoke, I felt I'd been sleeping all night. I woke to the distinct feeling that I wasn't by myself in that hotel room, which initially was reason for concern. I sat up in bed and looked around. I couldn't see anything, but I felt a definite presence there with me.

I don't know if the Lord at that point prompted me to get up and turn the TV on, or if I did it on my own to rid myself of these feelings. But I got up and turned it on and realized, as the picture came on the screen, that I hadn't slept long at all, because Jimmy Swaggart was still on, and he had just delivered the message of salvation and was having an altar call — where he invited people to come forward and invite Christ into their hearts. I realized in that instant that the presence in that room with me was the spirit of the Living God. I was being given the opportunity to bend my knee and invite Christ into my life.

Now, they say that when you die, your whole life passes through your eyes, and in a sense, my whole life passed before my eyes that night. I could see the number of times in the previous thirty years that, given the drinking and drugs and the kind of life-style that I was living, I was headed for destruction. I would be one step away from self-destructing, and this hand would materialize. It would gently nudge me back from the edge. At that moment, I intuitively knew that what I'd been longing for and what I needed was a relationship with God. I knew that the void in my life was a God-shaped void, and only God could fill it. I fell on my knees and wept and cried and invited Jesus Christ into my life.

I don't know how long I was on the floor. I finally got up and went back to bed. I do know that when I got up the next morning and went outside that it was a decidedly different world. The world hadn't changed, but I had. The Bible says that when you accept Christ into your life, you become a new creature. The old things pass away, and all things become new again, and I was a new creature in Christ.

Now, I couldn't have verbalized that and told you at the time. I've since come to learn and realize that what happened was I became born again through the spirit of the Living God. I went on about my business that day, and it was incredible. The grass seemed greener, the sky bluer. All of a sudden, my senses were so in tune with everything around me. Whereas I was so dulled with the drugs and alcohol and the life-style I'd been living, now everything has taken on a new brilliance.

So I went about my way that day and finished up the races and got on a plane to fly back to Colorado. After we got into the air, a stewardess came by and asked if I wanted a drink. When I was sober, I was really a pretty polite individual, yet I snapped at her. I said, "No!" She said, "Okay, fine." I can picture the look on her, the astonished and shocked look on her face that I would snap at her like that. Then I sat back in my chair and said, "Now where did that come from?" I started looking inside. I realized that not only did I not find alcohol appealing, but I found it repulsive. And I truly believe that at the moment I accepted Christ into my life, He broke the chains of bondage to drugs and alcohol.

I have never gone to rehab or had a relapse. I've been in the company of people doing drugs and alcohol, and it's not like I have to fight the urge. What I do is try to talk to people who are doing it into not doing it: "That's not the way to go. That's not what you need to be doing. This isn't the answer to your problems. Here, I have the answer, let me share it with you." The people that I was trying to witness to and minister to were the same ones that I had partied with. They were like, "Git owda here!" That caused me to have to find a new circle of friends. Whether you are reaching the pinnacle of success or falling on your back, until you want help, God Himself won't separate you from the habit or addiction that you don't want to get rid of.

A lot of people thought that the change that had taken place in my life was a momentary thing, and that I would come out of it, but Christianity to me is not a way of life, it is life. It is a continual, ongoing, ever-growing, intimate walk with the Lord. He is faithful. They now recognize that what happened to me was for real, that it wasn't a passing fancy. I recovered the day I accepted Christ. I was set free. When I sat down on the plane that night and snapped at the lady (and I apologized), the change had already taken place. As I said, when you accept Christ into your life you become a new creature.

I truly believe that if someone with an addiction of any kind has a heart's desire, a heart's cry, to be rid of that addiction, God will give that person the power to overcome. In my case, He instantaneously delivered me from the bondage of drugs and alcohol. Now, there's other areas of my life that the Lord and I together work on daily. I've always been competitive, but I wasn't a very good loser, and I was known to throw a temper tantrum if I got beat a nose in a race or if something didn't go my way. I had a vicious temper. But with the Lord's help, today I've got that in check.

And I realized right away that I was going to have a hard time witnessing for the Lord and living for the Lord if I used the kind of vulgarity that is second language — sometimes primary language! — in a locker-room environment. I was clear on that: Stay away from coarse talking. So the Lord has helped me and is continuing to help me to monitor my words and be careful about what I say and how I say it.

It's all a process, and God is continuing to work in and through me. God is faithful even when I'm faithless. So I'm not in recovery or recovering, I'm going in the spirit of the Lord and in the grace and knowledge of Jesus. As far as drugs and alcohol, I was set free from the moment I accepted Him. The Bible says that if you know the truth, then the truth will set you free. Elsewhere it says Jesus Christ is the Way and the Truth and the Life, and nobody comes to the Father except through Him. He is the Truth, and if you know the Truth, then the Truth will set you free. If you invite Christ into your life, you experience the power of God working in your heart and in your life. You experience the forgiveness of your sins, you are reconciled to God, and you have the power of God to tap into. It's not by might or by power, but by my spirit, sayeth the Lord. And it's the spirit of God working in and through me that allows me to be the person that I am and to be where I am today.

My life is better than it's ever been, and getting better by the day. I'd be lying if I said it was all just smooth sailing! I have good days and bad days — everybody does. That's part of being human. But my life is so incredibly better than it was twenty years ago.

I joke that I was like one of those life-sized cartoon characters, Popeye and all, air-filled but weighted at the bottom. That weight will finally bring them upright. For me, God was the weight at the bottom. My mother and father laid the foundation by raising me the right way, and I just waffled back and forth, back and forth, until on January 27, 1984, when I accepted Christ and finally came upright. By the grace of God, I have stayed that way for the most part.

My mother is still living; my father passed away in '86. Both parents saw me sober and straight. They had seen me at my worst, and it wasn't something they were proud of, yet at the same time, I think they recognized that they had raised me right — they had laid the groundwork. When the rubber meets the road, ultimately the choice has to be made. Needless to say, both my mother and father were ecstatic when the change occurred in my life. I wish my father was alive today to see the continuing change that has taken place, the success that the Lord blessed me with, and the positive influence that I trust I'm making on people I come into contact with in racing.

My daughter was born in 1986, so she never saw me under the influence of drugs and alcohol and never saw me in bad shape, but we have talked about the dangers of such. I've shared harrowing stories with her — near misses and close calls — and tried to impress upon her that I'm not proud of that. I only share with her for the reason I share with you, that she might learn from my mistakes.

I often share my testimony and tell people that if they're out there today and have a problem, know that there's help. I don't share to glamorize alcohol or drugs or make it look like what I did was all right — not by any stretch of the imagination! I despise what I did to myself, my family, and my friends — and what I very nearly did to the God-given talent and ability to communicate with horses and ride races that the Lord has blessed me with. To treat His love, grace, and mercy with disregard is disheartening to look back on, but I share in hopes that if there's someone on the verge of getting involved that they'd recognize it's the wrong way to go. That if they are involved, there's hope and help, and that they can turn away from that life.

A Chinese Christian

Christianity in China is more than 1,350 years old. In 635 Christians arrived in the Tang Dynasty capital of Xian and were allowed to create places of worship and propagate their faith. Despite its ancient lineage, Chinese Christianity has struggled for existence and definition for centuries, and that ordeal continues into the twenty-first century.

Symbolically, the Roman Catholic missionary effort in China begins with Jesuit Matteo Ricci's arrival in Beijing in 1601. The Protestant missionary endeavor begins with the work of Robert Morrison in 1807. By the end of the nineteenth century, the Protestant enterprise was dominated by the China Inland Mission, an independent missionary organization led by Hudson Taylor.

Both Catholic and Protestant efforts were characterized by evangelistic efforts that had modest results. But both also launched enormous cultural efforts to ameliorate poverty, increase education, and improve the health of the Chinese people. Ironically, the twentieth-century story of Christianity in China is the death of the missionary enterprise, the endurance of its educational and medical institutions, and the flourishing of an indigenous Christianity.

As historian John King Fairbank has written, "The missionaries [who] came as spiritual reformers soon found that material improvements were equally necessary, and in the end helped to foment the great revolution. Yet as foreigners, they could take no part in it, much less bring it to a finish. Instead it finished them."

Chinese Christianity in the twentieth and twenty-first centuries is largely the story of a church exploding in numbers and vitality with Chinese leadership and prospering in the face of persecution. An accurate estimate of the number of Chinese Christians is virtually impossible to make. But the overall picture is quite clear and dramatic. In 1900 Chinese Christians made up 0.4 percent of the population. By 2000, the number had reached 7.1 percent.

However, complicating this picture is the division of Chinese Christians into roughly two different groups. One is the state-sponsored churches (the Three-Self Patriotic Movement and the Chinese Christian Council for Protestants, the Chinese Patriotic Catholic Association and the Chinese Catholic Bishops Council for Catholics). Then there are the manifold house churches — for both Catholics and, especially, evangelical, charismatic/Pentecostal Protestants. By the first decade of the twenty-first century most of the growth seemed to be taking place in the house churches operating independently of government recognition. Two polls, done independently of one another in 2007, concluded that there were approximately 54 million Chinese Christians — more than 39 million Protestants and about 14 million Catholics — and more than 600 times the number in 1900.

Nicholas D. Kristof, the *New York Times* columnist, flatly concluded in 2006: "Although China bans foreign missionaries and sometimes harasses and imprisons Christians, especially in rural areas, Christianity is booming in China."

The worst of the persecution came under Communist rule by Mao Zedong, especially during the Cultural Revolution of 1965-68. State-recognized churches have always operated under strict restrictions, but in the midst of the Cultural Revolution even those churches were shut down. Despite the loosening of restraints on religious observance since Mao, churches are often monitored and even destroyed by government authorities.

The following account is the story of a young man whose journey from his family's Christianity to communism in his young adulthood and to deep Christian faith in his maturity symbolizes part of the pilgrimage of Chinese Christianity amid oppression. When this account originally appeared, his name was withheld to protect his identity — a sign of the continued persecution of Chinese Christians. And yet, the story itself is testimony to the vibrancy of faith and the endurance of discipleship.

∼

My grandfather, a country doctor in north China, became the first Christian in our family through a CIM missionary. Later, he also became the first member of my family to suffer persecution when he was tortured to death during the 1947-48 Communist land reform.

My father, the eldest son, graduated from a Christian high school just as the Japanese army invaded north China. He was severely beaten by Japanese soldiers for helping the church provide food and shelter to Chinese refugees. He made his way to southwest China, completed seminary training, and was ordained.

In 1954-55, when the government closed most churches, my father was denounced for propagandizing "spiritual idealism" and our family was given a "black" label, meaning we were to be totally ostracized. My mother divorced my father and left me at age five. Forced out of the parsonage, we lived in a shack at the back of the churchyard, which became a factory. Father was forced to do hard labor for the next 25 years. My only childhood memory is being hungry all the time.

As a young boy, I could only see that my family was responsible for my being bullied at school. When the Red Guards were sent out of the cities to the countryside, I volunteered to go. In November 1968, 12 teenagers arrived in a very remote mountain village. Working hard 12 to 14 hours a day, we barely survived. Since my father was a "criminal," I was usually alone. Many times, I sat on top of a mountain watching the sheep and wishing I weren't alive.

I kept up my hope for the future by secretly reading anything I could find. After I managed to leave the village to work in a factory, I studied even harder, but still in secret. After Mao died, college entrance exams were resumed. I passed, despite very sharp competition and only an eighth grade education. Deng Xiaoping's policies allowed us "black" elements to find a way back into society. I was even recruited by the Communist Party.

I always blamed my father for my troubles. Only after I was married, finished school, and had a good job did I reconnect with my father and his family. While I was a visiting scholar in the U.S. in 1990, he came to live with my wife and son.

That year was a major turning point in my life. When I learned the whole story of the June Fourth killings [in the 1989 Democracy Move-

Reprinted from *Christian History and Biography* 98 (2008): 4. © 2008 Christianity Today International. Used with permission.

ment], I felt terribly saddened by what the government did in Tiananmen Square. I now had to face the question, "Should I continue to serve the Communist cause?"

I visited churches everywhere I went and stood quietly observing how the Christians behaved. I could see they freely chose to believe, and many helped me without knowing a thing about me. I began to rethink my father's life. There was a stark contrast between June Fourth and my father — who never argued, never cheated, was always patient and kind, and was respected by all who knew him. I realized Marxism has no words to address a person's individual needs. Where does love come from? Where do goodness and evil come from? I enjoyed reading the Bible's answers to all these questions. God began to be real to me.

One special day I visited a Christian scholar who shared words from the Bible as a personal message for me. I was filled by the Holy Spirit as God spoke to me. I was so happy that I cried. A Communist with a heart of stone never sheds tears! Then I knew that the only explanation for my life's journey was that God loves me, gave me my father, and was blessing me today through this stranger. I humbly accepted Jesus Christ.

I decided I had to use my knowledge and life experience for God, not for myself. I would serve God, not the Party. The U.S. didn't need more Christians, but China did, so I would return to China.

When I saw my father, I immediately told him, "Now I'm a believer." He smiled and said, "I have prayed for you for 30 years." I realized I loved and respected my father because he lived his whole life true to his belief. Happily, my son loved his grandfather and respected my choice. So when he went overseas to university, he immediately was baptized and joined the church. He has become the fourth-generation Christian in our family.

Latin American Pentecostals:
Juan Gonzáles and Rosa

By the mid-twentieth century, Latin American Christianity was in trouble. The region, long dominated by the Roman Catholic Church, was marked by lax spiritual practice and widespread religious ignorance.

The Roman Catholic Church, spurred by initiatives from young priests, bishops, and lay people in Latin America and by Vatican programs, took dramatic steps to revitalize the moribund church. Vatican II, in particular, provided a platform for reform and renewal, and no continent saw the effects of the Council more than Latin America. A largely foreign-born priesthood was replaced by native-born clerics. Bible study exploded. Huge numbers of newly trained catechists bridged the gap between the illiterate or poorly educated masses and the church's teachings. The church frequently turned away from political passivity to challenge unjust social structures and corrupt regimes. By the end of the twentieth century, Latin American Catholicism had experienced a surge of new life unprecedented in its history.

An equally compelling, if not more important, story is the explosion of Pentecostalism in Latin America during the twentieth century. Although Western missionaries played a role, the birth and growth of Pentecostalism in Latin America is essentially an indigenous movement. By the twenty-first century, Pentecostalism transformed the continent's religion and culture and contributed to the most significant fact about contemporary Christianity: Pentecostalism is the most rapidly growing form of Christianity in the world.

Before 1900, there were occasional stirrings of the "second birth" of the Holy Spirit in various parts of the world. Signs of the Pentecostal movement were evident — speaking in tongues, healing, visions, and above all the experience of personal renewal. But early in the twentieth century, the movement began to build enormous momentum — in Europe and North America, but especially in Latin America, Asia, and Africa. By 2000, there were an estimated 141 million Pentecostal/charismatics in Latin America, 135 million in Asia, 126 million in Africa, 80 million in North America, and 38 million in Europe. The ostensibly Roman Catholic countries of Latin America were particularly affected, and they became fascinating to observers, who wrote books on Pentecostalism such as *Tongues of Fire* and *Is Latin America Turning Protestant?*

Both the Roman Catholic renewal and the Pentecostal/charismatic revolution brought Christianity to the Latin American masses. Historian Edward L. Clearly concludes, "By the end of the millennium Latin America was experiencing a great Christian and religious revival."

There are, of course, significant strains among the Pentecostal/charismatic groups (or "sects," as some would term them) and between them and the Latin American Roman Catholic Church and the historic Protestant churches. Some studies show that conversion to Pentecostalism is sometimes short-lived and that joining a Pentecostal church may be more like transferring membership than conversion. The political and social impact of the Pentecostal/charismatic movement in Latin America is likewise ambiguous, but it does appear that this Spirit-filled faith is providing new structures of meaning and individual identity for millions who are dealing with monumental social change and the transformation of the continent's entire culture.

The two accounts that follow demonstrate some of the dynamics of the Pentecostal/charismatic movement in Latin America. One comes from a Roman Catholic layman empowered by the Spirit to bring leadership to his church. His testimony illustrates the power of the movement even within the Roman Catholic Church. The other account is a sociological description of Pentecostalism in La Paz, Bolivia, that includes a testimony by "Rosa," an impoverished street merchant, whose story indicates how Pentecostal Protestant fervor and fellowship empowered her life with new meaning and purpose. Her narrative suggests the movement's potential for redefining and revolutionizing the role of women in Latin American life.

~

Juan Gonzáles ("Jany")

At 11 am on 7 February 1999 in the small town of Aibonito on the island, Jesus came into my life.

Blessings to all. I begin by saying proudly that I am a son of the Catholic Charismatic Renewal. I am now 23 years old, and I serve the Lord full-time. I would like to share with you young people what God did in my life. Not to glorify myself, nor for anything like that, only so that this testimony may edify the lives of others. This is my testimony, without much detail, short and precise.

I attended Catholic schools all my life, but my family was not active in the church. I went to Mass once a month since it was a school requirement. When I was sixteen, I was one of the most popular kids in school. Bright, athletic, and preoccupied with girls — that's how I would describe myself. I began to try drugs and tried them all. I joined a dance group that specialized in Regaeton concerts. What happened was that all this went to my head.

When I still had two years left to finish high school, one of my religion teachers, for the final assignment of the year, asked us to summarize each chapter of a book entitled "To the God of My Youth." I spoke with the teacher, and told him that I had no intention of reading that book because it was boring, clearly an excuse since I did not want to read it because it was about God. The teacher made me an offer and said to me: if you go on a three-day retreat next week, I'll give you an "A" for the final assignment, and you won't have to read it. An irresistible offer I couldn't refuse. I said to myself, three days are not that much, and for a good grade — I'm going to go. Already, I had fallen into the nets of the ship JESUS, and already I had bitten the lure.

On the fifth of February, I got to the retreat house of the Salesian Fathers of Puerto Rico. Some [participants] had brought marijuana to the retreat, and I was smoking it. Whatever anyone had to say didn't really matter to me, and I ignored them. It was soon Sunday, February 7th, and the retreat ended at noon. With one hour left for everything to end, Jesus called to me. It was the time for the manifestation of the Holy

---

Address by Juan Gonzáles ("Jany") in 2005 to young Catholics in Puerto Rico. It is reprinted from *Religion in Latin America: A Documentary History,* translated by Lee M. Penyak and Walter J. Petry (Maryknoll, NY: Orbis Books, 2006), 386-87. Used with permission.

Spirit, and every one was praying, crying, speaking in tongues, falling down backward — for me complete madness. I said: you're all crazy and I went to the back of the chapel. And there, in a little corner of that little chapel in the center of the island, Jesus touched me, called to me and spoke to me.

I could hear his voice, which said to me: you are mine, I have chosen you for myself, you are going to work with young people and you are going to become a preacher, a prophet for the nations.

I answered him: but, I, how? I don't know anything about you, I don't even know you. And I can't preach because I'm a stammerer.

Jesus [said]: Don't worry. You are going to preach my word and shout (expulsarás) my words out of your mouth. I thought I was going crazy, that the drugs were killing my brain, because I was hearing things and voices. I still couldn't believe what was happening to me.

And at a certain moment, I became paralyzed by an image of a person in front. I could only see eyes looking at me. I felt that look was coming to me little by little. It penetrated my eyes, ran through my body until it got to my heart. When I felt that sensation that struck my heart, it was like an exploding tire. Jesus had penetrated my heart and had enthroned himself in it. He was healing me, he healed my wounds, he healed the wound from my parents' divorce, he healed the damage done by drugs, he healed the wound of my loneliness, he healed the wound from a father who never sought me out. It was no longer I, it was Jesus in me.

I left that retreat a new man, renewed, changed and transformed. With nothing in my hands, but with my heart full to capacity and with a promise made by God. I did not begin to preach right away. I had to go through a process of conversion, slowly and effectively. And don't forget that I was a STAMMERER.

One year after this, it occurred to me that I had to decide to study and go to the University. After a long period of discernment, I enrolled in the school of Theology. When I acquired a little more knowledge, I again felt in my being that promise of God in my heart. The word of God held me captive, and God wanted to open my lips to proclaim it. I couldn't resist any longer, the fire of Jesus in my heart was burning me up. I had to preach. But I was a Stammerer.

On one occasion, some preachers from a Puerto Rican movement called the Cheo Brothers were at my parish. One preached while the other interceded for the preacher. That day I arrived late with a friend and the parish church was very full. We had to stay outside, and I took advantage of the opportunity to reveal to my friend what was happening to me.

He told me: Jany, you are a stammerer, you can't preach. I answered: I know, I'm aware of it; if it were solely on my account, I wouldn't preach. But it's something stronger than I. He kept on saying: Jany, you can't, you can't and you cannot.

But for the Glory of God, one of the Cheo Brothers was close by and heard part of the conversation; he approached me and put his hand on my shoulder and said to me:

Don't worry, you're going to preach.

My friend said to him: for him to preach, God will have to cure him first.

The Cheo Brother turned to him and told him: NOOO, God is not going to heal him. Smart and clever guys like YOU will go crazy in the face of the power of God when you hear him preach. You will say: How is it possible that when he preaches he doesn't stammer? This will make it clear (para que quede garantizado) that it is not HE [Jany] but rather GOD in HIM.

He turned to me and said: CONGRATULATIONS, today begins your ministry.

And from that day, God sent me to different places to preach, and now the stammerer can't keep his mouth shut, so that it's open to the four winds, proclaiming the grandeur of Jesus.

And it's amazing; many times I cry after I preach because it is humanly not possible, humanly it is impossible for me to speak that way. I realize that without him I am nothing.

Now I have a degree in theology and am studying for a master's in divinity and theology. Everything, my life, my future, my studies are about the Lord and for the Lord.

[I am] a young layman who serves the Lord and will serve him forever until he calls me. I am a member of Catholic Charismatic Youth of the Archdiocese of San Juan, Puerto Rico. I am coordinator of the prayer group of my parish. I conduct workshops and Bible courses and [I am a] preacher full-time.

I don't consider myself worthy of any of these honors. I only say all this so that you can see that God can indeed make use of a stammerer to proclaim his word. HE CAN USE YOU.

Put yourself in the hands of God and he will make powerful use of you.

Women and Pentecostalism in La Paz: Rosa

Organized religion represents perhaps the most common way that women in La Paz develop new relationships within socially prescribed boundaries, because they encounter more difficulties than men in finding emotional support and economic security once they move outside their kin networks. Household responsibilities lengthen their workdays; discrimination in the job market lowers their earnings; and the conditions under which most lower-class women work inhibit the formation of group solidarity. Domestic servants, for example, labor in isolation from their peers, and street vendors are forced to compete with one another in a milieu increasingly saturated with people desperately trying to earn a living. In addition, strong moral precepts regarding appropriate female behavior hamper the emergence of extra domestic activities centered around women and directed by them. . . .

The Pentecostal *culto* [service] offers women an institutional base for developing important and enduring social relationships, and it provides the rituals to validate these emerging bonds, which help to create a shared sense of community. The *culto* occurs five times a week and is an ongoing process of conversion whereby believers purge themselves of Satan's diabolical influence through collective song, prayer, and music. The human body, according to Pentecostals, is occupied either by Satan or by the Holy Spirit, and in order to evict Satan, one must be cleansed of sin. This requires the observance of a number of puritanical practices, which include abstaining from alcohol, tobacco, sexual intercourse for nonreproductive purposes, dancing, and the cinema, and also entails attendance of as many *cultos* as possible.

Participation in the *culto* is crucial to an individual's salvation, because the cleansing and healing powers of God can be mobilized most effectively by the active involvement of all believers. Indeed, attendance is so important that the pastor often asks church members to pray for those who are absent. But more than simple attendance is required.

From Lesley Gill, "'Like a Veil to Cover Them': Women and the Pentecostal Movement in La Paz," *American Ethnologist* 17, no. 4 (Nov. 1990): 712-15, 719, © 2004 by the American Anthropological Association and used with permission. This article subsequently appeared in Anna L. Peterson and Manuel A. Vásquez, eds., *Latin American Religions: Histories and Documents in Context* (New York: New York University Press, 2008), 191-97.

Congregants must also take part in the singing, shouting, hand clapping, praying, and testifying that characterize a typical *culto*.

A *culto* begins with praying and singing to the beat of musical instruments. The pastor, standing behind a pulpit with a lighted sign that reads "Jesus Heals and Saves," leads the congregation. Periodic shouts of "Hallelujah" and "Glory to God" punctuate the ceremony as congregants extend their hands toward heaven. The level of intensity gradually builds, culminating with the pastor's sermon, which, if successful, transforms the gathering. People start to writhe on the floor, speak in tongues, and even lose consciousness, all signs that the Holy Spirit is waging a successful battle with Satan for control of the individual. Individuals will then begin to testify about discovering God for the first time and the subsequent changes in their lives.

Women in this setting are not merely passive recipients of a religious message. They actively participate in the experience by singing and directing hymns, receiving the Holy Spirit, testifying, and even preaching on rare occasions. Such behavior contrasts with that characteristic of the traditional Catholic liturgy, which is much less participatory and in which the sermon may be given in a language that Aymara speakers do not fully understand. Women are also involved in a range of other church activities that include proselytizing on the streets, visiting needy church members in their homes, attending family services, and traveling to church meetings in other cities and foreign countries.

In the course of these activities, women meet other women like themselves with whom they share the intensity of the Pentecostal experience, and their dealings with men are governed by rigid puritanical rules that curtail abusive male behavior — such as drunkenness and the overt expression of sexuality — which is often tolerated in other contexts. This enables them to construct new social networks that are emotionally supportive and economically useful. These ties extend well beyond the church into the individuals' daily lives. Believers provide one another with information about living arrangements, jobs, medical assistance, and business opportunities in the city, and they are readily available for assistance and support in times of crisis. To varying degrees, these ties replace ties with kin left behind in the countryside or social and marital relationships in the city that are no longer viable because of divorce, abandonment, or the death of a spouse, and they enable women to develop greater self-confidence and personal integrity.

The Pentecostal church, then, and particularly the collective set-

ting of the *culto,* offers women the possibility of establishing new social relationships and reaffirming them on a regular basis. But the
church also requires them to adopt a new set of beliefs about the world
and their relation to it. These beliefs provide them with the means to
validate their membership in a new community and to reinterpret past
experiences in light of a changing social identity. This process begins
in the *culto,* and it continues with individual possession by the Holy
Spirit and the subsequent explanation of religious conversion in oral
testimonies. . . .

Although Pentecostal religious conversion demands continuous participation in the *culto,* it is also an individual experience that begins with
the baptism of the Holy Spirit. This is an extremely emotional event in
which a believer discovers . . . the road to eternal salvation by directly
encountering the power of Christ and establishing a personal relationship with him. The experience infuses converts with a new and stronger
sense of God. . . . If they submit to his will and acknowledge their sins,
he will lift them up to heaven when he returns to Earth on Judgment
Day, and they will be saved.

Believers describe their conversion experiences in highly emotional
accounts that sharply distinguish the pre- from the post-conversion
characteristics of the individual's life. They tell of the desperation and
despair that once plagued their lives and the peace and happiness that
they encountered after a surprise meeting with God changed them forever. These stories are based on actual experiences, but the meaning of
the past is reinterpreted by individuals in light of the new ideology and
their present social reality. The story of Rosa, a 50-year-old street vendor
and mother of four, illustrates how personal biography is reworked in
light of religious conversion and changing social relationships.

Rosa has been a member of the IPU [Iglesia Pentecostal Unida] for three
years and supports herself and her two youngest children by selling un-
derwear on a La Paz street. She was born in a rural community near La
Paz and migrated to the city with her parents at the age of eight. She attended elementary school in the city and, soon after becoming pregnant
at the age of 21, married a bricklayer, who was also a rural immigrant.

The marriage eventually deteriorated. Rosa grew extremely frustrated because her husband spent little time at home and was often
without work. She frequently lacked money for the family's domestic

needs, and his constant drinking squeezed the household budget even tighter. Sometimes he would come home drunk and beat her, and he stayed away from home for days at a time. The situation eventually grew intolerable, and the couple split up: Rosa remained with the children in the family's rented room, and her husband took up residence with another woman.

The break-up of her marriage initiated an emotional as well as an economic crisis for Rosa. She could no longer count on any financial assistance from her husband and was forced to support herself and her children on the meager returns from street vending. In addition, Rosa's social life underwent a dramatic change, because she was no longer able to participate in social events in the same way as in the past. These changes eventually moved her to seek refuge in the Pentecostal church. Rosa explains the circumstances that led up to her religious conversion as follows:

> My husband and I had always gone to fiestas and social gatherings of various sorts. I never drank, because I had to take care of him and make sure that he didn't fall down and hurt himself when he got drunk. I still received fiesta invitations after he left and decided to go to one or two because I liked all the food and dancing. I also wanted to see how much I could drink, since I'd never been drunk in my life.
>
> At one fiesta I was feeling a little tipsy after several rounds of drinks. But then the band started playing really lively music, and I wanted to dance. A man I didn't know asked me to dance. His wife was sitting nearby, and I asked her if she minded. She said to go ahead, so we did, but then he didn't want to stop. We continued with one dance after another. I was a little drunk, but I realized that his wife was going to get angry if we kept it up, so I went and sat down. I didn't want to start a big scandal right there in the middle of the party, and I finally just went home.
>
> On the way home I started to think "I don't like this. I wasn't born to make people gossip, and there is no man who can accompany me to these fiestas. It's not a good idea to go alone." I felt lonely. All the other women were with their husbands, and I realized that there was nobody who would take me home if I drank too much or watch out for me as I had done for my husband. I could end up sleeping on the street. It was then that I decided to

go to the church. People don't drink and dance there. They just pray to God, and I decided that that would be a better life.

Rosa finally settled on the IPU, after initially experimenting with another Pentecostal sect. She heard the pastor preach in a city plaza, and, at the urging of her son, decided to attend the *cultos* on a regular basis. She received the Holy Spirit six months after attending her first *culto* and this, according to Rosa, was an experience that profoundly changed her. As she explains:

> When you surrender to God with all your heart, you cry and cry, recognizing the errors that you have committed and all the things that happened before knowing him. Knowing God changes everyone. You attain a peace in your home even if there isn't work or money. If there is just one cup of tea, everyone drinks it together. There aren't all these problems that people have who ignore the word of God. If you love God, then you also love your family. How can the person who loves God offend his wife? It's impossible.
>
> If my husband had known God, I would not have lost him. But I was also ignorant. The enemy [that is, the devil] had grabbed me and would not let go of me. If I had understood the word of God, I would have married a spiritual man who feared God. Then I would have been able to live well and my marriage would not have been so difficult.

We can see from this story how Rosa's participation in the Pentecostal church and her encounter with God reshaped her understanding of preconversion life. During our interview, for example, Rosa told me that she had joined the Pentecostal church in large part because drinking and dancing were prohibited. Alcohol consumption in various forms was, indeed, a problem for Rosa: first, she had had to endure her husband's abusive behavior and the strain on the family budget caused by his excessive drinking; and second, following her husband's departure, she had suffered from ostracism in social situations where drinking and dancing were problematic for a single woman. But she had nevertheless participated in the festive drinking and dancing, because they were enjoyable activities and one way of belonging to the group.

It was only after her conversion to Pentecostalism that Rosa had

388

come to view dancing and the consumption of alcohol as sinful behavior, inspired by the devil. Falling under the influence of the devil, whom Rosa described as the "enemy," and the absence of God in her life and the lives of others accounted for past difficulties. These understandings reflected her current interpretation of past events and constituted an important new analysis of her life in light of Pentecostal doctrine. Her account was a post-conversion interpretation of the events that had led up to and constituted her religious transformation, and it represented a complex interaction of personal history and belief. . . .

The dramatic growth of Pentecostalism in La Paz over the past two and a half decades has been linked to profound changes in the social and economic fabric of life in the city. Female migrants from the countryside and lower-class urban dwellers, in particular, bear the brunt of a prolonged economic crisis as well as of class, racial, and gender discrimination. . . .

Through the experience of conversion, women address much of their gender- and class-based suffering by using religious ideology to recast the meaning of past events and revalidate their present social identities and relationships. This reflects a complex interaction of personal biography and belief that is an integral part of the process of change. They are also able to redefine their relationships with men because of the way in which Pentecostalism alters male behavior to suit their economic and emotional needs.

By creating new ties to one another, Pentecostal men and women overcome some of the mutual alienation that many experience every day as members of the lower class. These ties and the male resources that are channelled back to the domestic unit strengthen urban neighborhoods and help to create a new sense of community out of seeming disorder and chaos. In the process, these men and women are promoting values and practices that challenge aspects of the dominant society.

Bono

(b. 1960)

He's the lead singer of U2, the most famous and influential rock band in the late twentieth and early twenty-first centuries. By himself, he is regarded as perhaps the most noteworthy rock musician of the same period. Because of his music and his activism and philanthropy on behalf of Africa, he has been nominated for the Nobel Peace Prize three times, been knighted by Queen Elizabeth II, and been named as *Time* magazine's "Person of the Year" with a cover headline, "Can Bono Save the World?"

He was born into a religiously mixed family in Dublin, Ireland, wracked by religious conflict and violence. His mother was Protestant; his father was Roman Catholic. She died when he was fourteen; her death was an enduring source of grief in his life and shaped several of his later songs. His relationship with his father was troubled. He attended a progressive Protestant school, which left a deep mark on his faith and intellectual development. There some schoolmates gave him the name Bono, which he eventually accepted because it meant "good voice" in a loose translation of the Latin, "Bonavox."

Like all fledging musical groups, U2 did not find immediate success, but it did discover a crucially important bond: Christianity. All but one of the band members are Christian and became members of a fundamentalist and charismatic Christian group in Dublin — Shalom — where they found intense Bible study and fellowship. Early in the band's career, Bono wrote to his father, "You should be aware that at the moment three of the group are committed Christians. That means offering each day up to God, meeting in the morning for prayers, readings, and letting God work in our lives. This gives us the strength and joy that does not depend on drink or drugs. This strength will, I believe, be the quality that will take us to the top of the music business where never before have so many lost and sorrowful people gathered in one place pretending they're having a good time. It is our ambition to make more than good music."

U2 finally broke with Shalom and its leader over their desire to pursue a career in rock music, but religiosity and deep philosophical themes remained constant in their songs. They have consistently sought "to make more than good music," and as Bono once declared, "A rock star has two instincts: he wants to change the world, and he wants to have fun. If he can do both at the same time, that's the way to go." He has written nearly all of U2's songs. "You're in a rock band — what can't you talk about? God? OK, here we go," he maintained. "You're supposed to write songs about sex and drugs. Well, no, I won't."

As U2's and Bono's fame and wealth increased, he took up the cause of Africa after a visit to the continent with his wife. There they were deeply moved by the famine, poverty, and AIDS pandemic, as well as the structural problems of national indebtedness of developing nations. Through a variety of charity campaigns and especially through his own organization, DATA (Debts, AIDS, Trade, Africa), he has helped raise billions of dollars. He has demonstrated an uncanny ability to win a strange confederation of bedfellows to his cause, ranging from Pope John Paul II to Jesse Helms to Bill Clinton to George W. Bush.

Predictably, all of this has come with controversy. Some religious leaders — especially evangelicals — have been critical of his lifestyle, which includes alcohol and profanity, and his refusal to be aligned with a particular church. His philanthropy has been attacked for its reliance on capitalist contributions to alleviate human suffering, rather than focusing on the causes and long-term solutions to such deprivation.

Bono, however, remains unbowed and eloquent in his faith in God and his belief in the power of human benevolence. "I'm a believer. I don't set myself up as any kind of 'Christian,'" Bono has said with characteristic Irish self-deprecation. "I can't live up to that. It's something I aspire to, but I don't feel comfortable with that badge." To one church congregation, he declared, "This generation will be remembered for three things: the Internet, the war on terror, and how we let an entire continent go up in flames while we stood around with watering cans. Let me share with you a conviction. God is on his knees to the church on this one. God Almighty is on his knees to us, begging us to turn around the supertanker of indifference on the subject of AIDS."

At the heart of Bono's spirituality is God's grace. "The most powerful idea that's entered the world in the last few thousand years — the idea of grace — is the reason I would like to be a Christian," he has said. "Though . . . I sometimes feel more like a fan, rather than actually in the band. I can't live up to it. But the reason I would like to is the idea of grace. It's really powerful."

Perhaps the most famous of U2's songs is "I Still Haven't Found What I'm Looking For." It is subject to various interpretations. Some take it as a gospel song, especially the verse: "You broke the bonds/And you loosed the chains/Carried the cross/Of my shame/Oh my shame/You know I believe it." Others see the final agnosticism of the song's title and conclusion: "I still haven't found what I'm looking for."

The composition suggests the compelling appeal of Bono's songs — his own spiritual quest and the yearnings of a generation of fans drawn to music speaking to their deepest longings. Bono and his fans belong to the growing population that is "spiritual, but not religious," those who find deep resonance in faith but not its institutional expression. Bono's search for faith, however, is grounded in his experience of God's grace and the incarnation, which he described vividly in an interview with a French journalist at the height of his career. It may not have been the hour he first believed, but it was a defining experience of the love of God.

When was the first time something happened when you thought about a line from the Scriptures? When you first said to yourself: yes, I can see beyond that and see how it applies to such and such a situation?

Let me try to explain something to you, which I hope will make sense of the whole conversation. But maybe that's a little optimistic. [*laughs*] This was not the first time, but I remember coming back from a very long tour. I hadn't been at home. Got home for Christmas, very excited of being in Dublin. Dublin at Christmas is cold, but it's lit up, it's like Carnival in the cold. On Christmas Eve, I went to St. Patrick's Cathedral. I had done school there for a year. It's where Jonathan Swift was dean. Anyway, some of my Church of Ireland friends were going. It's a kind of tradition on Christmas Eve to go, but I'd never been. I went to this place, sat. I was given a really bad seat, behind one of the huge pillars. I couldn't see anything. I was sitting there, having come back from

Tokyo, or somewhere like that. I went for the singing, because I love choral singing. Community arts, a specialty! But I was falling asleep, being up for a few days, traveling, because it was a bit boring, the service, and I just started nodding off, I couldn't see a thing. Then I started to try and keep myself awake studying what was on the page. It dawned on me for the first time, really. It had dawned on me before, but it really sank in: the Christmas story. The idea that God, if there is a force of Love and Logic in the universe, that it would seek to explain itself is amazing enough. That it would seek to explain itself and describe itself by becoming a child born in straw poverty, in shit and straw . . . a child. . . . I just thought: "Wow!" Just the poetry. . . . Unknowable love, unknowable power, describes itself as the most vulnerable. There it was. I was sitting there, and it's not that it hadn't struck me before, but tears came down my face, and I saw the genius of this, utter genius of picking a particular point in time and deciding to turn on this. Because that's exactly what we were talking about earlier: love needs to find form, intimacy needs to be whispered. To me, it makes sense. It's actually logical. It's pure logic. Essence has to manifest itself. It's inevitable. Love has to become an action or something concrete. It would have to happen. There must be an incarnation. Love must be made flesh.

Afterword

I always considered myself one of the once-born, and one might say I was predestined to be a Presbyterian. I was born, baptized, and confirmed in the Presbyterian Church. I was ordained to be a Presbyterian minister. Aside from a brief and intense period in college when I entertained some serious doubts about my faith, there really was no time when I thought I was not a Christian or didn't want to be a Christian. When I got married, it was an interfaith ceremony. I married a Christian — although she belonged to the Reformed Church in America. What mattered is that we were both Dutch.

When our two children were born, they were baptized in the Presbyterian Church. I taught for seven years at Princeton Theological Seminary and then became the president of Louisville Presbyterian Theological Seminary. I published articles, reviews, and books about Christianity and the Presbyterian Church. I preached and taught in many churches. I raised a substantial amount of money for one of the fine seminaries of the Presbyterian Church and helped rebuild its faculty, administration, and Board of Trustees. Still, I thought of myself as once-born — a person who never knew himself as anything but a Christian.

Then, I crashed. It was September 11, 2002 — exactly one year after the World Trade Center towers came down. I was physically, emotionally, spiritually broken. My crash, I later learned, was the result of undiagnosed bipolar illness and a pattern of drinking that had progressed into full-blown alcoholism. But I was also morally broken. Alcohol had eroded my moral core and my moral code, and I had done things that were wrong and made me deeply ashamed.

I had to resign as president of Louisville Seminary, and in the following year I struggled to deal with the physical, spiritual, and moral wreckage of my life. I went to 12-step meetings, and I drifted in and out of abstinence — sometimes for four weeks, sometimes for six weeks, but never more than two months. All the while, I prayed, "Please Lord, forgive me."

Finally, a friend and fellow alcoholic, my doctor, and my wife convinced me that I could never get sober without going into treatment. With a heavy heart and an anguished conscience, I left for a rehab program in Atlanta. All the while, I prayed, "Please God, forgive me."

When I arrived, one of the counselors described me as carrying "a toxic level of shame and guilt." And I continued to pray, "Please Lord, forgive me."

Nothing happened. I had no sense of God's forgiveness. I had no sense of God's love. As another counselor said, I was "spiritually bankrupt."

After two months in treatment and after praying continuously for God's forgiveness and the forgiveness of others, I simply gave up that prayer. Instead, I prayed, "God open me up. Please open me up." I am not exactly sure why I prayed that prayer, except that I had reached the end of my rope and didn't know anything else to say.

On the morning of December 9, 2003, I was making breakfast in the little kitchenette of the apartment I shared with three other men. They were still sleeping. I was spreading peanut butter on an English muffin, when suddenly I was surrounded by white light. It was not blinding or frightening but warm and embracing. At first, there were no voices or sounds, but as the light subsided, I eventually heard, "You are not alone." And then the light faded.

The staff at the treatment center told me later that this event marked the beginning of my recovery. After I told my story in one of the small groups, the counselor, who was a Jew, said, "All right. Get on with it." That's an Old Testament way of summing it up: Turn around. Get on with it. And it's a perfect way of describing what it means to find God.

That encounter with God made a huge difference in my life. It was a return from what was surely a form of physical dying and a spiritual and emotional death. I had been dead to myself, to others, and to God. I had prayed for more than a year for God's forgiveness, but then I gave up and prayed: "God, open me up." Only after I prayed to be open to God did God again become part of my life.

Since then my life has been different. Most of the people I have wronged have forgiven me, and we have been reconciled. Those in my family, especially my wife, have recognized my sorrow at what I have done and welcomed me back to life and health.

What I knew intellectually about Christianity has traveled what's called the longest distance in the world — the 18 inches from my head to my heart. It's like talking about Jesus for years and then, suddenly, meeting him personally. What I have realized is that God didn't simply want my repentance in exchange for God's forgiveness. No, God didn't want a transaction; God wanted a relationship. With me. Just as I am. Only after experiencing God's presence did I know God's forgiveness.

Was it a conversion? Maybe, maybe not. My life and ministry have been so abundantly blessed by God, and surely that means I had some relationship with God. But at some point, I walked into the swamp, and there I found God again. With the help of my wife and my family and wonderful friends, I began to walk the path of discipleship again. Perhaps the best way of describing my experience is that it was the most powerful moment in my continuing conversion.

And it all began with a simple prayer: "God, open me up."

I offer this story as a footnote to the moving and insightful stories in this volume and as a personal explanation of why I think their experiences and their lives are so powerful and compelling.

These are the words of Jesus: "Ask, and it will be given you; search, and you will find; knock, and the door will be opened for you. For everyone who asks receives, and everyone who searches finds, and for everyone who knocks, the door will be opened" (Matt. 7:7-8).

We are not alone.

JOHN M. MULDER